33

Oil, state and industrialization in Iran

Oil, state and industrialization in Iran

MASSOUD KARSHENAS

Department of Economics
University of Warwick

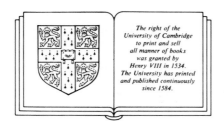

The right of the
University of Cambridge
to print and sell
all manner of books
was granted by
Henry VIII in 1534.
The University has printed
and published continuously
since 1584.

CAMBRIDGE UNIVERSITY PRESS

Cambridge
New York   Port Chester
Melbourne   Sydney

Published by the Press Syndicate of the University of Cambridge
The Pitt Building, Trumpington Street, Cambridge CB2 1RP
40 West 20th Street, New York, NY 10011, USA
10 Stamford Road, Oakleigh, Melbourne, 3166, Australia

First published 1990

Printed in Great Britain by The Bath Press, Avon

British Library cataloguing in publication data
Karshenas, Massoud
state and industrialization in Oil, Iran.
1. Iran. Industrialization
I. Title
338.0955

Library of Congress cataloguing in publication data
Karshenas. Massoud.
state and industrialization in Oil, Iran / Massoud Karshenas.
        p.   cam.
Originally presented as the author's thesis (Ph.D.–Churchill
College. 1988)
Includes bibliographical references.
ISBN 0-521-38351-X
1. Petroleum industry and trade–Government policy–Iran.
2. Petroleum industry and trade–Government policy–Developing
countries.   I. Title
HD9576.I62K375 1990
338.2'7282'0955–dc20

ISBN 0 521 38351 X

SE

To my mother and
to the memory of my father

Contents

Contents

Contents

Figures

Tables

Tables

Tables

Tables

Preface

A paradoxical aspect of the recent literature on industrialization in oil-exporting countries is that oil income is often seen as a hindrance rather than an aid to industrial diversification and growth. The experience of various oil-exporting developing countries during the 1970s and the 1980s, as well as those of industrialized countries such as the UK and the Netherlands in the aftermath of the discovery of North Sea oil, seem to lend credence to such views. In this book we argue that oil income, though by no means an unmixed blessing, can greatly contribute to industrial growth conditional on the adoption of appropriate policies by the government. It is further argued here that to have a realistic assessment of the policy alternatives facing the oil-exporting countries it is important to take into account the constraints imposed by the empirically given economic structure, as well as the political limits to state intervention. The specific case study of Iran makes it possible to examine the policy problems facing the oil-exporting economies in a historical setting which takes account of such constraints as posed by the structure and the organizational capacities of the economy and the state. Though the major part of the book consists of the case study of Iran, it is hoped that the general analytical framework discussed in chapter 1 may contribute to future research on other oil-exporting economies along similar lines.

Though the main focus of the book is on the process of growth and structural change in Iran during the 1953–77 period, it contains two relatively long chapters on economic developments during the pre-oil era. These historical chapters trace the roots of backwardness in the Iranian economy and help in an understanding of some of the key historical elements which shaped the impact of oil income on the industrialization experience in the post-1953 period. Having the character of interpretative economic history, the earlier chapters draw on an extensive body of literature on the economic history of modern Iran. The student of economic history may be therefore interested in these chapters on their own, as summaries of the existing state of knowledge on the economic history of modern Iran, and indicative of the numerous gaps which still remain to be filled by future research. Some of the points made in these historical chapters may have to be revised in the light of the findings of such future research. However, due care has been taken to base the main conclusions of these chapters, which inform our research on the post-1953 industrialization experience, on solid grounds supported by non-controversial evidence.

This book was originally submitted as a doctoral dissertation to the Faculty of Economics at the University of Cambridge. During my research years in Cambridge I benefitted from stimulating discussions with Hashem Pesaran as my supervisor. I wish to express my deepest gratitude to him for his ceaseless encouragement and advice. I also owe a profound debt to Mario Nuti for his encouragement and support during the earlier years of my research at Cambridge. A special note of gratitude is due to Nazy Sedaghat for her constant intellectual and moral stimulation and support throughout, and her indispensable help during the final stages of the work.

Different chapters of the book have been read and commented upon by various people whose help is greatly appreciated. Francesca Bettio, Sukhamoy Chakravarty, Ruchira Chatterji, Gavan Duffy, Hasan Hakimian, Ahmad Jazayeri, Iain Macpherson, Suzy Paine, Naser Pakdaman, Nazy Sedaghat, John Sender, and Pervez Tahir read various chapters of the book and provided valuable comments towards refining and shaping the ideas at various stages of my research. I am grateful to them all. I would like also to thank Bobbie Coe for typing much of the manuscript and for her expert word processing advice, and Anne Rix for her meticulous copy editing of the final draft.

Introduction

This is a study of the problems of economic growth and structural change in oil-exporting developing economies with special reference to the case of Iran. The analysis is organized around three interrelated themes which form the different aspects of the growth process: namely, the financing of accumulation, the sectoral balances in the process of growth, and the interrelationship between income distribution and growth. An attempt is made to go beyond the specification of the movement of the economic magnitudes involved, in order to investigate the interconnections between economic growth and the development of the economic structure as a whole. The study, therefore, is an historical investigation of the stages of accumulation in the Iranian economy, which highlights the interaction between economic growth and institutional change with particular emphasis on the role of the state in this process. The contribution of oil income to economic growth is investigated under different institutional arrangements at different stages of accumulation.

The book is divided into nine chapters. In chapter 1 we discuss the analytical framework of the book, first posing the question of the utilization of oil revenues within a structuralist framework where the process of growth, given the specific institutional framework of a developing economy, is said to be constrained by the shortage of certain key resources. The chapter goes on to argue that, in an oil-exporting economy, although such bottlenecks could be alleviated by the use of oil income in the short run, they can still reappear as strong impediments to growth in the longer run. The problem assumes added significance in view of the fact that oil is an exhaustible resource. At a time when oil income is rising fast, either due to buoyant international demand or rising prices, a short-sighted policy stance regarding the structural aspects of growth gives rise to a process of 'perverse growth' which may not be viable in the medium and long run.

The role of the state thus becomes crucial in an oil-exporting economy. In order to analyse the role of the state in the process of growth and structural change a distinction is made between the income generating and capacity

1

generating aspects of government policy. Though much of the literature on development planning has been focussed on the capacity generating aspects of government policy, we argue that within the context of an oil-exporting mixed economy the effects of the income generating side of government policy may be of equal if not greater importance in determining the structure of growth through its demand side effects. The chapter is concluded in section 6, where we try to extend our analytical framework by introducing certain key concepts which help in a descriptive analysis of the role of the state in the process of growth and structural change. It is argued that such an analysis is necessary for a critical appraisal of the role of state in the growth process and the formulation of effective alternative policies.

In chapter 2 we provide a historical study of the roots of backwardness in the Iranian economy by concentrating on the effect of two critical elements, the state and the structure of agrarian relations. These two key institutions continue to provide the vital clues to the process of growth in the later period (the oil period) in the Iranian economy. The chapter begins by giving a broad representation of the nature of state-economy interrelations in the pre-capitalist economy of Iran, and goes on to investigate the transformation of these interrelations under the impact of western capitalism during the late nineteenth and the early twentieth centuries. An analysis is provided of the transition of the state, from the traditional concept where the state was envisaged as a part of the natural order of the universe to the modern developmentalist state with its ideology of social engineering. The chapter, therefore, traces the evolution of the initial conditions which underlay the formation of the modern state in the inter-war period as well as the factors which broadly defined the role of the state in the economy of that period.

The formation of the modern state in the inter-war period is discussed in chapter 3, where the role of the state in the economy is traced from its *laissez-faire* phase in the 1920s to its strong interventionist phase in the 1930s. The chapter analyses the way accumulation was financed over this period and investigates the bottlenecks to growth within the structural framework set out in chapter 1. The contribution of oil income to economic growth is investigated within the same framework, taking into account not only the mode of utilization of oil income but also the factors which determined its size.

In the post-war period the Iranian economy entered a new phase of development, with oil income assuming a growing significance in financing accumulation. While in the inter-war period the major task of the state had been the mobilization of resources for investment within a predominantly agrarian economy, after the war the state faced the task of distribution and allocation of the already centralized economic surplus in the form of oil revenues. This radically changed the nature of state-economy interrelationships and marked the beginning of a period of rapid institutional change. In chapter 4 we discuss the emergence of the new political and institutional mechanisms of state intervention with particular emphasis on the credit system and the Plan Organization as important instruments of control over investment. The manner in which such controls were exercised to shape the structure of accumulation is discussed in the subsequent chapters.

In chapter 5 we outline the process of accumulation during the 1953–63 period, or what may be termed the semi-liberal phase of economic development in the post-1953 oil boom era. Over this period the Iranian economy was subjected to a massive inflow of external finance in the form of foreign aid and revenues from the oil sector. Recent theory on the 'booming export economies' maintains that, under such circumstances, the economy undergoes structural changes characterized by the crowding out of the traded goods sectors by non-traded goods sectors. In this chapter we counter this theory by demonstrating that over the period under study many of its assumptions regarding the tightness of the market for domestic resources and the nature of technological change did not hold and that the pattern of structural change can be better understood within the structuralist framework adopted in this book. In particular, government control over investment through the credit system and the Plan Organization is shown to have had a profound effect on structural change in this period. We further show how the structural features of accumulation brought about the impediments to growth which led to the crisis of the early 1960s. The crisis precipitated important institutional changes which re-establish the expansion of the economy on a new basis over the 1963–77 period.

The semi-liberal trade and industrial policies of the government during the 1950s were highly rewarding to the traditional ruling coalition – namely the merchant bourgeoisie of the Bazaar and the landlords – who in turn provided the social support which was crucial for the maintenance of the regime. These policies, however, led to severe balance of payments and inflationary pressures which created the acute political and economic crisis of the early 1960s. Using the terminology developed in chapter 1, the crisis could be viewed as the outcome of disproportionalities which resulted from the lack of co-ordination between the income generating and capacity generating aspects of government policy. To overcome these impediments to growth the government had to intervene to restructure the economy at different levels – one implication of which was the political break with its powerful traditional allies.

An important aspect of this restructuring was the transformation of agrarian relations, which had far-reaching implications for the growth of the economy as a whole. Iranian agriculture over the 1963–77 period

3

witnessed a phase of intense transformation through government intervention which was unparalleled in its modern history. Land reform was the hallmark of agrarian change which shaped all the other aspects of agricultural development in a significant way. Chapter 6 begins with a discussion of institutional change in the sector and proceeds to a detailed quantitative analysis of the resource flows into and out of the agricultural sector. It is shown that, contrary to common beliefs, there was a net inflow of resources of a sizeable magnitude into the sector, which combined with the institutional reforms to provide a positive output response. It is further argued that agrarian reforms removed one of the main sources of economic instability, i.e., the food price inflation which had previously hindered growth during the 1950s. The chapter concludes with a discussion of the income effects of agrarian reforms; it is argued that, although these reforms removed the supply constraints which backward agriculture posed to industrial growth, they intensified the maldistribution of income in the agricultural sector. This point is taken up in the next two chapters in discussing the implications of demand side factors in generating a process of 'perverse growth' over the period.

In chapter 7 we study the policies which were pursued to renovate the economy's industrial base during the 1963–77 period. Once again, the credit system and the Plan Organization play an important part in controlling the size and sectoral allocation of investment in the economy. The chapter also examines the question of the financing of accumulation. It is argued that the availability of oil income over this period allowed rapid accumulation to take place without the need to mobilize domestic savings through taxation or other policies aimed at curbing the consumption of high income groups. This, combined with the absence of any other conscious policies aimed at a wider distribution of income gains from growth, led to a concentration of income in the hands of a narrow section of the population which significantly influenced the structure of the home market and the final demand facing industrial producers.

Some of the implications of the lopsided structure of home demand for industrial growth are investigated in chapter 8, where it is argued that, although impressive growth rates were achieved over this period, the long- and medium-term viability of the growth path was suspect. The economy was subject to endemic balance of payments problems, which periodically interrupted the growth of the economy. The chapter provides a detailed study of the patterns of structural change in order to identify the sources of the balance of payments problems, where the root of the problem is found in the nature of structural change in the manufacturing industry. Chapter 9 provides the summary and conclusions of the book.

1

A framework for the analysis of the role of state in the oil-exporting developing economies

1.1 Introduction

The main impact of the oil sector on the economies of oil-exporting countries is through its income effect rather than direct linkages with other sectors of the economy. The state – being the main recipient of oil income in the national economy – therefore plays an important role in transmitting the impact of the oil sector to the rest of the domestic economy. The purpose of this chapter is to set up an analytical framework for studying, in a long-term perspective, the problems which the utilization of oil revenues may pose for the states in semi-industrialized mixed economies.

In the next two sections we shall consider the potential contributions which oil income can make to economic growth within a structuralist framework, where economic growth within the institutional set up of an underdeveloped country is said to be constrained by bottlenecks arising from the shortage of certain key goods and services. In section 1.4 we examine the possible ways of evaluating the utilization of oil resources by particular oil states. It is argued that, in complex economies undergoing fast growth and structural change, an optimization methodology may not be appropriate for such evaluation. Instead, alternative criteria are introduced in terms of the feasibility of the growth path, both over the lifespan of oil resources and in the long-run transition from an oil-based economy to a fully industrialized economy. In section 1.5 we analyse the specific policy mechanisms through which oil revenues may effect the process of growth and structural change in the context of semi-industrialized mixed economies. We argue that it is important to distinguish between two aspects of the impact of government policy in such economies; namely the income generating and capacity generating aspects. While most of the existing literature on planning in oil-exporting economies concentrates on the capacity generating aspects of government policy, we argue that the income generating impact of oil revenue utilization is equally important, both from the long-term and the short-term points of view. The chapter is ended in section 1.6, where we try to extend our analytical framework to incorporate elements which help in a *descriptive* analysis of the role of state in the growth process.

1.2 The meaning of utilization of oil income

Since oil revenues directly accrue to the central government in oil-exporting economies, an important aspect of the development effects of oil revenues may be sought by looking at their direct allocation in the public sector accounts. This, however, could produce a one-sided picture. Even in the countries – as was to some extent the case in Iran during the 1960s – where oil revenues are deposited in special accounts and utilized for specific development projects, one cannot discern the eventual impact of oil revenues from the pattern of their direct allocation by the government. The availability of oil revenues could for example influence the taxation and wage policies of the government with major implications for the pattern of resource allocation in the economy as a whole. What in the first instance appears as the utilization of oil revenues for investment purposes may in the final analysis turn out to be the substitution of oil for savings which were potentially mobilizable in the domestic economy. An adequate appraisal of the role of the state in the utilization of oil revenues has, therefore, to be conducted within an overall economy-wide framework, as an integrated treatment of government expenditure and revenue policies as a whole.[1] It is with this broader aspect of the utilization of oil revenues which we are concerned in this chapter.

1.3 Oil income and structural bottlenecks to growth

From an economy-wide point of view the role of oil income in the process of growth should be analysed in terms of its contribution to the mobilization and allocation of all productive resources in the economy. The existing development literature can be broadly divided into two groups on the basis of their closeness to two extremes in the treatment of the nature of scarcities which constrain the growth process. At one extreme lie what can be labelled the neo-classical theories with their common substitution and continuity assumptions and reliance on the price mechanism to bring about the necessary supply adjustments during the growth process. In a neo-classical model all resources simultaneously and continuously act as a bottleneck to growth. Oil revenues within such models, therefore, do not differ from other types of income and their allocation to alternative sectors does not possess any particular merits or demerits as long as the project which is financed

---

[1] This line of thought is developed in relation to the evaluation of the impact of foreign aid in Singer (1965), and Kalecki (1966).

6

thereby satisfies the marginal conditions necessary for 'optimal' inter-temporal resource allocation in the economy (see Dasgupta *et al.* 1978).

At the other extreme are the structuralist or bottleneck models in which growth at any particular time can be constrained by specific resources which, given the 'structural' rigidities in the less developed economies, cannot be resolved through the usual neo-classical substitution mechan-isms. In this literature, the major scarcities in productive resources which confront the developing countries in their growth process have been catego-rized into three major groups: (a) the supply of human resources, (b) the supply of domestic savings and (c) the supply of key goods and services. In principle, bottlenecks in the supply of key goods and services – such as capital goods, power and transport, food, raw materials and intermediate products – which arise from structural rigidities in the LDCs could be overcome through imports. This is not, however, feasible if the rate of growth of foreign exchange earnings is also constrained by structural obstacles to the diversification and expansion of exports. Thus the underlying rigidities which impede the expansion in production of specific commodities either for export or for domestic use, are usually manifested in the form of balance of payments constraints to growth.

A crucial point in the structuralist argument is the definition of what constitutes a 'structural bottleneck'. Structural bottlenecks should be dis-tinguished from the short-term rigidities which inevitably arise in any economy due to the fixed structure of productive capacities in the short run. The structuralist models emphasize the rather more persistent sources of disequilibrium between the pattern of resource availabilities and pattern of demand for resources in the process of development. The structuralist literature has mainly developed in relation to specific conditions prevailing in different LDCs and consequently a more general definition of the term 'structural' has yet to emerge. Drawing upon the various contexts in which the term has been used, here we may refer to a structural bottleneck in terms of the social and technical conditions of production in particular sectors of the economy, or the overall economic institutions of a country, which limit and condition both effective economic intervention by the government and the operation of the market mechanism. The causes of such structural bottlenecks lie in the long historical experience of development and thus could take various forms in different countries at different stages of their development. The structuralist approach, therefore, forms a broad analyt-ical framework within which different models have been developed to reflect the development experiences of particular countries, or to develop general policy prescriptions for specific groups of countries which face similar bottlenecks. Each model rests on specific presuppositions as to the limits of state intervention and the effectiveness of the price mechanism.

For example, Dobb (1969) and Sen (1968) analyse the problem of choice of technique for maximal growth in a surplus labour economy, where the size of the agricultural marketed surplus forms the main constraint to growth.[2] Their conclusion as to the capital intensity of production techniques for maximal growth crucially depends on their assumption of a strict institutional limit on the power of the government to increase the size of the agricultural marketed surplus, either through increasing total production or controlling food consumption in the rural sector. With a slightly different set of assumptions as to the realm of the state controls, namely when total agricultural output rather than the marketed surplus is the constraint and the state has effective control over real consumption both in the urban and rural areas, one can reach a completely different conclusion on the choice of technique for maximal growth in a labour surplus economy (see Kalecki 1972, chapter 10).[3]

Feldman (1928), Mahalanobis (1953), and Raj and Sen (1961) use structuralist models to analyse the growth implications of different sectoral patterns of investment in an economy with little or no import capacity and where the size of the capital goods sector is the main constraint to growth.[4] The limited availability of foreign exchange in these models could be due to various structural factors which limit the growth of exports. Primary commodity exports which form the major share of the LDC exports cannot keep pace with their foreign exchange needs, mainly due to low income elasticity of demand for such commodities. Agricultural primary exports could also be supply constrained due to institutional factors connected to the backward agrarian relations of production. Growth of manufacturing exports, which is a *sine qua non* for sustained growth without balance of payments problems in these economies, also depends on an ability to move successively from producing simple to more complex industrial goods – a process which itself is predicated upon the ability to sustain economic growth for a relatively long period of time. Under these circumstances price elasticity of real exports (in terms of international purchasing power) is very low and it might be more plausible to consider foreign exchange supply curves with a sharp cutoff point, rather than a smoothly increasing function of real exchange rate as in orthodox trade theory.

Another important area of application of structuralist models has been the interpretation of the inflationary processes in Latin American semi-industrialized mixed economies (see Baer and Kerstenentzky 1963, Furtado

---

[2] Of course Sen's model covers alternatives other than maximal growth, but the assumption of food supply constraint applies in all cases.

[3] Though Kalecki (1966) does not explicitly refer to the divergence between his and Dobb/Sen's assumptions.

[4] An additional assumption in these models is of course the non-shiftability of fixed capital between branches of production.

1970). Though these empirical case studies are based on specific conditions in the countries concerned, the broad structural similarities in these countries has given rise to more general structuralist formulations of the inflationary processes in semi-industrialized mixed economies (see Kalecki 1953, Seers 1962, Kaldor 1971, Diamond 1978, Wells and Malan 1981, Fitzgerald 1983, Taylor 1983). Four broad structural features of the semi-industrialized mixed economies form the underlying presuppositions to these general formulations. First, the food supply deficiencies arising from backward conditions of production in the agricultural sector. Secondly, the lack of integration in the manufacturing sector resulting in heavy reliance on imports for capital goods and intermediate manufactured goods. Thirdly, lack of diversification and relatively slow growth of exports arising from technological backwardness and inefficiencies in the manufacturing sector. These features are referred to as 'structural' in the sense that they cannot be corrected in the short to medium term by economic policies formulated in terms of the operation of the market forces through price adjustments. This is not solely due to low price elasticities arising from technical conditions of production but, more fundamentally, to social pressures which inevitably arise in resistance to the distributional effects of relative price changes. This lies at the heart of the structuralist explanation of the inflationary pressures in the semi-industrialized economies. Policy prescriptions are mainly formulated in terms of direct intervention by the state to restructure the manufacturing sector, change the production and exchange relations in the agricultural sector, and relax the barriers to the mobility of factors of production. The fourth structural feature of the semi-industrialized mixed economy, which completes the cycle of causal factors which lead to mounting inflationary pressures, is the rigid fiscal structure of the state which lacks the necessary flexibility to keep up with mounting public expenses in support of the development process. The ensuing fiscal imbalances further limit the ability of the state to perform its necessary restructuring functions during the process of growth, and give rise to recurrent cycles of medium to high growth rates followed by high inflation and balance of payments crises. The lack of flexibility in the fiscal structure of the state on the revenue side has been attributed to the nature of the political relations which limit the ability of the government to tax the capitalists and the modern middle classes who are the main beneficiaries of the growth process (see Fitzgerald 1977, 1978, Furtado 1970, p.97, Kaldor 1971).

Finally, the dual-gap models should be mentioned as the least sophisticated and most commonly used amongst the structuralist models. The dual-gap models are based on structuralist assumptions which involve a highly limited conception of the likely fields of effective economic policy by the state *vis-à-vis* the domestic economy, and concentrate on the foreign capital requirements to finance growth.[5]

What distinguishes the structuralist approach from the neo-classical and more generally the orthodox market oriented approach is not merely the recognition of the possibility of structural constraints which impede the full utilization of productive resources and restrict the size of the national product at any particular moment of time. They also attribute special *dynamic* significance to particular patterns of structural change, by focussing on the *complementarity* of the different sectors of the economy in the growth process. We shall shortly return to these dynamic considerations. Here it would suffice to point out that these dynamic aspects of different patterns of *sectoral* growth introduce additional reasons for state intervention to direct resources into particular sectors of the economy, which individual decisions based on price signals may not achieve (Kaldor 1964). Within the structuralist framework, therefore, the potential contribution of oil resources depends not only on the alleviation of the particular bottlenecks that happen to constrain the economy, but also on the dynamic effects that the expenditure of oil revenues can generate in a developing economy in the long run. Contrary to the neo-classical framework, here the fact that oil is an exhaustible resource and that oil revenues are in foreign currency acquires special significance, and furthermore the way the flow of oil revenues interacts with the domestic economy to shape the pattern of structural change is of crucial importance.[6]

At one level it may be correct to argue that the difference between the neo-classical and structuralist framework boils down to the magnitude of the relevant price elasticities, which is basically a matter to be resolved at the empirical level; while in some instances there may be high substitutability and a high elasticity of supply, in others the bottleneck model may provide a better approximation to reality. 'The reality is probably more complex than the pure neo-classicist or the bottlenecker would allow' (Stewart 1976, p.125). However, as we have tried to show in the foregoing argument, the two approaches have more substantive differences than this. The structuralist approach, by emphasizing the variety of social and technical conditions of production which shape the functioning of the market mechanism, can furnish a more general framework for the study of growth

---

[5] Dual-gap models are discussed in more detail in section 1.4 below.

[6] This is not to imply that in the neo-classical framework oil revenues do not exert any influence on the sectoral distribution of output and employment. In fact, a growing body of neo-classical literature on the so-called phenomenon of 'Dutch Disease' deals with precisely this sectoral reallocation of resources between the traded and non-traded sectors of the economy (see Mead and Russell 1957, Corden and Neary 1982, Corden 1984). Within the neo-classical framework, however, this reallocation of resources does not have any particular significance for the process of development.

processes in the LDCs than the neo-classical framework which is based on special assumptions about the behaviour of 'economic agents' and the flexibility of the price mechanism.[7]

Within the structuralist framework the immediate contribution of oil income to growth is related to the nature of the constraints which it helps to alleviate. Oil revenues, being predominantly in the form of foreign exchange, could help to alleviate imbalances between the structure of domestic supply and demand which could arise during the growth process. In other words, they could allow a higher rate of investment and growth in a balance of payments constrained economy. At the same time oil revenues amount to a net addition to the disposable resources in the national economy which could allow a higher rate of growth of investment and an acceleration in the overall rate of growth of the economy achievable without the need to curb consumption expenditure in the short run. In an economy where none of these bottlenecks act as an impediment to the rate of growth of the economy, then the rate of growth could be said to be constrained by the absorptive capacity of the economy. In a surplus labour economy the concept of absorptive capacity refers to the human skills bottleneck being binding. Extra oil revenues in this case would make relatively little contribution to growth, and after a point they could exert a negative impact. We shall return to this issue below.[8]

Of course, a continuous expansion of oil revenues cannot be relied upon to sustain the rate of growth of the economy in the long run, unless the necessary structural changes which should accompany the growth process are achieved. Oil is a depletable resource and sooner or later, depending on the rate of depletion, oil reserves will be exhausted. On the demand side also there are limits to the rate of growth of oil exports in the medium run.[9] Oil revenues, therefore, should best be regarded as a temporary catalyst which can help create the structural flexibility necessary for self-sustained growth. By alleviating the constraining effects of bottlenecks and allowing a higher overall rate of growth in the short run, oil revenues could help increase the structural flexibility of the economy in various ways. For example, in an economy where backward production relations in the agricultural sector hold down the rate of growth of agricultural production, oil revenues could increase the scope for intervention by the state, through neutralizing tempo-

---

[7] For example, a main emphasis in the structuralist literature has been the explanation of the variety of social and technical conditions of production in the different sectors of the economy which limit the range of variations in relative prices (see Kaldor 1971, 1972, 1977, Diamond 1978, Fitzgerald 1983, Wells and Malan 1981). On the 'rationality' of the economic agents under different forms of production in the Iranian manufacturing sector see appendix M.1.   [8] See below section 1.3.1 on the definition of absorptive capacity.

[9] Though in the short run this could be to some extent alleviated by foreign borrowing, the need for servicing the debt could soon exhaust this possibility.

rary disruptive effects (e.g., food shortages) which could arise from an agrarian reform programme. If it is overpopulation or the existence of surplus labour in the agricultural sector which retards the rate of growth in that sector, a higher overall rate of growth of the economy could incease the dynamism of the agricultural sector by absorbing the surplus labour into other sectors of the economy (Kaldor 1972a). The most important of these potential dynamic effects, however, relates to the manufacturing sector. The growth of the manufacturing sector entails a heavy initial reliance on imported capital and intermediate goods, and this sector needs time to 'grow' out of its 'infancy' and to become competitive enough to be able to export. Oil revenues can increase the rate of growth of the manufacturing sector by relieving the supply bottlenecks and by creating an expanding domestic demand for manufacturing output.[10] Growth of the manufacturing sector would itself result in important dynamic effects in the economy as a whole. The manufacturing sector is endowed with special attributes for the extension of capital and machinery, the application of science and technology and the introduction of new methods of work (Roseberg 1976). The sector is furthermore characterized by the existence of important dynamic economies of scale or economies of specialization (Young 1928, Kaldor 1967, Cripps *et al.* 1973). In addition, at low to middle stages of economic development the income elasticity of demand for manufacturing output tends to be greater than unity (UN 1979). As a result of the combination of these features, the manufacturing sector is capable of not only achieving rates of growth well above the rest of the economy, but also the growth of output in that sector goes hand in hand with the simultaneous growth of employment and productivity of labour. The manufacturing sector could, therefore, contribute to the growth of the other sectors of the economy in two ways. On the one hand, through the absorption of surplus labour it helps to restructure the social and technical conditions of production in other sectors of the economy and creates the conditions for accumulation of capital and introduction of modern technology in those sectors. On the other hand, by providing modern manufactured inputs, it makes such a technical change in other sectors possible.[11] The crucial importance of the establishment of a well integrated, competitive manufacturing sector for the attainment of self-sustained growth, means that the development

---

[10] Since here we are basically concerned with the 'potential' contribution of oil income to growth we shall mainly concentrate on the supply side effects. The demand side effects which become important within the institutional setup of a mixed economy are discussed in section 1.5.

[11] This is of particular significance with regard to the agricultural sector, where imported technology has to be readapted according to the local ecological relationships and resource availabilities (see Rosenberg 1976, chapter 9, part VI).

contribution of oil revenues, in an underdeveloped oil-exporting economy, virtually comes to an end with the achievement of this end.

The mere existence of oil revenues, however, does not by itself generate these dynamic processes. It requires planning and a long-term perspective on the part of the government. Oil can be used in short-sighted manner to increase the level of consumption in the short run without generating significant dynamic effects in the production structure of the economy as a whole. This is not, however, a likely outcome. Given the social and political pressures for economic growth and the developmentalist ideology of modern bureaucracies in underdeveloped countries, one would expect a high investment and rapid growth strategy to be adopted. The adoption of a 'maximal' growth strategy, however, in itself is not necessarily a sign of judicious planning for an oil-exporting economy. In an oil-exporting economy, given the absorptive capacity of the economy which sets limit to the maximum growth rate of investment, there are many such maximal growth paths, each implying a particular rate of depletion of oil resources and a particular pattern of structural change. The challenge which faces an oil-exporting economy is to choose that path of growth and structural change which is viable both from the long-term and medium-term perspectives. In the long run the challenge is to choose that particular growth path which creates the necessary flexibility in the production structure of the economy, so that the transition from the oil era can take place smoothly and evenly. In the medium run the problem is to ensure that the rate of growth of requirement for oil income is consistent with the growth of demand for the oil exports of the country in the international market. Otherwise, the growth process will be combined with severe cyclical fluctuations which, apart from its undesirable effects in the short run, would imply a loss of potential output during the down turn of the cycle which could not be compensated for given the absorptive capacity of the economy in the long run.

1.3.1 Absorptive capacity

The concept of absorptive capacity, as defined in the development literature, refers to the organizational and human skill capacities for undertaking new investment projects. Absorptive capacity, in this literature, is either characterized as a strict limit to the possible rate of growth of investment (see Chenery and Strout 1966, Marris 1970), or referred to as a limit beyond which extra investment would involve an increasing incremental capital-output ratio (see Adler 1965, Kalecki 1966, Eckaus 1972). These limits, which are taken to operate both in the short run and in the long run, are supposed to arise from a shortage of managerial and administrative capac-

13

ity and lack of skills in the LDCs. The justification for postulating a long-run ceiling on the rate of growth of investment in a surplus labour economy is based on the fact that the rate of acquisition of these skills is dependent upon the learning processes inherent in the very act of investment itself. Few of the above-mentioned sources, however, attempt to analyse the full implications of this 'learning-by-doing' hypothesis or examine the conditions under which it could result in the kind of investment limitations postulated. In this section we shall attempt a further elaboration of this concept by synthesizing the insights provided by the different strands of thought in the above-mentioned literature.

The dynamic relationship between the rate of increase of an economy's absorptive capacity and the growth of investment, which arises from the learning process involved in the act of investment, could be represented in the form of an 'absorptive capacity function', analogous to Kaldor's idea of a 'technical progress function' (see Kaldor 1957). The curve AA'' in figure 1.1 characterizes what may be regarded as the plausible shape of such a function for a typical developing economy. In this figure the horizontal axis measures the rate of growth of gross investment I, and the vertical axis refers to the rate of change of the index of absorptive capacity S which incorporates the rate of expansion of technical and organizational skills necessary for capital accumulation. These technical and organizational skills refer to the ability of the society to conceive, implement and effectively run the new investment projects. The index of absorptive capacity in this sense is representative of what Veblen (1932) has referred to as the 'common stock of knowledge' of the society. Individual learning processes are conditioned by, and derive their effectiveness in increasing the productive potential of the society from the existing common stock of knowledge of the society as a corporate body. The same applies to government's educational and technical training efforts. The capacity of educational planning by the government depends on the existing stock of knowledge, and the effectiveness of such planning in enhancing the productive potential of the economy, or adding to the existing stock of knowledge of the society, also depends on its congruence with the latter. For example, the educational institutions of an underdeveloped economy, which may emulate similar institutions in the advanced economies, or may play solely the function of rationing scarce, highly paid jobs in the modern sector of the economy, do not necessarily enhance the productive potential of the society. This brings into focus the significance of the practice of investment in the diffusion and assimilation of technological and organizational skills. The significance of investment in this regard is not only confined to the learning processes involved in each individual act of investment, but it also plays a broader social and macroeconomic function by signalling the direction in which the acquisition of

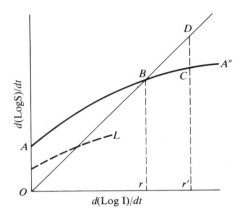

Figure 1.1 Absorptive capacity function

new skills, necessary for enhancing the productive potential of the economy, should go. Formal education, if planned appropriately, could play an important complementary role in raising the stock of knowledge in the society as a whole, but it cannot substitute for the learning processes which arise out of the practice of investment and production. The shape of the absorptive capacity function, which is meant to represent this latter category of learning processes, depends on the existing social and economic institutions of the country, and assumes as given the complementary skills which formal education could contribute to the common stock of knowledge of the society.

At a zero rate of growth of gross investment, the rate of change of the organizational and technical capabilities of the economy is at a minimum positive rate of OA. The positive value of the intercept of the function captures the effect of the learning processes which take place, partly due to the improved skills of those individuals and organizations who are already involved in undertaking investment activities at the current level (though this is subject to diminishing returns), and partly due to the creation of new skills which takes place independently of the investment activity itself. The slope of the absorptive capacity function is positive, which characterizes the fact that a higher rate of growth of investment activity implies a higher rate of growth of skill formation. The sign of the second derivative of the function – as long as the gradient of the function does not exceed one – is immaterial to our argument, but it could be plausibly argued that the function is convex from above.[12]

[12] This is due to the fact that a higher rate of growth of investment implies a higher ratio of newly acquired, and hence less experienced, skills in the existing stock of such skills.

For a surplus labour economy whose absorptive capacity function is characterized by the function AA'', the point of intersection of this function with the 45 degree line (i.e., point B) determines the rate of growth of investment consistent with the growth of capacity to invest in the domestic economy. This could be regarded as the long-term absorptive capacity of an economy whose absorptive capacity function, as determined by the sum total of its social and economic institutions, is characterized by the curve AA''. If the rate of growth of investment is to the left of point B, then the economy would tend to be characterized by a growing degree of slack in technical and organizational skills over time. As we noted in the previous section this situation is characteristic of an LDC facing a foreign exchange or a savings constraint. External resources could be used in such an economy to raise the rate of growth to the absorptive capacity limit (i.e., point B).[13] If the rate of growth of gross investment falls to the right of the point B, then the economy would be encountering a growing shortage of specific skills which cannot be procured from within the domestic economy.[14]

This representation of the concept of absorptive capacity could be used to highlight the two main definitions of absorptive capacity limit referred to above. On the one hand, those economists who consider it as an upper bound to the rate of growth of investment in the long run, should have strong reasons to believe that imports of skills cannot be relied upon to step up the rate of growth of investment on a permanent basis beyond the point B in figure 1.1. Kalecki (1966) puts forward two reasons for this. First, though it is possible (and in many cases necessary) to import some of the highly specialized services of foreign technicians, this is not politically feasible for a large number of intermediate skills. The political implications are grave specially in large immature economies where a major part of the indigenous labour force is underemployed.[15] Secondly, at such a high rate of growth the increment of imports of capital and intermediate goods for each additional unit of income is expected to be very high. Even in an oil economy it is, therefore, unlikely that the rate of growth of foreign exchange revenues could keep up with the mounting foreign exchange bill resulting from a large-scale inflow of foreign skilled workers. Since in the discussion

[13] This is the classic argument put forward in the development literature in favour of foreign aid.

[14] The possibility of the rate of growth of gross investment exceeding r, is of course very remote in non-oil LDCs, unless of course the development efforts of the government are so low that even at moderate rates of growth of investment the economy would face shortages of skills. This corresponds to the absorptive capacity function 'L' in figure 1.1.

[15] This is an important difference between the small surplus oil economies like Kuwait and Saudi Arabia where the shortage of labour is general, and large surplus labour oil economies like Iran. The political implications of a large-scale inflow of foreign workers are less severe in the former than in the latter.

of absorptive capacity the question of the foreign exchange constraint is assumed away, it is the first of these two reasons which should figure most prominently in postulating an upper bound to the long-term growth of investment. On the other hand, one can characterize point *B* as a long-term absorptive capacity limit in the sense that growth of gross investment exceeding that limit would involve decreasing returns. This could be due to a permanent over-stretching of the supplies of domestic skills and increasing use of foreign skills which are normally much more costly than their domestic substitutes.

According to the first interpretation, therefore, point *B* in figure 1.1 sets a ceiling to the rate of growth of gross investment in a surplus labour economy in the long run. Given the value of the capital-output ratio, it also determines a unique maximal growth path for such an economy. If for reasons related to the existence of other types of short-run bottlenecks in the economy there is a cyclical decline in the rate of investment, the new maximal path of growth of incomes would be permanently below the previous path. According to the second interpretation of absorptive capacity limit, while in principle such temporary disruptions to the growth of output could be compensated for, it would involve an unnecessarily high cost due to the rising capital-output ratio, and could exert undue pressures on the level of consumption in an underdeveloped economy in the short run.

The concept of absorptive capacity is basically meant to characterize the limit to the rate of growth of investment set by all the domestic factors of production which either cannot be imported or face rapidly rising import supply prices. In this sense, one can also include factors such as power, transport and general infrastructures. It should be noted, however, that the significance of the human skill bottleneck depends on the fact that its rate of growth is closely geared to the very process of development itself and, past a certain limit, cannot be appreciably expanded by additional investment: while the latter category of bottlenecks can be expanded in the long run without a limit by diverting the necessary investment towards them. The emergence of such bottlenecks in a modern economy could be mainly due to lack of foresight and policy mistakes by the government or unforeseen external shocks. We shall therefore refer to this latter concept of absorptive capacity as conjunctural or short term.

Such short-term bottlenecks – which on a moderate scale are in fact inevitable in a growing economy due to lack of perfect information on the part of the planners and the private decision-making units – could also appear due to disproportionalities in the supply and demand for specific skills. To the extent that they act as signals for directing the resources into desirable channels, and as inducements for the private institutions to invest in such activities, they could even be regarded as beneficial (see Hirschman

1958, Hirschman and Lindblom 1962). If an attempt is made, however, to increase the rate of investment appreciably in a short span of time through a rapid inflow of external resources, these bottlenecks would tend to lose their signalling function and turn into barriers to growth. An overheated economy would develop, characterized by abnormally high capital-output ratios, high inflation and the simultaneous appearance of various of the above bottlenecks – in the sense that the alleviation of one bottleneck would in a circular manner depend on the prior removal of another bottleneck and so on. In a moderately overheated economy the rise in the capital-output ratio is due to the delays which arise from infrastructural bottlenecks and the lengthening of the period of construction of the capital stock due to shortages in technical and organizational skills. Beyond a certain point extra investment leads to what Kalecki (1972, p.44) refers to as 'freezing of capital' rather than increased output. Extra investment under such circumstances could even produce negative returns due to the disruption of raw material supplies to existing production units, speculation and undesirable redistribution of income away from industrialists and producers in general and towards the middlemen and merchants. This situation, which characterized the Iranian economy after the 1974 oil boom, could be attributed to policy mistakes by the government rather than arising from lack of information or adequate control mechanisms in the economists' sense of these terms.

1.4 Government policy and long-term efficiency of oil revenue utilization

The dual function of oil revenues in the short run, namely their foreign exchange and savings contribution, is similar to the effect of an inflow of foreign capital. The structuralist framework summarized above formed the underlying framework for the two-gap models which were developed during the 1960s to estimate the foreign aid requirements of the LDCs and measure the productivity of foreign aid under different binding constraints (see, e.g., McKinnon 1964, Chenery and Strout 1966, OECD 1967). Such models are readily applicable to the case of oil-exporting countries as well. The underlying assumptions of the two-gap models, however, make them too restrictive for the evaluation of government policy in oil-exporting economies from a long-term perspective. Nevertheless, since the dual-gap models share in many of their assumptions with some of the recent planning models developed for the case of Iran (see, e.g., Razavi 1982, 1983, Motamen 1979), it would be useful to develop our argument through a critical appraisal of the conception in such models of the long-term efficiency of external resource use.

The two-gap models begin with the basic hypothesis of structural rigidities which characterize the underdeveloped economies, and which are not amenable to government policy in the short run. Lack of flexibility in the industrial structure is translated into an import function which makes the rate of growth of the GNP a fixed function of the minimum necessary (non-competitive) imports, and exports are taken as exogenous. The maximum potential mobilizable savings are taken as a fixed function of the GNP which incorporates the institutional and political limits to the ability of the state to increase the rate of savings.

Under these specifications of the economy any planned acceleration in the rate of growth of the economy generates a gap between the *ex-ante* national savings and the required investment, which only by coincidence would be equal to the *ex-ante* gap between export earnings and import requirements – although *ex-post* the two gaps have to be equal. The required external resources to finance a given rate of growth and the productivity of foreign aid in terms of growth of the GNP are calculated on the basis of the gap which happens to be binding in a particular economy. If the savings gap happens to be the binding constraint then the economy has to import more than the minimum rate necessary for a given rate of growth of the GNP. The extra imports cannot be utilized for investment purposes because of the lack of required domestic factors of production. If the trade gap is binding then domestic savings should be less than their potential value if a Keynesian type slump is to be avoided. The additional potential savings in this case cannot be invested because of shortages of required supplies of complementary foreign factors of production. Within this framework it can easily be seen that inefficiency in the utilization of external resources is only confined to a situation where there exists a divergence between the two *ex-ante* gaps – assuming that external resources are actually used to close the dominant gap.

The only possibility which the dual-gap models consider for pursuing a more efficient growth path in the long run is the possibility of closing the divergence between the two gaps when the trade gap is binding. In this case the potentially mobilizable savings (i.e., the gap between the two gaps) could be utilized, not to increase the rate of growth of the GNP as such, but to expand the import substituting and export promoting industries (both the rate of investment and the capital-output ratio rise with the effect of reducing the trade gap to the size of the *ex-ante* savings gap at a given rate of growth).

It is important to note that in the original formulations of dual-gap models and in much of the debate which followed,[16] the only source of inefficiency considered in the utilization of external resources, was the

[16] For a critique of dual-gap models along neo-classical lines see, Nelson 1970, Joshi 1970, Findley 1971, Michalopulous 1975.

inability to invest the potentially mobilizable savings when the *ex-ante* trade gap was binding. The policy prescriptions put forward were also directed towards the removal of this source of inefficiency. In this literature the possibility of desirability of government intervention to close the divergence between the two gaps when the savings gap is binding is implicitly ruled out. In a way this is tantamount to saying that, given the magnitude of inflow of external resources, a savings constrained growth path which is feasible always corresponds to a social optimum growth path, no matter what the rate of national savings happens to be. This assumes that either a higher rate of domestic savings is not feasible, that is factors such as distribution of income and government taxation which affect potential savings are assumed to be institutionally fixed and not subject to policy control, or that government's direct intervention to increase the rate of domestic savings would create inefficiencies and lead to a suboptimal intertemporal allocation of resources. This position is implicit in the neoclassical reformulations of dual-gap analysis (see Findley 1971) where, in a free market setup, domestic savings, given by the conditions of thrift and productivity in the economy, plus the inflow of external resources, determine the rate of investment, and competitive imports adjust to cover the trade balance.

An important precondition for the above postulates to have a claim to realism is that the government's direct economic involvement should be taken as marginal.[17] This is however far from reality in the LDCs, where public sector absorption generally forms a large share of total domestic absorption.[18] Especially in oil-exporting economies, where a considerable part of the national income directly accrues to the government in the form of oil revenues, the government exerts an important influence on the allocation of resources between consumption and investment both directly and indirectly; directly through the allocation of public sector expenditures between investment and consumption, and indirectly through the impact of government's expenditure and revenue policies on the distribution of income and the pattern of aggregate demand. There is no *a priori* reason to believe that the existing rate of domestic saving, being to such a large extent subject to political decision making, is either at its highest feasible rate, or is optimum by any non-arbitrary definition of the term. Once both the savings

---

[17] It should be noted that, even when all the underlying assumptions of neo-classical general equilibrium models are fulfilled and the economy is actually in full employment equilibrium, savings need not necessarily be at an optimum level from the social point of view (Dobb 1969, chapter 2).

[18] This is not due to bad economic policy or any such reasons. The high degree of direct economic involvement of the state in the LCDs is due to the functional need for state intervention on the supply side of the economy to remove the structural rigidities facing these economies (see Fitzgerald 1978, UN 1965, 1966).

and trade functions are made subject to policy control, the question of long-term efficiency of utilization of external resources involves much wider possibilities than the closure of *ex-ante* divergence between the two gaps.[19]

In a growing economy there is a complex interaction between different patterns of income distribution, savings, foreign trade and investment with different capital output ratios. Under these circumstances it would be simplistic to try to determine long-term optimum growth paths – specially with the use of structural relations estimated from the past performance of the economy and data available *ex-post* – for an economy undergoing a rapid process of growth and structural change.[20] It would be more reasonable, and from the point of view of policy evaluation more useful, to define long-term efficiency of utilization of external resources in terms of feasible growth paths. Here we shall define a path of growth in an oil-exporting economy as efficient if a reasonably high rate of growth, close to the absorptive capacity of the economy, is combined with a pattern of structural change which ensures the feasibility of the growth path both in the long run and in the medium run in the sense defined in section 1.3 above.

1.5 Policy framework for an oil-exporting mixed economy

So far we have been considering the potential development contribution of oil revenues and the possible ways of evaluating the growth performance in oil-exporting economies within the general context of the problems facing the LDCs in their growth process. We shall now proceed to further concretize the analysis by considering the specific long-term policy problems which the existence of oil revenues could give rise to in a *mixed economy framework*.

As we noted above, easy access to external resources in oil-exporting economies could allow a reasonable rate of growth to be achieved without the immediate need to bring about the appropriate structural adjustments in the domestic economy in the short run. This could lead to a process of 'perverse growth' – that is, a process of growth which is not viable in the long run and is subject to sharp cyclical fluctuations in the medium run.[21] Though the process of perverse growth which manifests itself in the form of periodic balance of payments crises is basically related to the supply maladjustments in the economy, a proper delineation of the causal factors giving rise to such a process and a critical appraisal of the role of the state

[19] This is particularly the case in middle-income LDCs where the government is not strictly constrained by the extremely low levels of income and the highly rigid structure of the economy.

[20] For an attempt to evaluate the performance of the Iranian economy in this period on the basis of comparison of different 'optimum' growth paths see Razavi (1983).

[21] The term perverse growth is due to Kalecki (1966).

therein, has to be conducted with a view both to the supply side and demand side factors. The impact of different forms of state economic intervention on the growth process shall be analysed both with respect to its immediate supply side effects and the effects mediated through the demand side.

The different forms of government economic intervention in a mixed economy can be broadly categorized under the direct and indirect headings, depending on whether government intervention takes place through direct control over the economic surplus, or it takes the form of various policy measures meant to influence the decisions of the individuals or institutions in the private sector. In both cases government intervention exerts a dual effect on the growth process. On the one hand it has an immediate effect on the creation of productive capacities in the economy. On the other hand it affects the process of income generation in the economy, and through changes in the absolute level and pattern of effective demand influences the pace and structure of economic growth.

The growing direct involvement of the state on the supply side of semi-industrialized mixed economies during successive phases of import-substitution industrialization, is a well-documented phenomenon. The economic role of the state in semi-industrialized mixed economies goes beyond the classical role of provision of the general pre-conditions for accumulation as in capitalist economies. Apart from its traditional support functions – namely the provision of social and physical infrastructure – the state has assumed an increasing direct role in commodity production in these economies through time. The growing direct involvement of the state in the process of accumulation in semi-industrialized economies is mainly concentrated in strategic sectors, such as heavy industry or high risk agricultural investment with long gestation periods, which do not attract private capital either because of private capital's own weakness or the low profitability or riskiness of such investments (see Fitzgerald 1977, 1978, 1983, UN 1979, chapter X, 1965, 1966). In undertaking such activities the state directly intervenes in the process of creation of new productive capacities in the economy.[22] These activities of the state would of course generate secondary effects on the process of capacity formation in the economy as a whole through the externalities they give rise to, as well as their demand generating effects. The extensive body of literature on public sector planning in the LDCs which has appeared during the post-war period mainly concentrates on the direct capacity creating functions of the state in the process of growth. In this literature the recurrent crises in the process of accumulation in the semi-industrialized economies is mainly related to the failure of the

---

[22] Under this definition one shall include other forms of direct capacity creating activities of the state such as, education and manpower training, research and development, and general infrastructure.

state in its direct restructuring functions in the economy – either due to its inability to mobilize adequate resources for that purpose or due to the misallocation of the resources at its disposal. Fitzgerald (1977, 1978) for instance attributes the main cause of recurrent balance of payments crises in the Latin American economies to the inability of the state to mobilize sufficient resources for the successful conduct of its direct restructuring functions in the economy, mainly due to tax resistance by the bourgeoisie. Much of the literature on public sector planning and oil revenue utilization in the Iranian economy also concentrates on the direct capacity creating activities of the state.[23] The immediate supply side effects of the direct economic involvement of the state is of fundamental importance to the growth process in the economies facing structural rigidities. They, however, do not exhaust all the different possible forms of government intervention in such economies, nor do they capture all aspects of the impact of direct government intervention on the process of growth.

The state can also bring about changes in the production structure of the economy through indirect policy measures which do not necessitate direct control over economic resources. Such policy interventions normally affect the economy through relative price changes (e.g., trade policy), or rationing the access of different agents to economic resources (e.g., credit policy), or changing/maintaining particular production relations and institutional forms (e.g., land reform, labour relations, etc.). The neo-classical policy framework is usually formulated in terms of the supply side effects of such indirect policy measures. The phenomenon of perverse growth, as referred to above, is mainly explained in terms of undue government interference or other 'imperfections' which distort the working of the market mechanism. The demand side of the economy is immaterial to the analytical models which underlie such policy diagnoses (Strassmann 1956, Pasinetti 1981).

However, as was noted above, both the direct and indirect forms of economic intervention by the state, apart from their immediate capacity generating impact, lead to the generation of new incomes and result in changes in the distribution of income between different social classes. The resulting demand side effects exert an important impact on the process of structural change in a mixed economy. In particular, in the oil-exporting economy, the income generating aspects of the expenditure and revenue policies of the government could turn out to be more important than is recognized in the existing literature. Policy frameworks which ignore the interdependence between the different forms of government intervention, or concentrate only on one aspect of the impact of government policy, could produce highly misleading prescriptions for such economies. The cause of

---

[23] For an interesting study of public sector planning in Iran from this perspective, see Baldwin (1967).

perverse growth in an oil-exporting mixed economy may be connected more to the income generating impact of direct government economic involvement and its demand side effects than to the shortcomings in the supply side planning or the 'distortion' effects of the import-substitution industrialization as such.

1.6 Role of the state in different stages of growth

The analysis has been so far concentrated on the potential contributions of oil income to economic growth, possible criteria for the appraisal of government policy with regard to the structural features of the process of growth, and the consideration of aspects of government policy which may have a significant bearing on economic growth and structural change in the context of an oil-exporting mixed economy. Using the terminology developed by Adolph Lowe (1976) it may be said that so far we have been by and large concerned with prescriptive economic analysis; that is, the necessary structural features of traverse from the situation of an oil-exporting underdeveloped economy to an industrialized economy over the lifespan of the oil resources. In this section we shall be mainly concerned with 'descriptive' analysis, that is, with concepts which may help to explain the actual role of the state in the process of growth in the Iranian economy. To stop at the level of prescriptive analysis presupposes a view of the state as an agent with perfect autonomy and a well-defined and consistent preference ordering which sets about shaping a formless or perfectly malleable economy. This is obviously in contradiction with the structuralist methodology we have been using so far. Our starting point rather is to treat the state as a relatively autonomous social institution which, at any moment of time, faces an economic system with a given empirical structure as well as political relations rooted in societal forces conditioning both the capacity of the state to intervene in the economy and content of such intervention. A critical appraisal of the role of the state in economic development and the formulation of realistic and effective policy alternatives requires a knowledge of these conditioning factors, both at the economic and political levels.[24] In what follows we shall thus try to extend our analytical framework to incorporate elements which may work as guidelines in the study of the role of state at different stages of growth in the Iranian economy.

Three broad sets of explanatory factors may be identified in the literature on the role of the state in economic development, which also characterize

---

[24] In an interesting study of the Indian planning experience, Chakravarty (1987) emphasizes the lack of attention to descriptive analysis, or 'force analysis' a la Lowe, as a main shortcoming of both the early planning experience in India as well as the arguments of its critics.

particular approaches to this question depending on which set is used as the central explanatory factor.

The first set of explanatory factors refer to the structural features of the economy, with regard to both the forces and the relations of production, which broadly determine the tasks that the state must undertake in support of accumulation. These tasks define the content of state intervention in different stages of accumulation and dictate the institutional arrangements that may be constructed to perform them. For example, as we shall see in the later chapters, in the case of post-1953 Iran the historical backwardness of industrial capital and the rigid agrarian structure called for the direct intervention by the state to launch the process of capitalist industrialization from above. This took place through provision and control of credit to the private sector, devising an effective incentive scheme for private investment, direct investment by the state in complementary lines of production such as heavy industry, and direct intervention to restructure the agrarian relations of production. However, when presented as the central or the sole explanatory factor, this leads to a theory of the state along the functionalist lines based on a narrow economic reductionism. The form of the state and its economic institutions in this theory are treated as a reflection of the economic base, and state interventions are viewed as a reflection of the needs of the economy at different stages in its development.[25] Although this approach has prompted many valuable studies on the role of state in different countries, it is subject to various criticisms at a general level. As Jessop (1982) has pointed out, once we drop the presupposition inherent in economic reductionism that the economy is a self-reproducing system with its own internal laws of development, then the approach exhibits obvious inconsistencies. In that case the economic structure cannot uniquely define its own path of development, and the state in adopting and implementing a particular strategy of development becomes subject to influence and resistance from socio-political forces as well as being constrained by its own organizational capacities. Without following the monocausal line of reasoning of economic reductionism, we may adopt a more flexible version of its central proposition by maintaining that the economic base sets only the broad structure of choices that confront the state and defines a range of

[25] This interpretation in terms of the 'base-superstructure' model is characteristic of a version of Marxist theories (see Cohen 1978) which builds upon the scattered writings of Marx and Engels, especially in Marx (1972, 1936), and Marx and Engels (1965). For a critical review of this literature see Jessop (1982). Nuti (1979) uses this approach very effectively in studying the different phases of accumulation in the Soviet Union, and Fitzgerald (1974) makes an interesting sketch in this fashion of the changing role of the Latin American states in different phases of import substitution industrialization. Gerschenkron's (1962) work, which derives the character of the state intervention on the basis of the technical requirements of industrialization, may be also classed in the same category.

workable strategies as possible ways of state economic intervention.[26] This would be also consistent with the other two sets of explanatory factors discussed below.

The second set of explanatory factors refer to the balance of class forces and the nature of the political coalitions in power. Different versions of the class theories of state have been put forward where the state institutions are either treated as a site of class struggle or they are seen as tools of administration and instruments of class rule. State intervention in this case is explained in terms of the interests of the political coalitions in power. This approach has sometimes been developed in a voluntarist direction by focussing on the independent political action in the transformation of the economic base. In this case it assumes a tautological dimension where it is always possible to explain state interventions *ex-post* in terms of the interests of the classes who benefit from such intervention. In some of its versions it has also come very close to economic reductionism discussed above, through the assumption that the economic base determines the balance of political forces in the struggle for state power (see Jessop 1982). The class-based theories have been criticized on the grounds of their inadequate conception of what constitutes a social class acting politically. It has been argued that class practices at the political level are filtered through the political organizations of the society and therefore the state structures have an autonomous influence on the constitution of class power, the definition of the class interests at the political level, and the formation of the objectives of the political coalition in power (Poulantzas 1973, Jessop 1982 and Przeworski 1985, chapter 2). This autonomy, however, is relative rather than absolute in two senses of the term; first in that the state structures are themselves historical products of particular socio-economic and political relations, and second in the sense that these same relations determine the possible forms of state intervention as well as conditioning the outcome of such intervention. This introduces the third set of explanatory factors which characterize the nature of the relative autonomy of the state.

The third set of explanatory factors refer to the state structures, namely the institutional forms of representation, internal organization and intervention of the state. The independent effect of the state structures and their overall pattern of activity may be viewed in two ways. First, as we have already mentioned, they may matter because of the way they influence the formation of certain class alliances and collective political actions, and

---

[26] In particular, in oil-exporting economies the existence of ample supplies of financial resources in the form of foreign exchange substantially expands the structure of choices in terms of both the goals and the strategies of development. In fact we shall argue that this widening of the structure of choices introduces a fundamental difference in the state-economy interrelationship between the inter-war and post-1953 periods, or what one may call the pre- and post-oil economy of Iran.

make possible the raising of certain political and economic issues to the exclusion of others. As we shall see in the case of post-1953 Iran, for example, the clientelistic form of representation of the state, based on the exchange of political support in return for the allocation of state resources, had an important impact on the nature of capital accumulation and its distributional implications over this period without being consciously intended by the government. On the other hand, state institutions may matter because of the way they effect the goal oriented interventions by the state.[27] The basis for such goal oriented interventions may be sought in the economic situation as discussed in the first set of explanatory factors. There could be, however, other factors which may prompt purposive state interventions. As Skopol (1985) has pointed out, modern national states are exposed to frequent challenges as well as a constant flow of new ideas and information, which may prompt state intervention to reshape the domestic economy from above. The state is believed to be particularly prone at times of political and economic crises to take the initiative and impose its own solutions over and above the interests of economically dominant classes.[28] Within this perspective, the state institutions would be clearly important both from the point of view of information gathering and policy formulation as well as from the viewpoint of the capacity of the state to implement its policies. In the literature on goal oriented state intervention some specific aspects of state institutions have been given the pride of place as preconditions for successful state action. A prominent factor in this regard is the state's sources of finance. According to a leading source in this literature, a state's means of raising and deploying financial resources tells us more than any other factor about the leverage a state may have for realizing any goal it may pursue.[29] The existence of a well-developed bureaucracy with a sufficient degree of corporate coherence is viewed as another important pre-condition for effective state action (Evans and Rueschmeyer 1985). This in turn depends on the way the state bureaucracy has evolved historically along with other socio-economic and political institutions, and the way it is articulated with the other state structures. For example, as we shall see in the case of Iran over the 1960s and 1970s, despite the appearance of an extensive and recently renovated bureaucratic machinery having access to

[27] This action oriented approach to the question of relative autonomy of the state is prominent in the recent neo-Weberian literature which investigates the various preconditions of the goal oriented state intervention through comparative historical research. See Evans *et al.* (1985).

[28] See Evans and Rueschemeyer (1985). The original formulation of this view is to be found in Marx (1859) in his discussion of the Bonapartist state, though Marx's perspective is far from the action oriented approach to the role of state in the above source.

[29] Skopol 1985, p.17. The origin of the idea, however, is to be found in Weber's discussion of modern bureaucracy. See Weber 1978, pp.963–9.

massive financial resources from the oil sector, the bureaucracy was still severely handicapped in its goal oriented activities due to its subordination to the court and the clientelistic nature of the form of representation of the state.

These three sets of explanatory factors, namely the economic conditions, class relations and the state structures, evolve in a complex and interdependent manner in historically specific settings. It would be therefore implausible to try to construct a deductive general theory of the role of state by giving logical or historical priority to any one of them in the determination of the other two (Jessop 1982, Evans *et al.* 1986). This is particularly the case in transitional economies like Iran, where the economy is composed of a complex articulation of different forms of production, superimposed by state institutions borrowed from the western capitalist countries. The purpose of the brief review of these different sets of explanatory factors has not been to construct a theory of the role of state in Iran or other oil-exporting countries, either. Rather the object has been to set up some preliminary guidelines to help to construct what Jessop (1982) has called a 'theoretically informed' empirical account of the role of the state in different stages of growth in Iran. The empirical task, therefore, is not to select between these explanatory factors, but rather to weave these notions together in an attempt to interpret the state-economy interactions in an analytically coherent manner.

To recapitulate, the salient features of the structuralist framework adopted could be summarized as follows. Instead of being an all-encompassing deductive theoretical model, the structuralist approach represents a broad analytical framework which is flexible enough to incorporate the specific factors underlying the experience of growth in different stages of accumulation. These 'specific factors' do not refer to unique events which come about accidentally and shape the experience of growth in a succession of disjointed chronological epochs. They rather refer to those economic relations and institutional factors which are the organic counterparts of the historical process of economic growth. Economic growth in each phase runs up against impediments which arise out of the historically given structure of economic relations, and each phase of accumulation is defined in terms of these impediments and the structural relations which underlie them. The transition from one phase of development into another is therefore characterized by the formation of new institutional arrangements which re-establish the growth of the economy on a new basis. This dynamics of growth and institutional change does not take place in a unilineal and predetermined fashion, but rather as a result of the response by social actors to the new economic problems within the constraints set by their material and organizational capabilities. The state, being 'the concentrated and organised force of society', inevitably plays a prominent role in this process. The analysis of the role of state is grounded in the actual historical experience, taking into account a multiplicity of factors related to the economic situation, class relations, as well as the 'relative autonomy' of the state. The impact of oil income on economic development is analysed in terms of its effect on the institutional setup of the economy and the state and the way these in turn determine the mode of utilization of oil income and the pattern of structural change and growth.

The breadth of the analysis has required a narrowing down of the focus of investigation to selected aspects of growth which have been particularly significant in Iranian economic development and may be so for other oil-exporting developing countries. The emphasis varies over different periods depending on the availability of data, but it remains within the three broad themes of: (i) the sectoral composition of physical capital formation and the resulting structure of output, (ii) the financing of accumulation and (iii) aspects of the interrelations between income distribution and growth. The role of the state is accordingly analysed in terms of its income generating and capacity generating impacts through direct means (involving extraction and direct utilization of the economic surplus by the state) or indirect means (through institutional changes, incentive schemes, etc.). Though our main concern is the study of growth over the oil period in the present century, many of the deep structural features of the economy and state had their origin in the transformations which took place in the last century, prior to the discovery of oil. In the next chapter, therefore, we shall begin with an analysis of these earlier transformations, which is also an investigation into the roots of economic backwardness as well as the pre-conditions for the rise of the modern state in the early twentieth century.

2

Capitalist development and the transformation of the Iranian state 1800–1920

2.1 Introduction

The purpose of this chapter is to study the structure of the medieval state in Iran and its transformation under the impact of capitalist west during the nineteenth and early twentieth centuries.[1] The chapter is divided into two parts. In the first part we examine the medieval socio-economic system in its broad outlines with special emphasis on the role of the state in the process of economic reproduction and change. The second part examines the different processes through which the penetration of modern western capitalism undermined the social bases of the traditional state. The main emphasis in this section is on the specific role of the state in the process of transition.

The question of the role of state in the political economy of medieval Iran has been a controversial one. The roots of this controversy to some extent lie in the paucity of empirical research and undue over-generalizations which this has given rise to. To a larger extent, however, it reflects the differences in outlook as to what constituted the 'essential' features of the medieval economy. Two broad tendencies could be distinguished in the literature. The first one regards the state as an epiphenomenon or as a superstructure whose functions are relegated to the secondary one of providing the general preconditions for socio-economic reproduction. Accordingly, it is main-

---

[1] The 'Medieval Period' here refers to the eight centuries from the rise of the *Seljuqs* in the eleventh century up to the nineteenth century. During this period, the main features of the socio-economic structure remained, more or less, intact. It coincides with the rise of the *Iqta* system of land tenure which, according to Lambton (1953, p.53), 'lasted in its essentials throughout the middle ages down to the 20th century'. Other aspects of the agrarian mode of production such as, form of rent, methods of organization of labour, techniques of production, type of crops, system of crop rotation and land utilization, according to the available evidence, also did not undergo any substantial transformations (see Lambton 1953, specially pp.1–9, 210–29, 295–392, Petrushevsky 1978, chapters 3, 4, 6–8, Khamsi 1968, Rawandi 1977, vol.3, pp.220–62). On the political level also this period exhibits certain continuity in being the period of dominance of Turkish and Mongol tribal dynasties; the so-called 'Touranian Period' (see Smith Jr. 1978, Berard 1910, Pegulevskaya *et al.* 1975).

tained that the medieval economy of Iran in its essentials was similar to that of the feudal system in medieval Europe. This is based on a minimal definition of the feudal mode of production as the combination of large landownership and small peasant production, where surplus extraction takes the form of extra-economic coercion and where commodity exchange and labour mobility are correspondingly restricted.[2]

The second tendency has been to consider the role of the state as determining, both in the reproduction of the economic system and its possible transformation over time. According to this view the character and position of the state in the medieval economy of Iran formed its main structural differential *vis-à-vis* the feudal system in western Europe, and therein lied the 'essence' of the divergent development paths in the two systems. For example Ashraf (1970), drawing upon the seventeenth-century experience of the Safavid state, emphasizes the centralized and bureaucratic aspects of the medieval state as the 'obstacle to the development of the bourgeoisie in Iran'; while Katouzian (1981), mainly blames the 'despotism' or 'arbitrary power' of the state and its juridical counterpart, i.e., the absence of 'private property'.

The position taken in this chapter is closer to the latter point of view to the extent that we consider the character and position of the state in the medieval economy to be of crucial significance for the dynamics of the system. We shall, however, try to avoid the kind of 'essentialism' which has characterized the above-mentioned debate. Any attempt at explaining the dynamics of a complex socio-economic system, over such a long period of time, in terms of some abstract attributes of the state is most likely to end up in simplistic generalizations. We shall instead try for a more concrete understanding of the character and position of the state in the medieval economy, by analysing the way it entered into the constitutive structure of production relations and its possible effect on the solidity of these relations.[3] This is attempted through a synthesis of the evidence and views expressed on both sides of the above debate. This serves as a background against which we can study the subsequent transformations in the form and

[2] For a brief review of this literature, see Ashraf (1970). See also Noamani (1972).

[3] This is in sharp contrast to the treatment of the impact of the medieval state of economic development in the above literature. For example, Ashraf (1970) mainly concentrates on the role of the state in the sphere of circulation, its control over merchant capital, and the barriers it created for the spread of 'capitalist rationality' which supposedly would have emanated from the expansion of market relations and trade. Capitalism is mainly regarded as an urban phenomenon and as an entity external to the medieval economy, which develops with the expansion of trade relations and gradually replaces the medieval mode of production. For a critique of this 'distributionist' tendency in the context of development of capitalism in western Europe, see Dobb (1972, pp.38–42), Merrington (1975), Hilton (1978), and Brenner (1977).

functions of the Iranian state during the nineteenth and the early twentieth centuries.

2.2 The role of the state in the political economy of medieval Iran

Similar to the feudal system in medieval Europe, political relations directly entered the internal nexus of the relations of production in the medieval economy of Iran. Nevertheless, the two systems processed their own specific characteristics which distinguish them both in terms of their internal structure and their evolution over time.[4]

A major distinguishing feature of the medieval society of Iran lay in the prevalence of pastoral nomadism. Even by the nineteenth century, after the Russian conquests in central Asia had pacified the indigenous nomadic tribes, it is estimated that about half of the remaining population of Iran was composed of nomads (Issawi 1971, p.20). The coexistence of the settled and pastoral modes of production, which was to a large extent conditioned by natural and climatic circumstances,[5] exerted an important influence on the overall structure of the political economy of medieval Iran.

In particular the military superiority of the nomads over the sedentary population, and the tendency of the small socio-economic units of nomadic tribes to form larger political alliances due to the practical needs of their migratory mode of life, had major political and economic consequences for the whole of the system.[6]

At the political level, the military potential of the normally dispersed nomads formed the backbone of the rise of various tribal dynasties which took power through the coalition of different tribal groups. The perpetual rise and fall of various tribal dynasties, during this period, created a peculiarly unstable political configuration which exhibited a regular pattern of centralization and decentralization of political authority during different phases of dynastic rule. Given the direct involvement of political relations in the internal structure of the relations of production in the pre-

---

[4] The following summary of the western European feudal system by Anderson (1979, p.407) could be used as a point of reference in this context: 'Feudalism involves the juridical serfdom and military protection of the peasantry by a social class of nobles enjoying individual authority and property, and exercising an exclusive monopoly of law and private rights of justice, within a political framework of fragmented sovereignty and subordinate fiscality. Further derivative aspects of this configuration were, 'the rural residence by the possessive class and . . . the growth of autonomous towns in the interstitial spaces between disparate lordships' (Ibid. p.409).

[5] Fisher (1961, pp.129–30, 213–17). The dichotomy, however, was not so strict, as the category of semi-settled agriculturalists filled the gap between the pastoral nomads and the sedentary agriculturalists (see Berard 1910, Garthwaite 1978).

[6] On the 'military differential' of pastoral mode of production over sedentary agriculture and the nature of nomadic political alliances see Smith Jr. (1978), Garthwaite (1978), Barard (1910, chapter ii).

capitalist economy of medieval Iran, this unstable political configuration had a direct bearing upon the structure of the economy. This was specially manifest in the structure of the land tenure system and the degree of control over economic surplus by the different strata of the ruling class.

The interaction between settled and nomadic modes of existence had given rise to a peculiar stratification of the ruling classes in medieval Iran. One could identify the following broad groupings within the ruling classes in medieval Iran: (a) the military aristocracy of the nomad tribes; Mongol, Turkish, Kurds, etc., (b) the settled local provincial nobility, not connected by service to the central government, (c) the civil service and (d) the Moslem religious cast, i.e., the clergy.[7] According to Petrushevsky 'These groups who struggled with one another to control the state, expressed two parallel political tendencies in Iranian society – that of tribal disintegration together with a system of military fiefs, and that of a centralized state together with a ramifying bureaucratic apparatus' (Petrushevsky 1968, p.515). The result of this power struggle between different strata of the ruling classes was highly correlated with the vicissitudes of the rise and fall of various tribal dynasties which ruled over the Iranian plateau from the tenth century AD up to the present century.[8]

Three phases could be distinguished in the processes of rise and fall of each ruling dynasty.[9] Phase one was the period of conquest and expansion when the dominant influence was the tradition of the tribe. In this phase bureaucracy was over-shadowed by the tribal structure of the polity and the traditional chiefs of the conquering tribes were independent rulers (Amirs) of the conquered provinces and only nominally affiliated to the central government.[10] The degree of control of the central government over the

[7] Petrushevsky 1968, Pegulevskaya *et al* (1975, p.347), Minorsky (1980, pp.14–19).

[8] The regularity of these political cycles which appears to have been a common feature of the whole region of the Middle East with its peculiar blend of settled and nomadic populations receives its most vivid expression in the works of Ibn-Khaldun, the fourteenth-century historian and public administrator in North Africa, who theorizes them in terms of the 'natural life cycles' of dynastic rule. Ibn-Khaldun's exposition of the life cycle of tribal dynasties corresponds with a high degree of accuracy to the vicissitudes of the changing political configuration in medieval Iran. See Ibn-Khaldun (1967, pp. 123–261). See also Berard (1910, p.54) where he maintains that the regularity of these political cycles could be captured with 'algebraic accuracy'.

[9] This general characterization is mainly based on the following sources: V. Barard (1910) and Ibn-Khaldun (1967) which give a broad overview; for pre-Mongol era see Ensafpour (1979), Pegulevskaya *et al*. (1975), for Ilkhani period see Petrushevsky (1968), and for Safavid era see Minorsky (1980). This three-phase characterization of dynastic rule assumes its most clear expression in the process of the rise and fall of the Safavid dynasty during the sixteenth and seventeenth centuries, to which we refer frequently for expositionary purposes.

[10] A typical example is the structure of polity during Shah Tahmasb (AD 1524–76) in the earlier part of the Safavid dynasty, where the 114 Amirs who filled the positions of commanders of the troops, governors and high officials, were all composed of the tribal aristocracy and mainly of Turkish origin (see Minorsky 1980).

provincial rulers during this phase depended on the ability of the sovereign to exploit the differences and collisions of interest of the local tribal chiefs. The concept of 'tribal feudalism' which is used by some authors (see, e.g., Keddie 1968, p.158, Minorsky 1980, p.14) to epitomize the medieval society of Iran could be justifiably applied to this phase of the dynastic rule.

The initial political coalition, however, would not necessarily last, i.e., by a gradual expansion of the civil and military bureaucracy, new alliances replaced the old ones which in effect implied the replacement of 'the unruly feudalism of the tribes and local dynasties' by centralization (Minorsky 1980, p.14). This second phase of the dynastic rule is usually referred to as that of 'Persianization' of the tribal polity (see, e.g., Lambton 1953, p.77, Petrushevsky 1968, p.495). In this phase we observe the transfer of the leading political role in the state from the nomad aristocracy to the Iranian officialdom. The central government, during this phase, attempted to bring the provincial tribal rulers under its own control by directly appointing the tribal chiefs, and reducing their autonomy by delegating many of their functions to a differentiated centralized officialdom.[11]

The civil and military apparatus in its centralized phase exhibited features akin to Weber's concept of 'patrimonial officialdom' (Weber 1978, pp.1006–71). To eliminate the local nobility, the king needed an administrative organization of his own which could replace them. Otherwise a new stratum of local notables would come into being with similar pretensions as their native predecessors. Thus the personal loyalty of the state officials to the central rulers had to be ensured. The use of the personal slaves (Ghulams) of the Shah as the chief military commanders and administrators who replaced the tribal nobility is a reflection of this need (see Minorsky 1980, pp.12–19). Thus in contrast to modern bureaucracy the position of officials, as a matter of principle, derived from their purely personal submission to their superior. Related to this was the lack of a clear cut separation between the public realm and the private domain of the sovereign who assigned his personal dependants as the heads of the political offices.[12] Furthermore, the area of jurisdiction of each official was not defined by impersonal norms and regulations, but delimited by the powers bestowed at the discretion of the King, the competing claims of other

[11] This process was by no means free from political struggle. According to Chardin, during the reign of Shah Abbas I (AD 1587–1629), 'in order to unify the kingdom which was split up amongst various tribal lords, the king had to conquer it as if it was a foreign land'. Quoted from Minorsky (1980, pp. 12–19).

[12] According to Minorsky (1980, p.25) 'Though the supervision of mamalek provinces was concentrated in a special Divan-i Mamalek, . . . in practise it could hardly be constructed into a state administration entirely distinct from the direct interests of the king and his court'. On this see also Lambton (1953, p.78), Noamani (1981, p.22), Sheikholeslami (1971, pp.104–7).

officials and tradition. The resulting fluidity of the area of jurisdiction of this patrimonial officialdom is in sharp contrast to the modern bureaucracy with its formal rules.

The reproduction of this pattern of political authority was, by its very nature, very precarious. With the territorial expansion of the empire, the centrifugal forces, both internal and external to the officialdom, would lead to the diffusion of political authority. The central state could not inhibit the gradual transformation of its officialdom, specially in the outlying regions, into a stratum of territorial lords which through time become independent of the central administration. Thus began the third phase of the dynastic rule which was the period of decline and political disintegration of the state.[13] Petrushevsky (1968) refers to this phase as the period of 'feudal dismemberment' of the polity. According to Lambton in this phase, 'the functions of the provincial governor, the provincial military commander, the tax collector, and the man to whom land was assigned tended to be combined in one person', leading to the 'emergence of large landed properties in which the holder carried out most of the functions of government to the virtual exclusion of central govenment' (1969, pp.21–2). This phase would normally lead to either violent internal upheavals or invasion by outlying nomadic tribes, bringing about a restructuring of the political configuration and the start of a new cycle.

This constant restructuring of the political configuration which did not allow the perpetuation and hence – to borrow a Weberian term – the 'typification' of political relations, is in sharp contrast to the structure of feudal polity in western Europe with its stable parcelization of sovereignty and contractually bound aristocracy.[14] This situation of unstable power relations between the different strata of the ruling class, is well reflected in the ideology of medieval state which envisaged the sovereign as a grand arbiter whose main function was 'to maintain the classes in their proper ranks' (see Lambton 1962, p.95).

The fluidity of political power and its cyclical change was directly reflected in the nature of the land tenure system which exhibited a similar kind of instability and fluidity. This was expressed in the category of *Iqta* (later known as *tuyul*), which was a form of land assignment, implying a

---

[13] Ibn-Khaldun (1967, p.245) calls this phase the period of senility of the dynasty and treats it as a phenomenon which occurs with natural inevitability.

[14] The abstract and usually undefined concepts of 'oriental despotism' and its counterpart 'arbitrary rule', which are commonly used to characterize the political structure in medieval Iran, refer to this fluidity of political power between different sections of the ruling class. As far as the relations between the ruling class and their subjects are concerned, western European serfdom typified an equally arbitrary power relation, as in Iran (see Brenner 1976).

non-routinized possession of land and/or claim to its revenue. Concerning the characterization of this category of land ownership Lambton writes:

> The most important medieval institution connected with the land was the land assignment, the Iqta . . . it was a grant of land or its revenue or both, with or without immunities made by government to its officers and others. The holder of the land assignment, although he often succeeded in transforming it into private property which he transmitted by inheritance, had his assignment solely at the will of the ruler. It might be revoked or assigned to someone else at any moment, in which case the only remedy of the original assignee was to defend it by force. (1969, pp.21–2)

Given the above discussed cyclical dynamics of the locus of political power, *Iqta* (the land assignment) would invariably run the same gamut from assignment of revenue for service to outright usurpation of proprietary rights.[15]

This also affected the relation between grantees and the population on the territory of their *Iqta*. As far as the theoretical rights of the grantees over their subjects were concerned, 'the principle was that the grantees were only entitled to collect the revenue due to them without interfering with any other rights of the population' (Minorsky 1980, p.28). The *Iqta* holder, however, 'at all times contrived to circumvent the theoretical distinctions and limitations so as to transform their holdings into a more permanent ownership and even to assume some seignioral rights on them' (*Ibid.*). Whatever the degree of delimitation of the rights of assignees over their subjects, the non-residence of the land holders in the rural areas as well as the structure of the natural economy of village communities in practice meant that the relation of the *Iqta* holder to his subjects was mainly a tributary one.[16]

The basic units of the rural socio-economic life were the village community and the tribal community of herdsmen. Organizationally, both the nomadic and settled rural societies appear to have been composed of communal units with their own internal autonomy and high degree of

---

[15] See Banani (1978). This interrelationship between landownership and political power further meant that the basic categories of land (such as, *Vaqf, Khasseh, Khalesseh, Arababi,* etc.) underwent a constant change of boundary and composition. For example, notice the expansion of *Khasseh* and *Vaqf* lands at the centralized phase of Safavid rule, or the confiscation of *Vaqf* lands and the expansion of state lands (*Khalesseh*) during the reign of Nadir Shah. For more examples see Lambton (1953).

[16] Lambton (1953, pp.5–6). The European manorial system and its counterparts during high middle ages, i.e., demesne farming and corve labour, were absent in medieval Iran and the landlords had little direct connection with agricultural production. The above-mentioned tributary relation was basically composed of different kinds of taxes and a customary type of rent based on share cropping (*Muzare'e*), with varying rates over different regions and in different periods. The peasantry was also subject to irregular corve labour in non-agricultural works.

communal jurisdiction over the internal affairs of the community. These communal units formed the mediatory links between the individual producers and the higher polity.[17]

Agrarian surplus was overwhelmingly disposed of in the cities by the ruling class who mainly resided in the urban areas. As a result the town did not possess the municipal autonomy of the city communes of the eleventh-to sixteenth-century western Europe, and did not develop any corporate political identity. The towns were rather characterized by a certain dismemberment with their residents organized in corporations called *Asnaf*. These corporations were mainly professional guilds, but, while their social functions were on the whole broader than those of the European guilds, their economic power and their control over their professions were less absolute than in the west.[18] Craft guilds had the same restrictive economic functions as the European guilds and the same hierarchic order of organization, but they were under strict state control (Lewis 1937, Ashraf 1970, 1980). A comparison between the socio-economic and administrative structures of the medieval western European towns and the towns in medieval Iran would at once make it clear how the overall social matrix in the two systems was structured around their respective agrarian modes of production. The autonomous medieval towns in Europe were as much a reflection of the fragmented sovereignty of the feudal system and its rural-based ruling class, as the Iranian towns were structured by an urban-based ruling class.

2.2.1 *Political power and economic stagnation*

So far we have been considering the broad outlines of the socio-economic system and political relations which constituted the political economy of medieval Iran. Two interrelated tendencies have been observed by histori-

---

[17] Information on the village level structure and organization of production is scant. The following features are, however, commonly accepted by all the writers. The unit of production was in general the small peasant holding but the possession of land was vested in the higher community of the village, and it was through the membership of the village community that the individual would get access to the land (Lambton 1953, pp.1–9). The communal possession of land is said to have been due to both natural and political conditions. The need for communal labour for producing some of the general preconditions of production (e.g., irrigation networks, *Qanats*, etc.), the need for defence, and finally the state's treatment of village as a corporate unit for taxation purposes are enumerated as the main cause of the rise of communal mode of production (Lambton 1953, Ono 1967). Administratively the villages in general appear to have enjoyed a considerable degree of autonomy and were organized as self-sustained and self-governing communities (Lambton 1954, pp.8–9).

[18] See Lambton (1954). According to Lewis (1937, p.20), since the cities of the Middle East never reached the degree of community organization that marked that of the west, the guilds had to take up some of the vacuum and took on functions that were not only professional as in Europe, but supplied the basic framework for the life of the cities as a whole.

ans with regard to the long-term evolution of this system over time. First is the long-term internal stability of the system and the persistence of its basic structures down to the nineteenth century when it began to disintegrate under the impact of western capitalism. The second tendency is the long-run deterioration in the forces of production, especially in the agricultural sector, which is believed to have been taking place throughout this period.[19] These two interrelated phenomena should be considered as the effect of the totality of the socio-economic and political relations which constituted the political economy of medieval Iran. Any attempt to reduce the effect of these complex social relations to some abstract essence – be it the lack of 'private property', 'despotism of the state', or the rule of 'arbitrary power'[20] – is bound to produce a one-sided and incomplete explanation of stability and change in the medieval socio-economic system. As we noted in the foregoing analysis, it is not possible to grasp the nature of property relations in medieval times in abstraction from the character of the political relations which were in turn structured by the peculiar nature of the agrarian mode of production – i.e., the spatial separation of the sedentary and pastoral modes of production.

The object of the present study is not to construct a theory of the long-term dynamics of the political economy of medieval Iran. Neither the state of the existing research nor the confines of the present study would allow such an attempt here. We may, however, draw upon the above analysis to bring into focus some of the elements which could contribute to the construction of such a theory, with emphasis on those factors which have been relatively neglected by the existing analytical models on the political economy of medieval Iran. One of the more influential of such models which has shaped the research project of many of the more specialized works on the Iranian medieval system is Marx's concept of the Asiatic mode of production (AMOP). A comparison between this concept, as it appears in Marx's later writings,[21] and our foregoing exposition of Iran's socio-economic system would help to underline some of these elements.

[19] See Issawi (1970), Keddie (1981 and 1980, chapter 7). This appears to have been a common feature of the whole region of the Middle East (see Hershlag 1964, p.7, Issawi 1966, p.12, and 1970). According to Issawi (1970, p.245), 'by any economic criteria, Middle East stood far lower in the 18th century than in the 10th or 11th'.

[20] These notions play a central explanatory function in many of the analytical works on political economy of medieval Iran. See Ashraf (1970), Khosravi (1979), Katouzian (1981).

[21] Here we are mainly dealing with the concept of the AMOP as developed in Grundrisse (Marx 1977, pp. 471–4) and dominated Marx's later writings on this subject. The alternative 'hydraulic' model found in the earlier writings of Marx and Engels and later developed in Wittfogel (1967) is not relevant to the case of Iran. For a review of the scattered writings of Marx and Engels on the AMOP, see Sawer (1977), H. Draper, vol.II (1978), Anderson (1979, pp.462–549).

Marx's account of the AMOP in Grundrisse is centred around the notion of 'self sustaining village communities' which form the basic social cells upon which an exploitative polity is superimposed. The communal form of appropriation of nature, which according to Marx is an 'initial, naturally arisen and spontaneous' form, pertaining to the pastoral and migratory period of human life, persisted in Asia even after the pastoral class settled on land.[22]

This communal form of property is, according to Marx, the real foundation for the whole socio-political edifice in the 'Orient'. He maintains:

> amidst oriental despotism and the propertylessness which seems legally to exist there, this class or communal property exists in fact as the foundation, created mostly by a combination of manufacture and agriculture within the small commune, which thus becomes altogether self sustaining and contains all the conditions of reproduction within itself. (Marx 1977, p.473)

Marx further constructs a theory of the dynamics of the AMOP based on the same idea of self-sustaining village communities. According to him they supply 'the key to the secret of unchangeability of Asiatic societies' (Marx 1977, p.479), and it is due to the simplicity of the production organization in these self-sustained communities that 'the structure of the fundamental economic elements of society remain untouched by the storm clouds of the political sky' (*ibid.*). The structure of the state, the relations between the ruling classes and the rural communities, and the form of the economic surplus are treated in a very general and abstract manner and given secondary importance in this conception of the AMOP and its tendency to change. The only specification on the form of surplus is that 'it takes the form of tribute' (Marx 1977, p.473), and the political structure could assume a 'more despotic or more democratic form' (*Ibid.*), without major implications for the dynamics of the system.

As could be seen the various features of this conception of AMOP do not contradict the evidence presented in our foregoing analysis in the case of Iran.[23] This concept of the AMOP, however, gives an incomplete picture of the manifold socio-economic and political relations which had a direct bearing upon the constitution of production relations and their solidity

---

[22] Marx (1977, p.472). The ossification of communal form of property, according to Marx, could be due to 'various, external, climatic, geographic, physical etc. conditions as well as their particular natural predispositions, their class character'.

[23] See specifically footnotes 16 and 17. It should be noted, however, that the notion of 'self-sustained village communities' which forms the basis of this version of AMOP has been recently criticized on the basis of empirical evidence from India (see Anderson 1979, p.488). The available evidence, however, seems to support it not only in the case of Iran but the whole of Middle East region (see Harshlag 1964, pp.17–18).

over time in the case of Iran.[24] One of the main aspects of the medieval society of Iran which is absent from Marx's concept of the AMOP, and which exerted a major influence on the overall structure of the economic system, is the coexistence of the settled and nomadic populations and the impact of this phenomenon on the political configuration of medieval Iran. The military differential of the nomadic mode of existence over settled agriculture could be argued to have played a major part in the consolidation of the dominant position of the ruling classes *vis-à-vis* the peasantry and the preservation of the prevalent relations of production. The absolute political and military superiority of the ruling class over the peasantry and the resulting over-exploitation of the countryside which is widely referred to in the existing literature (see Petrushevsky 1978, Lambton 1953, chapter xvii), should be considered as an important factor in explaining the stagnation of the agricultural sector. Another aspect of the political structure which enhanced the tendency towards over-exploitation of the peasantry, was its impact on the land tenure system. The fluidity of political relations and the lack of a stable landed aristocracy which created an inherent insecurity in the ownership relations prompted the landlord to over-exploit his temporary right of ownership and led to a general neglect of agriculture. Lambton concludes her detailed study of the landlord-peasant relations in medieval Iran by underlying these two phenomena as the main causes of agricultural decline in the following words:

> Over taxation and the tendency of government officials towards extraction, together with insecurity were the main causes of agricultural decay which became apparent on the disintegration of the Abbasid empire and has continued with certain breaks down to the present day. (1953, p.337)

It also appears plausible that the preservation of the autarchic economy of the village communities, which in Marx's theory of the AMOP is treated as the foundation of the whole system, could itself be to a large extent explained as a particular effect of the political structure.[25] Given the direct appropriation of the main part of the agricultural surplus in kind by the

---

[24] This aspect of Marx's concept of the AMOP – i.e., its inability to produce a concrete explanation of the dynamics of the system – has already been criticized, at a more general level, in the recent literature. See Hindess and Hirst (1975, pp.201–4), Anderson (1979, pp.484–520). Hindess and Hirst's criticism is of a more general character. They criticize the teleological pre-supposition of any attempt to derive the dynamics of concrete historical formations on the basis of the abstract concept of mode of production.

[25] As far as the communal structure of the village is concerned, as we noted above (see footnote 17), some historians maintain that the preservation of this form was largely maintained due to the state's treatment of the village as a corporate unit for taxation purposes. See also Hershlag (1964, p.17).

ruling classes and its transfer to the towns, the over-exploitation of the peasantry would have left little exchangeable surplus which could transform the natural economy of the villages.

There are, no doubt, other political, socio-economic, physical, etc. factors which could be identified as having a likely effect on the dynamics of the medieval system.[26] We need not however pursue this point any further, as the above would serve the purpose of highlighting the likely significance of the political relations in explaining the persistence of the medieval system over such a long span of time.[27]

The main object of this section has been to provide a concrete specification of the structure of the political economy of medieval Iran and the situation of the state in that structure. This would help to put into perspective the transformation of the system during the course of the nineteenth century under the impact of western capitalism, and to explain the specific role of the state in this process of transformation.

2.3 Impact of the west and the transformation of the Iranian state 1800–1920

During the nineteenth century and the first two decades of the twentieth century important transformations took place in the medieval socio-economic system, under the impact of modern western capitalism. The foundations of the traditional state were undermined and a totally new set of state institutions and a new form of state-economy interrelationship came into being. A fundamental mechanism in this process of transformation was the integration of the Iranian economy into the world market, which radically affected the position of the different social classes in Iranian society. This process of economic integration, however, did not take place independently of the transformations in other structures of the Iranian social formation. In particular, the traditional state, forming an important mediating link in this process of integration and playing a central role in the internal mechanisms of the medieval agrarian mode of production, left its specific imprint on the outcome of this process of economic transformation.

---

[26] One can mention absentee landlordism, perpetual state of chaos and warfare, aridity of the climate and the difficulty it created in sustaining draught animals, etc. This last factor could be of special significance even for later periods, as it rules out the 'ultimately revolutionary method of convertible husbandry' which is said to have been at the centre of the agrarian revolution in the eighteenth-century western Europe (see Chambers and Mingay 1966).

[27] The political factor mentioned in the text, specially the political and military resources of the peasantry *vis-à-vis* the landlords, are of special interest, because they form a central variable in the transition debate in western Europe (see Hilton 1978, Brenner 1976).

2.3.1 The structure of state in early nineteenth-century Iran

The political structure of the newly formed Qajar dynasty during the early nineteenth century corresponded to the first phase of the tribal dynastic cycles discussed in the previous section: where the tribal structure of the polity over-shadowed its bureaucratic aspects and political power was very diffuse. Tribal chiefs and provincial rulers governed without the direct intervention of the central authority.[28] The central state and its rudimentary officialdom could only exert its authority over the local rulers to the extent that it was successful in manipulating the factional rivalries between different independent tribal chiefs (Abrahamian 1974). Political fragmentation of the Qajar realm, however, had more deep seated structural causes and should not be considered as a normal phase of the old recurrent political cycles. This view is reinforced by the unsuccessful attempts during the reign of Fath-Ali Shah (1797–1834) to reconstruct the decentralized tribal polity. Although this led to a rapid growth of the traditional bureaucratic apparatus, the central state did not manage to exert much control over this apparatus (see Meredith 1971).

Some of the basic reasons for the political fragmentation of the early Qajar rule should be sought in the state of the economy during the early nineteenth century. Although the underlying socio-economic structure had not undergone any significant qualitative changes, quantitatively, as compared to the seventeenth century, there was a considerable decline in all aspects of the economic life of the country. The decline of the transcontinental Karavan trade, as well as a century of political chaos had led to a significant decline in foreign trade.[29] There was a considerable fall in the size of the population: the countryside even in comparatively fertile areas was underpopulated and urban population had also declined noticeably. The economy was composed of virtually self-sufficient regions and internal exchange had been reduced to a minimum.[30] The decline of money economy, paucity of means of communication, dispersion of the population over vast tracts of land, and the relatively low ratio of the settled to nomadic and urban to rural populations, all combined to hinder the centralization of political power during this period.[31]

---

[28] On the early Qajar state administration see C. Meredith (1971), Lambton (1953, pp.129–50).

[29] On foreign trade during this period, see the articles by Lambton (1970), Issawi (1970), and Hambly (1964).

[30] Economic conditions during late eighteenth and early nineteenth centuries are discussed in Hambly (1964), Hershlag (1964, part v), and Lambton (1953, chapter vi).

[31] Nowshirwani and Knight (1975), Abrahamian (1974), Keddie (1981). Of the other structural causes for the weakness of central state during the early Qajar rule, the following are emphasized in the literature: (a) the greater autonomization of the cast of the clergy since

It was at this conjuncture that the country was opened to the influence of modern western capitalism. This influence was exerted through different channels, from direct political and military intervention, to economic penetration and permeation of new ideas on modern modes of organization of socio-economic and political life. The immediate impact of western imperialism, however, was to further weaken the political power of the central state.

2.3.2 Imperialist domination and the state

Nineteenth-century imperialism in the case of Iran took the form of rivalry between its two powerful neighbours for political supremacy over the Qajar state. The Iranian internal politics during this period – down to the eve of the First World War – was highly conditioned by its being a buffer state between the fast expanding Russian empire in central Asia and the British empire in the south (India).[32] This resulted in yet another cleavage in the already weak administrative apparatus of the Qajar state by polarizing the already fragmented traditional political elite along the lines of competing interests of the two powers.[33] The two powers are said to have used their political leverage to 'prevent any major internal changes which they believed would effect their position in Iran' (Bakhash 1978, p.206). An immediate impact of the imperialist intervention was thus to deepen the already existing structural weakness of the central state and further limit the domain of its effective action, while at the same time keeping it from total collapse.

2.3.3 From the early reforms to the final decay of the state

The structural weaknesses of the Qajar state, arising in the first place from the internal conditions, and exacerbated by the interference and rivalry of the two imperialist powers, undermined the various reform movements which were initiated by the higher ranks of the state administration. Two distinct phases of reform movement could be distinguished – both initiating from within the state bureaucracy. The first one, which arose in immediate response to the threat that the military and technological superiority of the west posed to the authority of the traditional state, did not envisage any fundamental structural reforms either in the socio-economic organization

the seventeenth century (Berard 1910, Keddie 1981, pp. 1–23), (b) the breakdown of the slave institution (Meredith 1971) and (c) the duality of power within the Qajar tribe itself (Berard 1910).

[32] On the political and diplomatic history of imperialist intervention in nineteenth-century Iran, see Kazemzadeh (1968).

[33] See Bakhash (1978, pp.204–60), Kazemzadeh (1968, pp.148–240).

or in the organization of the state apparatus itself.[34] These reforms were mainly directed towards the strengthening of the state mechanism by making a more effective use of the traditional bureaucracy.[35]

What distinguished the second phase of the reform movement during the latter half of the century, was its more conscious and preconceived plan to restructure the whole state apparatus on the pattern of the modern western forms of government. These reforms which were theorized and put into effect by a small group of bureaucratic elite who also enjoyed the support of the Shah, could be viewed as the outcome of the cumulative process of contact with the west during the first half of the century. This, on the one hand, had made imminent an acute political and financial crisis for the traditional state, and on the other, had shown the possibilities for the reorganization of socio-economic and political life. The framers of these reforms, however, arising from the higher ranks of the traditional bureaucracy with its state centred ideology, had their own interpretation as to what constituted the essence of the modern social system in the west.[36] To these reformers what constituted the most essential and innovative feature of the western capitalist system was its form of state institutions. Accordingly, it was the renovation of the administrative apparatus of the state (e.g., the introduction of modern bureaucratic forms, separation of powers, promulgation of legal codes, etc.), which formed the central theme of the reforms envisioned during this period.[37] No structural socio-economic reforms were as yet conceptualized, apart from what seemed immediately relevant for the restructuring of the state machinery.[38] Although this second phase of reforms was pursued in a more purposeful fashion and with an increased sense of urgency, it did not have a better fate than the previous attempts, because this time they encountered a tougher resistance from within the traditional officialdom, who were the first group whose position would be endangered by such reforms.[39]

[34] On these early reform attempts, see Lorenze (1971), Farmanfarmayan (1968), Adamiyyat (1945).

[35] Amir Kabir's reforms represented the most serious attempt of this kind which ended unsuccessfully with his downfall in 1851, and culminated this phase of the reform movement. According to Adamiyyat (1945, vol.2), apart from the opposition of the indigenous vested interests – both within and outside the officialdom – the Russian intrigue also played a part in the downfall of Amir Kabir.

[36] For a study of the second phase of reforms, which is mainly identified with the name of Moshir o-Dowleh and Malkam Khan, see Bakhash (1978).

[37] See Bakhash (1978, pp.1–203).

[38] Here we are not taking the voluntaristic stand that, had these reforms envisioned a more thorough going idea of social change they would have succeeded in materializing them. The idea is rather to trace the evolution of the ideology of the Iranian state, from its traditional conception where the state was envisioned as a part of the natural order of the universe to the modern developmentalist state with its ideology of social engineering.

[39] This does not mean that the fate of these reforms was solely determined by intra-bureaucratic struggles. It had a wider socio-political context as is evident, on the one hand,

Failure of these attempts to restructure the state administration created a cumulative process of political disintegration which, by the end of the century, led to the total breakdown of central state's authority and legitimacy. The financial problems of the state and the underlying changes in the economy played a central role in this cumulative process. From the beginning of Naser ad-Din Shah's reign (1848) up to the constitutional revolution (1906–9), the central state's budget was in a perpetual deficit with a widening gap over time.[40] These financial problems, which originally stemmed from lack of control over the bureaucracy, assumed significant proportions with the expansion of trade and commercialization of agriculture towards the end of the century. The financial crisis of the state was related to the progressive monetization of the economy through various mechanisms. With the expansion of commercial agriculture, ownership of land became a main source of accumulation of wealth. This led to large-scale usurpation of state lands and *Tuyuls* by government officials and local power holders.[41] Furthermore the conversion of taxes in kind into cash, which took the form of specific lump sums on each village (*Tas'ir*), and the inability of the government to revise upwards these specific rates, combined with high rates of inflation,[42] increased the retained share of the landlords from the agrarian surplus at the expense of the government tax revenues (Jamalzadeh 1917, pp.123–4). In addition, during this period there appears to have occurred a substantial shift in the share of the agrarian surplus away from all the traditional land based ruling classes towards the rising merchant bourgeoisie connected with foreign trade. This process of primary accumulation in the hands of big merchants, who enjoyed a high degree of monopoly in export trade,[43] was specially noticeable during the export boom of 1860–1906.[44] Again, the central government did not have the power to impose any direct or indirect taxes on the merchants (Gilbar 1977). 'While the central government found itself with growing fiscal difficulties ... the big merchants became wealthier' (*ibid.*, p.288). These processes cut

in the attempts of Naser ad-Din Shah (1848–96) to use the powerful nationwide 'Assembly of Merchants Representatives' to check the autonomy of provincial governors, and, on the other hand, the coalition of the clergy with the local governors which successfully blocked this process. See Adamiyyat and Nategh (1977, chapter 7, especially pp.347–370).

[40] See Jamalzadeh (1917, chapter 13), Issawi (1971, chapter 8).

[41] See below, page 52.

[42] The high rates of inflation in the latter half of the nineteenth century were largely due to the depreciation of silver Kran *vis-à-vis* gold standard currencies. Kran declined from 20 units per pound sterling in 1834 to 22.5 in 1865, 50 in 1894, and 61.7 in 1914, *pari passu* with the decline in the gold price of silver in the international market (see Yaganegi 1934, chapter 4).

[43] 'Merchants engaged in the same line often formed a syndicate and thus subjected the market to their own interest', Abdullaev, quoted in Issawi (1971, p.45).

[44] On the activities of merchant capital during this period, see Ashraf (1980, pp.73–89), Abdullaev in Issawi (1971, pp.42–9), Gilbar (1977) and Adamiyyat and Nategh (1977, pp.299–375).

through the central government revenues, at a time when the financial needs of the state were rising rapidly.[45]

The deepening financial crisis of the state and the failure of the administrative reforms to remedy this problem led, on the one hand, to a systematic practice of sale of offices and titles, and farming out of state revenues to private individuals, and, on the other hand, to the granting of concessions to foreigners.[46] Sale of office and farming out of state revenues which during the seventeenth century – to the amazement of Chardin[47] – was unknown to Iran, now became the general practice.[48] Each act of alienation of state offices and farming out of state revenues further cut through the dwindling finances of the state and led to a cumulative process which ended in virtual breakdown of central administration. By the last decade of the nineteenth century virtually all state offices had turned into the private monopolies of a handful of individuals whose chief pre-occupation was, 'to recoup their initial outlay and additional profits as quickly as possible' (Bakhash 1978, p.264). The state as such had ceased to exist, and, in the words of one of its top officials, 'in the eyes of the people, the government and the crown suddenly appeared contemptible'.[49] The process of economic change during the latter half of the nineteenth and early decades of the twentieth centuries should be set against this social and political background.

2.3.4 Free trade and economic change 1850–1914

The integration of the Iranian economy into the world market and the resulting transformations in different production structures during the nineteenth century was in some of its important aspects highly conditioned by the above developments in the political sphere. In particular, the developments in the agrarian relations of production were very much affected by the nature of the transformation of the ancient regime.

The main channels of integration of the Iranian economy into the world capitalist system in this period was through trade. There was no foreign direct investments in productive activities such as plantations or mining,

---

[45] For example, government revenues declined from 1,900,000 pounds sterling in 1876 to 1,670,000 in 1886 (Issawi 1971, p.337). The rise in the financial needs of the state was not solely due to the rise in 'public' expenditures. Public treasury in this period was not distinguishable from the private purse of the Shah and his courtiers. In fact, the main part of this increase in state expenditures was due to the extravagances of the court. To these expenses one should add the payment of debt service to foreign creditors from the turn of the century, e.g., in 1913 debt service was 25 per cent of government expenditure (Issawi 1971, p.339).

[46] On the sale of concessions to Russia and Britain, see Kazemzadeh (1968, pp.149–385) and Issawi (1971, pp.358–61).   [47] See Minorsky (1980, p.27).

[48] On the sale of office during the late Qajar period, see Sheikholeslami (1977), Bakhash (1978, pp.260–300).   [49] Amin O-Dowleh, quoted from Bakhash (1978, p.265).

and all of the inflow of foreign capital – mainly concentrated in the latter quarter of the century – was directed towards commerce and related activities, or took the form of government loans.[50] In other words, nineteenth-century imperialism in Iran, unlike many other peripheral economies, did not take the form of direct intervention in the domestic production processes.

The economic history of Iran from mid nineteenth to early twentieth century was one of integration of a pre-capitalist economy into the world market under a free trade regime. With the system of capitulations imposed by the 1928 treaty with Russia, and subsequent treaties with other trading partners, the Qajar state lost its tariff autonomy, not to be regained until 1928.[51] From the early nineteenth century up to the eve of the First World War there was a rapid growth in foreign trade which particularly accelerated from the 1850s onward. Total trade (exports plus imports) in real terms is estimated to have increased by three times in the first half of the century, and by four times during the 1860–1914 period (Issawi 1971, pp.130–1). Though this rate of growth was lower than the increase in foreign trade of other Middle Eastern regions during the same period, it was nevertheless significant enough to bring about important transformations in the Iranian economy.[52]

The structure of foreign trade which was very much similar to other Middle Eastern regions, reveals the nature of participation of the Iranian economy in the world division of labour. By the turn of the century, imports were totally dominated by manufacturers – predominantly textiles – which together with tea and sugar formed more than 80 per cent of imports. Exports, with the exception of carpets, were chiefly composed of raw agricultural products (see table 2.1). The changing trends in the structure of exports to Russia, as depicted in table 2.2, clearly demonstrate the process

[50] 'Related activities' here include banking, road construction, real estate and communications (post and telegraph). Though there were a few exceptions, such as Caspian Fisheries and some agricultural processing activities, they had no major influence on the domestic economy. See Yaganegi (1934, chapter 2), Issawi (1971, chapter 8, especially pp.356–61).

[51] According to these treaties all imports and exports were subject to a single 5 per cent *ad valorem* duty, and foreign merchants were exempt from all inland and transit duties. The 5 per cent duty was, however, a maximum; competition between different customs farmers would normally drive the rates down to less than 2 per cent. In 1902 and during the 1920s separate tariff treaties were signed with Britain and Russia, but they did not substantially alter the import duties. For a detailed study of custom duties during this period, see Yaganegi (1934, chapter 3).

[52] During the 1800–1913 period, Egypt's foreign trade is estimated to have increased by 50 to 60 fold in real terms and that of Turkey by 15 to 20 fold, and 'the available figures for Iraq and Syria also indicate a much higher rate of growth than Iran' (Issawi 1971, pp.70–1). In 1915 per-capita foreign trade of Iran, Turkey, and Egypt, were $9, $15 and $24, respectively (Issawi 1981, p.68), while the figure for the underdeveloped world as a whole was $8 (Bairoch 1981, p.109).

of peripheralization of the Iranian economy under free trade. While in 1844 more than 70 per cent of Iranian exports were composed of handicraft manufacturers, by 1910 the share of manufactures, with the exception of carpets, was reduced to virtually nil. Two other features of the structure of trade during this period stand out. First, Iranian economy did not develop into a monoculture economy, that is, exports were not totally composed of one or two items as was the case in many other peripheral economies undergoing similar processes of integration into the world market during this period.[53] The second important feature of Iran's foreign trade was its total domination by Britain and Russia. More than 80 per cent of both commodity imports and exports originated from or were destined for these two countries (table 2.3). The two powers conducted their commercial and financial policies in Iran more as a means of political domination rather than commercial profitability, and at the end it was Russia with a higher degree of state involvement and lesser consideration for commercial profits which came to dominate the scene (Kazemzadeh 1968, Entner 1965). The rivalry between the two imperialist powers during the latter half of the century had reduced the prices of imported manufactured goods in the main Iranian cities – despite high transport costs – to well below those prevailing in some of the major industrial countries including Britain and Russia.[54]

Expansion of foreign trade and the spread of an exchange economy led to a high rate of growth of the urban population and relative expansion of non-agricultural activities.[55] The major part of the relative increase in the non-agricultural labour force was, however, absorbed in trade and related activities (Gilbar 1976, p.155, Issawi 1971, p.50). Despite the expansion of regional markets, specially in the latter half of the century, competition from cheap manufactured commodities led to large-scale destruction of traditional handicrafts particularly textiles which formed the largest subsector of traditional craft guilds.[56] Though, not all the traditional guilds faced the same degree of competition from cheap machine made imports,

---

[53] This was partly due to climatic diversity of different agricultural regions, and partly due to the rise of commercial agriculture as an adjunct to an already existing peasant subsistence farming, which set a limit to the degree of specialization in cash crops.

[54] Gilbar (1977, p.300). According to Entner (1965, p.70), in 1899 the Russian government's subsidy to its industrial exports to Iran amounted to at least 25 per cent of the value of total exports, and in later years 'subsidization became embarrassingly more extensive'.

[55] The proportion of urban population (in settlements with 10,000 inhabitants or more) increased from 8 to 9 per cent in the mid-nineteenth century to some 18 per cent of the total population in the early 1900s. During the same period the relative size of the rural labour force is estimated to have decreased by 10 to 15 per cent (Gilbar 1976, pp.149–56).

[56] See Issawi (1971, chapter 6, especially the extracts from Mirza Husein's book, *Jugrafya-i Isfahan* 1877), and Ashraf (1980).

Table 2.1. *Composition of foreign trade 1909*

	Exports			Imports[b]	
	Value[a]	%		Value[a]	%
Raw cotton	12602	22.0	Textiles	31785	41.3
Dried fruits	9573	16.7			
Carpets	8714	15.2	Sugar	21700	28.2
Cereals	4890	8.5	Tea	4468	5.8
Fish and products	3828	6.7			
Opium	3167	5.5	Metals and products	3488	4.5
Cocoon	3030	5.3	Kerosene	1443	1.9
Leather and hides	2146	3.7			
Others	9276	16.4	Others	13950	18.3
Total	57226	100.0	Total	76834	100.0

Notes and *Sources* as table 2.3.

Table 2.2. *Structure of exports to Russia 1844–1910*

	1844		1870		1910	
	Value[a]	%	Value[a]	%	Value[a]	%
Cotton products	1518	52.3	1088	25.3	12	0.0
Silk products	510	17.6	264	6.1	648	1.6
Woollens	103	3.5	69	1.6	220	0.0
Carpets	n.a.	—	n.a.	—	3412	8.6
Dried fruits	169	5.8	1030	24.0	9676	24.4
Rice and cereals	n.a.	—	144	3.3	5600	14.1
Raw cotton	19	0.0	848	19.7	12414	31.1
Fish	n.a.	—	127	2.9	3800	9.6
Hides	n.a.	—	114	2.6	2340	5.9
Others	583	20.8	611	14.5	1588	4.1
Total	2902	100.0	4295	100.0	39710	100.0

Notes and Sources as table 2.3.

Table 2.3 *Direction of trade 1906–1913*

	Exports		Imports	
	1906 %	1913 %	1906 %	1913 %
Share of Russia	65	72	52	56
Share of Britain[c]	11	14	31	28
The rest[d]	24	14	17	16
Total (000 Roubles)	62436	75936	76643	115367

Notes:

[a] Values in thousands of gold Roubles.

[b] Imports refers to 1910.

[c] Including India.

[d] Mainly, Turkey, France, Germany, Austria–Hungary, Belgium, Afghanistan, Italy.

Source: Entner 1965, pp.10, 64, 72, 78.

there was a general tendency towards dismantling of the guild system of production in all lines of handicraft.[57] The traditional functions of the guild system of production, ranging from the organization of sales, to quality supervision and entry prevention, etc., were gradually undermined.[58] The breakdown of the economic restrictions of the guild system, which appears to have led to a considerable decline in the income of individual artisans,[59] marks the origin of the simple commodity producing subsector of Iranian manufacturing – or the so called urban marginal sector – which even up to the present day employs the majority of the manufacturing labour force.

Only in a few lines of manufacturing activity – such as, carpets, leather products and processing of henna and opium, which were produced for the world market and enjoyed a dynamic demand – can we observe the development of higher organizational forms of capitalist production and the

[57] This could be explained partly by the expansion of market relations, and partly by the pressure on the supply side arising due to new entries from the ranks of the large class of urban unemployed, which undermined the restrictive practices of the traditional guilds.

[58] Parallel to the dismantling of the production organization of traditional guilds, one could also observe a discernible trend in the transformation of the labour process in traditional handicrafts production towards deskilling and simplification of the technological basis of production. See Issawi 1971 (extract from Polak 1865, pp.268–79 and extract from Hussein 1877).

[59] On the conditions of handicraftsmen in the latter half of the nineteenth century, see Polak (1865). According to Polak. 'The handicraftsmen ... show diligence and industry and often work at night, but their efforts are directed not towards improvement but only toward meeting their daily needs . . . I have never known any craftsman who had achieved a moderate degree of material well being' (*ibid.*, p.276).

achievement of a relatively high degree of division of labour within large capitalist workshops (see Issawi 1971, p.297). The limitation of both the number of such dynamic industries and the type of their products – mainly composed of processing export cash crops with very weak forward and backward linkages with other sectors of industry – would have obviously precluded the possibility of an integrated and dynamic industrialization process. There were also a few attempts during the last quarter of the nineteenth century and early 1900s to set up modern manufacturing industries, based on imported technology and employing wage labour, both by the indigenous merchants and foreign capitalists.[60] Very few of these factories could, however, start production and none could survive for long.[61] These latter attempts, though unsuccessful, point the way for what became the predominant trend in Iranian industrialization during the present century. The evolution of higher organizational and technological forms of production from within the small commodity producers having been blocked, the dynamics of industrialization takes the form of transplantation of modern industry from above – through the instrumentality of the state, indigenous merchant capital, foreign capital, or a combination of them – and based on imported technology.

Destruction of the old forms of manufacturing production and the failure to develop new and superior forms of production were, therefore, the central features of industrial change up to the early decades of the present century. Though free trade with the more advanced industrial economies was the main driving force in this process, one should not lose sight of the broader socio-economic and political context within which these changes were taking place. Of these latter conditions, the socio-economic conditions in the agricultural sector were of fundamental importance. For, agriculture was the predominant productive sector of the Iranian economy, and the main preconditions for industrial growth – such as demand, labour force, and other primary supplies – depended on the developments in that sector.

2.3.5 Transformation of the agrarian relations

Along with the rise of commercial agriculture, one can observe the following main tendencies in the transformation of agrarian relations during the

---

[60] For a detailed list of the modern factories which were set up during this period, up to the First World War, see Ashraf (1980, pp.89–104), Jamalzadeh (1917, pp.92–8).

[61] For the obstacles in setting up modern manufacturing establishments and the causes of failure of those which were attempted during this period see, Jamalzadeh (1917), Issawi (1971, pp.260–1, 275–6, 300–10) and Olson (1980). The reasons ranged from, paucity of markets both due to foreign competition and low income levels, lack of adequate legal and political superstructure, insecurity, archaic means of transportation, to dumping practices by Russian companies.

course of the nineteenth century: (a) the emergence of a class of large landlords who managed to consolidate their power over time, so that by the end of the century they had practically turned the traditional conditional land assignments (*Tuyuls*) into unconditional private property,[62] and (b) the greater personal subordination of the peasantry to the landlords, and the intensification in the rate of exploitation of the peasantry.

This process of agrarian change was intertwined with, and in some of its important aspects determined by the changes which were taking place at the level of the state during the same period. The emergence of large private landlordism was indeed the parallel outcome of the same process which led to the dissolution of the traditional state. This is well illustrated in Lambton's study of the evolution of agrarian relations in this period (1953, chapter vii, pp.151–8). According to her, the larger part of state lands during this period were usurped by the state functionaries. 'As the control of the government weakened, so the tendency grew to convert *Tuyuls* into de facto private property, inheritable and alienable by sale. The ranks of the landowners proper thus came to be swelled by erstwhile or actual government officials and *Tuyuldars*' (Lambton 1953, p.139).

The financial difficulties of the state also led to large-scale sale of state lands, sometimes directly to export merchants, in the last quarter of the century (Lambton 1953, p.152, Issawi 1971, p.208). There were certainly other mechanisms as well, which led to the rise of large private landlordism.[63] However, given the centrality of the state in the traditional relations of landownership, the outcome of this process was to a large extent dependent upon the nature of transformation of state power in this period.[64]

The emergence of private landlordism was only one aspect of the evolu-

---

[62] Although Moameni (1980, pp.35–6) regards the latter half of the nineteenth century as the period in which private land ownership acquired general official recognition, this whole period should be really regarded as a period of transition, when the traditionally fluid and non-typified land ownership relations were being practically transformed into private ownership due to the weakness of central authority. The constitution of 1906, by abolishing the system of *Tuyul* and recognizing the sanctity of private property, provided the first official recognition of the status quo. It was not, however, before the establishment of Reza Shah's modern bureaucratic state and the land registration act of 1928 that unconditional private property became the general legal form of land ownership. See Lambton (1953, chapters viii–ix).

[63] For an account of these other mechanisms, see Pavlovich (1910), Issawi (1971, pp.207–9) and Lambton (1953, pp.152–5).

[64] A comparison with the developments in the case of Ottoman Turkey during the same period would help help to shed light on this issue. The success of Mahmud II to break the power of janisaries (as early as 1826) and the relatively more successful attempts of this Sultan and his successors to build up a conscript army and a centralized state bureaucracy introduces an important divergence in the development of agrarian relations in Anatolia as compared to the case of Iran. Mahmud II's success in reasserting the central state's authority over Anatolia was a pre-condition for breaking the hold of the local notables (*A'yan*), who had

tion of the agrarian relations in this period. With the expansion of commercial agriculture, the latter half of the nineteenth century also witnessed important changes in the landlord-peasant relationship which were reminiscent of the Second Serfdom in eastern Europe. During this period, cash crop cultivation together with the penetration of cheap imported textiles led to a gradual erosion of the natural economy of the villages (Nowshirwani and Knight 1975, Gilbar 1978). The corporate structure of the traditional village communities was gradually undermined and the landlords came to exert increasing influence on the socio-economic life of the villages.[65] During the course of the nineteenth century one could observe a general tendency towards increasing personal subordination of the cultivators to the landlords, and by the turn of the century the peasants were left 'without any rights against the landlords having the character of serfs' (Gharatcheh-Daghi 1967, p.27). The following extract from a contemporary writer sums up the degree of subordination of the peasantry on the eve of the Constitutional Revolution:

> Anyone who owns a tract of land in Iran, is unquestionably the owner of the life and property of all the peasants on the land. This situation prevails all over Iran, though with different degrees of intensity. In Baluchestan and Kerman, the peasants with their family and their property are officially bought and sold along with the land; they are counted like the sheep and their value is added to the value of the land at the time of transaction. In other places, though the peasant is not directly transacted upon, his relation to the lord is intrinsically the same; it is one of extreme servitude. (Nazim al-Islam Kermani 1960, pp.113–14, my translation)

These transformations, though increasing the intensity and multiplicity of peasant obligations, did not fundamentally change the form of the rent. Share cropping remained the predominant form of surplus extraction.[66] These developments, however, appear to have intensified the exploitation

---

managed to turn the state (*Miri*) lands into *de facto* private property during the course of the eighteenth century. As a result, during the half century between the Tanzimat reforms and the Young Turks period, expansion of commercial agriculture goes hand in hand with the strengthening of central authority and the preservation of the state lands. This is said to have made 'the task of land reform simpler in Turkey than in other countries of Ottoman succession where large private estates predominated' (Hershlag 1964, p.29). See also Issawi (1980, pp.202–3), Karpat (1968).

[65] This appears to have been partly due to the introduction of cash crops which required greater contact and control by the landlords, and partly due to the breakdown of the mediatory role of the state in landlord-peasant relations. See Pavlovich (1910), Lambton (1953, pp.172–5 and 1954).

[66] There were, however, various other forms of surplus extraction by the landlords, such as corvee labour in non-agricultural works, military service in the landlord's private army, and various other contributions to the 'lord's larder' (Sursat). Moameni (1980, p.48), counts 300 forms of such extraction in different regions for the early present century.

of the peasantry to a large extent.[67] In 1899 the British consul in Isfahan, commenting on the transformations taking place in the agrarian relations, wrote, 'The peasants, in place of having an easy task master in the state, are now grounded down to the very last penny by their landlords' (Issawi 1971, p.210).

An important and revealing aspect of the process of consolidation of these semi-feudal relations of production during the nineteenth century was the passive role of the peasantry in this whole process. The political inertia of the Iranian peasantry, which was clearly known to the ruling elite during the nineteenth century and is reflected in the chronicles of that time (see Moameni 1980, p.83), has not received adequate attention in the recent literature on the political economy of modern Iran.[68] Most of the existing literature, either takes it as a matter of fact or relates it to the will of the landlords or the nature of the state.[69] In the later periods, once the landlords managed to establish their social and political power, they used both the newly created institutions at the village level[70] and the support of the state, to maintain the dependence of the peasantry and reproduce the semi-feudal relations of production. However, the initial consolidation of these relations which came about at a time of weakening of state power, could not be adequately explained without taking into account the factors which lay behind the lack of combativeness and political passivity of the Iranian peasantry.[71] One reason for this neglect in the existing literature may be the paucity of information on the factors which are of direct relevance to this phenomenon[72] – factors such as, organization of production and the

---

[67] Despite the probable rise in the productivity of agricultural labour due to the adoption of more expensive export cash crops (Gilbar 1978), as well as the secular improvement in the terms of trade of agricultural exports (Nowshirwani and Knight 1975), during the latter half of the nineteenth century, Lambton (1953, p.143) reports a gradual worsening in the conditions of the peasantry during this period. See also Moameni (1980, p.38).

[68] For a recent study, see Kazemi and Abrahamian (1978). Though this article emphasizes the importance of the above phenomenon, providing interesting empirical evidence, it nevertheless suffers from certain analytical shortcomings. Most of the factors which the authors put forward as explanations of this phenomena (e.g., low productivity of labour and paucity of development of exchange relations in agriculture) could well be interpreted as the consequences of this phenomenon rather than its causes.

[69] See Lambton (1953, pp.393, 174), Moameni (1980), Keddie (1972).

[70] For a study of the control mechanisms at the village level, used by the landlords to reproduce the semi-feudal relations, see M. Ono (1967).

[71] A valuable contribution of Kazemi and Abrahamian (1978) is their clear demonstration that the domination of the landlords over the rural population during the present century worked through internal control mechanisms independent of the strength or weakness of the central state.

[72] For example there exists little evidence on the differentiation of the peasantry during the latter half of the nineteenth century which may have arisen due to the expansion of commercial agriculture.

resulting stratification of the peasantry, their social organizations, the degree of internal solidarity amongst the peasantry and their general political and military resources.[73] Whatever its causes, the political inertia of the Iranian peasantry forms one of the important aspects of the political economy of modern Iran. It is indeed as a result of this phenomenon that the major landmarks in the modern agrarian history of Iran are induced by external factors – mainly initiated through the state and based on the changes in urban political economy.

The consolidation of the semi-feudal relations of production in the agricultural sector, which remained virtually intact up to the land reform of 1962, formed a major obstacle to productivity improvements in that sector. Even during the 1860–1914 period which was the most dynamic period from the point of view of growth of new export cash crops (Gilbar 1978), there was no noticeable improvements in the traditional techniques or forms of organization of agricultural production, and few successful attempts at introducing new seeds or any other new inputs which could appreciably alter the productivity of labour could be noticed.[74] The only noticeable source of improvement in the productivity of agricultural labour would have been confined, therefore, to those brought about by changes in the product mix towards the relatively more expensive export cash crops. The degree of commercialization of Iranian agriculture during this period, however, should not be over exaggerated. Given the fact that cash crop cultivation was conducted as an annex to peasant subsistence farming, the low levels of labour productivity in subsistence crops would set an upper limit to the degree of specialization and expansion of cash crops. To push the degree of specialization beyond this limit, under the highly monopolistic pre-capitalist market structure and the meagre means of transportation, would have endangered the very means of subsistence of the peasantry.[75] In fact the available evidence indicates that by the turn of the century this limiting barrier was already reached. The fast rates of growth of export cash crops (namely, cotton, tobacco and specially opium) during the last quarter of the century led to a process of substitution of such products for the main

---

[73] Brenner (1976) regards the power of resistance by the peasantry against the feudal lords, as determined by the above factors, the main dynamic force which led to the early dissolution of feudal relations in western Europe as opposed to the consolidation of these relations which gave rise to the second serfdom in eastern Europe. See also Hilton (1978).

[74] See Issawi (1971, pp.206–14), Khamsi (1968, pp.20–5), Seyf (1984).

[75] This obviously contradicts the premises upon which the post-Ricardian theories of comparative costs are based. However, the kind of mobility of factors of production and flexibility in production conditions which this class of theories presuppose are far from the prevailing conditions under the pre-capitalist production relations and the very low levels of labour productivity in peasant agriculture.

staple crops (i.e., wheat and barley).[76] As a consequence, the last decades of the nineteenth century witnessed a noticeable decline in the output of the main staple crops, and Iran, which was a net exporter of wheat and barley during the 1860s, became a net importer of these products by the turn of the century (Gilbar 1978, pp.315–19). One possible manifestation of this situation was the recurrent famines which occurred during the last decades of the nineteenth century, as well as the sharp rise in the prices of basic foodstuffs and the occurrence of bread riots in towns during the last two decades of the nineteenth and twentieth centuries. The first decade of the present century witnessed the peak of the expansion of agricultural exports, both in absolute and in per-capita terms (table 2.4). From the eve of the First World War onwards one could observe a long-term declining trend in the export of agricultural products *pari passu* with the increase in domestic requirements to feed a growing population.[77]

To sum up, though the integration of the Iranian economy into the world capitalist market brought about a once and for all increase in the level of output – specially in the agricultural sector[78] – it failed to create the conditions for the development of an internally dynamic economic structure. On the contrary, the forms of production which developed in the agricultural and manufacturing sectors, not only precluded the possibility of self-sustained and mutually interacting growth in these two sectors in the subsequent periods, but also constrained their capacity to respond to external demand. In the manufacturing sector, though the restrictive regulations of the traditional guild system were undermined, competition from cheap imported manufactures did not allow the development of industrial capitalism, nor did the simple commodity producing sector which replaced the traditional guild system achieve the kind of internal dynamism which characterized the European proto-industries.[79] The problem of lack of

[76] This process was clearly manifest in the expansion of the highly profitable opium cultivation in southern and central provinces (some of the main grain producing regions) where, according to the reports, 'almost all suitable ground was utilized for the cultivation of opium to the exclusion of cereals and other produce', British consul at Bushihr, quoted in Issawi (1971, p.315).

[77] It is true that in the inter-war period the rate of growth of world trade was itself much lower than the pre-war era (Maddison 1984), but given the absolute decline in the Iranian agricultural exports it is more likely that exports were supply constrained rather than demand determined.

[78] See Nowshirwani and Knight (1978), Gilbar (1978), Issawi (1971).

[79] Of course European proto-industrialization, due to the political strength of urban guilds, took place mainly in the rural areas. The three crucial elements which were of central importance to this early or proto-industrialization in Europe, were absent in nineteenth-century Iran. These were; the rise of demand for industrial products triggered by the development of long-distance trade and the growth of agricultural productivity, the breakdown of feudal relations of production, and generalization of exchange relations in the countryside. See Kreidt, Medick and Schlumbohm (1981).

Table 2.4. *Main agricultural exports 1913–1958*

(000 tons)

	1913	1938	1948	1950	1958
Rice	69.9[a]	3.5	1.5	13.8	1.3
Fresh fruits	55.8[b]	56.3	48.0	53.4	22.4
Tobacco leaves	1.8[c]	0.3	0.3	0.2	—
Raw cotton	24.5[d]	5.6	2.8	19.8	27.4
Opium	0.4[e]	0.3	0.0	0.3	0.1
Oil seeds	0.0	9.3	7.3	13.8	5.1
Tea	0.0	6.2	7.4	8.3	—

Sources:
[a] Jamalzadeh (1917, p.22), refers to the year 1910.
[b] Jamalzadeh (1917, p.19), refers to the year 1910.
[c] Jamalzadeh (1917, p.77), refers to the year 1910.
[d] Entner 1965, p.73.
[e] UK Department of Overseas Trade 1923, p.18. Other years, from UN, *International Trade Statistics* various years.

dynamism in the manufacturing sector, however, was not solely confined to the deficiency of demand. Even if external demand conditions were favourable, one would expect the prevailing semi-feudal relations of production and stagnant labour productivity in the agricultural sector to check the process of industrialization at an early stage.[80]

As to the factors which contributed to the emergence and consolidation of this particular production structure, certain observations may be made in the light of the above analysis. First, this specific outcome could not be solely attributed to some general effects of imperialism and/or penetration of the Iranian economy by western capitalism, independently of the internal socio-economic structures. Though the integration of the Iranian economy into the world market was the prime mover of the process of economic change, the specific outcome of this process was very much determined by internal conditions. Secondly, the development of this particular production structure could not be readily attributed to some inherent tendencies in the pre-existing mode of production which, once 'articulated' into the world capitalist market, would have necessarily produced such an outcome as a matter of course. As we have attempted to demonstrate, the nature of state power during the early nineteenth century, as well as the specific political

[80] In fact it could be argued that the low labour productivity in agriculture and the high rate of exploitation of the peasantry were amongst the main stumbling blocks for the expansion of manufacturing demand within the national market.

effects of imperialist domination did play a significant part in this process.

The socio-economic transformations in this period set the foundations for a new phase of state-economy interrelationships in the post 1920s era. With the rise of Reza Shah one can witness the emergence of a new form of state apparatus and a new configuration of political power and mode of intervention by the state in the social and economic processes. A review of some of the salient features of the Constitutional Revolution of 1906–9 would help to shed light on the socio-economic and political conditions which underlay the emergence of this new phase of state-economy interrelationships.

2.3.6 *Crisis of the state and the constitutional revolution of 1906–1909*

By the turn of the century the country was entangled in an acute socio-economic and political crisis. The over-expansion of export cash crops at the expense of subsistence crops – a process which in some instances was imposed by the landlords over a reluctant peasantry – had increased the possibility of famines which occurred frequently with moderate fluctuations in harvests (Olson 1981). The intensified exactions of the local governors cum landlords and the encroachment of money lenders and middle man had undercut the livelihood of the peasantry. This situation had by the end of the nineteenth century led to an exodus of the rural population to a few urban trading centres,[81] multiplying the already inflated ranks of the urban unemployed.[82] Food shortages and the sharp rise in the price of basic foodstuffs, fuelled by the monopoly practices of local governors and merchants, was a common problem in all urban centres,[83] which had become the scene of frequent bread riots. Competition of cheap imported manufactures had diminished the livelihood of thousands of traditional handicraftsmen without creating alternative industrial employment. Even the big merchants who emerged out of this process as the wealthiest and

[81] From the 1880s to the early 1900s, urban population is estimated to have grown by an annual average rate of 2.4 per cent, while the natural rate of growth of population both in urban and rural areas is estimated at a maximum of 1 per cent per annum. The proportion of urban population (in towns more than 10,000 inhabitants) increased from 8.9 per cent in the mid nineteenth century to some 18 per cent in the early 1900s (Gilbar 1976, pp.133–49). During this period there was also a large and steady outflow of migrant labour into the neighbouring countries, especially Russia. See Gilbar (1976), Hakimian (1985).

[82] During the last decades of the nineteenth century, 'travellers accounts abound in material showing that the streets and bazaars of the Iranian towns, specially the large commercial centres, were overcrowded with poor and unemployed persons ready to sell their labour for a piece of bread', Abdullaev, quoted in Issawi (1971, p.50).

[83] During the 1890s the price of bread in most major towns rose by as much as 200 to 300 per cent (Gilbar 1978, p.316). This period was, however, one of decline in wheat prices in international markets by about 20 per cent (Lewis 1978, p.280), and the rate of depreciation of silver Kran was only about 60 per cent (Issawi 1971, p.342).

most powerful social class in urban Iran, came to be increasingly constrained by the social dislocation which was caused by the uneven developments in different structures of the Iranian society.

Despite the high rates of growth of trade and high degree of monetization of the economy, the legal framework for commerce was still very underdeveloped. There were many instances of Iranian merchants adopting Russian or British nationalities both to escape the arbitrary practices of governors and Sharia courts and benefit from discriminatory privileges enjoyed by foreign merchants (Ashraf 1980, chapter 4, Entner 1965, Adamiyyat and Nategh 1977, chapter 7, pp.300–71). The archaic financial superstructure of the country also lagged far behind the needs of commerce. Modern banking was virtually non existent and the deficiency of silver currency which could not keep pace with the requirements of fast expanding commerce created a situation of acute shortage of money, particularly felt during the harvest time which was the boom in export activities.[84] The transport system was also in a very poor condition. Despite some improvements during the last quarter of the century the predominant means of transportation was the slow and costly pack animal (see Agah 1958, chapter 2, pp.10–40, Issawi 1971, pp.152–206). Nevertheless, the big merchants who managed to get round some of these difficulties through bribery and other means, took full advantage of the free trade situation to amass substantial amounts of capital free from any fiscal control and taxation by the government during the export boom of 1850–1914. It was mainly when the merchants came to engage their capital in industry and other productive activities that they found themselves severely handicapped by the chaotic political environment and inadequate institutional and infrastructural set-up.[85] The contradictions between the merchant bourgeoisie and the Qajar state took the form of open antagonism when Muzaffar al-Din Shah resorted to a roundabout method to tax the merchants through mortgaging the customs revenues for his fund raising activities abroad.[86] The reorganization of the customs in early 1900s with the help of Belgian administrators under the Russian patronage brought these contradictions to a head (Gilbar 1976).

Clearly the transformation of the Iranian economy during the nineteenth century had created new functional needs on a national scale which the

---

[84] On financial institutions during this period, see Yaganegi (1934), Rabino (1892, quoted in Issawi 1971, pp.348–56).

[85] See the case of Amin al-Zarb in Olson (1980).

[86] The more direct approach of sale of concessions to foreigners as the tobacco concession of 1891 had shown, was no longer practical. See Gilbar 1976, Adamiyyat and Nategh (1977). According to Jamalzadeh, during the early 1900s, two thirds of the customs duties which were in mortgage to the Russian and British governments accrued to the two countries (Jamalzadeh 1917, pp.132–52).

traditional state with its semi-tribal/semi-bureaucratic institutions could not fulfil. The unsuccessful attempts of the Qajar state to reform the government institutions was partly prompted by the awareness of these new needs. The failure of these reforms as we noted above led to a speedy disintegration of the traditional state. The Qajar state by the turn of the century had disintegrated into a hierarchy of private monopolies and all the political offices had turned into sources of personal enrichment for the officials. The state in failing to fulfil its traditional functions had itself become the main source of disorder and insecurity. As for the newly emerging public needs, the state was not even capable to cater for the basic infrastructural needs of the economy, let alone alleviating the appalling dimensions of the fast unfolding economic crisis.

The Constitutional Revolution of 1906–9 took place against this general socio-economic and political background. Various social groups with different and sometimes contradictory interests and outlooks took part in the revolution.[87] One of the uniting ideologies which, however, bound these different social groups in their fight for the constitution was that they all saw the constitution as a remedy for the deep economic crisis which prevailed on the eve of the revolution and a foundation stone for future economic progress. This theme runs through many of the agitatory pamphlets and speeches delivered on the eve of the revolution, and is cogently put in the following words by one of the prominent figures of the revolution in the first national assembly:

> We had never experienced constitutional monarchy before. But from what we had heard and trusting those who had seen other constitutional monarchies, it was believed to cause security and economic progress for the country. Thus, our enthusiasm in setting up the constitutional monarchy in this country.[88]

The remedy for the prevailing economic crisis which had deep-seated structural causes, however, required more than the 'night watchman' conception of the state which the semi-liberal constitution of 1906 and its supplementary amendments of 1907 envisioned.[89] This was all the more true as the Constitutional Revolution did not undermine the power of the dominant ruling classes in the countryside and had little impact on the prevailing agrarian relations. The stagnationary structure of the Iranian economy implied that none of the existing classes within the society had the

[87] For detailed studies of the Constitutional Revolution, see Berard (1910), Abrahamian (1982, pp.50–102).

[88] From the speech delivered by S.M. Tabatabai in the first National Assembly, quoted in Adamiyyat (1967, p.226), my translation.

[89] For an analysis of the Iranian constitution which was a combination of the Belgian constitution and Islamic law, see Berard (1910), Lockhart (1959).

capacity to lift the economy out of its crisis, and that the state had, sooner or later, to take a direct role in restructuring the economy. This, however, had to await the formation of the modern bureaucratic state during Reza Shah's reign in the post-1920s period, and a certain degree of autonomy of the state from the economically dominant ruling classes. All this has to be of course demonstrated in the following historical study of the nature of the post-revolutionary state and its evolution in the inter-war period.

The nature of the post-revolutionary state and its class base could be readily observed in the composition of the Constituent Assembly and the first parliament (Majlis), and in the immediate economic measures which it enacted. The parliament (together with the few regional assemblies formed in some major towns) was the only institutionalized apparatus of the post-revolutionary state and it was materially composed of the representatives of different classes which took part in the revolution, elected on a class representational basis.[90] An important determining factor with regard to the nature of the state power as reflected in the structure of the first national assembly was that the constitutional revolution was a purely urban phenomenon. 'The isolated mass of rural population did not play a part in establishing parliamentarianism' (Gharatcheh-Daghi 1967, p.27). As long as the power base of the post-revolutionary assembly remained in the urban areas, the merchants could exert their hegemony over the parliament. This was reflected in the first major economic act of the parliament, i.e., the establishment of the 'National Bank', with its main shareholders the big merchants and having the following monopoly rights.[91]

> [The Bank] would have the monopoly over all banking activities, mon-opoly right of issue of paper currency, the right to construct railways and roads, the monopoly of pearl mining in Persian Gulf (subject to payment of 10% of the profits to the Treasury), monopoly right of mining over all the state lands and other non agricultural lands (also subject to 10% royalty payment). (Adamiyyat 1976, p.436)

Although the bank project did not materialize, it highlighted a short period during which the merchant bourgeoisie was in the zenith of its economic power, as well as being in direct control of state power – i.e., the period of the first parliament (October 1906–June 1908). The power of the parliament, however, did not stretch beyond a few large urban centres, the rest of the century being effectively controlled by semi-feudal landlords and tribal chiefs. The reform of electoral law and introduction of universal suffrage after the third Majlis, marked the end of the hegemony of the

---

[90] On the electoral procedures and the composition of the constituent assembly and the first Majlis, see Abrahamian (1982, pp.86–92), Adamiyyat (1976, pp.347–82).

[91] For other economic acts of the first Majlis see Adamiyyat (1976, pp.431–51).

merchants in the parliament.[92] The first decade of the present century also marked the point of departure in the rising economic fortunes of the Iranian merchant bourgeoisie, when the uninterrupted half century of secular expansion in foreign trade came to a halt. The post-First World War period in fact witnessed a sharp cyclical decline in foreign trade,[93] as well as marking the beginning of the long-term secular decline in non-oil exports. According to Abdullaev, the bankruptcy of Amin al-Zarb, who was among the richest and most influential Iranian merchants, 'serves to trace a descending curve in the destiny of the nascent Iranian bourgeoisie' as early as in 1909. The revival of the Iranian bourgeoisie did not occur until the post-1953 period, and then not on the basis of its own initiative and the internal dynamism of the Iranian economy, but on the basis of increased oil revenues and in a clientelistic relation *vis-à-vis* the state.

The attempts of the first two post-revolutionary national assemblies to construct an adequately centralized and cohesive state apparatus, so as to institutionalize the revolutionary power mainly concentrated in the parliament, came to a naught. The first parliament met with strong resistance from the internal reactionary forces led by Muhammad Ali Shah, and ended in the bombardment and closure of parliament in June 1908. The second parliament, which was formed in November 1909 after the defeat of the counter-revolutionary forces by a nationwide armed uprising, though appearing to be more successful in overcoming the internal resistance, was finally forced to abandon its reforms by the intervention of Russia who occupied the northern parts of the country and forced the closure of the second parliament in 1911.

Between 1911 and 1921, the country was subject to immense political chaos and economic disruption.[94] There were, however, two major developments in this period – both arising from external causes – which had important implications for the subsequent course of political development in Iran. The first one was the October Revolution in Russia, and the second was the rise of the oil sector as a major source of foreign exchange and government revenue. They both contributed in their own way to the rise of the centralized authoritarian regime of Reza Shah. The first one through its effect on the social and political conditions and the second, by providing a source of independent finance for the state.

The October Revolution in Russia created a radical change in the

[92] 'By introducing a democratic law from modern Europe into the paternalistic environment of traditional Iran, it [the electoral law] . . . strengthened the conservative rural magnates who herd their peasants, tribesmen and other retainers into the voting polls', Bahar, quoted in Abrahamian 1982.

[93] Immediately after the First World War, foreign trade fell to its lowest value this century.

[94] On the political developments in this period see Miroshnikov (1964), Abrahamian (1982, pp.102–18). On the state of the economy, see Yaganegi (1934).

Russian policy towards Iran. Soviet government abolished the Tzarist capitulations, annulled all loans and obligations of the Iranian government, and recognized the rights of Iran as a sovereign state. Consequently, the British government, under internal popular opposition and international pressure, had to annul the 1919 treaty – whose terms were equivalent to the establishment of a British protectorate in Iran – and the British troops evacuated Iran. The old power rivalry suddenly ceased and Iran was freed from its semi-colonial status. The year 1921 opened a new page in the modern history of Iran – that of Iran as a sovereign state. The Russian Revolution also strengthened and radicalized the popular movements in Iran which were gaining momentum at a time of acute socio-economic and political crisis. This in turn contributed to the rise of Reza Shah's authoritarian regime, by rallying the support of conservative social forces behind the construction of a strong centralized state.

3
The rise of the modern state and capital accumulation: the inter-war period

3.1 Introduction

In this chapter we discuss the formation of the modern state in the inter-war period and trace the evolution of the role of the state in the economy from its *laisez-faire* phase in the 1920s to its strong interventionist phase in the 1930s. The use of oil income over this period was limited to the financing of government administration and made little direct contribution to domestic capital formation. The predominant role of the state, therefore, was the mobilization of resources from the domestic economy to finance accumulation. The chapter examines the various sources of finance for investment and the institutional mechanisms which were constructed to mobilize resources, given the constraints set by the domestic socio-economic and political relations as well as the international economic conditions over this period.

3.2 Emergence of the modern state

The *coup d'état* of February 1921 was conducted by Reza Khan, the commander of the only organized standing army – a force of 3,000 men – who initially relied on the support of the conservative forces within the fourth parliament to establish a centralized state apparatus and end the period of chaos and multiplicity of political power in the country. Fear of communist expansion from the north at a time of virtual breakdown of law and order, helped bring about a loose coalition between the conservative forces, the clergy-landlord-merchant oligarchy who dominated the fourth parliament, in support of the creation of a strong centralized state in Iran (Abrahamian 1982, chapter 3). This also happened to coincide with what the British government considered desirable for the safeguard of its interests in the region (Keddie 1981, p.87, Stork 1975, p.11).

After the February coup there were a series of measures taken by the state to rationalize and expand its central administration. At the core of these reforms was the creation of a centralized and unified national army which could end the widespread brigandage and political autonomy of the various regional governors and tribal chiefs, and defeat the popular movements in the north. With the creation of a professional and specialized officers corps, the hereditary officers and princes of the Qajar family were shorn of their ranks and the old provincial levies and tribal contingents were replaced by an organized and effective military establishment (Banani 1961, Kazemi 1980). By 1925, the army was the most powerful and centralized institution in the whole country, and Reza Khan as the commander in chief of the newly created national army could exert his authority over almost all the regions of the country. By controlling the military apparatus, Reza Khan's political power soon surpassed the power of the initial conservative alliance on the basis of whose support he had managed to consolidate his position. The power of the latter oligarchy, which, since the aftermath of the Constitutional Revolution shared in the control of central state with the Qajar crown, derived mainly from the regional clientelistic networks and traditional patronage links which enabled them to control the local voters and dominate the parliament. This loose coalition of parochial political groupings, each having its own particularistic interests and outlooks, however, was soon overtaken by the power of the nationwide military-bureaucratic establishment which upheld the ideology of national interest and modernization. Using the military to manipulate the elections of the fifth parliament, Reza Khan managed to replace the parliamentary majority of the conservative forces, who increasingly opposed his modernization policies and challenged the consolidation of his political power, by a working majority of his own supporters – mainly from the new intelligentsia (Abrahamian 1982, pp.131–5). By 1926 he emerged as Reza Shah, the founder of the new Pahlavi dynasty – the first dynasty of non-tribal origin coming to power without reliance on tribal support.

During the latter half of the 1920s, with the help of foreign advisers the finances of the state were reorganized and effective measures were taken to regulate the civil service by establishing educational standards, introducing life tenure, and providing a table of ranks and a regular scale of promotion with fixed salaries. The same bureaucratic criteria were applied to the judicial and educational systems. A comprehensive civil code as well as penal and commercial codes were devised which gradually transformed judicial practices from the private prerogative of the clergy, conducted according to their personal interpretation of *sharia*, into universal and formal rules. Bureaucratization of administration of law was completed by the 1936 legislation, introducing special examinations and university degrees for presiding over judicial courts (Banani 1961). Parallel measures were also taken with regard to the modernization of educational institutions (Arasteh 1962).

Rationalization of the state administration was accompanied by functional and structural differentiation of the state apparatus and the creation of specialized ministerial branches which could play a more direct and active role in the economy. In 1928, the National Bank (Bank Melli) was established by the state which took over the government's accounts as well as the monopoly right of banknote issue from the British owned Imperial Bank.[1]

The formation of this new centralized and unified bureaucratic machinery in a predominantly pre-capitalist economy and amidst a diversity of socio-political structures and vertical dismemberment of the society had important consequences for the distribution of power within the state itself. Bureaucratization of the state apparatus was tantamount to the institutional separation of the state from the medieval land-based economy and was the first pre-condition for the relative autonomy of the state from the economically dominant classes.[2] The degree of the autonomy of the state, however, depended on the prevailing socio-economic and political relations within the Iranian society. The absence of strong class structures and well-articulated class interests on a national scale, which was due to the backwardness of the Iranian economy, in the first instance entailed a high degree of autonomy for the state.[3] As we noted above, parallel to the centralization of the military–administrative apparatus of the state, the parliament diminished in its political significance and the balance of power between the traditional oligarchy in the *Majlis* and the Qajar crown which had been maintained since the Constitutional Revolution, totally shifted in favour of Reza Shah who formally exerted absolute control over the state apparatus. Once the control of Reza Shah over the state machinery was established and the organs of the modern state had acquired the necessary strength, the state machinery turned towards levelling out the vertical fragmentation of the society and destruction of what had remained of the traditional socio-political organizations. The traditional guilds which despite severe blows to their productive organization still performed an important role in the

[1] For the development of the modern banking and credit system in Iran. See Bharier (1971, pp.237–59).

[2] See Poulantzas (1973, part II, pp.157–67, and part V, pp.340–50). According to Poulantzas, it was the relative autonomy of the bureaucratic and highly centralized apparatus of absolutist state in western Europe which made it possible for the state to fulfil its functions during the transition period, despite the economic dominance of the feudal class.

[3] As we shall shortly see, the same conditions, i.e. the underdeveloped and peripheral structure of the Iranian economy, would themselves entail a high degree of structural constraint for the economic policies of the state.

political life of the cities were deprived of all power. The clergy which had, despite the lack of a unified political organization of their own, played an important ideological and political role through extensive traditional networks were severely weakened by the secularization policies of the regime.[4] The state machinery was next directed towards the 'integration' of the nomadic tribes into the modern social and political order of the nation. Tribal policy was directed, with high economic cost, towards the destruction of tribal organizations through forced settlement and prevention of seasonal migration. The 'nation building' policies of the state went as far as attempting to level out the multi-ethnic structures of the society; 'The policy towards the tribes was closely related to the long range ambition of transforming the multi-ethnic empire into a unified state with one people, one nation, one language and one culture' (Abrahamian 1982, p.142).

The social policy of the state during this period was not solely confined to the creation of the 'civil unity of the nation'. Any independent source of political power within the civil society was crushed. Political parties were banned and any social organization which could be a potential source of political opposition was broken.[5] The regime at the same time failed to establish a state political party of any sort which could work as a transmission mechanism between the increasingly atomized society and the centralized state, or function as a means of mobilization of political support for the state. Without having firm civilian foundations and legitimacy, the regime had to increasingly rely upon naked coercion.

The lack of urban civilian support could perhaps to some extent explain the weakness of the regime, despite its extensive bureaucratic-military organization, *vis-à-vis* the large landlords. The trend towards the consolidation of power of large absentee landlords over the countryside which was taking place from the mid nineteenth century, continued during the interwar period. The abolition of *tuyuls* in the first national assembly (1907) which was an attempt, albeit unsuccessful, by the urban dominated parliament to regain central control over the state lands and restructure the finances of the state on the basis of agricultural taxes did not succeed to reverse this trend. The abolition of *tuyuls*, however, inaugurated a new era in the social significance of land and the politico-legal attributes of landlordism. The civil code and the land registration laws of 1928–30 which provided a firm legal foundation for private land ownership, transformed

---

[4] The secularization policies of the state had many dimensions. Conduct of religious rites were highly restricted, legal and educational practices were freed from the monopoly of the clergy and transformed to the new bureaucracy, and the religious endowments (*vaqf*) were transformed in 1934 to the ministry of culture. See Gharatcheh-Daghi (1967, pp.29–31), Banani (1961), Abrahamian (1982, pp.149–60).

[5] 'It was the settled policy of Reza Shah to destroy any independent political organizations', Lambton (1943, p.44).

the status of the large landed proprietor 'from that of a territorial prince to that of an ordinary land owner' (Lambton 1953, p.260). The landlord formally became a private citizen of the state and his land assumed the character of unconditional private property. With the sale of large proportions of the remaining state lands to increase the government revenue for specific projects in different years during the inter-war period, large private landlordism became the predominant form of land ownership.[6]

The change in legal status of land ownership and the transformation of the status of the landlords into private subjects of the state did not, however, change the political authority and jurisdiction power of the landlords in the countryside. During the reign of Reza Shah the relation between the state and the landlords was one of political compromise. The landlords relinquished total control over the state machinery to the Shah, and the government did not intervene in the internal mechanisms of the agrarian relations. The countryside in a way formed a state within a state. 'There were some big landlords who would not even let the government agents enter their villages' (Ajami 1973, p.121). According to the law of December 1935, the *Kadkhodas* (village headmen), who were considered as the executive representatives of the government in the villages, were to be appointed and paid by the landlords (Lambton 1953, p.190). This was indeed the official recognition of the landlords political authority in the countryside. During the 1930s, the mutual reliance and support of the regime and the landlord class was perfected when, after the monarch, high bureaucrats and military officers by means of acquiring land – mainly through confiscation – closely associated with the landlords (Lambton 1953, pp. 259–62).

The occupation of the leading bureaucratic and military positions in Reza Shah's government by the large landlords, however, should not create the contention that the state was a mere instrument of the landlord class. There is no doubt that state support during this period did strengthen the landlord class, by safeguarding their property and suppressing the radical forces in the urban areas who opposed absentee landlordism and had put forward demands for land reform since the time of the Constitutional Revolution (see Moameni 1980, part ii, chapter 1, pp.82–90). During the reign of Reza Shah there was no mention of land reform or the need for transforming the landlord-peasant relations. Furthermore, land taxes and

---

[6] See Banani (1961, p. 114). The following is a rough estimate of the pattern of ownership of some 50,000 Iranian villages existing in the 1930s:
  1 Absentee landlords 58%
  2 Religious endowments (*vaqf*) 15%
  3 Reza Shah (private property) 5%
  4 State lands 4%
  5 Peasant ownership 18%
    It should be noted that the nature of agrarian relations on *vaqf* and state lands, which in any case were on long-term lease to private landlords, did not differ from large private holdings (Gharatcheh-Daghi 1967, p.62).

direct taxes on rents were abolished and the finances of the state, which up to then fundamentally centred around land revenue administration, were now based on indirect taxation. These phenomena which were reflections of the power of the landlords within the Iranian society, did not mean, nevertheless, that the state was a mere instrument of the landlords. The main drive of the state's economic policies during this period could be better explained with regard to its structural location within the Iranian transitional formation than by the control of the state by any particular class. These policies in their broad outlines could be related to different aspects of the economic crisis which the peripheralization of the economy during the nineteenth century and early twentieth century had given rise to. This should not, however, lead one to the other extreme of taking a simplistic functionalist standpoint. The way these economic imperatives impressed themselves upon the policy makers, the manner in which the policy makers envisioned the required course of state intervention, and finally the way in which these policies were implemented, depended on complex social forces which could not be analysed without a concrete historical study. For instance, the political and economic implications of the agrarian mode of production as we shall see, formed only one aspect, though a very important one, of these conditioning factors.

3.3 State and capital accumulation 1921–1941

The state economic policy during the 1921–41 period was not based on a coherent and systematic economic ideology. The general tendency, like the state's social policy, was towards the creation of a 'national economy' by providing the basic politico-legal and infrastructural requirements of a modern economy. Within this context, however, there were radical shifts in the form of state economic intervention. Two distinct periods, separated by the transitional years of 1929–30, could be distinguished with regard to the state economic policy.

During the 1920s the state adopted mainly a caretaker role in the economy. The free trade regime remained in force up to 1928, which led to the revival of foreign trade during this period with the same pattern as the pre-First World War era (table 3.1).[7] The attempts of the government

[7] A major change in the pattern of foreign trade in this period was the rise in the share of oil exports which after 1920 exceeded the value of total non-oil merchandise exports (see table 3.4). The actual foreign exchange proceeds of the oil sector composed of royalties and domestic expenditures of the Anglo-Persian Oil Company was relatively small during this period. Royalties constituted no more than a maximum 7 per cent, and the total foreign exchange contribution of oil no more than 25 per cent of the total value of oil exports (table 3.4). The proceeds from the oil sector during the 1927–41 period was set aside in a special revenue account and was largely spent on armaments (UN 1965, p.59).

during this period were mainly centred around reforming of the political and legal institutions and improving the means of transportation.[8] By the end of the decade, however, it was evident that the much-hoped for engagement of both domestic and foreign capital in the domestic productive activities, specially in the industrial sector, was not taking place. Iranian merchant capital had received a severe blow due to the recession in foreign trade during the First World War and its aftermath (Moghaddam 1956, chapter iv, pp.103–5), and foreign capital, except in the British owned oil industry enclave, was not forthcoming.[9]

Despite the institutional reforms which took place during the 1920s, by the end of the decade the economic prospects looked even bleaker than the early 1900s. Between 1913 and the mid 1920s, prior to the World Depression, there was already a noticeable decline in the terms of trade of the Iranian primary exports (UK, DOT 1925, p.17), while the volume of exports stood below the pre-war level.

The stagnation in the export sector which was an aspect of the inter-war phase of slow growth in the world market meant that the pre-war experience of export-led growth with its lopsided structure was no longer viable. Combined with the structural rigidities of the Iranian economy, the stagnation of the export sector created important structural tensions in the economy. An important aspect of the structural rigidities of the Iranian economy, and a good measure of its peripheral orientation, was its dependence on imports for the basic manufactured mass consumption goods (such as cotton textiles, kerosene, sugar and tea). These items formed more than 80 per cent of merchandise imports (see table 3.1), a fact which is a clear demonstration of the low productivity of labour and the extreme backwardness of the economy during this period.[10] The perpetual deficit on the current account of the balance of payments during the 1920s which by the end of the decade added up to at least $30 million[11] – chiefly financed by the outflow of precious metals – meant that even the prevailing low standard of living of the population was no longer sustainable. The Great

---

[8] On the developments in the transport system during the 1920s, see Bharier (1971, pp. 194–7).

[9] During the entire inter-war period there was no long-term capital inflow of any sort; neither of portfolio nor direct investment type (with the exception of the two enclaves of Caspean Fisheries and Anglo Iranian Oil Company, AIOC). The reason was not any lack of interest or need on the side of the Iranian government. It was rather due to the lack of supply of long-term capital in the inter-war period. See UK, Department of Overseas Trade (hereafter, UK, DOT), *Economic Conditions in Persia* April 1925, pp.1–9.

[10] According to the report of the British Board of Overseas Trade (1925, p.6) during the 1920s, '[Iran had] a smaller purchasing power per head of the population than any other country'.

[11] This $30 million was the deficit on the visible account (inclusive of oil sector). The invisible account was also in deficit during this period (see Moghaddam 1956, p.60).

Depression of the early 1930s which magnified these problems brought to the fore the urgent need for a radical restructuring of the economy. By the mid 1930s, the government had committed itself to a state-centred policy of economic development and a centrally controlled process of accumulation. This change in the government policy orientation was not based on a premeditated economic strategy, but rather it emerged in the form of a series of improvisations forced by circumstances.

The World Depression of the early 1930s and the implementation of the first five-year plan in the USSR which restricted the free access of Iranian merchants to Russian markets,[12] worked as a catalyst for the reorientation of the economic policy by the Iranian government. In Iran, similar to the experience of all primary exporters, the Great Depression accelerated the rate of deterioration of foreign terms of trade which was already taking place during the 1920s. This, together with the fall in demand for exports, created a significant decline in import capacity.[13] A more severe and immediately felt impact of the world crisis, however, was the sharp decline in the rate of exchange of silver Kran due to the slump in the price of silver in world commodity markets.[14] The sharp decline in the purchasing power of silver Kran and the instability of the exchange rate, in the latter half of the year 1929–30, brought the import trade to a virtual standstill (UK, DOT March 1930, p.13). Exchange controls were introduced in February 1930, followed by the foreign trade monopoly law of February 1931, which gave the government monopoly right of all foreign trade. Strict quantitative import controls together with a system of high tariffs and multiple exchange rates were imposed throughout the 1930s. Through the control of foreign trade the government pursued an energetic policy of capital accumulation and import-substituting industrialization.

During the 1930s the newly formed centralized state machinery was turned into a very effective means of mobilization and central control over economic resources. Government expenditure in real terms rose from Rls 392m in 1928 to Rls 810m in 1935 and Rls 977m in 1937; by an average rate of growth of 11 per cent per annum. More than 70 per cent of total government expenditure was financed through indirect taxation or deficit financing (see table 3.2). In particular, the state trading monopolies, which in some cases are reported to have made a rate of profit as high as 40 to 50 per cent of their turnover (Wilber 1976, p.130), played an important part in

---

[12] Due to high cost of transport the entire primary export trade of the northern provinces was tied to the Russian markets. This constituted about 40 per cent of total non-oil export.

[13] Imports in real terms dropped by about 50 per cent and exports by 20 per cent from 1929 to 1933 (see Moghaddam 1956, p.64).

[14] Following a 65 per cent drop in the gold price of silver in international markets during 1929–31, the Kran rate of exchange against the gold standard currencies declined by the same magnitude (see Yaganegi 1934, pp. 60–91).

Table 3.1. Composition of non-oil foreign trade 1910–1938

(annual averages)

	1910–13		1919–22[c]		1927–30[c]		1938–9	
	Value[b]	%	Value	%	Value	%	Value	%
Imports[a]								
Consumption goods	457.4	93.3	534.1	91.3	620.4	80.0	400.0	52.7
Textiles:	182.8	37.3	219.6	37.6	256.6	33.1	95.0	12.5
Cotton	159.3	32.3	201.6	34.5	206.8	26.6	60.8	8.0
Other	23.5	5.0	18.0	3.1	49.8	6.5	34.2	4.5
Sugar	129.0	26.0	125.9	21.5	101.9	13.1	87.9	11.6
Other	145.6	29.7	188.6	32.2	261.9	33.8	133.4	17.6
Capital goods	10.1	2.1	20.3	3.3	83.6	10.7	329.3	43.3
Motor vehicle and parts[d]	—	—	—	—	28.6	3.6	124.0	6.1
Machinery and equ.	—	—	—	—	25.2	3.2	80.5	10.6
Metal products	10.1	2.1	20.3	3.3	29.8	3.9	124.3	16.4
Raw materials	22.8	4.6	30.3	5.3	72.3	9.3	30.0	4.0
Petroleum[e]	8.7	1.7	14.1	2.4	38.0	4.0	18.9	2.5
Yarn	14.1	2.9	16.2	2.9	22.6	2.9	10.0	1.3
Cement	—	—	—	—	11.7	2.4	1.1	0.2
Total	490.3	100.0	584.7	100.0	776.3	100.0	759.3	100.0

Main exports[f]

Rugs and carpets	51.4	13.4	48.6	30.0	153.3	32.2	72.9	27.2
Opium	23.5	6.2	20.6	12.6	59.5	12.5	32.1	12.0
Raw cotton	79.4	21.0	3.3	2.0	46.5	9.8	29.6	11.0
Rice	35.4	9.3	5.7	3.5	38.2	8.0	2.4	1.0
Skins and hides	15.9	4.2	5.9	3.6	30.7	6.7	13.8	5.1
Gum	14.0	3.7	8.5	5.2	16.0	3.4	—	—
Fruits	55.8	14.7	23.8	14.5	48.3	10.1	68.6	25.5
Raw wool	11.1	3.0	1.7	1.0	15.0	3.1	12.7	4.7
Sheep casing	—	—	—	—	11.3	2.4	36.6	13.5
Total	286.5	100.0	118.1	100.0	418.8	100.0	268.7	100.0

Notes:
[a] Excludes the oil sector imports.
[b] Value is in million Rials.
[c] Includes some of the imports of AIOC.
[d] Excluding passenger cars.
[e] Mainly kerosene.
[f] Excludes monetary gold and silver.
Source: Moghaddam 1956, p.49. UN, *Yearbook of International Trade Statistics* (YITS) 1955.

Table 3.2. *Sources of government revenue 1928–1938*

	1928		1935		1937	
	Value	%	Value	%	Value[a]	%
Indirect taxes	277	71	693	65	1173	71
State monopolies[b]	64	16	320	30	340	21
State industries	—	—	27	2	74	4
Customs	112	29	170	16	362	22
Other indirect taxes[c]	101	26	176	17	397	24
Direct taxes	50	12	89	8	142	9
Public domains	22	6	27	2	41	2
Oil royalties	28	7	173	16	206	12
Miscellaneous	15	4	77	7	84	5
Total revenues	392	100	1059	100	1646	100
Total expenditure	392		1238		1916	
(at 1928 prices)[d]	(392)		(810)		(977)	
Deficit financing	—	—	179	16.9	270	16.4

Notes:

[a] Value in million rials.

[b] Year 1928 is the tea and sugar monopoly tax earmarked for railway construction.

[c] Includes road taxes, post and telegraph.

[d] Deflated by wholesale price index.

Sources: UK, DOT *Reports* 1930, pp.16–17, 1935, pp.6–7, 1937, pp.3–5.
Wholesale price index from Bharier 1971, p.46.

financing government expenditure.[15] The financial significance of the state monopolies for the process of accumulation cannot be fully realized from their share of total government revenue, which was about 30 per cent of the total. Apart from increasing the effectiveness of the fiscal machinery of the state in raising other forms of indirect taxation, a significant contribution of the monopoly companies in mobilizing resources was to tilt the internal terms of trade against the agricultural sector without generating a process of spiralling inflation which would have been inevitable otherwise (see

[15] Under the provisions of the foreign trade monopoly law of 1931, various trading companies were set up and granted exclusive right of wholesale marketing of major items of export, import and internal trade. Though not all the companies were directly owned by the state, their operations were tightly controlled by the government and through them the government was 'effectively in control of both internal and external trade' (UK, DOT 1935, p.26). The following wholesale trade monopolies were in existence in 1937: sugar and tea, opium, tobacco, cereals, dried fruit, cotton piece goods, silk and cocoons, carpets, cotton, wool and skins, jute, etc. For more detail, see UK, DOT (1935, pp.24–7) and 1937, pp.16–19.

p.79). Moreover, in many instances, through the encouragement of the government, large limited liability companies were formed by big merchants which were given total monopoly over some major items of foreign trade, and in some cases, over total trade of whole provinces.[16]

In the absence of any modern long-term credit organization and the lack of existence of large accumulations of money capital in the hands of the Iranian merchants, the concentration of funds through the state budget and private monopoly trade companies played an important part in financing fixed investment during the 1930s.[17] The pace of capital formation particularly accelerated in the latter half of the decade. The major part of investment during this period was concentrated within the state sector. More than 40 per cent of total government expenditure during the decade was invested: mainly in transportation and industry.[18] About 60 per cent of government investment was in roads and railways, which greatly contributed to the integration of the national market. By the end of the 1930s, the average duration of a journey fell to about one tenth of what it had been before the First World War, and the cost of transport was cut by some three quarters (Issawi 1971, p.375). The next important field of government investment was in the industrial sector. By 1941 industrial investment had reached a value of approximately £58m of which £28m had been contributed by the government.[19] Private investment in industry really got under way only in the latter half of the decade. The highly protected home market together with government encouragement in the form of tariff exemption, preferen-

---

[16] However, a large part of the original capital in many cases was supplied by the state. According to UK, DOT (1935, p.26), 'in some cases as much as three quarters of the capital was supplied by the Agricultural Bank which was a government institution'.

[17] Of course, an important pre-condition for this process to take place was the formation of the Bank Melli Iran, which had the effect of substantially increasing the level of liquidity in the economy. During 1933–40, the currency in circulation grew from about Rls 758m to Rls 1,264m, demand deposits grew from Rls 440m to Rls 1,119m, while government debt to BMI grew from Rls 65m to Rls 1,064m (Moghaddam 1956, p.160). This, however, does not reflect the full extent of the contribution of the Bank to increased liquidity in the economy. The demonetization of Silver Kran which ended the tendency for its speculative hoarding, the spread of modern banking facilities all over the country (by 1940 BMI had established eighty-four branches in the country) and the ease of transaction in the new instruments of payment, led to a rapid increase in the velocity of circulation. Taking into account the 10 per cent average annual rate of growth of money supply, and considering that the average rate of inflation during this period was about 12 per cent per annum, it would be readily observed that there must have occurred a rapid increase in the velocity of circulation – something of the order of at least 5 to 6 per cent per annum, assuming a 3 to 4 per cent real economic growth.

[18] During the 1934–40 period, 48 per cent of total government expenditure was on 'development projects' (not necessarily fixed investment). This was composed of 23 per cent on railways, 6 per cent on roads, and 19 per cent mainly on industry and mining. See Moghaddam 1956, pp. 158–69.

[19] The figures are current prices and converted at current rates of exchange. See UK, DOT 1957, p.76.

tial exchange premium, and exemption of transport fees for imported machinery, had made private manufacturing a highly profitable line of investment (see Moghaddam 1956, pp.170–9). By the end of the decade, more than 260 plants with no less than 63,000 installed horsepower, employing approximately 48,000 workers were established in both public and private manufacturing sectors (table 3.3). The main lines of manufacturing investment were in light industries such as textiles, sugar, matches, etc., for which the prior participation in world trade had produced a mass market, or industries such as cement and chemicals which found their market as a result of the investment in the 1930s.

The relatively high rate of capital accumulation during the 1930s was financed by domestic resources; foreign contribution was solely confined to technical assistance. The expanding government administrative expenditure and investment during this period were financed mainly through indirect taxation, such as tariffs and road taxes, profits of monopoly companies, and deficit financing which, under the conditions of inelastic supplies could be viewed as one form of indirect taxation. The main burden of indirect taxes – falling chiefly on the mass consumption goods which formed the bulk of foreign and domestic wholesale trade – was borne by the lower income groups. Though the distribution of the burden of taxation during this period was to some extent determined by the political considerations, one should not underestimate the impact of strictly economic factors on this issue. First, the choice between direct and indirect taxation under the extremely backward conditions in the Iranian economy was largely non-existent. The government did not have the extensive fiscal machinery needed for this purpose, and even if it could be set up its efficiency in raising net revenue (its revenue/cost ratio) would have been very low. Secondly, once the decision was made for indirect taxes, there was little to be chosen in terms of different items: the bulk of the wholesale trade was composed of basic consumption goods. These constraints on the structure of public finance and their implications for the distribution of the burden of taxation, largely arose out of the prevailing conditions in the real economy; namely the low productivity of labour and the general backwardness of the economy. This could be more clearly demonstrated if we look at the real side of the process of resource mobilization and examine the mechanism involved in accelerating investment and expanding government expenditure under the prevailing economic conditions.

Given the supply rigidities in the predominantly agricultural economy of Iran during the early 1930s,[20] the high rates of growth of employment in

[20] These supply rigidities were largely related to the persistence of semi-feudal relations of production and the backward technology of production in the agricultural sector which employed more than 70 per cent of the labour force. The absence of modern manufacturing

Table 3.3. *Manufacturing plants established during 1930–1940[a]*

Sector	Number of plants	Value of capital[b]	Installed horsepower	Number of workers
Textiles	72	1168	43026	29601
Sugar	8	582	9909	4501
Drinks	40	75	1360	565
Chemicals	11	637	2901	4458
Soap	16	15	85	231
Glass	6	22	574	1043
Leather	11	65	635	608
Matches	26	50	354	4033
Flour and rice milling	37	89	3072	1376
Cotton ginning	29	53	1382	590
Tea	9	42	348	399
Total	265	2798	63646	47405

Notes:
[a] Excludes government cement factories.
[b] Historical cost at current prices in millions of rials.
Source: Extracted from Ministry of Labour, *Statistical Survey of Iranian Industries* 1947 (in Persian).

both the government and investment sectors,[21] would have inevitably reduced the consumption per head of the rest of the population. This was not necessarily due to any reductions in the total supplies of basic consumption goods, which under the conditions of a surplus labour economy would be expected to rise as a result of the creation of new employment opportuni-

productive capacities formed the other aspect of supply rigidities. There are no reliable data on the production of different agricultural crops during the 1930s. The available evidence suggests some growth in the production of basic food crops during the 1925–35 period but a noticeable decline during the latter half of the thirties decade (see Bharier 1971, p.134). Though the reliability of this evidence is very poor, the overall picture it draws sounds plausible. The decline in the production of export cash crops during the earlier period would have increased the availability of land for food crops, while the constraints set by the backward conditions of agrarian production are highly probable to have checked the continuation of growth in the second half of the decade. There were other factors involved as well; on the one hand the improvements in the means of transport and higher security of roads favoured growth by improving the marketability of agricultural products, on the other hand the deterioration in the terms of trade of agricultural sector is said to have worked against agricultural growth or at least the expansion of marketed surplus (Moghaddam 1956).
[21] Government sector employees here refer to all in regular employment, e.g., civil and military administration, teachers, transport workers, etc. Investment sector refers mainly to the construction sector.

ties,[22] but rather due to the higher real income and consumption of the new employees and those upon whom they hitherto used to depend. Hence irrespective of the way their wages and salaries were formally financed, at any point in time, the new employees and workers would have benefitted at the expense of those who had already been employed and other classes of the economy.[23]

If we further consider the flow of resources, other than labour, which were commonly used by the investment and consumption goods sectors, it will be readily realized that accelerating investment in the short run was bound to lead to a reduction in total available supplies of consumption goods. The competing claims of the basic manufactured consumption goods and investment goods imports on the limited supplies of foreign exchange resources was a clear example of this phenomenon. During the 1929–36 period, while there was an absolute reduction in real imports, the share of investment goods rose from about 10 per cent to more than 40 per cent of total imports (table 3.1). This had to be accommodated by a substantial reduction in the imports of basic manufactured consumption goods, which virtually formed the rest of the import bill. It was not until after 1936 that the decrease in imports of consumption goods was compensated for by rather large increases in domestic production of substitutes (Moghaddam 1956, pp.72, 82).

The relatively high pace of accumulation and growth of government expenditure was, therefore, bound to be at the expense of the real consumption of the broad masses of the population. This was largely independent of the taxation policy of the state. Direct taxes on rents and land taxes were perhaps the only other alternatives within the domestic economy through which the reduction in the general standard of living of the population could have been to some extent alleviated. Through reducing the luxury consumption of landlords, any reduction in their real income would have released an equivalent amount of resources for employment in other sectors of the economy without creating any burden for the rest of the population.[24] The

---

[22] Surplus labour economy is used here in the sense of consumption per head of the workers being higher than their marginal product. The existing evidence supports the existence of disguised unemployment during the 1930s. If this were not the case, however, our argument would be *a fortiori* correct. New recruitment in the government sector would in that case lead to a decline in total available consumer goods.

[23] This does not mean that the new employees did in fact improve their standard of living. It means, rather, that in any actual situation of general decline in the standard of living of the population, they would lose relatively less than others.

[24] We have been so far implicitly assuming that the profits of big merchants, and the salaries of high government officials were saved. This was not, however, the case, especially with the latter category of income. The same argument therefore applies to the luxury consumption by these groups. As we shall argue in the next chapter, this aspect of the authoritarian regime, namely its attempt at co-optation of the new middle class by granting them high wages and salaries, assumes important proportions during the 1953–77 period and exerts a significant influence on the pattern of capital accumulation in that period.

political compromise with the landlords, however, ruled out this option. This, nevertheless, did not imply that the landlords were exempt from taxation. Under the circumstances, it could be argued that perhaps indirect taxation was a more effective means of taxing the landlords. This was implemented through heavy taxes on primary exports, and monopolizing the wholesale marketing of the domestic supplies of food grains which the landlords had to sell to the government at low administered prices (see Moghaddam 1956, p.17).

The available data do not permit a quantitative investigation of the financial burden on the landlords and other classes within the economy – namely, urban workers, petty producers and traders, and the peasantry. The distribution of the burden on different classes on the one hand depended on the taxation and the price policies of the state, and on the other hand reflected the ability of different classes to defend their income share by inflationary transmission of the burden to others. The remarkable fact is that the rate of inflation was moderate during this period: wholesale prices grew by an annual average rate of 9 per cent and retail prices by 12 per cent. Compared to the relatively large shift of resources to the government and investment sectors, this rate of inflation was low – it was probably not much higher than what the growth of indirect taxes would have implied. In Maynard's terminology, the efficiency of inflationary finance was very high (Maynard 1963, p.17). This reflected the inability of different classes to defend their income share through inflationary mechanisms – partly due to the very structure of the Iranian economy itself, but largely as a result of the political weakness of all the classes *vis-à-vis* the authoritarian state. During the 1930s, trade unions were banned and demands for higher wages and salaries were ruthlessly suppressed. Landlords were put into the strait jacket of monopoly trading companies which equally squeezed the peasantry by changing the terms of trade against them. The only mechanism through which the landlords could defend their share was through squeezing the peasantry even more – which according to the available accounts they did. The urban petty producers and traders had little market power to recourse to inflationary mechanisms. Ease of entry into these occupations under the conditions of surplus labour would ensure that these classes were always at the top in the hierarchy of sufferers from inflationary finance. As to the small merchants who were excluded from the private monopoly trading syndicates, high indirect taxes and the general squeeze on the standard of living of the population, was bound to squeeze their profits as well. The 3 per cent margin of retail price over wholesale price inflation was perhaps due to the higher market power and resistance of this class.

Through a combination of mechanisms, from outright political coercion to the creation of new economic institutions, the state thus became an effective instrument of primary accumulation in the Iranian economy. It was a task which none of the existing classes within the Iranian economy could perform, and was indeed predicated upon the state achieving a certain degree of autonomy from the economically dominant classes. The degree of autonomy of the state was, however, limited by the constraints which were rooted in the underdeveloped structures of the Iranian economy and its peripheral mode of integration in the world economy. We have already noted how state intervention during the 1930s was prompted by the pressure of circumstances arising from the World Depression and the adjustment problems it created for the Iranian economy. The state, however, should not be regarded in this context as a totally autonomous and free subject, set to bring about a new economic order with its efforts directed in a unilinear manner towards the 'modernization' of a 'traditional' economy. There were various contradictory features in the role of state in the process of capital accumulation during this period which reflected the complex and contradictory nature of the social forces which constituted state power. For example, while on the one hand the state conducted the process of primitive accumulation largely through the transfer of resources from the agricultural sector and partly at the expense of landlords, on the other hand it strengthened the institution of absentee landlordism and helped to perpetuate the semi-feudal relations of production which in the long run was a main obstacle to capital accumulation and growth. Various other such contradictions could be found at the more concrete level of analysis of the form of the regime and its interaction with the process of accumulation. For instance, while the highly autocratic and centralized form of the state was on the one hand instrumental in the process of capital accumulation, on the other hand the nepotism, favouritism, corruption and the lack of initiative which it encouraged was inimical to the pursuit of a planned and coherent industrial policy (see Hershlag 1964, and Groseclose 1947). Another important aspect of the relation between political power and capital accumulation which cannot be by-passed here was the highly exploitative relation between the Anglo-Iranian Oil Company and the Iranian state, and the potentially important role which the oil sector could have played in financing accumulation during the period under study.

The issue of the distribution of the profits of the Anglo-Iranian Oil Company (AIOC) formed an important aspect of the relation of state power to capital accumulation during this period. Though the share of the Iranian government in the profits of the AIOC formed a relatively small part of the total government expenditure, the total profits of the company compared to the entire investment outlays in the Iranian economy as a whole constituted a formidable sum. It is estimated that the profits of the

AIOC during the 1919–30 period added up to approximately £200 million, whereas the royalties paid to the Iranian government were no more than £10m (Hershlag 1964, p.205). The former sum was more than the entire value of capital formation in the Iranian economy, and equivalent to four times the total fixed investment in the Iranian industrial sector during the entire 1930–41 period.

The question of the distribution of oil income was a source of mounting conflict between the Iranian government and the AIOC during the late 1920s and early 1930s. The onset of the Great Depression created the climax, which led to the cancellation of the D'Arcy concession of 1901 by the Iranian government.[25] Though the new concession signed in 1933 did lead to some increase in the oil revenues of the government per unit of production, it did not bring about any significant changes in the extremely unequal shares (see table 3.4).[26] Nor did it create a substantial increase in the absolute value of the oil income of the government – not enough to make a dramatic impact on the process of accumulation in the rest of the economy. A rough comparison with the share of the Venezuelan government in the net profits of oil companies in that country during the same period would help to bring into light the relatively low bargaining power of the Iranian government *vis-à-vis* the AIOC. While the total receipts of the Venezuelan government during the 1913–47 period amounted to 35 per cent of the net profits of the oil companies operating in that country, the comparable figure in the case of Iran was only 20 per cent for the same period.[27]

The relatively low bargaining power of the Iranian state *vis-à-vis* the AIOC was largely due to the monopoly power of the company which was to a large degree maintained by the gunboat imperialism of the British government who was in full military and political control of the Persian Gulf (see Saikal 1980, pp.22–3). This issue nevertheless was not totally independent of the nature of the Iranian state and the configuration of political power within the country. Having alienated the majority of the urban and tribal populations and being by no means certain of the support of landlords, Reza Shah's authoritarian regime relied heavily on its coercive apparatus and support of its bureaucratic-military clientele to maintain its power. The regime, however, at a time of financial austerity could not risk the likely loss

[25] On the 1901 concession and the development of oil industry prior to the First World War, see Issawi (1971, pp.311–27).
[26] For the text of the new concession see Hurewitz (1956, pp.188–96). Payments to the Iranian government rose from an average of $0.2 million per ton during 1925–30 to $0.34 million during 1933–40 and $0.42 million during 1945–50. See Issawi and Yeganeh (1962, table 2.1, pp.18–19).
[27] Based on Issawi and Yeganeh (1962, tables on pp.188–9 and 194). Net profits of the companies refers to profits from the operations within the countries concerned.

Table 3.4. *Relative significance of the oil sector in historical perspective 1923–1977*

(annual averages)

	1923–6	1928–30	1935–7	1945–7	1955–7	1965–7	1975–7
1 Total quantity of oil exports (m. tons)	3.5	5.0	7.8	16.6	23.2	120.2	303.5
2 Value of oil exports (fob, £ m)[a]	13.0	23.7	26.6	38.8	43.9[c]	150.9	1164.0
3 Government oil income (£ m)[a]	0.9	1.3	3.8	4.2	20.0	75.0	1133.7
4 Net foreign exchange proceeds from the oil sector (£ m)[a,b]	3.2	3.1	6.8	12.0	25.2	81.3	1164.0
5 Government oil income as a % of the value of oil exports (3/2)	7.2	5.4	14.4	10.7	45.5	49.7	97.4
6 Government oil income as a % of total government revenue	13.8	15.1	16.8	16.4	45.1	50.8	75.4
7 Foreign exchange contribution of the oil sector as % of the value of oil exports (4/2)	25.0	13.3	25.1	31.0	57.4	53.9	100.0
8 Foreign exchange contribution of oil sector as % of total exports	21.0	22.5	37.3	53.6	65.0	74.4	83.8

Notes:
[a] All the values in the table are in 1923–6 pounds sterling, i.e., they have been deflated by the UK export unit values.
[b] Royalties plus domestic currency purchases of AIOC.
[c] For the years 1955–67 export values are calculated on the basis of posted prices.

Sources: Moghaddam 1956, UN 1955, p.73, CSO, *Statistical Yearbook* 1968, 1977, Amuzegar and Fekrat 1971, p.18, Bharier 1971, p.111, and Central Bank, *Annual Report* 1969, 1977.

of its oil revenues, even for a short period of time, which could arise had it taken a more militant stand against the company.[28] It was not until the advent of mass politics and the issue of oil becoming the central theme of the popular political and economic nationalism during the post-war period, that the Iranian government could bring about a significant shift in the distribution of oil income to her own benefit.

3.4 The post-war developments

With the allied occupation of the country in 1941, the sixteen-year period of authoritarian rule by Reza Shah came to an end. The disorganization and paralysis of the state apparatus resulting from the occupation of the country inaugurated a period of reentry of the masses into Iranian politics in the post-war era. Over the next thirteen years (1941–53), Iranian politics once more became the arena of open interaction between different social forces. This period of open politics in modern Iranian history is marked by political instability and perpetual change of alliances between different social powers. The prolongation of this period of political instability and its culmination in total exclusion of the masses from national politics after the 1953 coup, was due to a complex set of factors related to both the internal social structure and external interventions.[29]

The structural changes which had taken place in the Iranian society during the inter-war period had a distinct bearing upon the nature of political developments of the 1941–53 period. The process of social change in the inter-war period, which was predominantly concentrated in the urban areas, introduced important new dimensions to the nature of Iranian politics in this period, as compared to the early decades of the century.

An important aspect of urban social change was the levelling-out process, at work from the middle of the nineteenth century and specially intensifying during the inter-war period, which had removed the vertical dismemberment of the traditional urban society and created the possibility of horizontal mass political organizations. This loosening up process was reflected in the rapid growth of the Iranian communist party (Tudeh Party), organized along horizontal class lines and cutting through the traditional clientelistic political allegiances. The same phenomenon was also signified by the strong

---

[28] While negotiations for the 1933 concession were still in progress, the finance minister wrote to the Iranian minister in London: 'We haven't a single cent left. Send a telegram to Sir John Codman [the managing director of the AIOC] and ask him for an advance of 10,000 pounds against the new contract, so that we may be able to keep the country alive at least.' Quoted from Nirumand (1969, p.3).

[29] For detailed studies of the political events during this period, see Abrahamian (1982), Keddie (1981), Katouzian (1981).

nationalist movement led by the National Front during the 1949–53 period.[30]

The process of social change, however, as we noted above was solely confined to the urban areas. During the forties and fifties decades more than 70 per cent of the Iranian population still lived in the countryside and were under the total clientelistic domination of landlords and tribal chiefs. The broad national economic and class-based issues which were at the centre of mass politics in the urban areas, therefore, could not cut through the traditional patronage ties in the countryside. For example the Tudeh party which during the highly inflationary decade of forties could build up a mass following amongst the urban working and lower middle classes, could not mobilize the peasantry along the same lines of class politics as in the case of the dominated classes in the urban areas (see Abrahamian and Kazemi 1978). For the same reason a bourgeois liberal solution to the question of integration of the masses in the political process had become problematic. The independent peasantry, whose vote for example in the case of post-1950s Turkey and Greece formed the basis of restricted bourgeois democracies in these respective countries, in the case of Iran was strictly controlled by big landlords.[31] Another important factor was that, because of the oil question, Iranian mass politics had acquired strong nationalist dimensions which made a liberal compromise with the west virtually impossible.

A detailed study of the events which led to the defeat of both the urban middle-class and working-class movements and the reimposition of the autocratic rule of the Shah after 1953, falls outside the scope of the present study. The political developments during the transitional period of 1941–53, however, marked the beginning of a new phase of state-economy interrelationships and an entirely new role for the state in the accumulation process.

Though with the 1953 coup the main political aims of the new urban middle-class and leftist movements in broadening the base of political participation and challenging the dictatorial rule of the Shah remained unsuccessful, nevertheless the socio-economic reforms which formed the central issues of mass politics during this period could not be easily reversed. The demands for national control over the most vital economic resource of the country, and the utilization of oil revenues for development purposes

---

[30] National Front was an umbrella organization incorporating different factions of the traditional and modern urban middle classes. Under the leadership of Mosaddegh, it managed to control the executive power of the state and even the landlord dominated parliament on the basis of mass urban support mobilized around the issue of nationalization of the Anglo Iranian Oil Company.

[31] On the role of independent peasantry in the emergence of relatively stable bourgeois democracies of post-war Turkey and Greece, see Mouzelis (1980), Keyder (1979).

rather than its squandering over armaments and upkeep of a corrupt bureaucratic elite, the challenge to the power of the semi-feudal land-holding aristocracy which was seen as a major obstacle to economic and political modernization, and the demand for economic planning and more systematic attempts at economic development, were some of the important aspects of the new middle-class and leftist politics of this era which exerted a lasting influence – though not necessarily in the originally intended manner – in defining the new economic role of the state in the post-1953 period.

The transformation in the character and mode of economic intervention of the Iranian state in the post-1953 period was also to a large extent structured by the developments in the international economy and politics. The post-war restructuring of the world capitalist system under the US hegemony and the multinational-direct investment phase of western economic dominance, created totally different conditions of accumulation from those prevailing in the inter-war period. The first and perhaps most dramatic of these new conditions worked its way through the developments in the oil sector.

3.4.1 The oil era

In the post-war era the United States directly intervened to restructure the Middle Eastern oil industry, not only towards increased concessionary access for the US oil companies, but also in terms of geographical reorganization of the world oil markets and the allocation of the thus determined aggregate Middle East exports amongst the various oil-exporting countries (Stork 1975, chapters 2–3). This coincided with the strong nationalist movement in Iran, led by the National Front, against the British monopoly over the country's oil resources. The defeat of the Iranian oil nationalization attempt, after the CIA instigated coup of August 1953, and the 1954 consortium agreement according to which the US oil companies came to share in the control of the Iranian oil industry with the British Petroleum Company on a 40–40 basis, were the outcome of this conjuncture.[32] Though the 1954 concessionary agreement restored full management and commercial control of the oil industry to the foreign companies, the new 50–50 profit sharing formula led to a substantial increase in government oil revenues – by more than three folds per barrel of oil exports.[33] The

[32] For the details of the 1954 consortium agreement, see Fesharaki (1976, chapter 3).

[33] It is noteworthy that the increase in the share of the oil-exporting countries resulting from the 50–50 profit sharing agreement which came into effect during the early 1950s, was not at the expense of the oil companies. The increased payments to the host countries were almost entirely offset by tax credits in their parent countries.

significance of the developments during this period, however, goes far beyond this initial increase in government's share; it ushers a new era in the politics of oil and highlights a qualitative change in the role of the oil sector in the political economy of modern Iran.

Table 3.4, which provides a broad historical overview of the development of the Iranian oil industry during the three concessionary agreement periods, could help to highlight the distinct character of the post-1954 developments. The significance of political factors in determining the distributive shares between the oil companies and the government is well brought out by the quantum jump in the share of the government under the three successive concessionary periods (table 3.4). Despite the secular deterioration in the terms of trade of the Iranian oil exports *vis-à-vis* the exports of industrial countries from the late 1920s up to the late 1960s,[34] the Iranian government managed to increase its share, as a proportion of total value of oil exports, by ten times – from about 5 per cent to approximately 50 per cent. The bulk of the increase in the government's share was concentrated in the post-1954 period. In contrast to the two previous concessionary periods, the post-1954 period, referred to as the period of 'oil consciousness' in the Middle East (Stork 1975, chapter 4), is characterized by the growing bargaining power of the government *vis-à-vis* the oil companies leading to a continuous rise in the government's revenue share. The chief moments of the growing bargaining power of the government during the period which began with the abortive oil nationalization attempt in the early 1950s and culminated in practically total control of the oil industry by the government in the mid-1970s were characterized by: (a) the establishment of the National Iranian Oil Company (NIOC) during the oil nationalization dispute which created greater autonomy for the government in petroleum matters, (b) the 1956 Petroleum Act which laid the basis for the formation of joint ventures with independent oil companies in areas not covered by the consortium agreement on much more advantageous terms (Fesharaki 1976, pp.66–96), and (c) the creation of OPEC in the early 1960s to resist the reduction in the posted prices by the oil companies, which was the decisive step leading, in a decade's time, to total production and price control by the government (Stork 1975, Rustow and Mugno 1976, Fesharaki 1976). These developments, together with the rapid growth of

---

[34] See the first two rows of table 3.4. In fact in the post-war era, up to the late 1960s, the dollar price of Middle East crude oil had a declining trend in absolute terms. For example the posted price of Iranian crude (34 API) declined from $2.18 per barrel in 1947 to $1.78 per barrel in 1961. While further declines in the posted prices were resisted by the producing countries in the 1960s, the actual prices continued their downward trend until the end of the decade. See Issawi and Yeganeh (1962, chapter v), Stork (1975, chapters 2–3).

world demand for oil,[35] substantially increased the weight of the oil sector in the Iranian economy, and with the state being the main recipient of oil income, it radically transformed the role of the state in the process of accumulation.

[35] During 1950–74 period, the demand for energy in western Europe grew by almost three folds and demand for liquid energy by more than twelve folds. The growth of Middle East oil exports, however, was much higher than this – it grew by almost thirty-four times during 1948–74 period. This was due to the American oil conservation policies and the reorganization of the world oil supplies in the post-war period, which led to the replacement of the western hemisphere oil supplies in the eastern hemisphere markets by Middle East oil. Iran managed to capture a growing share of the market for Middle East oil – Iranian exports grew from 13.5 per cent of total Middle East exports in 1948 to 15.5 per cent in 1960, 22.8 per cent in 1966, and 25.6 per cent in 1974.

4

State, oil and the new institutions of accumulation 1953–1977

4.1 Introduction

In the post-1953 period the economy entered a new phase of development with oil income becoming the predominant source of financing accumulation. While previously the main role of the state was the mobilization of resources for investment within a predominantly agrarian economy, in this new phase the state faced the task of distribution and allocation of the already centralized economic surplus in the form of oil revenues. This radically transformed the nature of state-economy interrelationships and inaugurated a period of rapid institutional change. In this chapter we shall be mainly concerned with the state institutions which took shape over this period and which had a significant bearing on the accumulation process. In section 2 we examine the institutional forms of representation and internal organization of the state. Section 3 deals with two new institutions of state intervention, namely the Plan Organization and the Specialized Banks, which greatly enhanced the power of the state to control investment in the economy. A concrete analysis of the manner in which these institutional forms impinged upon the process of accumulation is conducted in the subsequent chapters.

4.2 Reemergence of modern authoritarianism

The overthrow of the popular government of Mosaddegh by the *coup d'état* of 1953 ended the period of open politics in post-war Iran and inaugurated the second phase of modern authoritarianism in the country. In many respects the conditions of the rise of the Shah to power and the social and political character of his regime were similar to those of the Reza Shah in the inter-war period. He initially relied upon the support of a conservative coalition of traditional merchant bourgeoisie of the bazaar, the high clergy and the landlords who, at a time of economic crisis, feared profound modification of society could lead to their elimination. The chief purpose of this initial coalition was to defeat the popular political organizations which sprang up during the era of open politics, notably the Tudeh party and the National Front. However, once this task was accomplished and after the Shah managed, with massive aid from the Americans, to strengthen the army and reinstate the unity of the state apparatus, like his father he became increasingly independent of this initial coalition. Two phases, separated by the crisis years of 1960–3, could be distinguished with regard to the political developments in this period. The first phase (1954–60) was one of reconstruction of the state's coercive and administrative apparatuses and the reassertion of the Shah's authority over these institutions. During this period the country became closely integrated into the western political and military system, with the Shah heavily relying on American financial and technical assistance to reconstruct the army and reorganize the state bureaucracy which subsequently became the two pillars of his political power in the country.[1] From the point of view of internal politics this initial period of consolidation of power crucially depended on the support from powerful propertied classes, namely the landlords and the big merchant bourgeoisie of the bazaar, and the high clergy (Westwood 1960, Walton 1980, Abrahamian 1982, chapter 9, Bashiriyeh 1984, chapter 1). In return, as a result of the suppression of the working-class and middle-class political movements and the reversal of the radical reform programmes put forward by the Tudeh party and the National Front, the economic and political standing of this conservation coalition strengthened.[2]

This initial political coalition, however, could not last long. The econ-

---

[1] On foreign and in particular the US military and economic aid in this period and the different aspects of the 'System of Iranian–Western Alliance', see Saikal 1980, chapter 2, and Baldwin 1967, pp.200–4. According to Baldwin, there was scarcely any area of institution building that did not have the benefit, or at least the presence of one or more foreign experts. This 'institution building' stretched from the creation of the notorious State Intelligence and Security Organization (SAVAK) with the help of the CIA in 1957, to the creation of the Plan Organization and the reorganization of various government ministries and agencies. Saikal (1980) estimates the total US military grants during 1954–63 at \$535.4m, 'which was the largest military grant that Washington had offered to a non-Nato country'. Baldwin (1967) puts the value of total American economic and military aid during 1950–64 at well over one billion dollars. According to him, in this period more aid went to Iran than to any other country in the western hemisphere, Africa or the Middle East except Turkey.

[2] In the aftermath of the coup the agrarian reforms introduced by Mosaddegh were reversed. According to Cottam (1979, p.287) the agrarian policies of the post-coup government were directed towards 'pulling the teeth out of Mosaddegh's agricultural reform'. For more details of the agrarian policies of the government during 1949–60, see Gharatcheh-Daghi (1967, pp.47–60), and Lambton (1969, pp.39–40). With regard to the bazaar middle class and the clergy also, the regime took a highly conciliatory posture during the 1953–60 period (Abrahamian 1982, pp.420–30). The revaluation of the Rial immediately after the coup and the gradual removal of trade restrictions and import quotas (see section 5.3) largely benefitted the bazaar merchants during the 1954–9 boom which followed the resumption of oil exports and large-scale foreign official capital inflows.

omic recession of the early 1960s created strong internal and external political pressures for social reform and change of the economic strategy of the government. The early 1960s witnessed mass demonstrations by teachers and students and a general resurgence of large-scale political opposition by middle-class groups. The inflationary boom of 1955–9 had already created major strikes by the workers and salaried employees and there were signs of peasant unrest in some areas, which intensified with the arrival of the recession (Ivanov 1977, pp.201–13, Ashraf and Banuazizi 1980, Bashiriyeh 1984, chapter 1). At the same time the American government which was getting alarmed at the Iranian situation, in particular in view of the 1958 Iraqi revolution and mounting propaganda attacks against the Iranian regime from the Soviet Union, began to exert pressure on the regime for social and economic reforms.[3] This necessarily implied a break in the coalition between the regime and its powerful conservative allies, which forced the Shah to challenge the entrenched social position of this group through forceful transformation of certain social relations from above. The six-point reform programme of the Shah, labelled the 'White Revolution', the centrepiece of which was land reform, marked this historic break of the regime with its powerful traditional allies, and indeed the elimination of an important fraction of this group, i.e., the absentee landlords. The effect of the land reform at the national and regional political levels was that 'the traditional landowners who occupied the key positions in the bureaucracy and legislature in the pre-land reform era lost their power basis qua landowners' (Ashraf and Banuazizi 1980, p.54). The final violent confrontations of June 1963 also marked the end of political compromise with the traditional merchant bourgeoisie of the bazaar and the clergy.[4]

This shift in the political alliances of the regime, which marked the second phase of post-1953 authoritarianism, led to the strengthening of the process of bureaucratization and centralization of power which had been taking place since 1953. Two parallel developments were involved in this process. First, the continued expansion of government bureaucracy and its growing

---

[3] According to A. Meyer the US ambassador to Tehran at the time, 'the idea was that Iran's demise was about to take place . . . and we just had to take some dramatic and drastic steps'. Quoted from Saikal (1980, p.75). See also Abrahamian (1982), Ashraf and Banuazizi (1980) and Bashiriyeh (1984).

[4] The participants in the June 1963 demonstrations comprised a broad spectrum of the Iranian urban society from the clergy to the shopkeepers, office employees, teachers, students and workers. The call for the protest came from the guild leaders, bazaar merchants, the National Front and the clergy in this instance led by the Ayatollah Khomeini (Abrahamian 1982, p.424). The suppression of these demonstrations marked not only the break in the regime's alliance with the traditional social forces, but also the end of any form of independent political action by the new middle classes who had managed to reorganize under the leadership of the National Front during the 1960–3 period. For detailed accounts of the developments during this period see the sources quoted in the above footnote.

power of control over the society, and secondly, the increasing shift of power within the state from the legislature to the executive and within that to the court and the monarch.

The elimination of traditional absentee landlordism led to the penetration of state bureaucracy into the countryside as it undertook various economic functions in the agrarian sector such as the provision of credit and other inputs, marketing and distribution of output and increasingly the reorganization of the production process itself (see chapter 6). In the urban economy also bureaucratic controls substantially expanded when the state, in an attempt to redirect capital into industrial activities, reversed the semi-liberal economic policies of the 1950s (see chapters 5 and 7). The over-expansion of the state bureaucracy was not only connected to the needs of the economy, but it also acquired a momentum of its own as the regime sought to strengthen its social power through central control of collective organizations of society. Trade unions, employers associations, bazaar guilds and the associations of civil servants were deprived of autonomy and/or replaced by official organizations under the control of the central government (Bashiriyeh 1984, pp.29–53). All independent political organizations were suppressed and an official party structure was created which, however, failed in its aim of mobilizing mass support for the regime's 'White Revolution' (Benab 1979).

As for the internal structure of the state, these developments once more shifted the locus of power from the parliament to the monarch who ruled the country through the control of this extensive military/bureaucratic apparatus.[5] After 1963 the court became the centre of power and dominated all the other structures of the state, including the government, the parliament and the party structure. The parliament lost its importance in representing social interests in an organized manner and access to political power became restricted to a small elite at the centre of which was the Shah and his family.

The socio-political background and the character of the autocratic regime of the Shah during the 1953–77 period was to some extent reminiscent of that of Reza Shah during the inter-war period. As Abrahamian (1982, chapter 9) has pointed out both dictators relied on their over-extended bureaucratic and military establishments – which, largely being their own creations and lacking strong ties with the prevailing social forces, functioned as subordinate tools in the hands of the two monarchs – and the system of court patronage which was at the centre of the clientelistic relations which characterized the channels of access to public institutions and policy for private interests. Both monarchs rose to power on the

[5] The historical process and the mechanisms through which the Shah came to control the bureaucracy are detailed in Halliday (1979, pp.45–59) and Zonis (1971, pp.18–117).

shoulders of conservative ruling classes and foreign powers who feared the spread of communism in the country, and in both cases economic crises led the regimes to turn against their conservative allies in an attempt to restructure the domestic economy. Despite these similarities in the political forms, however, there existed essential differences in the nature of the state's economic involvement and the forms and functions of its economic institutions between the two periods. These differences pertained both to the capacity of the state to intervene in the economy and the content of such intervention. In both respects a major determinant was the nature of the new economic conditions that confronted the state, and the type of institutional and political arrangements that were constructed to resolve the economic problems which arose. The most notable aspect of these new conditions was the substantial rise in oil revenues and easy access to foreign capital in the post-1953 period. This diametrically altered the role of the state in the process of accumulation. While in the inter-war period the main task of the state had been the mobilization of the economic surplus within a predominantly agrarian economy through the control of trade, in this new era the state – being in direct control of a substantial share of the national income in the form of oil revenues – faced the task of distribution and allocation of the already centralized economic surplus. Accordingly, new institutions such as the 'Plan Organization' and the 'Specialized Banks' replaced the monopoly trading companies as the main institutional mechanisms of capital accumulation. Of course, the creation of these institutions was not directly connected to the need of the state to dispose of its oil revenues. In line with Gerschenkron's (1962) well-known thesis and like other late industrializers, these institutions were created at a time when the requirements for centralized finance to launch modern industry was beyond the capacity of the domestic bourgeoisie. The existence of oil revenues in the case of Iran, however, substantially increased the effectiveness of these institutions and enhanced the capacity of the state to control the allocation of resources.

4.3 New economic institutions

In this section we shall consider the formation of the Plan Organization and the new credit institutions within the historical context of the development of the Iranian political economy and examine their respective roles in capital accumulation during the 1953–77 period. The aim of this section is to examine the extent to which these new institutions provided the state with effective levers of control over investment. The manner in which these levers of control were used to shape the process of accumulation by the state is examined in the following chapters.

4.3.1 The Plan Organization

Attempts at 'development planning' in Iran, like in almost all other Middle Eastern countries, started in the immediate aftermath of the Second World War (see UN 1955, chapter 5, pp.111–40). Post-war 'development planning' in the Middle East was initially little more than a collection of public sector investment projects which were set up as a prerequisite for receiving aid from the IBRD and the American government. In this respect, planning in most Middle Eastern countries started as a part of the post-war reconstruction of the capitalist world and was in sharp contrast to the idea of planning based on the socialization of means of production as practiced in the centrally planned economies. In Iran also, IBRD and the American government played an important part in establishing the Plan Organization after the war (see Baldwin 1967, p.24). To ensure the effectiveness of government 'development' efforts at a time of political instability and administrative disorganization, the Plan Organization which was established in 1949 was originally conceived as a financially independent institution outside the regular administrative machinery of the government. During the first two plan periods (1949–62) Plan Organization was mainly concerned with the formulation and execution of its own investment projects independent from other government agencies.[6] According to Baldwin (1967, p.198), the initial autonomy of the Plan Organization was a 'necessary structural accommodation to Iran's political situation'. However, with the greater political and administrative unification of the government after 1963, Plan Organization relinquished its functions of formulation and execution of individual investment projects to other government ministries and agencies. From the beginning of the third plan, with the formation of the Supreme Economic Council, the Plan Organization was brought under the control of the Prime Minister's office in an effort at greater co-ordination of government economic policy. Under the new arrangements there was a complete review of the responsibilities of the Plan Organization, where it mainly concentrated on national planning, supervision over the implementation of the projects by responsible ministries and agencies, and financing of the approved programmes through the plan budget. With the beginning of the fifth plan in 1973 Plan Organization lost its financial autonomy when the development and current budgets of the government were merged.[7]

---

[6] Though according to the first and second plan laws the execution of the projects was to be through other government ministries and agencies under the supervision of the Plan Organization, in actual fact the Plan Organization, 'which never developed effective power of supervision over ministry execution of the Plan projects', directly executed the larger part of the plan in this period (Baldwin 1967, p.29).

[7] For a comprehensive study of the evolution of the government budgetary practices in Iran in this period, see Sharafi (1977, vols.1–5).

From the outset, the oil revenues of the government were tied to development investment either directly implemented or supervised by the Plan Organization.[8] Over the 1956–72 period on average about 71 per cent of the total oil revenues of the central government were allocated to the Plan Organization. With the rapid growth of oil revenues, and increasing reliance on foreign borrowing which was equivalent to mortgaging the future oil revenues, the Plan Organization increasingly assumed a central role in capital accumulation during this period. As table 4.1 indicates, *pari passu* with the growth of oil revenues and the increasing possibilities of foreign and domestic borrowing which it created, the development outlays of the Plan Organization grew by ten times on an annual basis between the second and fourth plan periods. The oil price rises in the post-1973 period led to another five fold increase in government development expenditure between the fourth and fifth plans.

It is important, however, to distinguish between government development expenditure as shown in the table and public sector investment. Not all the development expenditures contributed to capital formation in the public sector. Included in the former were transfers in the form of Plan Organization's loans to the private sector and other development expenses which did not directly enter into public sector capital formation.[9] On the other hand, not all public sector investment was financed by development expenditure, various public sector agencies and ministries were involved in investment activities through their own funds – e.g., public enterprises through the amortization funds. To get a more accurate picture of the direct involvement of the state in capital formation and form an idea of the quantitative correspondence between this and government development

[8] In the first plan law (Article 5) all government oil revenues were allocated to the Plan Organization (PO). This constituted no more than 37 per cent of the financial requirements of the plan; the rest was to be provided by a loan from IBRD and domestic borrowing. According to the second, third, and fourth plan laws between 60 and 90 per cent of oil revenues were to be allocated to the PO in different years (see PO 1968). In practice, however, the share of the PO was constantly below that envisaged in the plan laws. In particular during the second plan period when various other government ministries were independently involved in investment activities and when the unbridled expansion of government current expenditure absorbed an increasing share of the oil revenues, this share fell to 49 per cent as opposed to 80–90 per cent projected in the plan law (Article 8). From 1963 onwards, with the concentration of most government investment activities within the plan frame, this share rose to 66 per cent (third plan) and 78 per cent (fourth plan), which was still below that envisaged in the respective plan laws. In absolute terms, however, the financial allocations to the plans were normally above those originally envisaged in the plan laws, due to an unexpectedly high rate of growth of oil revenues and easy access to foreign borrowing in this period.

[9] These categories are defined in detail in Central Bank (1969, pp.111–13) as used in the estimation of the consumption and fixed investment outlays of the Plan Organization. In what follows we shall use the same categorization.

Table 4.1. *Receipts and payments of the Plan Organization 1956–1972*

(In billion Rials)

	1956–62[b]	1963–7[c]	1968–72	1973–7[a]
Total payments	<u>103.0</u>	<u>220.4</u>	<u>621.3</u>	—
Development expenditure[g]	82.5	197.3	574.7	2555.1
Other payments[d]	20.5	23.1	46.6	—
Total revenues	<u>69.4</u>	<u>144.9</u>	<u>454.5</u>	—
Oil	64.3	141.5	436.9	—
Other	5.1	3.4	17.6	—
Deficit	<u>33.6</u>	<u>75.5</u>	<u>166.8</u>	—
Domestic bank credits[e]	5.8	48.2	77.7	—
Foreign loans[f]	27.8	27.3	89.1	—
Public sector				
Gross Fixed Investment	<u>128.6</u>	<u>180.5</u>	<u>535.2</u>	2908.2
(As % of total GDFCF)	(41.0)	(42.9)	(53.7)	(54.9)

Notes:

[a] From 1973 the development and ordinary budgets were merged.

[b] It differs from the second plan period by including the last six months of 1962/3.

[c] It differs from the third plan period by excluding the last six months of 1962/3.

[d] Consists mainly of debt service payments and administrative expenses.

[e] Periods 1962–7 and 1968–72 include Rls 13.8m and Rls 1.9m sale of treasury bills respectively.

[f] Includes advances from the oil companies.

[g] Excludes recurrent development expenditures for 1973–7 period.

Sources: Central Bank, *Annual Report* 1968, 1972, 1977. Plan Organization 1964.

expenditure the last row of table 4.1 gives the aggregate figure for gross fixed investment in the public sector. These figures clearly indicate the predominant role played by the public sector in domestic accumulation, with its share in total gross fixed investment rising from 41 per cent to 55 per cent over the period.[10] Within this, a major part was financed by the development expenditure of the government. After allowing for the discrepancies mentioned above, it turns out that during these four plan periods respectively, 52.4 per cent, 75.8 per cent, 93.7 per cent and 67.9 per cent of gross fixed investment in the public sector was undertaken within the framework

[10] To put it in comparative perspective these shares may be set against the share of public sector investment in Latin American countries as a whole which grew from 30 per cent in 1955–9 to 37 per cent in 1965–70 (Fitzgerald 1974).

of the successive plans.[11] The low ratio for the second plan period, as mentioned above (see footnote 8), was due to the fact that in that period various other central government ministries competed with the Plan Organization for new investment projects and government investment took place in a highly haphazard and uncoordinated manner. From 1963 onwards, a much higher degree of central control over public sector investment was exerted; most of the investment activities of central government ministries were incorporated into the plan expenditure, and strict controls were imposed on the access of public enterprises to bank credits for financing their investment. By the fourth plan period, more than 90 per cent of public sector investment was brought under the control of the Plan Organization. During the fifth plan period (1973–7) these trends were once more reversed, when the enormous liquidity expansion in the economy resulting from the fiscal activities of the government and relaxation of control over bank credits to public enterprises and municipalities led to the rapid expansion of public sector investment outside the plan frame.[12] The share of the fifth plan in total public sector investment declined to about 68 per cent. Despite these fluctuations the share of government development plans in financing public sector investment remained quite substantial. We shall build upon this fact in the following chapters to infer the changing composition of government investment – disaggregated data on which are not available – on the basis of the changing pattern of development expenditure during different phases of accumulation.

It should be emphasized, however, that the growing predominance of public sector investment in domestic accumulation in this period was not due to deliberate policy aimed at greater direct state control over the mobilization and allocation of the domestic economic surplus. On the contrary, a fundamental feature of the post-1953 state was its repudiation of the etatist policies of the 1930s and active support for private enterprise, both foreign and domestic. The role of the Plan Organization in the accumulation process could best be understood in terms of the close partnership which developed between the state and private capital in this

[11] To arrive at these figures we have deducted the transfers to the private sector and the 'consumption expenditure' of the Plan Organization as calculated by the Central Bank, from the development expenditure data given in the table. The values of fixed investment thus arrived at for the second to the fifth plan periods respectively are: Rls 67.4bn, Rls 163.0bn, Rls 502.1bn, and Rls 1976.2bn (sources used are, Central Bank, *Annual Report* 1968, 1972, 1977, Central Bank 1974, and CSO, *Statistical Yearbook* 1977).

[12] The over-expansion of investment activities which led to major disequilibria in the economy during the fifth plan period is often in the literature related to the disproportionate increase in the size of government development expenditure. As we shall see in the next section, however, the monetary consequences of government fiscal activities played an equally, if not more, important role in this phenomenon.

period. Reliance on external finance, namely oil revenues and foreign borrowing, meant that the investment activities of the state did not necessarily encroach upon the interests of private capital (see table 4.1). Far from encroaching on private sector interests, the concentration of government investment in activities not favoured by the private sector created a highly complementary relation between the state and private capital.[13] In this partnership, however, it was the state which played the major role, as the post-1953 private capital – specially in the industrial and agricultural sectors – came into being largely due to the conditions that the state created in its favour.

In this period effective measures were introduced by the government to strengthen private capital and in particular to initiate its entry into industry and agriculture in a major way. These measures ranged from the changes in the nature of state regulation of markets, to the award of substantial direct and indirect subsidies to private capital, social reform and the establishment of specialized agencies to provide direct technical and financial aid to private industry.

After 1954, the post-war trend in abolishing the state monopoly trading companies continued, and by 1957 the policy of trade monopoly by the government was in principle abandoned (see UN 1951, pp.47–9, Agah 1958, p.80). Of course, the direct involvement of the state in trading activities through its commercial companies such as the Cereal Organization, Fertilizer Distribution Company, etc., continued.[14] However, the activities of these latter trading companies, being concerned with price stabilization and subsidization of wage goods and strategic inputs used in the private sector, were on a totally different footing from the revenue-raising state monopolies of the inter-war period. The market intervention of the state during the post-1953 period was largely indirect – mainly taking the form of foreign trade and exchange regulations, credit rationing, indirect taxes and tariffs – with a view to the protection/subsidization of particular sectors of the economy rather than revenue-raising motives.

While the state regulation of the commodity markets played a major role in accelerating primary accumulation in the hands of the newly emerging industrial capitalists, it was the state's contribution in the field of industrial finance which played the decisive role in initiating the large-scale entry of private capital into modern industry. The 1950s was a decade of rapid development for the Iranian financial institutions, and by the early 1960s

---

[13] This issue is further elaborated in chapter 7 where we give a more detailed account of the interactions between public and private investments.
[14] For a complete list of these trading corporations and their activities, see Plan and Budget Organization of Iran (1969, 1977).

the banking system had acquired a much higher degree of differentiation than existed a decade earlier.[15] A significant development during this period was the emergence of close collaboration between bank capital and industrial capital through the formation of industrial finance banks. In this field also the state played a significant role in initiating, and more important in supplying the capital for, the establishment of the industrial finance institutions. After its own investment activities, control over credit became the second most important lever of controlling domestic accumulation for the state.

4.3.2 *The specialized banks*

The most effective measure taken by the state, in terms of its initial impact on private investment in the 1950s, was the creation of the Revaluation Loan Fund (RLF) in 1957. The revaluation of foreign reserves in 1957 made available Rls 7.1bn (equivalent to more than 34 per cent of total money supply as it stood at the end of 1956), which was earmarked for granting long-term loans to private industry and agriculture.[16] During the 1957–9 period, the RLF provided Rls 6.6bn long- and medium-term credit at highly

[15] In 1950, the Iranian banking system was composed of six banks, four of which were owned by the government, one was a Russian owned bank specializing in trade between the two countries, and the remaining one was the only private commercial bank which was formed in 1950. By 1960 the number of banks had increased to twenty-six including four specialized banks – of which seventeen banks were private, nine with foreign participation. The share of the private banks (more than half of which represented joint foreign banks) rose to 39 per cent of the total assets of the banking system by the end of 1962. By 1976 the number of banks had increased to thirty-five which included ten specialized banks. Despite the proliferation of private banks, in 1976 the government banks still owned more than 50 per cent of the assets of commercial and specialized banks (for more details see, Benedick 1964, Bharier 1971, chapter 2, Amuzegar 1977, chapter 9). While during the 1950s government exerted no effective control over the activities of the private banks, with the formation of the Central Bank and the Currency and Credit Council within that institution in 1960 the government tightened its surveillance over the formal credit market. Through a policy of differential interest rates and different forms of credit controls, the Central Bank could exert its control over the total amount and distribution of funds within a 'regulated' credit market. See the circulars of the Currency and Credit Council in various issues of Bank Markazi Iran Bulletins. Relevant aspects of the monetary and credit policies of the Central Bank will be discussed in the following chapters as appropriate.

[16] A dual exchange rate system based on the use of export certificates was in effect until a unified exchange rate system was put into place in March 1956. Up to May 1957, foreign reserves (including gold and IMF accounts) were converted at the old principal import rate which was 32.5 Rls per US dollar. In May 1957 foreign reserves were revalued at the new unified rate of 75.5, the proceeds of which (Rls 7.1bn) were allocated to the RLF at the National Bank (see IMF 1963, p.294). It should be noted that this unification of the exchange rates did not amount to a devaluation of the exchange rate as far as the private sector traders were concerned. The rates applicable to them before March 1957, including the export certificates rate, was 76.5. The main effect of this act was in the public sector by more than doubling the Rial value of government oil export revenues, and turning the disguised subsidies on the import of essential goods into open subsidies.

subsidized rates to private industry, which according to the existing estimates added up to about 24 per cent of gross fixed investment in private industry.[17] Compared to the Rls 6.7bn total direct expenditure for industry by the Plan Organization during the entire seven year period of the second plan (1956–62), the substantial privatization of public funds through the RLF in this period stands out as an unprecedented expression of government support for the private sector. After 1959, the management of the RLF was entirely entrusted to the private sector itself.

Throughout the 1960s and 1970s, the policy of financial assistance to private industry continued on a more massive scale through the two powerful industrial finance banks, namely the state owned Industrial Credit Bank (ICB) and the privately owned Industrial and Mining Development Bank of Iran (IMDBI). ICB was formed by the Plan Organization in 1955 with the explicit purpose of providing long-term financial assistance to private industry. The original capital of the bank, which was fully owned by the government, was Rls 600m which grew rapidly to reach the level of Rls 4.3bn by the end of 1972 and Rls 5.1bn by the end of 1975. More than 90 per cent of the financial resources of ICB came from the government, the rest being government guaranteed foreign loans.[18] The bank, therefore, played an intermediary role between the public sector as the supplier of funds and the private sector on the receiving end, without any attempt to directly mobilize funds from the private sector itself. This entire reliance on public funds was in fact a by-product of government policy of subsidization of private capital accumulation.[19] During the 1960s and 1970s ICB, providing about 30 per cent of long- and medium-term loans, became the second largest supplier of funds to private industry after IMDBI (see table 4.2).

Although IMDBI was a private joint stock company, the initiative for its creation and a major part of its capital came from the Iranian government

[17] See table 4.2. More than 56 per cent of funds went to new establishments. The interest charges ranged from 4 to 6 per cent for long-term and 6 to 8 per cent for working capital loans, which should be set against the 'free market' (bazaar) rates ranging from 12 to more than 36 per cent. For more details on the operation of the RLF in this period see, Benedick (1964), Baldwin (1967, chapter 4).

[18] Financial resources of the ICB grew from Rls 5.1bn at the end of 1966 to Rls 29.2bn by the end of 1975. Up to 1970 all of the financial resources of the bank were composed of government loans (including the Plan Organization's managed funds) or paid up capital by the government. From 1971, when government legislation allowed the bank to increase its loan capital ratio to 300 per cent, increasing reliance was made on foreign markets to enhance the financial resources of the bank. By 1975 government funds furnished 90 per cent of financial resources of the bank, the rest being government guaranteed foreign loans (ICB, Annual Report 1967, 1975).

[19] Interest charges of the ICB ranged from 6 to 7 per cent until the late 1960s, rising to 8 to 10 per cent by 1974. Tax exempt yields on long-term government bonds on the other hand amounted to more than 12 per cent (IBRD 1974, Benedick 1964, p.88). This made the raising of long-term loans from the domestic money markets virtually impossible both for the ICB and the IMDBI.

and the World Bank. The initial equity ownership of the bank was Rls 400m (40 per cent foreign, 60 per cent Iranian), which formed about 12 per cent of the initial capital of the bank, the rest being long-term government and foreign loans. Immediately after its establishment IMDBI took over the administration of ICBs complete industrial loan portfolios as well as RLFs remaining cash and many of its projects. These (managed loans), together with Rls 600m interest free loan from the central bank, comprised more than 70 per cent of the initial capital of the bank. The contribution of government funds to the financial resources of IMDBI grew rapidly from Rls 2.0bn in 1959 to Rls 7.3bn at the end of 1971 and Rls 56.8bn by the end of 1977. These loans were more than twice the entire financial resources granted by the government to the state owned ICB over the same period. A substantial share of IMDBIs financial resources also came from state guaranteed foreign loans.[20]

The formation of IMDBI in 1959 was a landmark in the development of industrial capital in Iran. The bank was created when Iranian industrialization was entering a new phase of its development, i.e., when production of consumer durables and intermediate products, which required new and relatively more sophisticated technology, large initial investment and ample supplies of long-term foreign exchange loans, were becoming the growth engines of the industrial sector (see chapter 7). IMDBI played a crucial role in all aspects of this process of industrial restructuring. The functions of IMDBI in this respect went far beyond those of a normal financial intermediary. It played an active role in promoting new investment projects, performed an important intermediary function between the state, domestic capital and foreign capital, and was highly influential in the formulation of the industrial policies of the government (see IBRD 1974, Nowshirwani and Bildner 1973, Benedick 1964). In quantitative terms also the scale of the involvement of IMDBI in financing private industrial investment was enormous. During the 1963–77 period it provided about 68 per cent of industrial loans granted by industrial finance institutions (80 per cent excluding working capital loans), and it is estimated that during 1959–72 alone the bank was directly involved in the mobilization of more than 55 per cent of total private fixed investment in industry.[21] More than 50 per cent of IMDBIs loan and equity participation went to the projects promoted by the

---

[20] Up to 1971 the foreign currency resources of IMDBI were almost exclusively supplied by the World Bank. From 1971 IMDBI increasingly relied on borrowing from private foreign banks, and in particular after 1973 the favourable conditions in the Eurodollar market permitted the bank to substantially increase its foreign currency resources through variable interest loans in that market.

[21] See IBRD (1974), Sadigh (1975). These estimates are based on the assumption that each loan contributed to capital formation three times its size.

bank itself. The significant involvement of IMDBI in the development of modern manufacturing in this period becomes more evident if one considers that the activities of the bank were solely, and in fact exclusively, confined to the very large-scale firms with relatively more sophisticated technology.[22] With ICB mainly specializing in small- to medium-sized loans, IMDBI was left with the virtual monopoly over government subsidized loans to the large-scale manufacturing sector.

The major private shareholders of IMDBI, therefore, enjoyed substantial powers of control over industrial accumulation which was by far greater than their contribution in terms of the equity capital of the bank. The foreign shareholders consisted of a syndicate of twenty American and European multinationals whose main interest in the bank was the future investment possibilities which it opened for them in the expanding Iranian economy, rather than immediate financial profits.[23] For the first five years of the operation of the bank the syndicate was in total control of IMDBIs Board of Directors and Executive Committee which was the ultimate loan granting body in the bank. By 1973 the domestic equity of the bank was owned by more than 3,000 shareholders. However, more than 49 per cent of the domestic equity of the bank belonged to the ten largest industrial and commercial interests in the country who, together with their foreign partners, were in effective control of the loan policy of the bank.[24] According to a World Bank report (1974), over 25 per cent of the approved loans of IMDBI went to the companies partly or wholly owned by the directors on the Board of the bank. The structure of capital and ownership of IMDBI highlights one of the salient features of the post-1953 capitalist development in Iran, namely the emergence of a small group of businessmen with clientelistic ties to the state, who, by virtue of their monopoly access to the state funds and close collaboration with foreign capital, managed to multiply their capital in a hothouse manner.

Table 4.2 provides aggregate data on the contribution of industrial finance by different institutions during the 1956–77 period. As the table

---

[22] For example, during the 1959–72 period 80 per cent of IMDBIs approved industrial loans went to 191 loans of greater than Rls 50m size, while at the end of this period the total number of private manufacturing establishments with a book value of fixed capital of greater than Rls 100m was only 143 units (Ministry of Economy 1972, IMDBI, annual report 1972). This signifies the involvement of IMDBI in almost all private large-scale manufacturing establishments which were set up during this period.

[23] Accordingly, the financial commitments of the twenty syndicate members was very small. The largest commitment was from the two American co-sponsors, Chase International and Lazard Ferers, with $241,667 each. The capital contribution of the other members varied between 50 thousand to 100 thousand dollars. See Benedick (1964, pp.120–30).

[24] For the structure of the equity ownership of IMDBI and a list of major shareholders in 1973, see IBRD 1974.

Table 4.2. *Industrial finance by different institutions 1956–1977[a]*

(billion Rials)

	1956–62	1963–7	1968–72	1973–7
Industrial Credit Bank (ICB)	0.9	3.4	10.9	67.2
Revaluation Loan Fund (RLF)	6.6	—	—	—
Industrial and Mining Development bank of Iran (IMDBI)	1.7	6.2	19.4	156.9
Total[a]	9.3	10.5	31.1	225.5
As % of gross private fixed investment in industry and mining	29.7[c]	n.a.	30.7	40.4[d]
Gross investment in private manufacturing based on:				
Operation licences	n.a.	13.9	40.1	169.2
Establishment licences	n.a.	58.2	89.0	210.3

Notes:
[a] Disbursed loans including working capital loans of the ICB and share participation. Excludes non-industrial loans and loan guarantees, and working capital loans by Bank Melli Iran.
[b] Includes the Industrial Guarantee Fund and the Development and Investment Bank of Iran's loans to the manufacturing sector.
[c] Refers to 1957–9. Private investment estimates are based on Mahdavy 1970.
[d] Refers to the years 1973–5.
Sources: ICB, *Annual Report* 1964, 1969, 1975, IMDBI, *Annual Report* 1967, 1977, Benedick 1964, p.256, Central Bank, *Annual Report* 1963, 1972, 1977, Ministry of Industry and Mines, *Trends in Industrial and Commercial Statistics*, 1976 Q4, UN 1979.

shows a notable aspect of industrial finance over this period was its total domination by the two major banks, IMDBI and ICB – particularly the former. The contribution of other industrial finance banks in this field was marginal.[25] The second important aspect of industrial finance in this period was the relatively large and rapidly growing share of bank loans in financing private investment in the manufacturing sector. There are little accurate data on the private sector manufacturing investment and virtually none on its financing over this period. In the table we have used the available data on gross fixed investment in the private sector manufacturing and mining for selected years to provide a rough indication of the significance of bank

[25] These other banks consisted of the Industrial Guarantee Fund which was set up in 1961 and later transferred to the Omran bank, and the Development and Investment Bank of Iran which was created in 1973. The share of these two banks in long-term industrial finance over the entire 1956–77 period was no more than 4 per cent.

capital in financing private industrial investment. According to these estimates the ratio of long-term industrial loans to private fixed investment in industry and mining rose from about 30 per cent in the 1956–62 period to over 40 per cent in the 1973–7 period. Two sources of upward bias in these ratios may be pointed out. First, the data for private sector fixed investment which are national accounting estimates omit a large part of what from the point of view of private investors are considered as investment – e.g., the value of land and purchased premises. Secondly, the omission of working capital from the investment data leads to an over-exaggeration of the ratio of loans to industrial investment as implied by the figures in the table.[26] On the other hand, two sources of downward bias could be also identified in the above ratios. First, the numerator refers to manufacturing loans while the denominator includes investment in mining as well as in manufacturing. Secondly, the industrial loans were solely supplied to the large-scale or corporate manufacturing sector, while the investment data refer to both small and large production units. These problems do not, however, arise in relation to the data on gross investment in private manufacturing provided by the Ministry of Industry and Mines on the basis of the operation and establishment permits. These estimates which are presented in table 4.2 represent all investment outlays in private manufacturing, including working capital investments, and exclude the very small-scale manufacturing sector (employing less than ten persons) only. As they stand, however, these data are not directly comparable with the loan disbursements of the industrial banks, as gross investment based on the operation permits refer to completed investments in a particular year rather than the investment actually undertaken in that year, and those based on establishment permits are, if at all, only indicators of planned investment which would be spread over several years to come. Assuming a two year average construction period for investment projects, and taking into account the fact that the periods over which investment aggregates are being considered here are relatively long, one could set up a plausible correspondence between gross investment data derived from the operation permits and the loans related to such investments with a reasonable degree of accuracy. On this basis the loan investment ratios which could be calculated for the 1963–7, 1968–72, and 1973–7 periods respectively are, 36.5 per cent, 44.1 per cent and 57.7 per cent. These ratios are even higher than the above ratios calculated on the basis of national account estimates of gross investment, and show a similar

---

[26] The bulk of loans by the industrial banks in this period, however, was composed of long-term loans. If we omit the working capital loans of the ICB which are included in the aggregate figures of the table, the above ratios would be marginally reduced to, 24.6 per cent, 25.2 per cent, and 37.8 per cent for the 1956–62, 1968–72 and 1973–7 periods respectively.

rising trend as the latter. Considering that industrial loans were mainly given to the large capital intensive firms, these ratios would indicate a remarkably high degree of utilization of long-term bank loans by the corporate sector of private manufacturing, particularly during the post oil boom era of 1973–7.[27] On this basis it may be plausibly assumed that at least from the mid 1960s between 60 to 70 per cent of the financing of gross investment of the private corporate manufacturing sector came from the specialized banks.[28]

High rates of external financing are a common feature of the early stages of industrialization when the corporate manufacturing sector is relatively small and industrial investment has to be largely financed by surpluses generated in other sectors of the economy.[29] The financial arrangements through which such surplus transfers can take place in the private sector are: (1) direct transfers drawing upon the existing funds, as when the merchants or other property owners turn industrialist, (2) selling primary securities in the stock market and (3) borrowing from financial institutions. The absence of an efficient capital market – efficient in the sense of providing liquidity for long-term debts presupposing the existence of a large volume of securities and high rates of turnover – which was itself due to the lack of development of the corporate sector of the economy, ruled out the second option in Iran as in most other LDCs.[30] The first mechanism, which was

[27] The average size of the loans given by IMDBI and ICB during the 1956–77 period as a whole were Rls 134m and Rls 58m respectively, while the average size of fixed capital in private manufacturing establishments based on operation licences was Rls 29m. For more details and further elaboration of this point see chapter 7.

[28] It should be noted that here we are only concerned with the financing of real rather than financial investments of the corporate manufacturing sector, and it is for this reason that only the long-term credits from the specialized banks are being considered. The available data do not allow entering into the complications involved in the latter category of investments which in any case would lead us far afield. It is nevertheless important to keep in mind that the availability of cheap finance may have well led to the diversion of these funds into financial investment, real estate speculation, etc. and hence the high observed loan/physical investment ratios.

[29] See Eshag (1971). In the case of Iran this is well attested by the very high ratios of manufacturing investment to the internally generated surpluses in the sector itself. The ratio of gross investment to quasi rent (i.e., value added less wages and salaries) in the large-scale manufacturing grew from about 50 per cent in 1968 to 55 per cent in 1971 and about 90 per cent in 1973–4 when the pace of investment rapidly accelerated. Considering the rents, interest payments and the consumption of the capitalists, which must be deducted from the quasi rents to arrive at the potentially available internal finance, these ratios could well rise to a range of 150 to 200 per cent (according to the Central Bank estimates (1974 p.23), for example in 1974 rents and interest payments amounted to about 40 per cent of the quasi rents in private industry).

[30] The Tehran Stock Exchange was only established in 1967 and up to the mid 1970s, when the government introduced the law of Expansion of Industrial Ownership, its activities were still very limited. For example in 1976, at the peak of its activities the total value of transactions in non-bank company stocks was no more than Rls 3.1bn (Central Bank, *Annual Report* 1976, p.63). For further details of the development of capital markets in the 1970s, see Amuzegar 1977, chapters 9, 17.

historically the main channel of industrial finance mobilization down to the late 1950s, also lost its significance with the large-scale appearance of modern banking and cheap long-term credits by specialized banks. From the late 1950s a new breed of industrialists with close ties to the state and to the new financial institutions flourished, who increasingly relied on cheap loans from the industrial banks to invest in new industries. The rapid pace of industrial investment as well as the type of the new industries which spearheaded the new phase of industrialization, rendered the traditional mechanism of industrial finance mobilization obsolete. The bank-dominated structure of industrial finance in Iran, like in other LDCs at a similar stage of industrialization, was therefore the outcome of the prevailing real economic conditions. This structure of industrial finance, as compared to a capital market dominated one, makes private investment more amenable to government control. In particular in the case of Iran, where the government supplied the bulk of the funds to industrial banks from its oil surpluses, control of finance was an important potential source of controlling the pace and structure of private investment.

The contribution of specialized banks in the field of agricultural finance was also substantial. Agricultural finance was mainly provided by the two government owned banks, namely the Agricultural Co-operative Bank (ACB) and the Agricultural Development Bank of Iran (ADBI). More than 75 per cent of the agricultural loans over the 1956–77 period were extended by the ACB which specialized in small loans to peasant farmers, mainly through the rural co-operative societies (see table 4.3).[31] The ADBI was established in 1968 and mainly catered for the credit needs of large commercial farms and agrobusiness ventures which became the priority sectors in the agricultural policy of the government with the beginning of the second stage of land reform in 1967. Consequently the funds extended by the ADBI in the form of loans and equity participation grew rapidly to about 30 per cent of total agricultural credits during the 1973–7 period. As table 4.3 shows, government credits to agriculture expanded significantly after the land reform of 1962, and as in industry they received a massive boost after the 1973 oil boom.

4.4 The new institutions and potential control over investment

Table 4.4 brings into a comparative perspective the size of the disbursed funds through the government development plans and the specialized

---

[31] About 70 per cent of ACB loans were disbursed through the rural co-operative societies, mainly used for small short-term consumption loans with 3 to 4 per cent interest rates, amongst the co-op members. The rest were directly disbursed by the bank to individual farmers at 6 per cent interest rate.

Table 4.3. *Agricultural credits by specialized banks 1956–1977*

(billion Rials)

	1956–62	1963–7	1968–72	1973–7
Agricultural Co-operative Bank	7.7	23.4	43.6	180.3
Agricultural Development Bank	—	—	2.3	84.9
Total^a	7.7	23.4	48.9	285.2

Notes:
^{a} Includes loans by rural co-operatives from their own funds.
Sources: CSO, *Statistical Yearbook* 1966. Central Bank, *Annual Report* 1968–77.

banks, in relation to the accumulation effort as characterized by the size of the fixed capital formation and potential internal surpluses within the agricultural and manufacturing sectors. The table gives a clear indication of the significance of these two external sources of finance in capital accumulation in both sectors. The ratio of these funds to total fixed investment in manufacturing and mining grew from 44.1 per cent in 1963–7 to 64.9 per cent in 1973–7, and in agriculture it grew from over 160 per cent to more than 178 per cent over the same period.

These ratios are subject to the same qualifications made above when we were discussing the relative significance of the overall plan expenditure and industrial credits. In the case of agriculture in particular, where the likelihood of inaccuracies in fixed investment data is high and a significant part of gross investment is composed of working capital and subsistence funds for the peasant cultivators, such comparisons may not be very suggestive. A more appropriate variable for such a comparison may be some notion of internally generated funds potentially mobilizable for investment in the two sectors. In the manufacturing sector, quasi rents (value added minus wages and salaries) furnish the best measure for such a variable on the basis of the available data. In the agricultural sector an analogous concept is that of net agricultural surplus which measures the value added in the sector net of the consumption of direct producers and their families.[32] As the table shows, the inflow of the total 'government managed funds', namely the specialized banks' credit plus Plan Organization's expenditure, into the manufacturing sector grew from 10.3 per cent of the quasi rents in 1963–7 period to 33.1 per cent in 1973–7, and in agriculture they grew from 61.3 per cent to 87.2 per cent of net agricultural surplus over the same period. If it is considered that a large share of quasi rents and net surpluses in the two sectors goes to

[32] For more details see Appendix A.1.2.

Table 4.4. *Government development spending and credits by specialized banks to industry and agriculture 1956–1977*

(billion Rials)

	1956–62	1963–7	1968–72	1973–7
Manufacturing				
Government development exp.[a]	6.7	12.6	94.5	288.9
Credits by specialized banks	9.3	10.5	31.1	225.5
Total	16.0	23.1	125.6	514.4
GFCF in manufacturing[b]	n.a.	52.4	170.1	792.6
Quasi rents[b,c]	n.a.	224.5	468.3	1552.3
Agriculture				
Government development exp.[a,d]	26.1	36.6	73.6	244.0
Credits by specialized banks	7.7	23.4	48.9	285.2
Total	33.8	60.0	122.5	529.2
GFCF in agriculture	n.a.	31.1	73.8	296.4
Agricultural surplus[e]	n.a.	97.8	271.4	606.7

Notes:

[a] Excludes credits granted to the private sector from the development funds.

[b] Includes mining.

[c] Refers to value added minus the wage and salary bill.

[d] Includes irrigation.

[e] Refers to value added minus consumption in agriculture.

Sources: Tables 4.2 and 4.3, and table A1.1, Appendix A1.

interest, taxes and rentier and capitalist consumption, then the significance of government funds to, and its potential control over, accumulation in these two sectors becomes evident.[33]

4.5 Concluding remarks

In this chapter we examined the evolution of the political structure of the regime and its main institutions of accumulation within the historical context of the development of the Iranian political economy. Two major themes were highlighted in the above analysis. First, the high degree of autonomy of the state executive from the legislature and by implication

---

[33] Of course these figures do not reflect the net contribution of government in the supply of finance for capital formation in different sectors. The data required for a complete flow of funds analysis are not available.

from the underlying society, and within that the concentration of power in the hands of a small elite centred around the court and the monarch. Secondly, the central role of the state in the distribution of a sizeable share of the investable funds in the economy. These two factors greatly enhanced the power of the state's economic intervention and conferred upon it a high potential for controlling the pace and pattern of investment in the economy. The manner in which these controls were exercised, that is the socio-economic project which defined the content of state intervention, is the subject of the following chapters.

5

The role of the state in capital accumulation, the semi-liberal phase

5.1 Introduction

The purpose of this chapter is to examine the role of the state in capital accumulation during the 1953–63 period. As we have already noted in the previous chapter, the 1950s was a period of mutual support between the newly established authoritarian regime of the Shah and the traditional proprietary classes, namely the coalition of landlords, merchant bourgeoisie of the bazaar and factions of the high clergy. The semi-liberal trade and industrial policies of the government, which in a period of rapid inflow of external resources was highly beneficial to this traditional coalition, led to severe imbalances in the economy which brought about the crisis of the early 1960s. In this chapter we shall analyse the nature of structural changes which accompanied the boom of the 1950s and the subsequent recession of the early 1960s.

5.2 Three phases of accumulation

The process of growth involves a constant change in the structure of demand, technical coefficients of production and the pattern of real capital formation in different sectors of the economy. In particular, in economies which are subject to severe external shocks, as was for example the case in the post-1953 Iranian economy following the resumption of oil revenues and the inflow of foreign capital on an unprecedented scale, the need for such restructuring of real capital formation assumes major proportions. Obviously, the capacity of an economy to achieve this necessary change in the composition of real capital depends upon its economic organizations, and in the case of underdeveloped economies at the early stages of industrialization it invariably involves the creation of new economic institutions and the transformation of some of the prevailing relations of production. This process of capital restructuring would necessarily involve social conflict in which the state plays a prominent role.

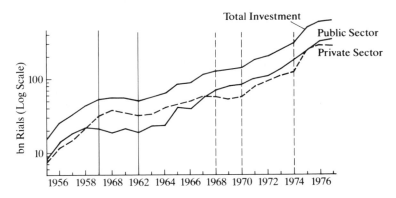

Figure 5.1 Real gross fixed capital formation: 1959 prices
Sources: As for table 5.1.

Three phases could be broadly distinguished with regard to the rate and structure of capital formation in Iran during the post-1953 period. Though a more detailed account of the changing role of the state during these different phases of accumulation will follow, it would be helpful at this stage to give a brief overview of the basic characteristics of each phase:

1 The first phase (1955–9) was one of rapid growth of real investment following the massive injection of external funds (namely oil revenues and foreign capital) into the economy (see figure 5.1 and table 5.1). This was a period of compromise with the merchant bourgeoisie and landlords during which the state followed a semi-liberal economic policy.

Government investment in this period was largely confined to infrastructure and light manufacturing industries, and private investment concentrated in construction, transportation and light manufacturing. The uncoordinated growth of investment and incomes in this period, which resulted in a substantial divergence between the structure of demand and supply in the domestic economy, gave rise to the balance of payments crisis of the early 1960s.

2 The second phase (1960–2) was the period of political crisis of the regime leading to the break in its alliance with the powerful traditional proprietary classes. The period witnessed a rapid decline in the pace of investment in particular in the private sector, following the Stabilization Programme of the government and the political uncertainties which characterized the period. The political and economic changes which took place in this relatively short span of time reflected different aspects of state intervention

Table 5.1. *Growth and structure of gross fixed investment 1956–1977*

Real annual average growth rates	1955–9	1960–2	1963–77	1963–8	1968–70	1970–4	1974–7
Public GFCF	26.6	0.0	21.6	25.5	8.8	21.4	24.6
Private GFCF	39.3	−9.9	16.5	11.3	0.3	21.6	31.3
Total GFCF	36.0	−5.7	18.9	19.8	5.2	21.5	27.4

Percentage shares[a]

Share of GFCF in GNP	1955–6	1959–60	1962–3	1967–8	1971–2	1973–4	1975–7
Public GFCF	4.5	6.7	5.4	11.3	12.4	10.9	18.0
Private GFCF	3.7	11.9	8.7	10.3	11.0	7.8	14.6
Total GFCF	8.2	18.6	14.1	21.6	23.4	18.7	32.6
Share of GFCF in non-oil GDP	9.1	22.1	16.9	26.5	30.9	32.7	51.7

Notes:
[a] At current market prices.
Sources: For 1955–9, Plan Organization 1965, Mahdavy 1970. Investment at current prices from these sources is deflated by investment price index calculated from Central Bank's price series on construction and imported capital goods with 80% and 20% shares respectively. For the rest of the years, Central Bank, *Annual Report 1962–77.*

to deal with the contradictions which resulted from the previous phase of accumulation, and created the basic elements for the new model of accumulation which took shape in the post-1963 period. Various trade and credit restrictions and regulations which were devised to deal with the balance of payments problems were used to redirect private capital from mercantile activities, construction and real estate into new import-substituting industries. Land reform did away with the semi-feudal production relations in agriculture which were a major obstacle to accumulation and growth not only in the agricultural sector but in the economy as a whole. By then the specialized banks were firmly established and played a vital role in this redirecting of real capital formation. The state autonomy from the established proprietary classes, namely the landlords and the merchant bourgeoisie, was a pre-condition for this restructuring of capital. A new capitalist class closely connected to foreign capital and with slender social ties was virtually grafted into the economy and formed the focal point of the industrial strategy of the state.

3   The third phase (1963–77) formed the longest period of sustained accumulation in recorded economic history of Iran, with a real annual rate of growth of 18.9 per cent for gross fixed investment. The share of gross fixed investment in non-oil GDP rose from 16.9 per cent in 1962–3 to 30.9 per cent in 1971–2, and reached the phenomenal rate of 50.7 per cent in the post-1973 oil boom years (see table 5.1). Public sector investment in particular accelerated in this period as the government assumed the role of producer in basic and heavy industries such as steel, machine making, chemicals and petrochemicals. There was also a change in the structure of private investment as it moved into new consumer durables and intermediate products, which catered for the rapidly expanding domestic market composed of urban middle classes, rich peasantry and sections of the urban working class. Regarding the fluctuations in the rate of growth of investment, two further sub-periods may be distinguished in this phase. The first one refers to the minor recession of 1968–70, and the second to the over-expansion of investment after the oil price rises of 1974 (domestic investment ratio grew by 20 per cent between 1974 and 1975) and the over-heating problems which it gave rise to. From the point of view of structural features of accumulation and the role of the state, however, this phase may be treated as a homogeneous one.

5.2.1 The semi-liberal phase

After the 1953 coup, the Iranian economy was subjected to a massive inflow of external finance. With the 1954 concessionary oil agreement oil exports resumed and revenues from that sector grew at an unprecedented pace. During the five year period of 1956–60 government oil revenues amounted to $1228m, compared to $483m during the entire thirty-six year period of 1913–49. There were also substantial inflows of foreign capital in the form of official aid and grants during this period. Between 1953 and 1960, the Iranian government received more than $890m in the form of aid and grants from the US government alone (Bharier 1971, p.119). Such large inflows of external funds were bound to have a significant impact on the rate and structure of domestic investment. The impact was, however, mediated through government policy – either directly through the choice of the rate and composition of government investment or indirectly through the policies which affected private investment.

5.2.2 Public sector investment

The available data suggest that those new external resources were immediately translated into government expenditure and exerted a highly expansionary impact on the economy during the 1955–60 period (see section 5.5). Public sector investment in this period, starting from a very slender base, witnessed an annual rate of growth of 25 per cent in real terms. There are no data available on the composition of public sector investment in this period though. The composition of the Plan Organization's development expenditure (which as we noted in the previous section comprised more than 50 per cent of public sector investment in this period) could be taken as a reasonable indicator for this. According to the development expenditure data, more than 68 per cent of government investment in this period went into economic infrastructure which was mainly composed of transportation and water. Allocations for water went mainly into bulky investments on three large dams which were not completed until the mid 1960s. More than 90 per cent of the government expenditure on transport and communications went into the construction of inter-city roads, railways and the expansion of ports which principally facilitated the connection between main urban centres and foreign trade ports. The existing road and port facilities which had badly deteriorated during the Second World War, could have hardly coped with the rapid growth of import trade which followed the expansion of domestic demand and the liberal trade policy of the government in this period. Such large-scale projects were also favoured by foreign consultants and contractors who, in the absence of the indigenous know-how, were mainly in charge of planning and implementation of the projects (Mahdavy 1970, PO 1964). The only field in which government investment directly contributed to expanding productive capacities in a significant way was the manufacturing sector.[1] More than 77 per cent of government direct invest-ment in the manufacturing sector was allocated either to traditional light industries such as textiles and sugar, or to cement. The latter was to cater for the needs of the massive construction projects of the government, and the former two industries were to substitute for imports which by the mid 1950s constituted a large share of supplies in these industries.[2] The concentration of government investment in large infrastructural projects with long gesta-tion lags played not an insignificant role in intensifying the inflationary pressures and the balance of payments disequilibrium in the latter half of the 1950s.

5.2.3 Private sector investment

The rapid expansion of domestic demand following the overhaul of external funds by the government in the economy, led to a spurt in private invest-ment. Between 1955 and 1960, the share of the private sector's fixed investment in GNP more than doubled, and by 1958 it had already over-taken public investment (table 5.1). Clearly, such an acceleration in the rate of growth of private investment was not possible without the availability of abundant bank credit in this period. Table 5.2 shows the rapid increase in bank credits to the private sector which particularly accelerated after the revaluation of foreign reserves in 1957. There were various factors underlying the growth of the supply of bank credits in this period. The first one was the fast expansion of the banking system itself and the growing use of bank instruments as a means of payment. This was signified by the declining share of currency in total money supply (M1), from 60.7 per cent in 1953 to 51.1 per cent in 1959 and 38.6 per cent in 1961 (IMF, *IFS* 1963). Secondly, in this period there was little control or supervision over the activities of the commercial banks, and in fact Bank Melli Iran which was in charge of supervision over the banking system, was at the same time the largest commercial bank in the country. This is said to have led to an

[1] In the agricultural sector the state refrained from any direct intervention in production and much of its development expenditure was of an infrastructural nature such as the building of silos, research and education projects, and rural reconstruction (see PO 1964). The rest of the allocations to the agricultural sector which went into agricultural extension services, provision of subsidized machinery, fertilizer, pesticides, etc., formed only 4 per cent of total expenditures and had a negligible impact on the sector.

[2] In 1954, sugar and textiles formed 35.5 per cent of the total value of merchandise imports. In the case of sugar, imports constituted 77.5 per cent of the total quantity of domestic supplies, and in the case of cement in 1954, even before the beginning of the investment boom, imports contributed 49.3 per cent of domestic supplies. The domestic output of cement in 1954 (65,000 tons) was actually lower than its level in 1938 (80,000 tons). This phenomenon which was probably also the case with regard to textile factories, was due to the wear and tear and lack of replacements in the post-war period (see Ministry of Industry and Mines 1955, and PO 1964).

Table 5.2. *Domestic credit expansion 1954–1961[a]*

(billion Rials)

Changes in banking systems	1954	1955	1956	1957	1958	1959	1960	1961
Net claims on the public sector	0.56	0.15	1.54	2.06	2.09	−1.27	6.91	−3.26
Net foreign assets	−0.36	0.35	1.33	10.13	0.56	−3.01	−2.26	0.23
Claims on the private sector	1.66	1.67	1.10	3.16	8.63	9.63	8.91	6.73

Note:

[a] End of period except for 1961 which refers to 1961Q1–1962Q1, due to the incompatibility of the 1960 and 1961 data.

Source: IMF, *International Financial Statistics (IFS)*, 1963.

expansionary bias in the credit policies of the bank in this period (PO 1964). The third factor influencing the expansion of the supply of credit to the private sector was the growing net public sector debt to the Bank Melli Iran which implied a net addition to the deposits of commercial banks with the Bank Melli or an equivalent increase in the monetary base in the economy (table 5.2). The last and most important factor was the change in the Rial value of the net foreign assets of the banking system. Two periods could be distinguished in this respect. The first period (1953–6) was a period of genuine rise in the dollar value of net foreign assets of the banking system, as the economy had not yet adjusted to the sudden inflow of foreign exchange resources.[3] The second period which began with the revaluation of foreign exchange assets in 1957, witnessed a fictitious rise in the net foreign exchange assets denominated in domestic currency.[4] To moderate the expansionary effects of the revaluation funds the government spread disbursement of revaluation fund loans over a three-year period, yet the money multiplier effect of these funds gave rise to a phenomenal growth in private credit over the 1957–60 period (table 5.2).[5] It must be mentioned that much of the bank credits in this period were used to finance trade, and in particular, with the growing inflationary pressures in the economy, they

---

[3] In fact, the Rial value of the change in foreign assets, as shown in table 5.2, does not fully reflect the rise in the dollar value of foreign assets, as in this period the Rial was being gradually revalued against the dollar. From the point of view of domestic credit expansion, however, it is the Rial denomination which matters.

[4] The dollar value of foreign exchange assets in 1957 rose by only $25m, which at the current rate of exchange was no more than Rls 1.8bn.

[5] The revaluation fund amounted to a net addition to the supply of high-powered money, equivalent to 36 per cent of the money supply (M1) as it stood at the end of 1956.

increasingly fuelled the thriving speculative activities in real estate and commodity hoards (see Central Bank, *Annual Report* 1962). However, the establishment of long-term industrial loan agencies by the government helped to attract a relatively substantial amount of these funds into productive activities. This leads us to the question of the composition of private investment and its main determinants over this period.

5.3 External resources and the composition of private investment

The composition of private sector investments has various complex determinants both at the supply and demand sides. It may be helpful to begin with the textbook accounts of structural change in economies subject to sudden inflows of external funds. According to these accounts which are usually expounded by the aid of full-employment equilibrium comparative static models, an economy which is subject to a sudden inflow of external finance would witness the crowding out of its traded goods sectors such as manufacturing and agriculture by non-traded goods sectors such as construction and services (Corden and Neary 1982, Corden 1984). The medium-term transition process therefore involves booming investment in the latter category of industries and disinvestment in the former. The mechanism through which this takes place is the revaluation of the real exchange rate which tilts the relative prices in favour of the non-traded goods sectors. Under a fixed exchange rate system this takes place through the inflationary impact of the expenditure of external funds in the economy which leads to a real revaluation of the exchange rate. The logic of the underlying argument could be simplified as follows: to effectively transform the inflow of external finance into higher real incomes in an economy which is in a state of full-employment equilibrium, it is necessary to increase the share of imports in total domestic supply of tradeable goods so that labour – or any other tight resources which constrain the expansion of total domestic output – could be released to be employed in the non-tradable goods sectors of the economy. It should be clear, however, that there is nothing inevitable about the restructuring process expounded in this simple account of matters; it all depends on the degree of 'tightness' of the different markets, given the technological possibilities open to the different sectors of the economy. In the case of the Iranian economy in the early 1950s, there existed a relatively large slack in the labour market, investment activity was at a low ebb, and the possibilities of introducing more advanced technology in the manufacturing sector were immense. Under such circumstances what happened to the structure of private investment very much depended on the government policy stance and the different measures which it could take to direct private investment into particular channels.

Between 1953 and 1955 the nominal exchange rate was revalued by about 15 per cent (table 5.3, column 1). This was not due to the automatic response of the foreign exchange market, but it rather resulted from deliberate policy by the government which maintained strict exchange controls in this period. A dual exchange system based on export certificates was in force up to 1956, whereby essential imports (largely imported by the government itself) were subject to the preferential official exchange rate of 32.5 Rls per dollar and the rest of imports were subject to an additional charge, i.e., the price of export certificates. Since government received a major part of the foreign exchange proceeds of the export sector in the form of oil revenues, it frequently intervened in the export certificate market, thereby regulating the effective nominal exchange rate for the private sector. It was this principle import rate (including the export certificate rate) which was revalued during the 1953–5 period and formed the basis for the unified exchange rate which came into effect from March 1956 with the abolition of the export certificate system. Another measure, which had a more significant impact on import prices, was the reduction of customs duty charges from 71.2 per cent of the value of the dutiable imports in 1953 to below 30 per cent by the end of the 1950s (table 5.3, column 2). In addition, the government relaxed quantity restrictions on the import of various commodities which led to a rapid expansion of domestic availability of such commodities.[6] These measures, together with the inflationary pressures resulting from the investment boom, did in fact result in a noticeable revaluation of the real exchange rate – as is signified by the opposite movements of the general index of wholesale prices and that of the imported commodities. As table 5.3 (columns 3 and 4) shows, while the wholesale price of imported goods declined by about 20 per cent between 1953 and 1960, the general index rose by more than 15 per cent over the same period. On an aggregate basis, therefore, it appears that the textbook predictions hold. At a more disaggregated sectoral level, however, the matters were much more complicated than the orthodox textbook view – based on the simplistic assumption of traded and non-traded goods forming two homogeneous categories of products – would lead us to believe. To present a more realistic view of the relative price and profitability changes and the

[6] Throughout the post-war period the government set annual quotas on foreign exchange allocated to different commodities which was rationed amongst the import merchants on a first in first served basis (see UK, DOT 1948). These quotas which became much more restrictive during the oil nationalization dispute of the early 1950s were substantially relaxed after 1953 but not totally abolished (Agah 1958, UN 1956, p.24). There was a second round of relaxation of quantity restrictions when in April 1957 the government attempting to stabilize the inflationary pressures in the economy removed the specific quota limits on all 'non-essential imports' (see Bank Melli Iran, *Balance Sheet* 1957, UN 1958, p.46). The impact of the relaxation of trade restrictions is seen in the rapid growth of private sector merchandise imports, particularly after 1957, in col.12 of table 5.3.

Table 5.3. *Exchange rates tariffs and relative prices 1953–1960*

			Wholesale price index 1953 = 100							Cost of living index		Merchandise imports[c]	
Year	Nominal exchange rate[a]	Tariff[b] protection	General index	Imported goods	Food grain	Animal foods	Textile	Building materials	Metals	General index	Rent	Private sector	Public sector
	1	2	3	4	5	6	7	8	9	10	11	12	13
1953	90.5	71.2	100.0	100.0	100.0	100.0	100.0	100.0	100.0	100.0	100.0	n.a.	n.a.
1954	84.5	66.0	110.7	106.1	115.6	139.0	110.5	134.7	113.6	115.9	126.5	138.2	7.5
1955	76.5	60.9	106.8	97.8	136.6	133.8	104.8	141.4	114.1	117.9	145.4	206.7	43.3
1956	76.5	33.2	115.1	91.0	155.8	144.0	102.6	152.3	116.1	128.3	166.5	229.6	70.1
1957	76.5	29.8	112.9	81.6	141.3	159.4	103.4	157.5	106.3	133.9	179.5	280.2	84.4
1958	76.5	29.7	111.6	80.0	131.8	158.0	101.2	162.9	100.1	135.3	190.9	370.7	88.1
1959	76.5	30.3	113.6	81.3	155.8	185.5	95.2	172.7	101.7	152.9	202.0	440.5	89.9
1960	76.5	27.7	115.9	82.8	167.1	203.0	95.7	173.2	108.4	165.1	213.1	473.7	70.6

Notes:
[a] Rials per US dollar, principle selling rate including exchange certificates.
[b] All customs revenues including commercial profit taxes, as percentage of dutiable imports.
[c] Excluding military and oil concessionairs' imports. Values in million US dollars

Sources: For column 1, IMF, *IFS* 1957–63. For column 2 Bahrier 1971, tables on pp.71 and 105. Trade data from Baldwin 1967. The rest of the data from Central Bank, *Quarterly Bulletin*, vol.2, No.11, January–February 1964.

response of private investment to these changes at a disaggregated level of analysis the following considerations should be taken into account. First, during the 1950s the Iranian government still maintained quantitative controls over certain categories of imports (notably cereals which remained a government monopoly), through which it protected particular industries on a selective basis. The same applied to tariffs, which at 30 per cent of total dutiable imports represented relatively high rates of protection for certain competitive imports. Secondly, and connected to the first point, is the question of the structure of imports. If these mainly consist of non-competitive imports, such as intermediate and capital goods used as inputs in domestic industries, then their cheapening relative to the price of final output may increase the effective protection afforded to domestic industries. Thirdly, the changes in money wages and prices in the traded and non-traded goods sectors are not in themselves sufficient indicators of profitability and therefore relative attraction for private investment in these sectors. The possibilities for the introduction of more advanced technology in different sectors, which increases the productivity of labour and economizes on the use of raw material inputs and working capital requirements, is of equal significance. In particular, the relative backwardness of Iranian industry in the 1950s meant that there existed an immense backlog of more advanced technology which, with the expansion of imports and higher degree of openness of the economy, would have been made more accessible in this period.[7]

The next two considerations relate to the effect of the relative price and the profitability changes on the structure of private sector investment, assuming that the economic boom had in fact increased the profitability of non-traded relative to traded goods sectors. The fourth consideration refers to the 'tight resources' or factors over which high profitability sectors compete with the other sectors and on the basis of which they crowd out the latter. As we have already mentioned, in the period under study there was no indication of a general shortage of labour. Highly trained labour was, however, in short supply throughout the period and for this reason substantial use of foreign skills and know-how had to be resorted to. This, however, could not have formed a strong basis for the crowding out of the tradable sectors by non-tradable ones, as these two sectors (e.g. construction and manufacturing) are likely to draw upon specific skills which at least in the short run, when the supply of such skills is more or less fixed, may be treated as non-competing. With abundant supply of foreign exchange, access to foreign skills also could be assumed to be open to all sectors irrespective of

---

[7] For a general formulation of this hypothesis and its testing in relation to countries at different relative positions to the 'technological frontier' and different degrees of openness, see Gomulka (1971).

their profitability. Even under the assumption of foreign exchange scarcity, it was in principle the government who decided which sectors were to have access to the scarce foreign skills rather than the market. Under such circumstances the only 'tight' factor which could have acted as a principal argument for the crowding out hypothesis was the supply of finance.

In an *unregulated* credit market, the supply of credit, which under the condition of an externally induced strong boom in a developing economy always remains scarce, would flow into high profit activities and in particular the lucrative speculative activities that normally accompany such booms. This effect, however, can be mitigated to a smaller or larger degree by different types of government intervention in the credit market. Such intervention could take the form of subsidizing private bank credits to particular lines of activity, imposing quantitative restrictions on sectoral allocation of bank credits, or setting up specialized funds or agencies to channel credit into priority sectors of the economy. Though the Iranian banking system in this period remained largely 'unregulated', the setting up of industrial loan agencies significantly affected the composition of private sector investment.

The fifth and final consideration is the prevailing relations of production in the different sectors of the economy. These relations determine to what extent investment in each sector responds to favourable market conditions and also the extent to which the state can effectively control the utilization of credit within each sector. For instance, the distribution of credit and control over its use in a sector of the economy which is dominated by a plethora of petty commodity producers is not practical. Similarly, favourable relative price movements would not necessarily stimulate investment activities in an agricultural sector which is dominated by semi-feudal relations of production.

These conditions furnish important elements in the explanation of the observed relative price and profitability changes and the related change in the composition of private investment in the period under study. By focussing on the central role of government policy in directing private investment, as well as the limits to such state intervention, they constitute a much more powerful analytical framework than the orthodox market oriented approach.

A salient feature of relative price movements in this period was the rapid increase in the relative price of agricultural products compared to other traded goods. The wholesale price indices of food grains and animal foods grew by 73.8 per cent and 109.8 per cent respectively as compared to 16.1 per cent increase in the general index between 1953 and 1960 (table 5.3, columns 4 and 5). This highlighted the constraint which the backward conditions in Iranian agriculture posed to the growth of investment in the urban economy. What is more interesting in this respect, however, is the absence of any attempt by the government, which had monopoly over the import of food grains, to augment the domestic availability of food supplies through imports. Import of food grains remained at the same average annual level of 43.4 thousand tons between the 1954–6 and 1957–9 periods (UN, *YITS* 1959, 1962). This was clearly not due to the shortage of foreign exchange or any such like considerations on the part of the government. In fact, to alleviate inflationary pressures, in 1957 the government removed quantity restrictions on various manufactured imports which led to the rapid growth in the CIF value of such imports from $245m in 1957 to $455m in 1959: while during the same period food imports which were mainly a government monopoly remained stagnant at $59m.[8] The political influence of landlords seems to have had a major impact on this aspect of the foreign trade policy of the government, as this was the main channel through which the landlords could appropriate a share of the rising oil revenues and foreign aid.

The available data do not allow a comprehensive analysis of the relative price and cost changes in the manufacturing sector over this period. It is, however, possible to make certain inferences on the performance of the textile and building material sectors which were two of the largest branches of the manufacturing sector. The divergence in the relative price and cost movements between these two sectors could also serve as an indicator of the range of possibilities that different branches of manufacturing must have experienced in this period. The wholesale prices of textile manufacturing both in absolute terms and relative to other traded goods followed a continuously downward trend during the 1954–60 period; so that by 1960 they were 4.3 per cent below their 1953 level (table 5.3, column 7). There are no data available on money wages in this period. However, assuming a constant or even a moderately declining real wage, and considering that the cost of living index increased by 65.1 per cent over the period, it may appear plausible to argue that there was a profit squeeze in textile manufacturing. There were, however, strong countervailing tendencies at work. First, the relative price and profitability in textiles in 1953 was abnormally high due to the severe restrictions on imports during the oil nationalization dispute (Agah 1958). Secondly, the greater availability of foreign exchanges in the post-1954 period which eased access to more advanced imported technology would have contributed to greater profitability by increasing productivity of labour and reducing the working capital requirements in the modern textile manufacturing sector. Greater availability of imported raw

---

[8] This was mainly composed of sugar and tea which played a minor role in domestic agricultural production. Food imports, excluding sugar and tea, rose from $7.9m in 1957 to $10.7m in 1959, which implied a decline from 2.5 per cent to 1.9 per cent of total value of imports.

material inputs and rapid expansion of demand would have had a similar result by increasing capacity utilization in the sector. Thirdly, the cheapening of imported machinery and raw material inputs, resulting from the relaxation of import restrictions and reduced tariffs, would have also contributed to higher profitability.[9] The available data on the import of finished textile products also support the view that the reduction in textile prices was more due to cost reductions rather than profit squeeze resulting from import competition. Between 1954 and 1959, despite the rapid expansion of domestic demand for textiles, the CIF value of textile imports actually declined from $42.9m to $40.5m, falling from 19.4 per cent of total value of imports in 1954 to 7.5 per cent in 1959 (table 5.7). This is indicative of the fact that the import liberalization policies of post 1953 were directed more towards non-competing imports such as machinery, transport equipment and intermediate products, rather than the established traditional industries such as textiles.[10] Though the available data do not allow a definite conclusion on the variation in profitability of textile manufacturing, it may be plausibly argued that the small producers who were not the main beneficiaries of the new imported technology and cheaper raw material imports were severely squeezed through declining prices of the products and rapidly rising cost of living.[11] On the other hand, large-scale modern textile manufacturing is most likely to have improved its profitability due to increases in labour productivity and reduction in its capital and raw material input costs.[12]

[9] The cheapening of industrial raw material after the removal of quantitative import restrictions in 1957 is clearly seen in table 5.6.

[10] While imports of textiles, sugar and tea declined from 40 per cent to 16 per cent of the CIF value of total imports between 1952 and 1959, the import of capital goods, largely composed of transport equipment, and intermediate products such as chemicals, rubber, paper and metal products, grew from 29 per cent to 54 per cent of total value of imports during the same period (table 5.7).

[11] The available data indicate that small-scale producers, working in workshops which on average employed 2.7 persons each, accounted for 75.3 per cent of total employees in textile manufacturing in 1964. During the 1950s their share of employment could have been well over 80 per cent. It is also shown that labour productivity in this small-scale sector was virtually stagnant (see appendix M.1). During the 1955–9 period, the rapid growth of cheap factory produced textiles and the sharp increase in the cost of living and prices of domestically produced raw materials led to a sharp decline in the real incomes in this small subsector of textile manufacturing. In the case of cotton textiles for example, the Ministry of Industry's data indicate that output in this small subsector remained stagnant at 40m metres, with a declining share in total domestic output from 54 per cent in 1955 to 20 per cent in 1959. Taking into account the absolute decline in the textiles price index and the increases in the cost of living index, this implied 50 per cent decline in the real incomes in the small-scale manufacturing sector. Considering the low mobility of labour which normally characterizes such traditional handicrafts, an equal rate of decline in per-capita real incomes is implied by this.

[12] Assuming constant real wages, a 7.4 per cent annual growth of labour productivity would have been sufficient to keep unit wage costs constant in the face of the 65.1 per cent increase

The experience of the building material industry was totally different from that of textiles. Between 1953 and 1960 the wholesale price index of construction materials grew by 73.2 per cent which was 8.1 per cent higher than the cost of living index and 57.3 per cent above the general index of wholesale prices (table 5.3, column 8). If we allow for the low variation in the price of metals which formed the imported component of building materials (table 5.3, column 9), then the price increases for the building material industry become even more paramount.[13] The building material industry, except for cement, was principally composed of small- to medium-sized producers who used little imported inputs and machinery, and faced no competition from imports due to high costs of transportation (see Ardahali 1966). The sizeable increases in the relative price of the building material industry were due to the combined effect of low rates of technical advance and productivity growth, the absence of competition from imports and the rapid growth of demand. Given that the rates of growth of building materials prices were higher than the cost of living index, the real incomes in the small subsector of this industry appear to have been growing – contrary to what was the case in textile industry. Unit profits in the large-scale subsector of the industry must have also been increasing, even with the assumption of moderately rising real wages and raw material prices, and no productivity improvements.[14] Obviously, if we allow for the growth of labour productivity and economies in the use of raw material inputs – both

in the cost of living index during the 1953–60 period. Taking into account the 4.7 per cent decline in the prices of textiles during the same period, and disregarding the effect of other variable costs, to keep unit profits constant a labour productivity growth ranging between 9 to 10.9 per cent was required – the variation depending on the assumption about wage shares in the base year varying between 40 to 20 per cent. The available data, however, suggests that during the 1955–9 period growth of labour productivity in mechanized textile factories, which by 1959 produced well over 60 per cent of total domestic output, was much higher than this range. According to the Ministry of Industry's data, employment in mechanized textile factories grew by 26 per cent while the volume of output grew by 350 per cent, representing an annual productivity growth of 37.5 per cent (Benedick 1964, tables on pages 241 and 242). Such substantial productivity gains indicate that modern textile factories could have accommodated large increases in money wages while increasing their unit profits, even at a time of rapidly worsening terms of trade. Considering that capital-output ratios would have been most probably declining over this period due to a higher degree of capacity utilization, cheapening of imported machinery, and economies in working capital requirements, profit rates would have also been increasing in modern textiles over this period.

[13] Unfortunately, the Central Bank data do not provide the weights used for the construction of price indices for the period under review.

[14] It could be easily seen that by assuming constant real wages, raw material prices and labour productivity, the 73.2 per cent increase in the industry's prices and 65.1 per cent increase in the cost of living index would have implied a unit profit increase within the range of 76 to 80 per cent between 1953 and 1960 – the variation depending on the assumption about wage shares in the base year varying between 30 and 50 per cent.

of which could be plausibly argued to have experienced modest growth over the period concerned – then unit profits would *a fortiori* be higher.[15]

The experience of other manufacturing sectors in this regard would have been closer to that of textile or building material industries depending on the possibility and speed of introduction of more advanced technology, the degree of effective protection which they enjoyed, either naturally or due to the foreign trade policy of the government, and the rate of expansion of demand for their products relative to their supply response over the period of the boom. An important point which emerges from the above analysis is the significant role of technical change in determining profitability in the face of adverse terms of trade movements. Even on the basis of the slender evidence which exists, it could be reasonably established that high rates of productivity growth in the mechanized textile sector allowed a reduction in output prices to be combined with growth of unit profits and possibly real wages, at a time of rapid increase in the cost of living.[16] This point has to be taken into account before making any inferences on relative profitability changes on the basis of relative price movements between traded and non-traded goods. In particular, non-traded goods sectors such as services and construction which are characterized by slow rates of technical advance and productivity growth, are bound to have experienced much higher increases in their output prices than manufacturing, but not necessarily in their profit rates.

[15] There are no data available on growth of labour productivity over the 1953–60 period. The major source of labour productivity growth over this period, in building materials excluding cement, was the rapid propagation of Hoffman Kilns which were used for the mass production of bricks. Mechanized units in the building materials industry, including brick production, only made their appearance in the 1960s and 1970s (Ardahali 1966). Labour productivity in the large-scale building materials sector (employing more than ten) during the 1968–73 period, which was another period of construction boom in the economy, grew by an annual rate of 5.8 per cent. If we consider that this latter period was one of rapid mechanization in the building materials industry (see IMDBI, *Annual Report* 1968–73), then a 5 per cent maximum annual rate of labour productivity growth for the 1953–60 period would be a reasonable estimate.

[16] There are no data on wages in this period, but the arithmetic of cost-price relations can show to what extent higher real wages could have been accommodated in mechanized textiles without affecting unit profits. On the basis of the above discussed data on cost of living and labour productivity growth in mechanized textiles, it could be established that unit wage cost could have remained constant while accommodating an annual real wage rise of 28.0 per cent over the 1953–1960 period. Taking into account the reduction in textile prices and disregarding the effect of other variable costs, unit profits could have been maintained while accommodating real wage increases ranging between 23.7 and 26.4 per cent per annum – the variation depending on the assumption of wage shares in the base year varying between 20.0 and 50.0 per cent. There are no data available on variable costs per unit of output, but when it comes to the comparison between different sectors, there is little doubt that the technologically dynamic sectors such as textiles would have experienced much larger savings on such costs, or suffered less from inflation of such costs, relative to other sectors.

Profit rates play an important part in determining the rate and composition of private investment by both creating the incentive for private capital to move into particular lines of activity and producing the finance for such investment. This movement of capital is in fact the classical mechanism through which the rates of profit in different lines of activity are expected to tend towards equality in the long run under competitive market conditions. However, in an underdeveloped economy where the corporate sector forms a very small part of the economy, as was the case in the Iranian economy during the 1950s, the mobility of capital is highly restricted. The large-scale mechanized factories are particularly handicapped in this regard since they need large concentrations of money capital and their profits are only potential and incumbent upon their establishment in the first place. Before their establishment, such potential profits either accrue to the countries where the imports originate or are spread amongst many small producers in the domestic economy. One function of the modern financial institutions is the creation of such concentrations of money capital necessary for modern industrial investment. The private commercial banks which proliferated during the 1950s, and the bazaar which accounted for loans at least as much as all commercial banks, together formed the formal and informal components of the private financial institutions of Iran during this period. These institutions, however, were mainly involved in extending short-term credits to finance inventory accumulation, hire purchase, and with the building up of inflationary expectations, increasingly commodity hoards and real estate speculation (Benedick 1964, pp. 13–16, 51–3, 65–79, Central Bank, *Annual Report* 1962). Long-term industrial finance had to compete with such short-term commercial loans which charged interest rates up to 40 per cent over this period (*ibid.*). Under such circumstances it fell upon the state to provide the funds and the appropriate institutions for long-term industrial finance. The provision of cheap long-term industrial loans by the state had a remarkable catalytic effect on private industrial investment after 1956, as is shown in table 5.4.

Looking at table 5.4, it appears that between 1952 and 1955 growth of private investment was more biased towards construction and transportation which increased their share from 65.3 per cent to 75.5 per cent at the expense of industrial and, in particular, agricultural investment. From 1956, however, with the appearance of government industrial finance provisions there was a sharp reversal in this process, whereby the industrial sector increased its share from 19.4 per cent in 1956 to 45.7 per cent in 1959, and construction witnessed a drastic decline of almost 30 per cent in its share. Though there are no data available on the composition of private manufacturing investment over this period, it is possible to make a fairly accurate estimate of it on the basis of the composition of government

Table 5.4. *Composition of private fixed investment 1952–1959*

(percentage shares)

Year	Agriculture	Industry	Construction	Transport	Total	(bn Rials)[a]
1952	12.1	22.5	63.3	2.0	100.0	(2.3)
1955	5.1	19.4	63.6	11.9	100.0	(6.5)
1956	5.9	36.9	38.0	19.0	100.0	(10.8)
1957	6.6	37.6	37.4	18.4	100.0	(13.3)
1958	11.2	39.2	34.3	15.3	100.0	(20.9)
1959	8.8	45.7	33.0	12.5	100.0	(30.8)

Notes:
[a] In constant 1959 prices. Method of construction of price index as in table 5.1.
Source: Mahdavy 1970, and table 5.1.

industrial finance granted to the private sector (RLF plus ICB loans).[17] About 80 per cent of industrial loans went into food processing, textiles and construction material industries, in which the market conditions and technological possibilities open to Iranian industrialists were conducive to rapid growth of modern mechanized factories.[18] Modern cotton textile, sugar and cement factories were the principal absorbers of private investment within these three sectors. The rest of the funds were distributed in the form of small loans amongst numerous small- to medium-sized producers in various manufacturing activities (see Benedick 1964, chapters 10–11, Plan Organization 1964, Baldwin 1967, chapter VI).

Though in terms of government long-term credit the agricultural sector – receiving half of the revaluation loan funds – was more or less on the same standing as the manufacturing sector, its investment performance lagged far behind that of the manufacturing sector. Though the share of agricultural investment recovered from the low level it had fallen to in the 1955–6 period, it could not regain its 1952 peak levels – despite the massive injection of the revaluation loan funds and the sharp improvement in its terms of trade relative to the manufacturing sector (see table 5.4). The agricultural loans were mostly received by absentee landlords and were largely utilized in the lucrative business of urban real estate speculation and luxury housing (Ahari and Johnson 1963). The direct agricultural produc-

[17] These loans amounted to 24 per cent of the total private sector's fixed investment in manufacturing over the second plan period. Considering that these loans may have helped mobilize a capital twice as their own size in the private sector, their distribution would give a fair index of large-scale private manufacturing investment.
[18] Since the government did not set any priorities for the utilization of loans in particular industries, the distribution of industrial loans within the manufacturing sector was principally determined by the demand from private industrialists (Benedick 1964).

Table 5.5. *Comparative agricultural indicators: Iran, Turkey, Egypt 1959–1960*

	Iran	Turkey	Egypt
Tractors (per 000 hec. of cultivated land[b])	0.53	1.68	4.60
Fertilizer (ton per 000 hec. of irrigated land)	2.9[a]	18.8	51.7
Yields (ton per hec.)			
Wheat	0.86	1.07	2.39
Barley	0.87	1.25	2.44
Rice	1.91	3.86	5.00
Pulses	0.65	1.18	1.81
Cotton lint	0.29	0.30	0.61
Tobacco	0.34	0.72	—
Oil seeds	0.64	0.60	1.16

Notes:
[a] Refers to 1960.
[b] Including orchards.
Source: UN 1961.

ers neither had the collateral which was strictly demanded by the Agricultural Bank[19] nor did they have easy access to the branches of the bank in the main urban centres (Bharier 1979 pp.245–9). This lack of effectiveness of government credits to enhance agricultural accumulation was one aspect of the impact of the prevailing agrarian relations in hindering the development of productive forces in that sector. Table 5.5, which brings into a comparative perspective the historical backwardness of Iranian agriculture, indicates the degree to which the development of productive forces in Iranian agriculture lagged behind Middle Eastern norms as characterized by those of Turkey and Egypt. Though it would be too premature to give a general judgement on the causes of such productivity differentials, a major factor which stands out and should figure prominently in such an explanation is the large-scale eradication of absentee landlordism in the early stages of modern state formation in the latter two countries (see chapter 2).

5.4 Supply constraints and economic waste

Apart from the wastage of a large part of government's agricultural loans, the prevailing agrarian relations formed a more important source of waste at the national economic level as a result of relative price increases of

[19] The Agricultural Bank changed its name to Agricultural Cooperative Bank (ACB) after the land reform of 1962.

foodstuffs and industrial raw materials in the period under study.[20] Such price increases would have entailed considerable income redistributions away from the industrialists, workers and the government, in favour of sterile classes such as the absentee landlords, middlemen and money lenders. Clearly, the middle to rich peasant farmers and sharecroppers who had a marketable surplus at their disposal and could master adequate market power *vis-à-vis* the middlemen would have also gained. The poor response of the agricultural output to such 'price incentives', however, is indicative of the predominant wastage of the income transfers.[21] The rise in the income of these sterile classes, due to sluggish growth of agricultural output and protectionist policies of the government, would have a second round magnifying effect on economic waste as the savings of these classes are normally channelled into commodity hoards and speculative activities. The first round of increases in the relative prices of agricultural products which is due to a genuine shortage of such products, thus becomes magnified and spreads into other commodities. Though it is not possible to empirically distinguish between these two effects on the basis of the available data, a comparison between the changes in the retail and wholesale prices as presented in table 5.6 may help to shed light on aspects of this issue related to the increase in the commercial margins in retail trade. Looking at the table, it can be readily observed that, despite the large increases in the wholesale prices of food grains and animal foods, the general wholesale price index for foodstuffs showed only a slight increase over the 1953–60 period (row 3). This was due to the consumer subsidies which the govern-

[20] In the absence of accurate data the following hypothetical situation could give the minimum income transfers involved in these relative price increases. Assume agriculture in this period formed a constant 30 per cent share of the national income in real terms, and that 30 per cent of agricultural output throughout this period was sold to the non-agricultural sector. Both of these are clear underestimates. Further assume that the wholesale price index of cereals applied to all agricultural commodities, which is again a clear underestimation (see table 5.6). On the basis of these assumptions and the national income data provided by Plan Organization (1965), it turns out that the increase in agricultural incomes due to relative price increases would add up to Rls 52.7bn at current prices as compared to the Rls 5.1bn of government credits during the 1956–60 period. Surely, this estimate has no claim to precision. However, by providing an approximate estimate of the *minimum* income transfers, it can give some idea of the orders of magnitude involved. Obviously more accurate estimates of the income effects resulting from such relative price changes would not only require precise data on the variables used above, but would also have to take into account the quantity responses both on the demand and supply sides resulting from the change in relative prices. This, however, falls beyond the confines of the present study and also what the available data permit.

[21] For example, between the 1950–4 and 1960–4 periods, the output of wheat which was the main food grain (65 per cent in quantity terms) grew at an average annual rate of 2.3 per cent which was below the population growth estimates of 2.8 per cent per annum (Bharier 1971, tables on pp.27, 134).

Table 5.6. *Relative price changes 1953–1960*

	1953–7 %	1957–60 %	1953–60 %
Wholesale prices			
1 General index	12.9	2.6	15.9
2 Raw materials	25.5	− 14.1	7.8
3 Food	5.8	9.7	16.1
Food of animal origin	59.4	27.3	103.0
Food of vegetable origin	− 14.2	2.7	− 12.0
Food grains	41.3	18.3	67.1
4 Textiles	3.3	− 7.4	− 4.3
Cost of living			
5 General index	33.9	23.3	65.1
6 Food	21.2	25.5	52.1
7 Clothing	18.0	18.3	39.6
8 Rent	79.6	18.7	113.1

Source: Central Bank Iran, *Quarterly Bulletin*, 2, 11, January–February 1964.

ment provided mainly through the operations of the Cereal Organization.[22] However, as the comparison between the wholesale and retail prices of food shows (table 5.6, rows 3, 6), most of these subsidies were absorbed into the commercial margins of the retailers. This was an inevitable result of the inelastic supplies of food products: it was not before the land reform of the early 1960s that the government attempted to stabilize food prices by increasing their availability through imports. A similar divergence could be observed between the change in the wholesale price of textiles and retail price of clothing which was not so much due to inelastic supplies as to the rising costs in the distributive trade arising from increasing cost of living and stagnant labour productivity (rows 4, 5, 7). During the 1957–60 period, when, as compared to 1953–7, there was a deceleration in the growth of the cost of living index while the divergence between the wholesale and retail prices of textiles considerably widened, increasing commercial margins might have been more responsible for this.

Whatever the source of the widening wedge between the retail and wholesale prices, it amounts to a similar type of economic waste as when the relative price changes lead to an increase in incomes of sterile classes such as

[22] The huge amount of consumer subsidies given through the Cereal Organization could be seen from the nearly 80 per cent wedge between the change in the relative prices of food grains and 'food of vegetable origin' during the 1953–60 period (table 5.6, row 3).

absentee landlords. By driving up the prices of final consumer goods, they amount to a redirection of productivity gains in industry, incomes received from the oil sector, and foreign capital inflows, into channels which are not conducive to economic development.[23]

To sum up, the accumulation process over the 1954–60 period came across glaring contradictions which were embedded in the prevailing social and political relations in the country. Despite the availability of an abundant supply of foreign exchange resources, inelastic food supplies became a major source of disequilibrium as reflected in the rapidly rising cost of living and growing income inequalities which accompanied it. The liberalization of foreign trade did little by way of alleviating the food price increases: instead, by increasing the availability of capital goods and intermediate and luxury consumer products, it further exacerbated the unequal distribution of the gains from economic growth. The rapid price inflation of foodgrains which formed the major item in the cost of living of the majority of rural and urban population, meant that the process of accumulation, as in the inter-war period, was accompanied by a declining standard of living for a large section of the population.[24] Unlike the case in the inter-war period, however, this was not a necessary by-product of financial requirements for accumulation. As we have already noted, a large part of such income transfers went into speculative hoards with a detrimental effect on productive accumulation. One aspect of this was the growing urban discontent and

[23] In the long run one would expect a moderately widening wedge between the wholesale and retail prices due to relatively slow growth of labour productivity in distributive trades. The above notion of economic waste could in the short run refer to the divergences from this long-term norm. Increases in the commercial margins in the retail trade, which normally arise in inflationary times or at a time of sudden acceleration in demand, are distributed amongst a host of small traders and are normally invested in commodity hoards. Over time, the higher commercial margins would attract a growing number of small operators who could not find employment in the productive sectors of the economy and who managed to carve out a small share of the market at some stage of the distribution chain. In the long run, when this process had worked itself out one would have expected commercial margins and the wedge between the retail and wholesale prices to have returned to their long-term 'norms'. It is not, however, inconceivable that the insertion of a large number of operatives and the accompanying rise in the working capital requirements would create a permanent increase in distributive costs. This could be referred to as the long-term aspect of above notion of economic waste.

[24] According to the 1959 urban household budget survey of the BMI, food accounted for 65 per cent of total consumption for the bottom 60 per cent of urban households. In the rural areas this ratio could have been well over 80 per cent. Our calculations on the basis of UN data on production and imports of major foodgrains (wheat, barley, rice and pulses), indicates that per-capita supplies of these products (imports plus production) grew by an annual rate of 0.84 per cent between 1954–5 and 1959–60 (source UN, *YITS* 1957, 1962, UN 1961). Considering the rapid growth of incomes in the top 40 per cent of households, composed of the large and small property owners, government employees and possibly sections of the organized urban labour force, the bottom 60 per cent must have witnessed a decline in their standard of living.

the rapid increase in the number of strikes by factory workers (notably textile and brick-making factories) and the lower-scale government employees towards the end of the decade (Ivanov 1977).

A longer-term aspect of the unequal distribution of income was the rapid diversification of demand in the upper strata of income receivers who witnessed a substantial increase in their real incomes over this period. The rapid growth of demand for new consumer products, such as motor cars, electrical appliances, consumer durables, pharmaceuticals, cosmetics, paper, etc., together with the increase in the demand for investment goods and intermediate manufactured products, such as steel, machinery and chemicals, created a widening disjuncture between the structure of domestic demand and supply which increasingly spilled over into imports. As table 5.7 shows, more than 92 per cent of the increment in imports between 1954 and 1959 was accounted for by these new products, the domestic production capacity for which was virtually non-existent.[25] The balance of payments crisis of 1960–1, which was the most immediate manifestation of the growing divergence between the structure of domestic demand and supply, impressed the need for the transformation of the structure of industry and trade if the process of accumulation was to be continued. This in turn entailed a break in the alliance of the regime with the powerful traditional proprietary classes, namely the landlords and the bazaar merchants.

5.5 The economic recession

The 1955–9 boom was followed by the economic recession which continued up to mid 1963. Though the recession was triggered by the 1960–1 balance of payments crisis and the deflationary measures taken by the government to stabilize the foreign exchange situation, the period signified adjustment processes of important long-term consequences.

The balance of payments crisis of the early 1960s was caused by the over-expansion of commodity imports during the 1955–9 economic boom, with heavy reliance on foreign borrowing. The main items of foreign exchange receipts and payments over this period are shown in table 5.8. As can be seen from this table, the period witnessed a continuous decline in the significance of non-oil exports in financing commodity imports – from 50 per cent in the late 1940s to below 18 per cent in 1959. The dollar value of non-oil exports, after exhibiting a 50 per cent increase over the 1948–55 period, remained

---

[25] The 70.3 per cent import ratio for 'other manufactures' reported in the last column of the table should be treated with care. The domestic production data used for calculating this ratio is almost entirely composed of output of very small workshops which should be more realistically grouped under services rather than manufacturing. For the great majority of these imports no domestic substitutes existed. See also chapter 7.

Table 5.7. Structure of imports 1948–1960^a

	1948		1954		1959		Import ratios* 1961
	m $	%	m $	%	m $	%	
Food, beverages and tobacco	25.7	18.7	46.5	21.0	59.0	10.9	12.2
Tea	11.6	8.9	9.5	4.3	16.6	3.1	
Sugar	10.0	7.6	35.5	16.1	30.4	5.6	
Textiles	35.9	27.5	47.9	21.7	45.9	8.5	20.4
Non-metalic minerals^b	0.5	0.3	1.6	0.7	1.6	0.3	23.2
Other manufactures	64.8	49.6	115.8	52.4	408.9	75.8	70.3
Paper and products	2.8	2.1	3.5	1.6	12.5	2.3	72.7
Rubber and products	4.0	3.1	10.1	4.6	18.7	3.5	69.1
Chemicals and pharmaceuticals	9.0	6.9	11.8	5.3	36.1	6.7	67.7
Basic metals^c	10.2	7.8	20.9	9.4	74.0	13.7	63.1
Capital goods	13.7	10.5	36.7	16.6	136.7	25.3	83.5
(electrical machinery)	(3.9)	(3.0)	(5.7)	(2.6)	(30.4)	(5.6)	
(mechanical machinery)	(1.7)	(1.3)	(1.1)	(0.5)	(39.9)	(7.4)	
(transport equipment)	(8.1)	(6.2)	(29.9)	(13.5)	(66.4)	(12.3)	
The rest	2.7	2.1	10.8	4.9	25.6	4.7	
Total	130.7	100	221.0	100	539.4	100	

Notes:
^{a} CIF value, excluding imports by concessionaires and passengers.
^{b} Imports, except for the last column, refer to cement only.
^{c} Includes metal products.
* Imports as per cent of total domestic supplies. Conversion of SITC to ISIC code is based on UN 1966.

Table 5.8. *Foreign exchange receipts and payments 1948–1963*

(million dollars)

Year	Non-oil exports[a]	Oil[b] exports	Commodity imports[a]	Long-term loans[c]	Loan[d] repayment
1948	42.3	29.2	100.0	—	3.1
1949	54.0	36.9	104.7	—	2.4
1950	33.0	40.0	176.9	—	1.6
1951	61.6	58.9	145.2	—	1.8
1952	53.7	8.4	145.7	—	2.0
1953	59.5	—	71.7	—	2.4
1954	78.1	—	94.4	41.9	—
1955	94.9	22.5	200.2	72.6	4.5
1956	70.1	92.2	279.1	83.4	6.0
1957	89.6	140.5	345.4	106.7	16.9
1958	98.4	207.8	371.4	116.6	31.0
1959	86.3	244.9	479.7	61.3	43.4
1960	94.7	258.7	495.2	103.0	62.2
1961	105.6	285.0	512.7	64.1	63.1
1962	88.5	289.9	490.1	134.0	55.7
1963	82.1	342.2	458.1	54.5	49.3

Notes:
[a] Excluding trade with the USSR and frontier barter trade.
[b] National export revenues from the oil sector, excluding foreign exchange sales by the oil companies. Oil revenues for 1959 exclude $25m bonus from concession to Pan American oil company.
[c] Including US aid and grants except for military grants.
[d] Principal plus interest.
Source: Central Bank, *Quarterly Bulletin*, 1, 2, July–August 1962, and Plan Organization 1965.

stagnant over the period of the economic boom.[26] The stagnation of non-oil exports was due to the rapid expansion of domestic demand and the removal of export subsidies which the abolition of the dual exchange system implied. In view of the rapid expansion of alternative sources of foreign exchange, namely oil revenues and foreign capital, the diminishing significance of non-oil exports in financing commodity imports over this period was to a large extent inevitable. What gave rise to the balance of payments crisis was rather the haphazard and unplanned manner in which foreign

[26] The growth of the value of non-oil exports during the early 1950s was due to the favourable conditions that the Korean War boom created for primary commodity exports. In Iran the stimulating effect of the Korean War boom was reinforced by the oil crisis which created a premium for non-oil exports (see Agah 1958).

loans were accumulated and the way in which the new inflows of external resources were utilized. The rapid growth of oil revenues during the 1954–7 period, when Iran was regaining its pre-oil crisis share in the oil market, together with the large net inflows of foreign capital, led to a rapid accumulation of foreign exchange reserves in this initial four-year period.[27] This was the background which prompted the government to liberalize foreign trade and venture the massive domestic credit expansion through the revaluation loan fund in 1957. These measures together with the large expenditure programme of the government under the second plan created a rapid acceleration in the rate of growth of imports at a time when the pace of growth of oil export revenues had already stabilized and the servicing of accumulated foreign debt was increasingly becoming a heavy drain on foreign exchange revenues (table 5.8).[28] From 1958 the country had to increasingly draw upon foreign exchange reserves to finance imports. During the three years of 1958–60 there was a cumulative drain on foreign exchange reserves of more than $210m (Baldwin 1967), so that by mid 1960 the country faced a severe balance of payments crisis with foreign exchange reserves almost depleted.

During the period of the boom the government showed little consideration about the disequilibrating effect of its financial and monetary policies, nor did it have the institutional setup for undertaking the necessary regulatory tasks at the macro-economic level. There was little appreciation of the role of fiscal policy in harnessing the required resources for investment and in controlling the level and composition of effective demand. Easy access to oil revenues and foreign borrowing substituted for the need to reform the tax system for domestic resource mobilization. As table 5.9 shows, during this period between 50 and 60 per cent of government expenditure was financed by oil income or by domestic or foreign borrowing. Government current expenditure over this period grew rapidly and absorbed an increasing share of oil revenues. The current expenditure of the general budget of the government grew from Rls 11.6bn in 1955 to Rls 34.7bn in 1960, representing a rate of growth in real terms (deflated by the wholesale price

[27] Baldwin (1967, p.57), estimates the cumulative increase in foreign reserves during 1953–6 at $225.1m.

[28] As it was noted above, the extremely high rates of growth of oil export revenues during the 1954–8 period were due to Iran's regaining of its share in the international oil market after the 1952–3 oil crisis, and the once-and-for-all effect of the 50–50 profit sharing agreement with the oil consortium. The slow down in the rate of growth of oil export revenues after 1958 was thus predictable. During the years 1959 and 1960, however, these rates of growth were exceptionally low due to the decline in posted prices of crude oil. In 1959 the posted prices declined by 8 per cent and in 1960 by another 5 per cent. During the rest of the 1960s posted prices remained stable and the dollar value of oil revenues grew *pari passu* with export volumes, at the trend rate of 17.4 per cent per annum. This temporary dip in oil export revenues during the 1959–60 period could be said to have exacerbated the balance of payments crisis but was not its main cause.

Table 5.9. *Consolidated state budget 1955–1962[a]*

	As percentage of total expenditure			
	1955–6	1957–8	1959–60	1961–2
Revenues:				
Oil revenues[b]	22.5	38.5	39.4	41.8
Direct taxes[c]	5.2	5.5	8.7	8.5
Indirect taxes[d]	34.5	36.5	36.9	40.6
Total[e]	62.2	80.5	85.0	90.9
Expenditure:				
Current expenditure[f]	56.6	55.3	62.6	68.6
(Defence)	(20.1)	(21.2)	(31.0)	(26.1)
Capital expenditure	43.4	44.7	37.4	31.4
(Plan organization)	(12.5)	(25.5)	(24.2)	(23.7)
Total expenditure	100.0	100.0	100.0	100.0
(bn Rials)[g]	(22.8)	(35.0)	(48.6)	(52.7)
Deficit financing	37.8	19.5	15.0	9.1
Domestic budget deficit[h]	44.3	39.0	42.8	41.5
(bn Rials)[g]	(10.1)	(13.7)	(20.8)	(21.9)
Domestic budget deficit as per cent of GNP	6.5	7.2	7.9	6.7
Domestic budget deficit as per cent of money supply[i]	49.9	49.4	52.0	56.6
In billions of Rials				
US grants[g]	3.4	2.8	4.2	4.9
Public debt (beginning period)				
Domestic	10.2	11.4	16.0	18.5
Foreign	8.0	15.0	24.7	28.2
Total	18.2	26.4	40.7	46.7

Notes:
[a] Consolidated accounts of general budget, Plan Organization and public enterprises accounts.
[b] Excluding NIOC revenues which are included in indirect taxes.
[c] Includes income tax, inheritance and property taxes.
[d] Including customs duties, administrative receipts and investment income.
[e] Net revenue of public enterprises is included as a deficit item in current expenditures.
[f] Includes price subsidies, the net losses of state enterprises, and the interest on public debt.
[g] Annual averages.
[h] Defined as the budget deficit plus oil income, minus direct imports by the government.
[i] Averages of the ratio of domestic budget deficits over the money supply (M1) as they stood at the beginning of each year.
Sources: UN *Statistical Yearbook* 1957, 1960, 1963.

index) of 22.5 per cent per annum. The share of oil revenues allocated to development expenditure declined to 49 per cent, from the 80–90 per cent envisaged in the second plan law. Accordingly, a high degree of utilization of domestic and, in particular, foreign borrowing had to be made to finance the massive investment programme of the government. Free access to foreign and domestic borrowing allowed various government ministries and agencies, including the Plan Organization, to initiate new investment projects independently from each other and in an uncoordinated manner. At the micro-economic level this led to several instances of duplication and waste (see Plan Organization 1965, chapter 1, 1963), and at the macro level it contributed to the severe internal and external imbalances which appeared in the economy towards the close of the 1950s. The expansionary impact of the government budget could be measured by the size of the government *domestic* budget deficit which represents total injections of the public sector in the domestic economy minus withdrawals through different forms of taxation.[29] Looking at table 5.9, one can see that the domestic budget deficit formed about 40 per cent of the total government expenditure and close to 7 per cent of the GNP throughout the period, which signifies the extremely expansionary impact of the budget. In addition, such huge domestic budget deficits exerted further expansionary impact on the economy through their effect on the money supply and the availability of credit. Indeed, in the absence of a capital market, and given that the domestic borrowing of the government – which in any case was relatively low (see table 5.9) – was mainly from the Central Bank, there existed a one to one relation between the domestic budget deficits and the injection of high-powered money into the economy. As can be seen from the table, such annual injections of high-powered money through the government budget were on average equal to 50 per cent of the money supply in all the years over the period under study. It was not only the case that the institutions for sterilizing the monetary impact of the domestic budget deficits were non-existent, but also, as the experience of the revaluation loan fund showed, there was an absolute lack of concern over such matters on the part of the government. The expansionary impact of the domestic budget deficits and the revaluation loan fund would have set in motion inflationary pressures of explosive proportions had they not found an outlet in the form of the expansion of private sector imports. In fact, the rapidly growing balance of payments deficit of the private sector, after the substantial liberalization of foreign trade in 1957, could in a sense be interpreted as the mechanism of sterilization of the monetary impact of the domestic budget deficits and the revaluation fund while at the same time relieving the pressure of excess

[29] Domestic budget deficit as defined above is thus equal to the budget deficit plus oil-revenues of the government minus import of goods and services by the government.

demand through greater availabilities in the goods market. This process, however, was taking place by building up substantial public sector foreign debts. In the years immediately following the revaluation of foreign exchange reserves in 1957, when the pressure of monetary and fiscal expansion on foreign exchange resources were at their highest, public sector foreign debt service obligations were also mounting. At the time no one knew the total size of public sector foreign debt incurred by different government agencies nor the future debt service obligations. This was the case *a fortiori* for private sector foreign debt, specially after the liberalization of foreign trade when vast amounts of commercial credits were utilized by import merchants through collection bills, over which the government had no control or supervision (Central Bank, *Annual Report* 1962). It was not until the foreign exchange situation attained crisis proportions, when in September 1960 the country was left with foreign exchange reserves barely sufficient to finance one or two weeks value of essential imports, that the government was forced to take action through the introduction of an IMF prescribed stabilization programme.[30]

The stabilization programme consisted of a series of contractionary fiscal and credit policies and import controls, put into effect over the 1960–1 period.[31] It managed to stabilize the balance of payments situation by creating an economic recession which persisted far beyond the period in

[30] In the year 1960 the Central Bank was forced to use $58m of the IMF credit facilities. In spite of this, and the receipt of relatively large amounts of long-term foreign loans ($103.00m), according to the governor of the Central Bank 'foreign exchange reserves were at times so low that they could only cover the requirements of a few days'. See Central Bank, *Bulletin*, vol.2, no.7.

[31] The texts of the September 1960 stabilization programme and its two further revisions of July and December 1961, which formed the basis for the standby arrangements with the IMF, are given in Central Bank, *Bulletin* 1963, vol.1, no.5. The 1960 programme consisted of a Rls 3bn ceiling on total credit expansion (Rls 5bn expansion in private credits and Rls 2bn contraction in net public sector credits), a 2 per cent increase in Bank Melli's minimum lending rate and rediscount rate, and import restrictions through the imposition of higher commercial profit taxes. A surplus of Rls 1.8bn in the ordinary budget of the government was envisaged in place of the budgeted Rls 0.9bn deficit for 1960, to be achieved by Rls 2.7bn expenditure cut and Rls 1bn increase in tax revenues. Certain transfers from the ordinary budget to the Plan Organization were also envisaged to reduce the burden of credit restrictions on government investment. In the event, however, the programme achieved limited success in its aims. The expansion in the credits of the banking system declined from 19.6 per cent in 1959 to 7.0 per cent in 1960, but this was still well above the ceiling set by the programme and was at expense of a considerable curtailment in public and private investment. Though the net indebtedness of the Plan Organization and state enterprises declined by Rls 0.6bn, the treasury generals' net credits from the Central Bank showed an unprecedented growth of 29.3 per cent (Rls 3.2bn) in 1960. Expectations of further import restrictions and a possible devaluation intensified stock accumulation by import merchants through greater use of foreign commercial credits, and in the absence of exchange restrictions it led to increased capital flight, thus exacerbating the balance of payments problems (Central Bank, *Annual Report* 1962). By early 1961 the balance of payments situation remained even more critical than the previous year with substantial delayed foreign debt

which the programme was in force. The burden of the stabilization programme fell primarily on the investment activities in the public and private sectors. During the last two years of the second plan (1961–2) no new investment projects were initiated by the government, and real private investment dropped by more than 16 per cent. Since the bulk of the imports consisted of final consumer products and investment goods, the slowdown in the pace of investment and restrictions over luxury consumer goods imports appeared as the only practical means of averting the foreign exchange crisis. The impact of these measures on the growth of output in the industrial sector, which as yet did not heavily depend on imported inputs, was minimal; real output in manufacturing and mining, relying on the expanded capacity during the recent investment boom, continued to grow by an annual rate of 11 per cent over the 1960–2 period. From the point of view of domestic economic activity it was the construction sector (the domestic investment goods sector par excellence) and domestic trade and related services such as transportation which were most adversely affected. Domestic trade exhibited a negative rate of growth of − 4.3 per cent per annum in real terms over the 1960–2 period, while the output of the construction sector remained more or less stagnant over this period. In terms of real incomes, therefore, it appears that the brunt of the recession was taken by the low-income, urban wage earners, such as the construction workers and the mass of workers involved in trade and related services, through a reduction in their rate of employment and in their real wages,[32] as well as the powerful traditional bazaar merchants (see also Walton 1980). A significant feature of the stabilization programme was that, irrespective of its massive import restrictions and the large increases in customs duties and import taxes, it did not create any inflationary pressures in the economy,

service payments in both the private and public sectors (*ibid.*). More stringent measures and stricter control mechanisms had to be introduced in the July 1961 revision of the stabilization programme. According to the revised programme the credit ceiling of Rls 3bn was maintained for 1961 as well, but this time implementation was stricter under the supervision of the newly established Central Bank. Ceilings were imposed on individual banks' lending to the private sector, and in an attempt to increase the surveillance over public sector borrowing, the banking operations of all government establishments were centralized at the Bank Markazi. Strict exchange and quantitative import controls were also imposed. Imports of all goods considered to be luxury goods (214 items) were prohibited, and financing arrangements for a major part of imports were changed to the documentary letter of credit system with 20 to 100 per cent deposit requirement depending on the priority of the goods. These measures brought about a considerable improvement in the balance of payments by reducing the pace of investment and checking the import of luxury consumer goods. By December 1961 the foreign exchange situation had so improved that the Central Bank relaxed restrictions over private sector credits by introducing the second revision of the stabilization programme, and by March 1962 the stabilization programme was officially terminated.

[32] For example, the index of real average annual wages of construction workers declined by 15.2 per cent between 1960 and 1963.

and more importantly it did not even reverse the 1950s trend of declining relative price of imports. For instance, while the wholesale price index of foodgrains and the cost of living index grew by 15.0 per cent and 9.2 per cent respectively between 1959 and 1962, the wholesale price index of imported commodities grew by no more than 6.9 per cent. This was due to the existence of large inventory accumulations in the hands of import merchants which they had to dispose of under the pressure of the credit squeeze over this period (Central Bank, *Annual Report* 1962).[33] These trends further reinforced the growing income inequality experienced in the preceding economic boom, or to say the least, they did not create any dramatic reversals in the existing income and consumption patterns. The stabilization programme therefore managed to improve the balance of payments situation partly by curbing the investment goods imports, and partly by curbing the new 'luxury' consumer goods imports without substantially altering the structure of final consumer demand. This structure of demand formed the basis for the growth of the new import substituting industries during the 1960s and the 1970s.

5.6 Concluding remarks

Though the stabilization programme was officially terminated in March 1962, and already from December 1962 the government had tried to revive private investment through the relaxation of credit controls, grants of tax incentives, and the removal of tariffs and quantitative restrictions on the import of investment goods, private investment did not revive until late 1963 (see Central Bank, *Annual Report* 1963–5). This signified deeper adjustment processes taking place during the recessionary period, which were aimed at resolving some of the contradictions of the previous phase of accumulation and setting the economy on a new growth path. Two major areas of such restructuring, both of which involved direct intervention by the state, could be distinguished. The first area of state intervention was the restructuring of the industrial sector through directing private and public investment into new lines of manufacturing production, which were in greater conformity with the structure of domestic demand, and the second one related to the agrarian reforms. Both of these transformations involved challenging the entrenched social position of the strong traditional proprietary classes, and the political uncertainties which resulted further prolonged the recession in investment activity.

---

[33] It should be noted that, even after the recession, with the government persisting in its import restriction measures on a more or less similar scale as a means of protecting the new import substituting industries, there were no upward pressures on the prices of home produced or imported industrial products. This may be partly explained by the large government subsidies to the industrial sector, and be partly indicative of the high profit margins of the import merchants during the 1950s boom.

6

The role of agriculture in the industrialization process

6.1 Introduction

In this chapter we shall examine the transformation of Iranian agriculture during the 1962–77 period, focussing on the implications of agrarian change for the process of industrialization. Iranian agriculture over this period witnessed a phase of intense transformation through government intervention which was unparalleled in its modern history. Land reform was the hallmark of agrarian change which shaped all other aspects of agricultural development in a significant way.

A dominant theme in the literature on Iranian agriculture is the relative neglect of agriculture by the government in this period. It is sometimes even claimed that the industrialization bias of the government's economic policies led to a 'squeeze of resources' out of the agricultural sector which was the cause of the poor growth performance of the sector. However, no attempt has yet been made at a clear definition and quantification of the net resource flow into or out of the agricultural sector. In this chapter we argue that there was a net positive resource inflow into Iranian agriculture, and that contrary to the received view in connection with the land reform such inflow did produce a positive output response, though a limited one. We shall further argue that agrarian reform removed one of the main sources of economic instability, i.e., the food price inflation, and paved the way for fast industrial accumulation and growth. The real problem was different in our view. For, although agrarian reforms contributed to the removal of major bottlenecks to industrial growth on the supply side, their implementation led to a worsening distribution of both land and income. This created a new source of instability in so far as it induced a lopsided industrial growth through its demand side effects, the consequences of which will be explored in the subsequent chapters.

In section 2 we shall give an overview of the land reform programme and its impact on agrarian relations. In section 3 we shall attempt to quantify the net resource flow into agriculture and its impact on agricultural production.

Section 4 deals with the issue of marketed surplus of the agricultural sector, and section 5 briefly reviews the processes of employment and income generation in Iranian agriculture. Section 6 concludes the chapter by examining the possible policy alternatives and by exploring the likely implications of agrarian change for industrialization.

6.2 Land reform and the transformation of agrarian relations

The restructuring of agrarian relations through the land reform programme and its supporting reform measures was one of the most important aspects of state intervention in the Iranian economy during the 1960s and the 1970s. These reforms had far-reaching impacts on the conditions of production in the agricultural sector, as well as having important implications for the nature of structural change and growth in the economy as a whole.

On the eve of the 1962 land reform the semi-feudal relations of production in Iranian agriculture remained intact and there was little sign of internal tensions seriously threatening their solidity.[1] Absentee land-lordism was the dominant form of landownership – where more than 55 per cent of the cultivated land was owned by 1 per cent of the population residing in the cities.[2] The large landlords were practically the rulers of their villages and kept rigid control over the social and economic life of the peasantry (Ono 1967). Thanks to their control over 65 per cent of the population residing in the rural areas, the landlords also mustered substantial political power at the regional and national levels (Hadary 1951, Ashraf and Banuazizi 1980).

The village land was let in small sub-units to the tenants who farmed the land on the basis of share-cropping or fixed rental arrangements. Traditional share-cropping formed the backbone of the land tenure system, encompassing more than 62 per cent of the cultivated lands of the country (see table 6.1).[3] Insecurity of tenure, reinforced by population pressure on

[1] According to Ivanov (1977, pp.209–10) in certain regions there were signs of peasant unrest during the years of the crisis. This was, however, only confined to certain northern regions and, as yet, posed no serious threat to the predominant agrarian relations in the country as a whole (see Ashraf and Banuazizi 1980, Kazemi and Abrahamian 1978, Halliday 1979, pp.108–9).

[2] Fisher, *Cambridge History of Iran* (1968, vol.1, chapter 21). The question of landownership on the eve of the land reform, in the absence of proper land records, has remained controversial. However, of the 51,300 villages enumerated in the 1956 census, the public domain lands accounted for 10 per cent, the crown lands for about 4 per cent, the *Vaqf* lands for about 10 per cent and private holdings for the remaining 76 per cent (Ajami 1973). It is estimated that above 55 per cent of the cultivated land of the country belonged to large absentee landlords, i.e., those owning the equivalent of one or more villages (*ibid.*).

[3] Dividing the area of land in the Mixed Tenure category between the first three categories of tenure in table 6.1, the distribution of total area between share-cropping, fixed rent and owner-occupier types would be 62.1 per cent, 9.5 per cent and 28.4 per cent respectively.

Table 6.1. *Composition of tenure for different sizes of holdings: pre- and post-land reform*

Size of holding	Pre-land reform (1960)					Post-land reform (1974)			
	Owner occupier %	Share-cropping %	Fixed rent %	Mixed tenure %	Total %	Owner occupier %	Fixed rent %	Mixed tenure %	Total %
Area of holdings by type of tenure									
<2	38.7	29.6	20.3	11.4	100.0	91.0	2.1	6.9	100.0
2–5	28.4	47.8	12.3	11.5	100.0	92.5	2.2	5.3	100.0
5–10	22.4	60.0	4.7	12.9	100.0	93.3	1.8	4.9	100.0
10–50	19.8	65.8	3.9	10.5	100.0	92.3	2.8	5.0	100.0
50–100	29.5	55.0	5.1	10.4	100.0	89.4	5.0	5.6	100.0
>100	57.0	9.0	18.8	15.2	100.0	83.0	6.6	10.4	100.0
Total	26.2	54.8	7.4	11.6	100.0	90.7	3.1	6.2	100.0
(000 ha)	(2976)	(6222)	(844)	(1315)	(11365)	(14878)	(516)	(1023)	(16418)
Number of holdings by type of tenure									
<2	46.4	24.9	18.9	9.8	100.0	90.9	2.4	6.7	100.0
2–5	29.1	46.5	13.2	11.2	100.0	91.3	2.0	6.4	100.0
5–10	22.5	59.3	5.1	13.1	100.0	93.4	1.9	4.7	100.0
10–50	18.8	66.2	4.2	10.8	100.0	92.7	2.3	4.9	100.0
50–100	28.6	57.1	4.9	9.4	100.0	87.5	5.0	7.5	100.0
>100	55.0	15.0	25.0	5.0	100.0	81.1	7.8	11.1	100.0
Total	33.2	43.4	12.5	10.9	100.0	92.0	2.2	5.8	100.0
(000)	(624)	(814)	(235)	(204)	(1877)	(2282)	(54)	(143)	(2480)

Sources: Ministry of Interior Affairs, *National Agricultural Census*, vol.15 1960 and CSO, *Results of the Agricultural Census: Second Stage 1974*, 1976.

land, had reduced to extreme dependence and servitude the relations between the peasant share-croppers and the landlords (Ono 1967, Keddie 1968). In addition to the share of the crop, the peasant share-croppers were also subject to labour services and various other types of dues.[4] Fixed rental arrangements prevailed in less than 10 per cent of the cultivated land, mainly concentrated in small family operated farms in the rice growing region of the Caspian littoral and large-scale commercial farms. Within both types of tenure, peasant family holding was the predominant form of possession of land.[5] As table 6.2 shows, within the different forms of tenure there existed a highly uneven distribution of land amongst the different landholding groups, indicating the highly differentiated stratification of the peasantry (see Keddie 1968). About 60 per cent of agricultural land belonged to 17 per cent of holdings (above-10-ha class), while more than 60 per cent of holdings (below-5-ha class) accounted for just over 18 per cent of the total area of holdings. This degree of concentration of landholding was not due to the technical requirements of production. As table 6.3 indicates, within each holding group, and specially in the above-50-ha category, there was a high degree of fragmentation of land. The average size of land plots, which were the operational units of production, was below one hectare for the country as a whole.

There was also a limited degree of development of large-scale capitalist farming and plantation type enterprises. These were mainly concentrated in regions, such as the Gorgan plains, where the availability of highly fertile lands, free from traditional farming practices, encouraged the introduction of mechanized farming during the agricultural price boom of the 1940s and the 1950s (see Okazaki Shoko 1968). Such modern farming practices, however, had experienced only limited development. The prevailing agrarian relations restrained the development of productive forces, as well as

---

[4] The traditional share-cropping arrangement was based on the division of output between the peasant and the landowner according to the ownership by each of the five factors of production, i.e., land, labour, water, draft animals and seeds. Though this formed the principle of crop sharing, the practice varied according to the type of crop, the kind of land and variation in inputs. The landlords share varied between 20 to 80 per cent of the crop (see Demin's article reproduced in Issawi 1971, pp.221–4, and Lambton 1953, pp.306–9). On labour services and other dues see Lambton (1953, pp.330–6). It is commonly maintained that the various exactions of landlords and money lenders left the peasants generally with bare minimum subsistence (Demin 1961, Lambton 1953, pp.379–2, Vreeland 1957, pp.194–5).

[5] Though the organization of labour, particularly amongst the share-croppers in central, eastern and southern regions was based on the formation of farming groups known as boneh, sahra, etc., the right of possession (Nassagh) was invested in individual family holders. The origins of group farming in these semi-arid regions has been traced to the traditional communal organization of villages, but they still continued to perform a functional role in the provision of water (particularly upkeep of *qanats*), and in their use as an instrument of control by the landlords (see Safi Nezhad 1977 and Ono 1967).

143

Table 6.2. Size distribution of holdings for different forms of tenure: pre- and post-land reform

Size of holding	Pre-land reform (1960)					Post-land reform (1974)			
	Owner occupier %	Share-cropping %	Fixed rent %	Mixed tenure %	Total %	Owner occupier %	Fixed rent %	Mixed tenure %	Total %
Area of holdings by size									
<2	7.4	2.7	13.7	4.9	5.0	4.3	2.9	4.7	4.3
2–5	14.8	11.9	22.7	13.5	13.7	10.6	7.1	8.9	10.5
5–10	18.2	23.2	13.6	23.6	21.2	18.5	10.2	14.2	18.2
10–50	35.0	55.7	24.4	42.0	46.3	46.6	38.4	37.0	45.7
50–100	5.6	5.0	3.5	4.5	5.0	6.3	10.3	5.8	6.4
>100	19.0	1.5	22.1	11.5	8.7	13.7	31.1	25.1	14.9
Total (000 ha)	100.0 (2976)	100.0 (6222)	100.0 (844)	100.0 (1315)	100.0 (11365)	100.0 (14878)	100.0 (516)	100.0 (1023)	100.0 (16418)
Number of holdings by size									
<2	55.8	22.9	60.2	33.8	39.9	38.1	42.8	44.8	38.6
2–5	22.1	27.1	26.7	26.0	25.3	21.8	20.6	24.6	21.9
5–10	12.3	24.8	7.2	21.6	18.1	17.6	14.9	14.3	17.2
10–50	9.1	24.5	5.3	16.0	16.0	17.5	18.7	14.8	17.4
50–100	0.4	0.6	0.2	0.4	0.5	0.7	1.6	0.8	0.6
>100	0.3	0.1	0.4	+0.0	0.2	0.3	1.4	0.7	0.3
Total (000)	100.0 (624)	100.0 (814)	100.0 (235)	100.0 (204)	100.0 (1877)	100.0 (2282)	100.0 (54)	100.0 (143)	100.0 (2480)

Sources: As for table 6.1.

Table 6.3. *Fragmentation of agricultural holdings 1960*

Holding size Group (ha)	< 2	2–5	5–10	10–50	50–100	> 100	Total
Ave. holding size (ha)	0.76	3.3	7.1	17.5	67.1	247.7	<u>6.0</u>
Ave. size of plots (ha)	0.22	0.3	9.0	15.3	4.2	9.9	<u>0.99</u>
No. of plots over no. of holdings	3.4	10.4	0.8	1.1	16.0	25.0	<u>6.1</u>

Sources: As for table 6.1.

improvements in agricultural productivity and the full utilization of the available land and labour resources in the Iranian agriculture at large. In 1960, no fertilizer was used on 83.2 per cent of the area under cultivation of annual crops. Double cropping was practiced on only 0.4 per cent of cultivated land, and only 3.8 per cent of farm units regularly used a tractor for ploughing (Mahdavy 1965). According to the 1960 census of agriculture, about 60 per cent of agricultural households belonged to the poorer classes who either had no land at their disposal or had less than 2 hectares to cultivate.[6] At the same time, 69 per cent of the agricultural lands (including fallow lands) remained uncultivated. The co-existence of such massive amounts of underutilized land and labour was an indication of the degree to which the prevailing agrarian relations hindered the realization of the agricultural potential, even with the traditional methods of production.[7]

The land reform of 1962, as we have already noted in chapter 4, originated in economic and political developments outside Iranian agriculture itself. The outcome of the land reform programme, which took more than a decade to complete, depended on these external factors as well as the constraints which the structure of Iranian agriculture imposed on possible forms of government intervention. Of particular importance was the fact

[6] These households could only scrape a living at bare subsistence by performing casual labour at peak seasons. This epitomized the massive underutilization of labour in Iranian agriculture at the time. Cf., the results of the 1954 survey, 'A reconnaissance survey to determine the possibilities of a more equitable distribution of farming population on the arable lands of Iran', reported in Keddie (1968).

[7] It is often argued that shortage of water is a main cause of the underutilization of land and labour in Iranian agriculture. However, there is strong evidence to suggest that during the 1950s and the early 1960s, there was a substantial underutilization of water resources as well, even with the traditional methods of extraction and use. One of the leading experts in the field noted in the early 1960s that, 'about a fourth of the *qanats* are out of use or abandoned; if those which are being used were properly taken care of and those that are unproductive were restored – which can almost always be done – the total flow of water could be tripled. Such a flow would be almost equal to that of the Nile in Cairo ... and could supply [equivalent] to more than half of the country's agricultural output.' (Gablot, 'Le probleme de l'eau en Iran', 1962, in Issawi 1971, p.219).

that the reform was implemented with minimal participation of the peasantry at the village level, and no involvement of the urban working and middle classes. It was a reform from above, which had to be implemented by an inept and inexperienced bureaucracy. As a consequence, the land reform programme amounted to a surgical operation whereby the absentee landlords were removed from the apex of agrarian socio-economic hierarchy through a gradual four stage process, without creating major changes in the distribution of holdings and with minimum disturbance at the village level.[8] The drastic change in the form of tenure resulting from the implementation of the land reform programme is shown in table 6.1.[9] By 1974 more than 90 per cent of both the area and number of holdings belonged to the owner occupiers, as compared to about 26 per cent and 33 per cent respectively before the reform.[10] Peasant farmers received land on the basis of their pre-land reform possession rights (*Nassagh*). This reinforced the pre-existing structure of holdings and left intact the socio-economic hierarchy at the village level. Family sized peasant proprietorship with highly unequal sized distribution, which derived from the unequal distribution of holdings prior to the reform, became the predominant form of production in Iranian agriculture (see table 6.2).

The landless labourers, who constituted more than 30 per cent of the rural

[8] For detailed studies of the four stages of the land reform programme see Lambton 1969, Ashraf and Banuazizi 1980, Shams 1973 and Keddie 1968. The final outcome of the reform, in terms of its impact on the land tenure system, was either the sale of land to share-croppers under long-term credit arrangements, or the division of land between the landlord and the tenant on the basis of the old crop sharing arrangements. The government acted as an intermediary in the purchase of land from the landlords and its sale to the peasantry in fifteen annual instalments. In the absence of appropriate cadaster surveys, and for the sake of promptness, the distribution of land took place on the basis of old possession rights (*Nassaghs*) in the villages. It should be noted, however, that even in the absence of administrative inadequacies it was highly unlikely that the government would intervene to change the distribution of holdings at the village level, given the nature of the regime and the political situation of the country. Such a redistribution would have led to serious disturbances in the villages and necessitated the mobilization of the poorer sections of the peasantry which was anathema to the nature of the Iranian regime.

[9] Of course the transformation in the form of tenure shown in table 6.1 is not completely explained by the land reform. The reform affected 90 per cent of the villages, 30 per cent of which were only partially affected. It is estimated that 40 per cent of land was transferred to share-cropping peasants as a result of the land reform (Ashraf *et al.* 1980).

[10] Due care should be taken in interpreting the category of 'owner occupier' in the table, which the agricultural census refers to as 'wholly owned' holdings. It is very likely for the rich farmers to lease at least part of their holdings for part of the year to the poor peasants. The prevalence of below-subsistence holdings together with the low ratio of wage labour to family labour amongst the rich farmers (see note 24), indicates that such practices were probably highly common. The problems involved in the supervision of wage labour in backward agriculture makes land lease more attractive to the rich farmers than the employment of wage labour. This is not, however, reflected in the data given in tables 6.1 and 6.2. The tables nevertheless adequately highlight the drastic eradication of traditional absentee landlordism in Iranian agriculture.

households, received no land. The land reform left unaffected the situation of the poorest 60 per cent of rural households who either received no land or received very small plots of land (below 2 hectares): insufficient even for the subsistence of the household. The reform per se did not alleviate the under-utilization of the land, labour and water resources of the country. On the contrary, it has been argued that by destroying the old practices of group farming (*Boneh*), which were particularly essential for the upkeep of *qanats*, the land reform programme removed an important traditional institution which could effectively be used for the redeployment of resources within traditional agriculture without replacing it with effective alternative institutions (Mahdavy 1965). The Rural Cooperative Societies which were created as an integral part of the land reform programme were more concerned with providing external assistance, notably credit, to their members rather than mobilizing the internal resources at the village level (see Ashraf and Safai 1977, ILO 1972, appendix H).

From the latter half of the 1960s, parallel to the land reform programme, a series of reforms were introduced with the ambitious aim of restructuring the organization of production in Iranian agriculture. The main thrust of these reforms was towards the consolidation of holdings of entire villages, and the introduction of mechanized agriculture with the use of wage labour and modern inputs. Apart from giving encouragement to the private sector for land consolidation and mechanization through various forms of subsidies (see Nowshirwani 1976), the government also directly intervened to hasten the mechanization process by creating new forms of production units such as Farm Corporations, Production Co-operatives and large agro-business enterprises.[11] Despite the rapid proliferation of the latter

---

[11] The establishment of farm corporations was one of the major measures of the third stage of the land reform aimed at consolidation of small family plots. The entire lands of peasant farmers in selected villages were taken over by the corporations which were managed by a government-appointed director. The peasants were given shares proportional to the size of their land. The corporations were higly mechanized and made use of wage labour only. By 1976 there were eighty-five Farm Corporations comprising 778 villages with 32.5 thousand shareholders and an area of 310 thousand hectares. By 1975 the utilization of tractors and combines had reached 100 per cent and 95 per cent of the area under cultivation in the existing corporations. Production Co-operatives were basically similar to the Corporations in their aims and farming methods, with the difference that the peasants retained the title to their land and played a more active role in the management of the enterprise. By 1970, thirty-four Production Co-operatives covering 181 villages were established, encompassing 58 thousand peasant holders and covering an area of 46 thousand hectares of arable land. Agro-business enterprises were joint stock private, public, or mixed companies, mainly with participation of foreign capital, which were set up in the late 1960s and the early 1970s for the purpose of cash crop cultivation on a very large scale (above 5,000 hectares), mechanized farms in the large areas becoming cultivable under the dams. Despite the receipt of massive subsidies from the government, the agro-business enterprises turned out to be largely unsuccessful, mainly due to labour and managerial problems (see Ashraf *et al.* 1980, 1977, Afshar 1981).

types of production units during the late 1960s and the 1970s, they still constituted no more than a very small part of Iranian agriculture by the mid 1970s. It is estimated that in 1974, the land actually cultivated by these three production types was no more than 1.2 per cent of the total cultivated land and they produced no more than 2.4 per cent of the marketed surplus of the agricultural sector (Satwatmanesh 1980). Nevertheless, such new ventures still absorbed a substantial share of government resources in the form of cheap credits, grants and subsidies, infrastructural facilities and trained personnel.

6.3 Net resource flow and the growth of agricultural output

After the 1962 land reform there was a surge in the inflow of financial and real resources into Iranian agriculture. The three channels through which financial transfers normally take place – namely the terms of trade effect, the credit system and budgetary transfers – all registered a net positive inflow for the agricultural sector over the post-1963 period. Table 6.4 shows the net income gains through terms of trade improvements in the agricultural sector.[12] As can be seen from the table, the net income gains through terms of trade improvements in the agricultural sector between 1963 and 1977 amounted to Rls 81.8bn which was more than 46 per cent of real value added in the sector in 1977 (measured at 1963 prices).[13] Table 6.5 gives some indication of the net financial flows into Iranian agriculture through the credit system and budgetary transfers during the 1963–77 period. The first two rows of the table show the substantial gross inflow of funds through these two channels, which particularly grew during the oil boom years of the fifth plan (1973–7). As data on the outflow of funds through the credit system are not available,[14] we have compared the sum of these two inflows with a measure of maximum possible outflow of funds which is given in the last row of the table. The latter equals the net agricultural surplus, as the value added in the sectors minus the

[12] The definition of the income terms of trade and its methods of calculation is detailed in appendix A.1.
[13] This includes the effect of net transfers through government subsidies and indirect taxes, see appendix A.1. Our finding about the substantial income gains due to the terms of trade improvements in Iranian agriculture during this period is contrary to the popular belief on this issue and even to the views expressed in some of the scholarly works on Iranian agriculture (see Ashraf and Banuazizi 1980). Such misjudgements may have been caused by lack of due attention to the large subsidies which the agricultural sector received, over both the consumer and the intermediate goods, as well as the rapid growth of labour productivity in the manufacturing sector which may have been partially transmitted to the consumers.
[14] As far as the outflow through the budgetary transfers is concerned, it may be noted that land taxes and direct taxes of agricultural incomes over this period were virtually non-existent (see Grove 1970).

Table 6.4. *Terms of trade of the agricultural sector*

| Year | Net barter terms of trade | | | Income terms of trade of the agricultural sector[d] |
	Intermediate products[a]	Final products[b]	All[c] products	
1963	100.0	100.0	100.0	0.0
1964	102.1	109.8	108.2	5.2
1965	99.5	112.0	110.1	6.7
1966	101.7	111.1	109.6	7.1
1967	104.0	108.3	108.1	6.5
1968	107.1	107.5	107.8	7.1
1969	110.3	110.4	109.9	9.6
1970	111.5	111.0	110.3	10.7
1971	108.3	121.0	118.8	17.4
1972	115.5	121.7	120.5	21.6
1973	131.9	124.9	125.7	30.3
1974	149.4	153.4	151.3	57.5
1975	150.2	139.3	141.7	53.3
1976	145.4	149.7	147.5	65.7
1977	149.3	160.8	157.2	81.8

Notes:

[a] It refers to the percentage ratio of the composite price index of intermediate products sold by the agricultural sector over that of the agricultural sector's purchases for intermediate use.

[b] It refers to percentage ratio of composite price index of agricultural sales for final use over that of purchases of the sector for final use.

[c] Terms of trade of all products sold and purchased by the agricultural sector. A detailed list of these products is given in appendix A.1 at the end of the book.

[d] It refers to income gains in the agricultural sector arising out of the terms of trade improvements from the base year of 1963. For a discussion of the different definitions of this concept and the methods used, see appendices A.1 and A.2 at the end of the thesis.

Sources: Appendix A.1, table A1.6.

Table 6.5. *Major categories of inflow and outflow of funds in Iranian agriculture 1963–1977*

(billion Rials)

	1963–7	1968–72	1973–7
Inflow			
Government development expenditure[a]	36.6	73.6	244.0
Gross credit inflow by			
Specialized banks[b]	23.4	48.9	285.2
Commercial banks[c]	20.0	54.9	185.5
Informal institutions[d]	41.7	99.7	201.7
Sum total[e]	121.7	277.1	916.4
Outflow			
Maximum possible outflow[f]	97.8	271.4	606.7

Notes:
[a] Excludes credits granted to private sector from the development funds.
[b] Includes loans by rural co-operatives.
[c] The figure for 1963–7 period is calculated on the basis of percentage given in ILO 1973.
[d] The figure for 1963–72 period is calculated on the basis of 51–49 per cent share between formal and informal sources of finance given in ILO 1973. For the 1973–7 period a 30–70 per cent share is assumed.
[e] Excludes transfers due to interest rate subsidies by the government, and current budgetary expenditure on agriculture.
[f] Refers to net agricultural surplus, i.e, value added minus consumption expenditure of direct agricultural producers, as calculated in appendix A.2.
Sources: ILO 1973, Central Bank, *Annual Report* 1971 1971, 1974, 1977. Appendices A.1 and A.2, and tables 4.3. and 4.4 in this text.

consumption of the direct agricultural producers. Since a large part of the net agricultural surplus is expected to have been invested in the sector itself, this gives a measure of maximum possible outflow of funds from the sector. Even with this qualification in mind, the comparison between the last two rows of the table gives a clear indication of the large, and rapidly increasing, net inflow of financial resources into Iranian agriculture over this period.[15] Using Millar's (1970) terminology, the 'finance contribution' – or its counterpart on the real side, i.e., the net product contribution – of the

[15] Obviously, the measurement of the net resource flow would be affected by how one defines the agricultural sector. It is important to note in this regard that relatively significant budgetary transfers such as the current government administrative expenditure for the agricultural sector and subsidies through low interest credits have not been taken into account in the table – the latter due to data problems and the former due to the definitional objections which may be raised against its inclusion.

agricultural sector to development over this period of rapid accumulation was negative.[16]. This was made possible by the existence of substantial surpluses in the oil sector and the rapid growth of labour productivity in the manufacturing sector.

The flow of modern technical inputs such as chemical fertilizers, pesticides and agricultural machinery and implements into Iranian agriculture also grew rapidly over this period. The use of chemical fertilizers grew from about 32 thousand tons per annum in the early 1960s to 675 thousand tons by the mid 1970s, while investment in agricultural machinery experienced a seven-fold increase in real terms over the same period (table 6.6). The distribution of the flow of real and financial resources and their impact on agricultural production was, however, very uneven. Government's development expenditure by and large benefitted only the large agro-business concerns and farm corporations which made little contribution to the growth of output and were created at the expense of displacement of thousands of peasant households.[17] Close to 30 per cent of the credits granted by the specialized banks were also absorbed by large capitalist farms – mainly consisting of the state sponsored farm corporations and agro-business concerns. A large body of research on Iranian agriculture testifies to the lack of commensurate response of agricultural production – and particularly production in the new government sponsored projects – to the considerable amount of human and financial resources allocated to the sector. Over-centralization of the decision-making processes, apathy and corruption of the bureaucracy, and the overbearing power of individual private interests close to the court and the high bureaucracy, which in many instances led to the adoption of projects of dubious technical viability, are

[16] In formal terms the finance or net product contribution of the agricultural sector (F) could be represented as:

$$F = (x_1 - m_1) = f_1 + t_1 + TT$$

where x_1, m_1, f_1, t_1, and TT are respectively the marketed surplus, outside purchases, net outflow of funds through the financial system, net outflow through budgetary transfers and net income losses through terms of trade effect in the agricultural sector – all measured at the end of previous year's prices (see Millar 1970). Due to lack of accurate data on the real side for the whole period, we have approached the measurement in the above through the right-hand side of the equation or the financial side.

[17] See ILO (1972) appendix D, Katouzian (1978), Shefa-eddin (1980), Ashraf (1982). According to the ILO report, 'large private capital (e.g., agro-industrial companies) is given the most assured supply of irrigation water, lands and government protection and subsidies (specially investment in infrastructure) most of which is denied to the smaller private (and domestic) individual entrepreneurs in agriculture'. For example, the bulk of development expenditure allocated to agriculture during the 1960s (which comprised twice the expenditure on the other sectors of agriculture) was utilized for dam construction, and the land made available below the dams was handed over to mega-sized agro-business. During the fifth plan also about 40 per cent of the development expenditure in agriculture (excluding irrigation) was directly allocated to agro-business and farm corporations.

Table 6.6. *Use of technical inputs and the volume of output of Iranian agriculture 1959–1977*

	Annual average			Average annual growth rates[a]
	1959–61	1968–70	1975–7	1959–77
Use of chemical fertilizers (000 tons)	31.7	212.3	675.3	21.1
Real investment in machinery and implements[b]	2.3	3.6	16.4	13.0
Volume of output (*major products, 000 tons*)				
Wheat	2876	4253	5667	4.3
Barley	854	1128	1377	3.0
Rice	698	1020	1500	4.9
Cotton	332	522	505	2.6
Sugar beet	741	3240	4673	12.2
Tea	37	79	95	6.0
Oil seeds	16	53	112	12.9
Real value added[b]				
Farming	58.5	90.2	111.7	4.1
Animal husbandry	27.0	32.0	45.5	3.3
Total agriculture	86.8	124.1	161.3	3.9

Notes:
[a] Cumulative growth rate between 1959–61 and 1975–7 mid periods.
[b] In bn Rials, 1959 prices.
Sources: Central Bank, *Annual Report* various issues, CSO, *Statistical Yearbook* 1970, 1981.

said to have been the main causes of wastage of a large part of government expenditure in the agricultural sector (Moameni 1980, Katouzian 1978, Ashraf and Safai 1977).[18] It has been also argued that the absorption of the bulk of government expenditure by these few white elephants was at the expense of rural co-operatives, attending to the needs of peasant farmers, by depriving them of valuable trained personnel and finance (ILO 1972, Madjd 1983, Ashraf and Safai 1977). This notwithstanding, the available

[18] According to Mahdavy (1970), the organizational inadequacies in making efficient use of economic resources is a common characteristic of the 'rentier' states, caused by the ability of the state to compensate organizational deficiencies by increasing oil revenues. In this sense the abundance of financial resources and the easy option of recourse to international markets for procurement of necessary food supplies, could be argued to have alleviated the urgency for organizational effectiveness in efficient use of resources in agriculture. In support of this kind of argument one may notice the fact that a conspicuous feature of

evidence suggests that the extensive network of rural co-operatives played an important part in the supply of credit to the peasant farmers who had received land under the land reform programme.[19]

Despite the mismanagement of a large part of the government's direct investment in agriculture, the sector as a whole showed moderate rates of growth which prompts a favourable assessment, considering that it was a period of major institutional change and reform. The average annual rate of growth of output of major agricultural products over the 1959–77 period varied between 3 to 4 per cent, with cash crops such as tea, sugar beet and oil seeds achieving particularly high rates of growth (table 6.6).[20] These rates of growth appear to have mainly resulted from the positive response of peasant farmers, especially the above-subsistence subsector or what ILO (1972) refers to as the 'viable subsector' of peasant agriculture,[21] to relatively favourable domestic market conditions over this period.

official publications on planning in this period was that sectoral plans were normally appraised in terms of the amount of spending which the related ministry or agency could undertake over the plan period without due consideration to the outcome. A sectoral plan would be regarded as unfulfilled if the related ministry could not disburse all the allocated funds over the plan period.

[19] Most of the literature on Iranian agriculture justifiably highlights the shortage of funds and personnel which plagued the rural co-operatives, as well as their organizational shortcomings and deficiencies related to the size and duration of their loans – which is justified in view of the poor performance of alternative uses which government's agricultural expenditure was put into. One should not, nevertheless, underrate the considerable quantity of credit which reached the peasantry through the co-operative network. This could be only duly appreciated in an historical perspective. The membership of rural co-operatives increased from 750 thousand in 1963 to 2 million in 1972 and 3 million in 1977. Just above 70 per cent of credits by specialized banks was distributed to peasant farmers through the co-operatives. Of a sample of 339 villages surveyed by the Plan Organization in 1975, 30 per cent of the peasants obtained co-operative loans while 32 per cent used the middlemen. This should be compared to the figures for 1960, where according to the Ministry of Interior Affairs, *National Agricultural Census* (1960, p.59) only 4 per cent of total agricultural holdings received loans from government sources.

[20] It is often argued that the 3 to 4 per cent overall rates of growth given in the official publications for this period is an overestimation and the actual trend rate of growth was no more than 2 to maximum 3 per cent. Our estimates of the growth rates of marketed surplus, which are derived independently from output data, however, support the higher official estimates of output growth. The trend rate of growth of marketed surplus in real terms over the 1963–77 period was about 6 per cent (see appendix A.1). Considering that marketed surplus/value added ratio in 1963 was 0.52, and assuming that all the increment in output over the period was marketed, we arrive at an annual average rate of growth of value added of about 4.4 per cent which is closer to the official estimates. As we shall shortly observe, during the 1970s there was an acceleration in the growth of food consumption by agricultural households which led to a reduction in marketed surplus/value added ratio, and therefore the above rate should be regarded as a conservative estimate of output growth.

[21] The substantial variations in regional productivity of land, still largely arising from different ecological conditions, makes it very hazardous to attempt a general definition of the 'viable sector' which may be applicable to all regions. According to ILO (1972, appendix D, p.29), this sector roughly refers to above 4 to 10 ha farms for irrigated lands and above 14 to 30 ha for dry land depending on the cropping pattern chosen.

Table 6.7. Output and use of technical inputs by the size of holding 1974

			Holding class (hectares)					
	<1	1–2	2–5	5–10	10–50	50–100	>100	Total
Use of chemical fertilizer (kg per ha)	329.3	110.2	45.7	25.0	21.9	30.8	42.3	35.9
% of land tilled with tractor	16.8	24.7	37.6	48.1	56.1	73.0	82.9	56.3
% farm area	1.6	2.7	10.5	18.2	45.7	6.4	14.9	100.0
% share of gross[a] output		34.0		15.0	44.0		7.0	100.0
% share of[a] marketed surplus		20.0		15.0		80.0		100.0

Note:
[a] Excludes holdings not owning land and pastoralists.

Sources: CSO, *Results of Agricultural Census: Second Stage 1974*, 1976, and Price 1975.

This subsector, which by and large fell within the above-5-ha size holdings, controlled more than 70 per cent of the farming area and contributed over 60 per cent of the output and 80 per cent of the marketed surplus of the farming sector in 1974 (table 6.7).[22] The movement of terms of trade in favour of the agricultural sector, the ample supply of the so-called 'incentive goods', and the availability of subsidized inputs and credits (albeit the latter's inadequacy), appear to have provided both the finance and the incentive for accumulation in this farming subsector. Unfortunately there are no reliable data available on accumulation in the agricultural sector.[23] The data on the use of technical inputs such as tractors and chemical fertilizers shown in table 6.7, however, indicate the widespread use of such inputs amongst different farming groups by 1974. In particular the 'viable subsector' of peasant farming (5–100 ha class), accounting for about 70 per cent of tractor hours and 50 per cent of chemical fertilizers used, appears to have been the real dynamic core of Iranian agriculture over this period. This may be indeed attributed to the eradication of absentee landlordism and the effects of owner-farmer management brought about by the land reform.[24]

6.4 Agricultural marketed surplus and urban food supply

One of the most significant aspects of the post-land reform developments, as compared to the experience of the 1950s, was the availability of ample

[22] As we have already noted, the extreme fragmentation of holdings implied that a large section of the above 100ha farms fell within the category of prosperous peasant agriculture rather than the very large-scale mechanized capitalist farms. Here, due to the classification of the official data by the size of holdings, we shall refer to the 'viable subsector' of peasant agriculture as the 5 to 100ha size group, with the proviso that this may include a large number of holdings (but not significant in terms of output and marketed surplus) in the lower end which fall into the subsistence farming group, and that it does not take into account a small number of holdings (which are relatively more significant in terms of output and marketed surplus) in the above 100ha class which belong to the prosperous peasant sector.

[23] As table A2.2 (appendix A.2) shows, net agricultural surplus in real terms (after allowing for the terms of trade effect) grew from Rls 14.4bn in 1963 to Rls 107.5bn in 1977, or by an annual average of 15 per cent. Considering the structure of Iranian agriculture, where more than 90 per cent consisted of owner-occupiers, and noting that apart from interest on loans there were no other major sources of leakage of the surplus out of the sector, and furthermore that the bulk of the sector consisted of peasant farming where mobility of capital is expected to be low, these figures may indicate a relatively high rate of growth of investment in the sector.

[24] The core of this group is composed of independent peasant farmers: 50 per cent of the holdings in this group made exclusive use of family labour, and in 44 per cent the major part of work was done by family members. Only in 6 per cent of the holdings in this group was the major part of work done by wage labour. Unfortunately very little research has been done on accumulation in this important subsector of Iranian agriculture, with the exception of Mahdavy (1982) who provides an interesting case study of the dynamic nature of the rich peasant holdings.

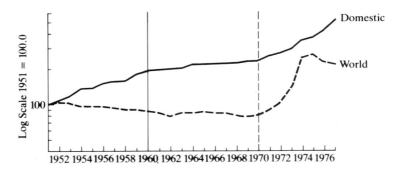

Figure 6.1 Indices of world and domestic food prices

Notes: The index of world food prices (1960–77) is the FAO dollar index of food import prices in the Middle East. For 1951–60 it is based on the UNs index of world food exports.

Sources: Bank Markazi Iran, *Annual Reports*, FAO, *Trade Year Book* 1972, 1979, UN, *Monthly Bulletin of Statistics* June 1961.

supply of foodstuff at stable prices, which was maintained partly through food imports, but largely through the growth of marketed surplus in Iranian agriculture itself. Figure 6.1, which compares the behaviour of the domestic and international food prices over the 1951–77 period, brings to light the manner in which the problem of food price inflation was alleviated after 1963. During the 1950s, a period in which international food prices were actually declining, the Iranian economy witnessed a rapid rise in food prices. This situation was reversed in the 1960s and 1970s when domestic food prices showed a much higher degree of stability, and managed to considerably narrow the gap with the world price index during rapid inflation of international food prices of the early 1970s. During the 1960s the stability of domestic food prices was maintained mainly thanks to the rapid growth of real marketed surplus of food in Iranian agriculture. Imports fluctuated at around 3 per cent of real food consumption of the non-agricultural sector, with a slight downward trend over this period, while the increase in marketed surplus was more than sufficient to maintain extremely high rates of growth of food consumption (over 8 per cent per annum) in the non-agricultural sector (table 6.8, and figure 6.2).[25]

The 1970s decade witnessed comparatively high rates of food price

[25] Since the data in the table do not take into account the increase in inventories over this period, the real growth of marketed surplus may have been even higher than the 8.3 per cent indicated in the table.

156

Table 6.8. *Urban demand, marketed surplus and imports of food 1963–1977*

(1963 prices, billion Rials)

	1963	1970	1977	Trend growth rates	
				1963–70	1970–77
Real food consumption by non-agricultural sector[a]	74.2	130.7	238.2	8.3	9.3
Real food imports[b]	2.0	2.9	32.1	1.9	28.0
Import ratio %	2.7	2.2	13.5	—	—
Real marketed surplus of food[c]	51.4	60.8	114.0	8.3	5.5
Real value added of agricultural sector	98.4	140.2	177.3	3.9	4.3

Notes:
[a] Refers to all food items including sugar and products, coffee, tea and beverages, vegetable oils and salt, at 1963 consumers prices.
[b] Imports of food products excluding the items enumerated above, at 1963 CIF prices.
[c] Refers to all food items enumerated above, at 1963 producers prices.
Source: Appendix A.1.

inflation in Iran,[26] partly due to the transmission of extremely high rates of food price rises in the international market. By providing large food subsidies the government managed to alleviate the effect of imported food prices on the domestic economy – particularly over the 1970–4 period.[27]

The 1970–7 period witnessed a rapid growth of food imports (by 28 per cent per annum in real terms), so that by 1977 imports had risen to nearly 15 per cent of consumption of non-agricultural households (table 6.8). As table 6.8 shows, it appears that the main reason for the acceleration of food imports over this period was the rapid growth of food consumption by both the agricultural and non-agricultural households. While the lack of accurate data for rural areas undermines any attempt to provide an exact estimate of the rates of growth of food consumption by agricultural house-

[26] The average annual rate of increase in food prices rose to 11.6 per cent during the 1970–7 period as compared to 1.8 per cent over the 1963–70 period. World food prices grew by an annual rate of 30.3 per cent over the 1970–4 period compared to 0.1 per cent during the 1963–70 period.
[27] After 1974 domestic food price inflation accelerated despite the decline in the imported food price index. Over this period of 'oil boom', domestic food prices grew under the general inflationary pressure in the economy.

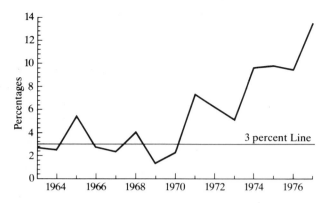

Figure 6.2 Ratio of food imports to consumption of the non-agricultural sector
Sources: As for table 6.8.

holds, the deceleration in the trend rates of growth of marketed surplus from 8.3 per cent in the 1960s to 5.5 per cent in the 1970s may be taken as an indication of the rapid increase in food consumption by agricultural households in the latter period – particularly since the period exhibited relatively higher growth rates for agricultural output.[28] The sharp increase in food imports over this period is often referred to as an indication of poor growth performance, implying a sharp reversal in the growth of food output in the 1970s. The data presented in table 6.8, however, does not support this proposition.[29] According to the data, this phenomenon seems to have been

[28] Using the data on average household consumption of food in rural areas provided by the CSO household budget surveys, we estimated trend rates of growth of 1.1 per cent and 5.2 per cent for agricultural households real consumption of food in rural areas for the 1960–70 and 1970–7 periods respectively. The erratic behaviour of the CSO data in some years and the negative growth of per-capita food consumption over the 1960s decade which is not plausible, shed doubt on the accuracy of this data. The rapid increase in the trend growth rates is, however, too pronounced to be doubted. This is also supported by other evidence. The 1970s was a period of relatively high rates of growth of real incomes in rural areas, and particularly amongst the poorer agricultural classes. The period witnessed a strong boom in the side-activities, such as carpet weaving and brick making in rural areas (Madjd 1983), as well as urban construction activity which drew heavily on rural migrant labour. Over the 1970–7 period real wages of unskilled construction workers rose by an annual rate of 19.5 per cent.

[29] Only during the years 1975 and 1977 was there a noticeable decline in the growth rates of value added in agriculture, while food imports began their steep climb from 1970. Though a discernible decline in the growth of cash crops such as cotton and sugar beet could be observed from 1970 (see appendix A.1, table A1.3). In the case of these commodities, particularly cotton which was an export cash crop, the main causes of decline in growth rates have been attributed to the rising cost of production, overvaluation of the exchange rate and the lack of adequate price support by the government during the oil boom years of the early 1970s (see Madjd 1983, Jazayeri 1987).

caused, partly by the acceleration of the rate of growth of demand for food in the non-agricultural sectors, but largely due to the supply pressures arising from a deceleration in the growth of marketed surplus, itself due to higher rates of growth of food consumption in the agricultural sector.[30] The availability of ample supplies of foreign exchange, however, helped alleviate the pressures on the supply side through imports and even to reduce the impact of international inflationary pressures through high food subsidies. In terms of its contribution to the growth of the economy on the supply side, one of the major aspects of the post 1963 developments in Iranian agriculture was, therefore, the alleviation of food price instability and the removal of the adverse effects of rising food prices on industrial wage costs.

6.5 Employment and income distribution

Other features of agricultural change over this period, which had important bearing on growth and structural change in the economy as a whole, were its income distribution and employment generation effects. As we have already noted, the pattern of land ownership which emerged after the land reform, inherited the already highly unequal distribution of holdings from the pre-reform era. Government policies, such as the exemption of mechanized farms from land distribution and the encouragement of land consolidation, further exacerbated the unequal distribution of land holdings. Table 6.9 brings into clear relief the rapidly worsening distribution of land holdings over the 1960–74 period. As the table shows, of the approximately 5 million hectares of new land brought under cultivation between 1960 and 1974, about 84 per cent was concentrated in the top 20 per cent of the largest holdings, with the bottom 60 per cent of holdings accounting for only 4.1 per cent of the increment and the bottom 40 per cent actually losing land in the process. Land being the most important asset in the agricultural sector (particularly given that animal husbandry in Iran was mainly concentrated on pastoral nomadic regions), its distribution would have a direct bearing upon the distribution of income in this sector. Of course the distribution of income is expected to be less skewed than land ownership, due to higher productivity of land in small holdings as well as the contribution of labour income which contributes substantially to total income among the poor peasant households. The trend of income distribution over time would however be significantly affected by changes in distribution of land. There were also other factors which contributed to the worsening income distribution in the agricultural sector over this period, in addition to that implied by the worsening distribution of land holdings. The income gains from terms

---

[30] The change in the structure of food consumption due to the rapid increase of incomes may be pointed out as another possible reason for the growth of imports over this period.

Table 6.9. *Decile distribution of land by holding class 1960–1974*

Holding class	Size of[a] holding (ha)	Share of[b] cultivated land		Share of the increase in cultivated land 1960–74
		1960	1974	
Lowest 40%	less than 2	5.1	3.4	− 0.4
Lowest 60%	less than 5	14.0	10.9	4.1
Second 40%	2–10	28.7	25.0	16.7
Lowest 80%	less than 10	33.8	28.4	16.3
Top 20%	greater than 10	66.2	71.6	83.7
Total		100.0	100.0	100.0
Gini coefficient of Land Holdings Distribution		1960 0.6490	1974 0.6955	

Notes:

[a] The size of holding groups are approximations, since there is generally an overlap between decile and size classifications.

[b] Decile shares have been calculated by fitting cumulative distribution curves to the group data given in the sources below. Pareto distribution curves were fitted to the lowest and highest open intervals and third degree polynomials to the rest of the intervals. Methods of fitting the curves as in Kakwani (1980).

Sources: As for table 6.2.

of trade improvements is expected to have benefitted the rich farmers with a higher marketed surplus and who made high purchases from outside the agricultural sector, proportionately more. Also, as shown by Ashraf and Safai (1977), the major part of subsidized credits and other inputs which were distributed through the rural co-operatives were utilized by the rich farmers who dominated the management committees of these organizations. Government's encouragement of mechanized farming which reduced the demand for labour relative to the expansion of newly cultivated land (see Nowshirwani 1976), is also expected to have *pari passu* reduced the income of wage labour which was mainly drawn from the poorer sections of agricultural households.[31] Because of the virtual absence of land taxes and

[31] There were of course other countervailing factors, mainly originating outside the agricultural sector, such as the strong boom of 1973–7, which, by providing employment in the construction sector and other side activities in the rural areas, must have increased the overall renumeration to the poor agricultural households. This, however, did not reverse the trend towards worsening income distribution in the rural areas.

direct taxes on agricultural incomes, the government also did not have any direct means to redress the growing maldistribution of income, had it been deemed desirable at all. Since reliable data on income distribution in the agricultural sector are not available, we have used the distribution of household consumption expenditure in the rural areas as an indicator of changing agricultural income distribution over the 1963–76 period.[32] As here we are mainly concerned with the role of agriculture in the industrialization process, the distribution of consumption expenditure provides more relevant information on the structure of demand facing the industrial sector than the distribution of income. As the data presented in table 6.10 clearly indicate, over this period there was a rapid concentration of income in the top decile groups of rural households[33] – in particular the top 20 per cent of households who increased their share of expenditure by nearly 10 per cent over the period.[34]

Another aspect of agricultural development over this period, which was also related to the issue of income distribution, was the weakness of the employment generating effect of agricultural growth. Despite an increase of almost 50 per cent in the area of arable land during the 1959–74 period, employment in the agricultural sector remained stagnant. The most accurate data on employment are the population census data which indicate that between 1966 and 1976 employment in the agricultural sector actually declined by 11.5 per cent, from 3.38 million to 2.99 million, while over the same period land under cultivation of different crops grew by more than 25 per cent. Even with such a rapid rate of increase in the land/labour ratio, by the mid 1970s landless labourers and very poor peasant farmers with casual seasonal employment, extremely low productivity, and a meagre standard

[32] Of course, the distribution of income in any year would be much more skewed than what the expenditure data in the table indicate – due to the substantial amount of dissaving which has been observed for the lower expenditure deciles in rural Iran and the rising saving ratios at increasingly higher expenditure deciles (see ILO 1972, appendix C). The expenditure data here are more suggestive of the changing income distribution over time.

[33] Of course not all rural households are agricultural households. Nevertheless, the distribution of income across rural households is a close proxy for agricultural households as well. Our decomposition analysis of income inequality in rural areas has shown that more than 70 per cent of inequality is explained by inequality within agricultural households, and that the Gini coefficients of income distribution within the agricultural and non-agricultural households in rural areas are very close.

[34] With a constant average propensity to consume across the different income groups over time, there would be a one to one correspondence between the percentage changes in consumption expenditure shares and income shares. Given the likelihood that the rapid growth of income in the upper deciles may have increased their saving propensities, the concentration of income could well have been more rapid than indicated in the above table. On the other hand, since there is a limit to the period of dissaving by the lower classes, the expenditure for these classes may not have risen as fast as their income due to debt repayment in the later years, which acts as a countervailing tendency to the above factor.

161

Table 6.10. *Distribution of household consumption expenditure in rural areas 1963–1976*

Household expenditure decile class[a]	1963	1970	1973	1976
Lowest 40%	19.4	17.1	15.9	13.5
Lowest 60%	35.9	31.3	30.1	27.3
Top 40%	64.1	68.7	69.9	72.7
Top 20%	42.4	46.6	47.5	52.2
Gini coefficient	0.3440	0.4140	0.4153	0.4743

Note:
[a] Methods of calculation as in table 6.9.
Source: CSO, *Household Budget Survey of Rural Areas* 1963–76.

of living, formed more than 60 per cent of the rural households.[35] They formed a substantial reserve of labour which was continuously drawn upon by the urban sector throughout the period of rapid investment of 1963–77.[36]

6.6 Summary and conclusions

To sum up, the first notable outcome of agrarian transformations in the post 1963 era was its contribution to the removal of food supply constraint which had been a basic source of instability during the 1950s. This was achieved primarily through the rapid growth of marketed surplus of the agricultural sector, and increasingly through the growth of imports during the 1970s. The growth of food imports during the 1970s appears to have been largely caused by the growing food consumption of agricultural households and the consequent reduction in the rate of growth of marketed surplus, rather than by a sharp reversal in the growth of output as is often alleged. Besides providing the urban sector with a food supply (which was a major item in the urban wage basket), the agricultural sector also contributed to the growth of the economy by providing a large addition to the urban labour supply. Contrary to the common belief, the agricultural sector was not financially squeezed on account of the government's industrializa-

[35] Ashraf and Banuazizi (1980), see also appendix M.1, section 2. According to the 1968 Survey of Employment the average number of days worked by the agricultural labour force was 108 days a year. This figure was actually decreasing over time, and for the landless labourers was probably even much less than 100 days a year (ILO 1972, p.26).
[36] See appendix M.1 for the measurement of rural-urban migration and the share of migrant labour in the urban labour force.

tion bias over this period. The existing evidence suggests that there was a net financial inflow, or net product inflow, into Iranian agriculture throughout the period. Though the adequacy and efficiency of use of these external resources, in particular government's direct investment, has been seriously questioned, the existing evidence nevertheless suggests that the middle to rich peasant proprietors – who dominated the agricultural sector in terms of land ownership and output in the post-land reform era – showed a positive response by substantially increasing their use of modern technical inputs and generating moderate rates of growth of output. However, the land reform did not contribute to the alleviation of land hunger which existed in the rural areas – if anything, the developments in the sector during the first decade after the reform even intensified this phenomenon, as is indicated by the absolute decline in the area of land belonging to the lowest 40 per cent of peasant holdings. The distribution of income in the agricultural sector also worsened, as the new lands brought under cultivation and the income gains in the sector were concentrated in the upper strata of agricultural households.

The development of the agricultural sector over this period appears to have followed the classic path of development in capitalist agriculture, where one is expected to witness increasing differentiation amongst the peasantry, growing concentration of land holding, and both a relative and an absolute decline in the agricultural labour force. It would be a speculative exercise to compare this path of growth to that of an alternative mode of organization of agricultural production, such as a communal form – for such radical alternatives would be too far fetched from what the political realities in Iran at the time could have accommodated. Even a more egalitarian distribution of land by imposing ceilings on the area of land holdings (which would have implied a challenge to the established power structure within the villages) was not possible without a full-scale mobilization of the poorer strata of rural society. However, even within the prevailing 'capitalist' framework there was ample room for government intervention to alleviate some of the undesirable aspects of agrarian change and improve the growth performance of the sector. In this respect the existing literature on Iranian agriculture emphasizes: (a) the need for the allocation of a greater share of government development expenditure and credits to the agricultural sector, (b) the improvement in the channels of disbursement of funds to ensure that the benefits reach the actual producers, (c) redirection of government expenditure from showpiece projects of dubious economic viability into more productive use, and (d) the decentralization of the decision-making processes and the introduction of more democratically controlled rural institutions as a prerequisite for achieving these ends. Other more specific shortcomings which could have been remedied to some extent even without the need for fundamental institutional and political change may be also pointed out. One such shortcoming which has not received due attention in the existing literature was the absence of an effective system of income and land taxation in the agricultural sector. Such an effective tax system would not only help bring about a more equal income distribution, but in the case of land taxes which were also administratively more feasible, it would have helped bring about a more efficient use of agricultural land (see Kaldor 1962). Other measures could have been also introduced to increase labour absorption in the agricultural sector. The large area of new lands which were brought under cultivation below the dams could have been converted into 'viable peasant holdings' instead of mega-sized agro-business concerns. Instead of encouraging mechanization and the adoption of labour-saving technology, the government could have also encouraged the adoption of land-saving technology through the creation of small-scale irrigation networks and more intensive use of fertilizers, pesticides, improved seeds and encouragement of multiple cropping.[37] The utilization of underemployed agricultural labour in public works programmes in the rural areas, such as road-building and irrigation works, would have also helped increase productive employment amongst the landless labourers and poor peasant farmers.[38] An obvious pre-condition for the success of such policies is that land yields should increase such that the productivity of labour may grow faster than the consumption of the newly employed labour and those upon whom they hitherto used to depend – otherwise there would be a slow-down in the growth of marketed surplus, which would check the growth of employment in the other sectors of the economy at the prevailing real wages. However, in the case of Iran where such marginal changes in the urban food supply could have been easily compensated for through imports – financed by oil revenues – even this pre-condition was not strictly binding, at least in the short to medium run. The combination of the above measures, i.e., taxing the affluent and generating productive employment for the disadvantaged

[37] It should be noted that the increasing application of labour-saving techniques was not entirely due to the encouragement by the government (e.g., subsidies on agricultural machinery, provision of ample and cheap credit to the large mechanized farms, creation of farm corporations, etc.). As it has been argued by Lefeber (1972) for the case of Indian agriculture, other factors such as peak season labour shortages in certain regions, and the growing savings in the hands of the rich farmers with lack of alternatives for asset accumulation, may have reinforced the tendency to invest in agricultural machinery. It should be also pointed out that not all forms of agricultural mechanization are labour saving. For example agricultural mechanization in the form of mechanized irrigation and threshing is likely to increase labour absorption by increasing multiple cropping (see Ishikawa 1978).

[38] Expenditure on rural development and reconstruction during the fourth and fifth plans (1967–77) respectively constituted only 1.9 and 0.9 per cent of total development expenditure.

strata, may even have had a positive balance of payments effect, by curtailing conspicuous consumption of the former and boosting agricultural production.

It should be noted, however, that such policies by themselves could not have remedied the central long-term problem of Iranian agriculture, namely the underemployment, low productivity, and the resulting poverty of 60 per cent of the rural labour force. Historically, major improvements in labour productivity in the agricultural sector have been accompanied by a shift of labour away from agricultural production and towards industry and services. In Iran even by the mid 1970s more than 40 per cent of the labour force was still engaged in the agricultural sector which signified the need for a substantial shift of labour out of the sector *pari passu* with the growth of the economy. Such a shift, both in relative terms and in absolute numbers, would also contribute to the accelerated growth of labour productivity in the agricultural sector itself.[39] The above policies, therefore, should be viewed as medium-term measures to improve the employment situation and income distribution, while in the long-run surplus agricultural labour has to be absorbed through the growth of the other sectors of the economy.[40] Given the rapid rate of population growth (2.9 per cent per annum), this posed a formidable task in terms of labour absorption for the other sectors of the economy. The adoption of the above policies in the medium and short run was not only desirable with a view to social welfare considerations, but also by creating a mass-based home market for the industrial sector, it would be essential for stable industrial growth and the long-term growth of employment in the non-agricultural sectors of the economy. As we shall argue in the subsequent chapters, while on the supply side the agricultural sector did not create major bottlenecks to the growth of industry, on the demand side it reinforced the lopsided growth of the industrial sector which was inherently unstable.

[39] The necessity for an absolute shift of labour out of the agricultural sector is signified by the fact that even in the mid 1970s the ratio of total arable land over total number of agricultural households was no more than 7 hectares, which in the semi arid regions did not even suffice for the subsistence of the household. Although it may have been possible to increase output per head by extending the area under cultivation through substantial increases in agricultural investment, such a policy may not have been efficient from the point of view of the economy as a whole due to much lower rates of return on agricultural investment compared to the other sectors.

[40] The labour market in Iranian agriculture, particularly during the oil boom years of the 1970s, had a strong seasonal element where, in the peak season, the market for labour in certain regions was tight while during the rest of the year a major part of the labour force remained severely underemployed. Taking this element of seasonality into account, surplus labour is here defined in a dynamic sense; that is, the amount of labour which could be removed from the sector without loss of output with the extension of the more advanced techniques already known and used in the sector. However, according to the ILO estimates in 1972 even 'under the prevailing conditions and with current techniques of cultivation', it was possible to remove 1 million workers (just under 30 per cent of the agricultural labour force) from the agricultural sector without reducing the level of output (ILO 1972, p.26).

7
State intervention and restructuring of industrial capital 1963–1977

7.1 Introduction

Concomitant with the transformations in the agricultural sector, the 1963–77 period witnessed important changes in the industrial structure which were mainly initiated by the state. The aim of this chapter is to examine the main aspects of state intervention which shaped the process of industrial change over this period. These consisted of a direct restructuring of government's industrial investment, as well as the adoption of other direct and indirect measures to control the rate and structure of private investment through both the supply side and demand side influences. In analysing the effect of government policy on industrial growth through its demand side influences, it is necessary to look beyond the industrial policy of the government and take into account broader aspects such as its overall expenditure and taxation policies which influenced the structure of demand through their impact on income distribution.

In the next section we shall discuss briefly the initial conditions which prompted government intervention and shaped the overall industrial strategy which was adopted. The subsequent three sections discuss the growth and structure of public and private investment and their influence on the structure of industrial output and employment. These sections largely focus on the supply side influences of government industrial policy. In section 6 we shall focus mainly on the influence of the demand side factors on industrial growth. The section begins by examining the implications of the overall expenditure and tax policies of the government for income distribution, and goes on to investigate the likely effects of the resulting pattern of consumption on industrial structure. The chapter is concluded in section 7 which provides a summary of the salient features of industrial growth over the period under investigation. The implications of the industrial structure for the long-term feasibility of the growth path is investigated in the next chapter.

166

7.2 The initial conditions

The various elements which contributed to shape the industrialization strategy of the government after the recession of the early 1960s have already been pointed out in chapter 5. The rapid diversification of demand for industrial products during the 1950s, combined with the sluggish growth of new industries due to the liberal trade policy of the government, had created an immense gap between the structure of domestic demand and supply for industrial products. In a few traditional industries relatively high growth rates were achieved during the 1950s – though even in these old established industries production capacity in the early 1960s was still very limited. Table 7.1 draws a comparative picture of the performance of selected branches of Iranian industry over the 1950s with two other Middle Eastern countries of comparable size, namely Egypt and Turkey. As the table shows, despite the impressive growth rates in certain industries in Iran during the 1950s, by 1960 the level of production even in the old established industries, such as cotton fabrics and cement, was between 30 and 50 per cent of the other two countries.

The apparent backwardness of Iranian industry even by regional Middle Eastern standards may to some extent explain the vigorous industrialization drive which was initiated by the government in the post-recessionary period, through massive public sector investment and a high degree of reliance on foreign capital to renovate the industrial base. The recession of the early 1960s, which was the culmination of the chaotic and un-coordinated growth of the economy during the previous decade, acted as a catalyst in shaping the new import-substituting industrialization drive by the government. Given the degree of backwardness of Iranian industry in the early 1960s, an initial phase of industrialization based on a protected home market may have appeared inevitable. This it was hoped would allow the build-up of the necessary industrial skills and know-how for a later stage of export-led industrialization. Politically also, the government would have favoured the import-substituting industrialization strategy, as it was bound to show impressive results at least in the medium term, while at the same time accommodating a relatively high wage and salary policy which, as we have already noted, was the basis for the co-optation of the modern middle classes and sections of the organized working class employed in the modern industrial sector.

The import restrictions and high tariffs which were imposed during the balance of payments crisis of the early 1960s induced the growth of a host of new industries catering for the highly protected and rapidly expanding home market. The availability of cheap finance and ample supplies of

Table 7.1. *Indicators of industrial performance: Iran, Turkey, Egypt 1953–1960*

	Levels		Annual growth rates
	1953	1960	1953–60
Sugar (000 tons)			
Iran	78	89	1.9
Turkey	189	618	18.4
Egypt	245	361	5.7
Cigarettes (billion)			
Iran	5.8	8.3	5.2
Turkey	20.5	26.3	3.6
Cotton fabrics (m metres)[a]			
Iran	34	236	47.3
Turkey	330	520	9.5
Egypt	380	482	4.9
Automatic cotton looms installed[b]			
Iran	640	8526	38.2
Turkey	3356	14788	20.4
Egypt	40301	47000	19.4
Cement (000 tons)			
Iran	53	782	46.9
Turkey	531	2038	21.2
Egypt	1097	2047	9.3
Sulphuric acid (000 tons)			
Iran	0	1.6	—
Turkey	20	23	2.0
Egypt	40	103	14.5
Production of electricity (m kwh)			
Iran	492	1070	11.7
Turkey	1201	2886	13.3
Egypt	1197	2639	11.9
Commercial consumption of energy (000 tons coal equivalent)[c]			
Iran	1780	3990	17.5
Turkey	5410	6390	6.3
Egypt	4730	6150	5.4

Notes:
[a] Refers to 1955–60 period.
[b] Refers to 1952–60 period.
[c] Refers to 1953–8 period.
Sources: UN 1956 and 1961.

labour and foreign exchange made a relatively long period of sustained and rapid industrial accumulation possible. This new phase of industrialization was characterized by important changes in the structure of both public and private investment.

7.3 Public sector investment

The only available source of information on the sectoral composition of public sector investment are the data provided by the Central Bank on the composition of development expenditure.[1] A distinct feature of the structural shift in the government's development expenditure in the post-1963 era was the increasing concentration of government investment in the industrial sector and related activities. As can be seen from table 7.2, the share of government investment allocated to the industrial and energy sectors grew from about 16 per cent to 41 per cent between the second and fifth plan periods, over the same period the share of physical infrastructure, such as transport and communications, and water and agriculture, declined from 71.0 per cent to 28.1 per cent. The growing direct involvement of the state in industrial production in the post-1963 period was accompanied by a more clear definition of the public and private spheres of industrial investment. Government investment was confined to heavy industries such as basic metals, mechanical engineering, chemicals and petrochemicals, which were beyond the investment capacity of the private industrialists. The share of government investment allocated to traditional light industries fell from 77.3 per cent during the 1956–62 period to 3.8 per cent by the fifth plan period (1973–7), while the share allocated to heavy industry over the same period grew from 5.7 per cent to 80.0 per cent (see table 7.2).

The role of state as the supplier of heavy industrial goods in this new phase of industrialization opened up new areas of government investment and led to a rapid acceleration in the pace of public sector investment. Real gross fixed investment in the public sector grew by an average annual rate of 22 per cent over the 1963–77 period, and by 1967 it had surpassed the level of private investment. Such rates of growth of course could be only sustained thanks to the rapid increase in oil revenues of the government. As we have previously mentioned (see chapter 4), the size of the government's development plans was largely determined by the expected oil revenues over the plan period. The possibilities of financing government investment through domestic resource mobilization, either by taxation or other forms of government intervention, were not instrumental in determining the size of the

---

[1] The degree of correspondence between the value of public sector investment and the government's development expenditure over this period is discussed in chapter 4.

Table 7.2. *Sectoral allocation of government development expenditure 1956–1977*[*]

(percentages)

	1956–62	1963–7	1968–72	1973–7
Productive sectors	87.5	73.4	79.2	69.0
Industry and mines	11.7	8.4	22.3	16.5
Energy[a]	4.8	15.6	18.8	24.4
(Sub-total)	(16.5)	(24.0)	(31.1)	(40.9)
Agriculture[b]	7.7	12.4	8.1	6.1
Water	23.5	10.7	8.3	5.6
Transport	39.8	26.3	21.7	16.4
(Sub-total)	(71.0)	(49.4)	(38.1)	(28.1)
Social sectors[c]	12.5	26.6	19.8	31.0
Total[d]	100.0	100.0	100.0	100.0
Total (bn rials)	(75.2)	(204.6)	(506.8)	(2555.1)
Industry and Mines				
Traditional industries[e]	77.3	11.7	4.6	3.8
New industries[f]	5.7	57.9	73.9	80.0
Credits to private sector	7.9	25.7	6.7	15.5
Other	9.1	4.7	14.8	0.7
Total	100.0	100.0	100.0	100.0
Total (bn rials)	(8.8)	(17.1)	(113.1)	(421.1)

Notes:
[a] Includes power, oil and gas.
[b] Excludes water.
[c] Includes housing, education, health, urban and rural development and tourism.
[d] Excluding recurrent development expenditures.
[e] Includes textiles, food products and cement.
[f] Including basic metals, chemicals and petrochemicals, paper, machinery and military industries.
[*] Periods refer to planning periods.
Sources: Central Bank, *Annual report*, 1967, 1972, 1977. Plan Organization 1964.

government's development expenditure. It was rather the availability of external finance, namely oil revenues and foreign credits, which determined the magnitude of government investment. Since foreign credits were by and large a function of expected future oil revenues, the latter became the main determinant of planned investment.[2]

As the experience of the three development plans implemented over the 1963–77 period shows, the size of development expenditure was frequently revised due to unexpected fluctuations in the oil revenues of the government.[3] During the periods – often lasting for no more than one or two years – when large unexpected increases in oil revenues alleviated the pressures of balance of payments and fiscal deficits, the government would respond by quickly increasing the size of its development expenditure and by starting various new investment projects. During the subsequent periods, however, when oil revenues grew at or below average rates, new investment projects had to be postponed and resort to foreign borrowing had to be made in order to finance the many projects in the process of completion. This state of affairs implied that, irrespective of the existence of medium-term planning at the formal level, actual government investment was closely correlated to the proceeds from the oil sector even at the short-term annual level. Our economic estimates of the elasticity of real public sector investment with respect to government oil revenues indicate a short-term (annual) elasticity of 0.3 and a long-term elasticity of 1.0, with variations in oil revenues

[2] Oil being the main source of foreign exchange earnings in Iran, it was bound to play a determining role in the debt servicing capacity of the country in the long run, both for the foreign creditors and the government.

[3] For example, the original version of the third plan proposed a total development expenditure of Rls 190bn over the plan period. The balance of payments crisis of the early 1960s led the Council of Ministers to reduce the size of the plan to Rls 140bn by a decree passed on 6 September, 1962. With the acceleration in the growth of oil revenues and easing off of the balance of payments problems, the size of the plan was once more increased to Rls 230bn halfway through its implementation. The actual size of development expenditure in the third plan was Rls 204.6bn. In the case of the fourth plan, the original size of planned development expenditure was Rls 457.1bn, which given the balance of payments problems of the late 1960s was too ambitious. The original plan relied heavily on foreign borrowing (by Rls 150bn), which was believed to be made available by the American government in supporting the Iranian government in its new role of 'policing' the Gulf after the evacuation of the British troops from the region. During the two last years of the plan, with the Tehran Oil Agreement, oil revenues of the government grew by an unprecedented rate of 80 per cent which led to an upward revision in the size of the plan to Rls 554.5bn. The actual development expenditure over the fourth plan was Rls 506.8bn. The original version of the fifth plan which was conceived amidst the euphoria of rapid oil revenue increases of the early 1970s, envisaged a development expenditure of Rls 1,560bn which was three times the size of the fourth plan. However, with the immense oil revenue increases of 1973–4, the size of the plan was almost doubled to Rls 2,848bn. The actual development expenditure during the fifth plan was Rls 2,555.1bn.

explaining more than 98 per cent of variations in government investment.[4]

Considering the cumulative effect of high rates of growth of fixed investment on government recurrent expenditures as well as the growing requirements of government expenditure on social overheads in support of accumulation, in order to sustain such high elasticity values in the long run it was clearly necessary to take effective measures to increase revenues through taxation. As we shall shortly observe, failing to take such measures, the government was faced with chronic fiscal problems which constantly threatened the stability of the accumulation process.

7.4 Private sector investment

The rapid growth of government investment over this period produced a strong impetus for private investment, both from the demand side and the supply side. On the demand side, it contributed to the rapid expansion of the home market, both directly and indirectly through the multiplier effect. The fact that government investment was mainly financed by external resources substantially increased its domestic multiplier impact. Private investors were encouraged to increase their investment with the highly buoyant conditions of demand and the availability of resources for investment, namely labour, foreign exchange and capital. On the supply side also the growth of government development expenditure is expected to have contributed to the profitability of private investment through direct cost reduction and other indirect positive externalities. Government investment in infrastructure such as transport, communications, energy and irrigation, and its development expenditure on social overheads such as education and health would have obvious positive effects in this respect. Even government investment in heavy industry is expected to be conducive to the growth of private investment on the supply side through its positive externalities (e.g., on-the-job training of labour, diffusion of new technology, etc.).

Such complementary and dynamic interactions between public and private investment are expected to be particularly strong in economies with ample supply of surplus labour and substantial possibilities for increasing

---

[4] The following OLS estimates were obtained, regressing real public sector investment (IG) on real oil revenues (ROIL), deflated by government investment price deflator, and one period lagged real public sector investment (IG_{-1}), for the 1959–77 period:

$$IG = 0.06 + 0.69\ IG_{-1} + 0.30\ ROIL - 0.03\ D * ROIL \qquad R2 = 98$$
$$\quad (0.03) \quad\ (5.02) \qquad (2.60) \qquad (-1.08) \qquad\qquad h = -1.18$$

The values are in natural logarithms, and D is a dummy variable which captures the effect of the 'extraordinary' oil revenue increases in 1974 on the coefficient of ROIL.

the productivity of labour through the introduction of advanced technology. With the classical assumptions of full employment and given technology, however, public investment rather than being complementary becomes a substitute to private investment. The conventional arguments of 'crowding out' effect of public investment strongly rely on such assumptions.[5]

In the case of Iran, with the availability of an ample supply of labour and possibilities for increasing labour productivity by introducing more advanced technology, such real crowding out effects are expected to have been minimal. Furthermore, the financing of government investment by external funds also ruled out the possibility of financial crowding out by private investment.[6] Though the government budget over this period showed a tendency towards growing deficits, the mode of financing was through monetary expansion which did not directly lead to a squeeze of supply of credits to the private sector.[7] This is clearly shown in table 7.3 which reflects the underlying mechanisms of credit expansion in the economy. As the table shows (column 10), the supply of bank credits to the private sector grew by relatively high rates ranging between 15 and 28 per cent per annum over the 1963–72 period, and accelerated to the phenomenal rates ranging between 30 to 60 per cent during the oil price boom of 1972–7. The supply of bank credits to the private sector depended on government borrowing requirements and the balance of payments as they affected the liquidity of the

[5] For a review of the crowding out literature based on full employment and fixed technology assumptions, see Von Furstenberg and Malkiel (1977). It is important to note that with these assumptions, even when public sector expenditure is financed by 'external' funds as was the case in Iran, the crowding out effect would still be present: as the private sector has to accommodate greater public absorption of *domestic* resources by curtailing its own expenditure. The degree to which this curtailment actually falls on private *investment* depends on the marginal propensity to save of the private sector and labour intensity of public sector investment (*ibid.*). This group of 'crowding out' models has a close resemblance to the full employment models of 'Dutch Disease', discussed in previous chapters.

[6] For a critical review of the literature on financial crowding out, see Friedman (1978). Apart from the assumption of non-accommodating monetary policy, the 'crowding out' results in the literature crucially relying on specific assumptions regarding relative substitutabilities between money, financial assets and real assets in the private sector's aggregate portifolio. In the case of Iran with an undeveloped capital market, deficit spending financed by domestic borrowing could produce direct crowding out results under the assumption of non-accommodating monetary policy.

[7] It could be argued that this situation may produce indirect 'crowding out' effects by creating balance of payments problems which prompt a restriction of credits to the private sector investors. This is analogous to the full-employment crowding out theories discussed above, with the difference that rather than labour, it is the foreign exchange which forms the constraining factor. The crisis of the early 1960s, and the mild recession of 1968–9 could be cited as examples. As we shall argue in this chapter and the next, however, these effects were more the outcome of the lopsided industrial structure of the economy as well as the lack of demand management through taxation, rather than high rate of government investment.

Table 7.3. *Changes in the claims of the banking system on private and public sectors 1963–1977*

Year	Change in net claims on public sector			Change in net foreign assets			Change in claims on private sector					
							Billion Rials			% of end of last period claims		
	Total	Central Bank	other banks[a]	Total	Central Bank	other banks[a]	Total	Com. banks	Spec. banks	Total	Com. banks	Spec. banks
	1	2	3	4	5	6	7	8	9	10	11	12
1963	3.0	3.3	−0.3	1.6	2.3	−0.7	11.4	9.2	2.1	19.6	20.0	17.9
1964	7.9	8.2	−0.4	−5.0	−5.1	0.1	14.8	11.7	3.1	21.4	21.1	22.2
1965	2.0	4.1	−2.1	5.8	4.8	1.0	12.7	7.9	4.8	15.0	11.7	27.9
1966	0.5	2.6	−2.1	−0.6	1.3	−1.9	18.5	13.5	4.9	19.1	18.1	22.5
1967	11.4	12.2	−0.9	0.8	2.5	−1.7	17.1	13.5	3.6	14.8	15.3	13.3
1968	12.5	12.2	0.3	−8.6	−8.6	0.0	27.4	22.1	5.3	20.7	21.7	17.4
1969	25.2	20.0	5.3	−7.5	−7.3	−0.2	22.3	18.6	3.7	13.9	15.0	10.2
1970	28.7	37.0	−8.3	−21.6	−21.7	0.1	39.2	31.6	7.6	21.5	22.2	19.3
1971	17.1	11.7	5.4	17.9	22.9	−5.1	36.8	30.2	6.6	16.6	17.3	14.0
1972	13.3	9.7	3.5	40.6	48.1	−7.5	75.9	61.3	14.6	29.4	30.0	27.3
1973	62.6	49.7	12.9	16.8	29.6	−12.8	118.5	103.4	15.1	35.5	38.9	22.1
1974	−190.3	−236.2	45.8	460.4	471.8	−11.4	162.1	111.0	51.1	35.8	30.1	61.3
1975	132.0	45.0	87.0	28.1	59.9	−31.8	356.9	258.0	98.9	58.1	53.7	73.5
1976	193.9	137.1	56.8	−41.3	32.0	−73.3	429.4	302.6	126.8	44.2	41.0	54.3
1977	119.4	−2.2	121.6	164.8	241.9	−77.1	318.5	181.6	136.9	22.7	17.4	38.0

Note:
[a] Includes commerical banks and specialized banks.
Source: IMF, *International Financial Statistics* 1983.

banking system, as well as the monetary policy of the Central Bank.[8] During the 1960s government domestic borrowing was totally financed by loans from the Central Bank and in fact there was a relatively sizeable reduction in the net claims of commercial banks on the government (table 7.3, columns 1–3). The mode of financing the budget deficits over this period, therefore, had a highly expansionary effect on the banking sector liquidity. Though this was partly neutralized by the decline in the net foreign assets of the banking system (table 7.3, columns 4–6), the overall effect was an increase in the monetary base which led to relatively high rates of private credit expansion over this period. In the 1970s private credit expansion assumed explosive proportions as a result of the expenditure of the substantial government oil revenues in the economy. The large increase in the net foreign assets of the banking system over this period (table 7.3, column 4) is an indication of the extent to which oil financed government expenditure expanded the domestic monetary base. The rapid build-up of government loans from the commercial banks (table 7.3, column 3) was a belated policy measure to wipe out some of the domestic liquidity and could by no means be interpreted as a financial squeeze on the private sector arising from the government borrowing requirements.[9] The financial crowding out hypothesis, therefore, is ruled out over this period too.

The strong inducement of both government investment and bank credits for private investment is clearly captured in the following private investment function which was estimated for the 1963–77 period.[10]

$$IP_t = 23.7 + 0.99IG_t + 0.36CR_t - 0.08K_{t-1} \qquad R^2 = 0.98$$
$$\quad\; (3.10)\,(3.83) \quad\;\; (2.13) \quad\;\; (-1.80) \qquad\qquad DW = 1.92$$

where: IP = real private fixed investment, IG = real government fixed investment, CR = bank credits to private sector deflated by private investment price deflator and K = private sector's capital stock. t-ratios are given in brackets.

[8] Of course the decline in the cash/deposit ratio in the non-bank private sector due to the expansion of the banking network and the greater use of bank instruments as means of payment, would have a similar impact as the increase in the supply of high powered money. This, however, would work through a long-term and gradual process and does not seem to have been important during the period under study. The ratio of the supply of base money outside banks to the money supply (M1) declined from 0.34 during the 1962–3 period to 0.31 during 1976–7.

[9] It is important to note that this measure, together with other measures taken by the Central Bank, such as increasing legal deposit requirements and the reserve ratio of the commercial banks, remained largely unsuccessful in checking the unbridled private credit expansion over this period. The removal of exchange controls over this period enabled the commercial banks to expand their liquidity by increasing resort to foreign borrowing. This is reflected in the rapid build-up of foreign debts of the private banks, as shown in column 6 of table 7.3.

[10] For the method of derivation of this investment function from a stock adjustment model of investment, and the sources of data and methods of estimation see appendix I.1.

7.5 Capital formation and structural change in industry

There are little reliable data on the structure of private investment over this period, but the available evidence indicates that a relatively large part of private investment was channelled into new import substituting industries, which together with government industrial investment gave rise to a rapid change in industrial structure. Private sector fixed investment in the manufacturing sector is estimated to have had an annual rate of growth of about 14 per cent in real terms over the 1965–77 period, accounting for about 60 per cent of total investment in the sector over the period as a whole.[11] The availability of external finance, channelled through the industrial banks and the Plan Organization, contributed to a rapid acceleration in the rate of manufacturing investment over this period. As table 7.4 shows, the rate of investment in the manufacturing sector increased from about 14 per cent of manufacturing value added in the early 1960s to over 65 per cent by the mid 1970s. Considering that the investment figures in the table do not include working capital investments, these figures indicate extremely high investment rates which clearly could not have been sustained without the contribution of external funds. In particular during the oil boom years of the early 1970s, when due to the overheating of the economy there was a spurt of speculative activity similar to that of the late 1950s,[12] the channelling of funds through the specialized banks and the Plan Organization played a crucial role in accelerating the rate of manufacturing investment.

The high rates of capital formation in the manufacturing sector brought about a rapid change in the structure of production. As it is shown in table 7.4 manufacturing production in the mid 1960s was dominated by the light consumer goods industries such as food, textiles, clothing and wood products, which accounted for more than 75 per cent of total output. By 1976, however, the manufacturing sector had achieved a much higher degree of diversification, with the new consumer durable, intermediate, and capital goods industries, claiming about 50 per cent of total output. Government investment in heavy industry made an important contribution to structural change in intermediate and capital goods industries, while the private sector

---

[11] These are only approximate estimates based on the following method of estimation. Government's fixed investment in the manufacturing sector was estimated by multiplying total government fixed investment by the share of the manufacturing sector in total expenditure of development plans. This was subtracted from the data on the value of total manufacturing investment provided by the Central Bank, to arrive at the private sector's fixed investment in the manufacturing sector. These results on public and private sector investment were also found to be in line with the figures on total long-term industrial loans granted to the private sector compared with the development expenditures in the sector as reported in table 4.4. [12] See chapter 5.

Table 7.4. *Structural change in the manufacturing sector 1963–1976*

	1963–4	1970–1	1975–6
Manufacturing investment			
Value added ratio[a]	13.7	42.5	66.5
Share of manufacturing[b]			
Value added in non-oil GDP (%)	15.6	18.6	20.0
Composition of manufacturing output (% shares)[c]			
	1965	1970	1976
Food, beverages and tobacco	40.0	37.9	22.4
Textiles and clothing	32.8	26.8	20.6
Wood and products	2.7	2.1	1.5
Paper and publishing	1.1	1.8	1.9
Leather and rubber	2.2	2.1	1.9
Chemicals	3.2	5.1	7.5
Minerals	4.6	3.8	3.9
Basic metals and products	5.1	8.1	18.9
Mechanical engineering	0.3	0.9	7.3
Electrical appliances	1.6	3.2	5.7
Transport equipment	5.0	6.0	6.8
Others	1.4	1.2	1.6
Total	100.0	100,0	100.0

Notes:
[a] Refers to fixed investment in machinery, tools and buildings divided by gross value added at current prices.
[b] At constant prices. Includes mining.
[c] Percentage share of gross manufacturing output at current prices.
Sources: Central Bank, *Annual Reports* various isuses, Ministry of Industry and Mines, *Iranian Industrial Statistics* 1969, Ministry of Industry and Mines, *Time Trends of Iranian Industrial Products* 1977.

contributed to the diversification of the industrial structure by investing in consumer goods branches and in particular in the new consumer durable goods. While the government played a major role in determining the overall size of private industrial investment by controlling the size of industrial credits, the pattern of investment in the private manufacturing sector was left to the profit motives of the individual industrialists. There was no conscious policy to direct private investment into selected industries through a selective application of government import protection policy or of the numerous subsidies which it granted the private investors.[13] Protection from competitive imports was granted across the board for all the major products in the final consumer market. The pattern of investment in the private manufacturing sector thus became crucially dependent on the growth and structure of domestic consumer demand. We shall discuss in more detail the relation between the structure of demand and manufacturing output at the end of the chapter.

There were, however, other important structural changes taking place through the introduction of new products and technology within each branch of the manufacturing sector, which are not reflected in the overall sectoral composition of output shown in table 7.4. An important aspect of structural change in the manufacturing sector concerned the size composition of manufacturing establishments and the nature of the new technology embodied in the manufacturing investment in this period. A striking feature of Iranian manufacturing in this period was its extreme duality. As table 7.5 shows, in the mid 1960s Iranian manufacturing, in terms of employment, was dominated by small artisan workshops which on average barely employed more than one wage labourer each. More than 65 per cent of the entire manufacturing labour force in the urban areas was employed in these small workshops with extremely low labour productivity and wages.[14] As we have demonstrated in appendix M.1, these wage and productivity differentials could not be explained by the specific characteristics of labour in the two sectors, nor could they be due to the concentration of small workshops in specific low wage and low productivity regions. They were rather general to all industries in all regions.[15] The low productivity of

[13] For a review of government tax and subsidy incentives to private manufacturing and its protection policy, see Ministry of Economy, *Industrial Development of Iran* 1967. Apart from the credit subsidies which we have already discussed, the industrial companies were exempt from income tax on 50 per cent of their profits, which increased to 100 per cent exemption for the first five years for companies outside Tehran. In addition, industrial companies were totally exempt from customs duties on imported machinery and raw materials and were protected on the output side by high tariffs on, or total prohibition of, competitive imports. According to the above source, 'any enterprise can apply and receive protection from competitive imports in the form of increased tariff rates in addition to complete prohibition against import of goods directly competitive to those produced by domestic enterprises provided that the local producer proves ability to supply adequately for local demands' (*ibid.* p.41).

[14] Of course there were exceptions such as the highly skill-intensive artisan workshops where real incomes and the value productivity of labour were relatively high. These, however, could not have consisted of more than a relatively few number of artistic activities where no mass produced substitutes existed. To the extent that these activities were prevalent, the remaining majority of workshops would have had even lower levels of productivity than shown in the table above.

[15] The hourly wages of unskilled labour in these two subsectors of manufacturing are perhaps a more appropriate indicator of the extreme duality of the urban labour market. According to the Ministry of Labour's survey in 1964, the hourly wage rates for unskilled labour in the large and small sectors were 6.5 and 2.5 Rials respectively (Ministry of Labour 1964). These

Table 7.5. *Size composition of urban manufacturing sector 1964*

	Small scale[a]	(%)	Large scale[a]	(%)
No of establishments	108920	(97)	3219	(3)
No. of employees[b]	328220	(66)	164897	(34)
Gross value added (m Rials)	19559	(44)	25011	(56)
Value added per employee[b] (Rials)	59.7		151.7	
Wage rate[c]	23.3		42.2	
Average no. of employees per establishment[b]	3.0		51.2	
Average no. of paid employees per establishment	1.6		49.1	

Notes:
[a] 'Small' refers to establishments employing less than 10 workers and 'large' to those employing 10 or more.
[b] Total persons engaged.
[c] Wage bill divided by total numbers of paid employees.
Source: Ministry of Industry and Mines, *Iranian Industrial Statistics* 1964.

labour in the small manufacturing subsector was a characteristic of the backward technology and work practices prevalent in this sector, which mainly arose from the extremely small size of the workshop. The growth of output in this small subsector, as we shall shortly see, mainly took place in the form of duplication of workshops with similar conditions of production and the same level of labour productivity. The real dynamic manufacturing enterprises, which absorbed almost all of the new investments and generated the structural changes which we observed above, fell within the large-scale manufacturing subsector. As table 7.5 shows this large-scale subsector in 1964 employed 34 per cent of the urban manufacturing labour force and produced 56 per cent of the value added.

The demarcation of the large-scale manufacturing on the criterion of employing more than ten persons, though very informative in shedding light on aspects of duality in Iranian manufacturing, is still very arbitrary and is chosen here because of the way in which the official data are presented. A more detailed differentiation of 'large-scale' manufacturing is necessary for a better understanding of the nature of accumulation and technological change in the subsector over this period. Table 7.6 gives a breakdown of the large-scale manufacturing sector according to the number of persons employed and the size of the fixed assets, and compares it

show much wider wage differentials than the wage rates reported in the table above, mainly because the latter does not take into account the longer hours worked per man-year in the small workshop.

Table 7.6. *Size structure of urban sector large-scale manufacturing and IMDBI loans 1972*

Employment[a]		Size of fixed assets[b]		IMDBI loans[c]			
Class[a]	No. of plants	Class[b]	No. of plants	Class[c]	No.	% value of loans	(cum. 1960–77)
10–49	5230	<25	5211	<25	12	3.8	(2.2)
50–99	282	26–50	276	25–45	9	5.7	(3.1)
100–499	243	51–100	150	45–75	14	12.9	(4.7)
500–1000	61	101–150	42	75–150	9	16.4	(11.0)
>1000	34	>150	171	>150	12	61.2	(79.0)
Total	5850	Total	5850	Total	56	100.0	(100.0)

Notes:

[a] Total number of persons engaged.

[b] Value of fixed assets in million Rials.

[c] Value of industrial loans in million Rials.

Sources: Ministry of Industry and Mines, *Iranian Industrial Statistics* 1972, and IMDBI, *Annual Report* 1972.

with the size of industrial loans granted by the Industrial and Mining Development Bank of Iran (IMDBI). As we noted in chapter 4, the IMDBI loans constituted more than 70 per cent of total long-term industrial credits granted to the private sector over the 1963–77 period. As the table shows, about 90 per cent of large-scale manufacturing establishments fell within the lowest bracket, employing between ten to fifty workers and with the value of fixed assets less than 25m Rials. This group, however, received only 2.2 per cent of the value of IMDBI loans over the 1960–77 period. More than 95 per cent of the IMDBIs lending over this period went to a relatively small number of large factories, which comprised the modern 'corporate' manufacturing sector, employing more than fifty workers and with a capitalization of above 25m Rials each.[16] This corporate sector formed the dynamic core of Iranian manufacturing, which absorbed the major share of manufacturing investment and was the main beneficiary of the preferential credit, foreign trade and fiscal policies of the government over this period.

While the availability of abundant supplies of cheap credit and foreign

[16] Hereafter for convenience of expression we shall refer to the subsector of 'large-scale' manufacturing as the 'corporate' sector. In the rest of this chapter, therefore, the following terminology would be adopted; 'small scale' (large scale) would refer to establishments with less than (more than or equal) ten employees as in the official publications. 'Corporate sector' would refer to establishments with more than fifty employees, and 'medium size' would refer to those employing between ten and fifty persons.

exchange created the conditions for rapid accumulation and technological change in the corporate sector, at the same time it encouraged an increasing degree of mechanization of the manufacturing sector which intensified the duality within the sector. As table 7.7 shows, there was a seven-fold increase in the incremental capital/labour ratio of manufacturing investment between the third and the fifth plan periods. This was partly a result of the increasing weight of the modern corporate sector in manufacturing investment, and partly because of the increasing capital intensity within the corporate sector itself as every new vintage of machinery incorporated the latest automated technology.[17] This later trend was particularly intensified during the fifth plan period (1973–7), when as a result of the shortages of skilled labour, which arose because of the overexpansion of investment activity, the firms had to resort to increasing automation.

The modern corporate manufacturing sector exhibited impressive growth rates in terms of output, productivity and employment (table 7.8). The extremely high rates of growth of output allowed a rapid expansion of employment to take place – by about 7 to 8 per cent per annum – despite the relatively high rates of growth of labour productivity. High labour productivity growth rates in turn allowed a rapid increase in real wages, which grew by about 4 per cent per annum over the 1960s and accelerated to the extremely high rate of 11 per cent per annum over the 1970s, in line with productivity growth. The modern corporate sector, however, embraced only a very narrow section of manufacturing employment. Despite the relatively high rates of employment growth in the corporate sector, because of its narrow base, its contribution to the increase in manufacturing employment was relatively low. As table 7.7 shows, the contribution of the corporate sector to the increase in manufacturing employment declined from 18 per cent over the 1963–7 period to 13 per cent in 1968–72, and to merely 10 per cent in 1973–7. Throughout this period it was the small-scale manufacturing subsector which absorbed the major bulk of new entrants into the labour market, which multiplied rapidly due to high rates of population growth and transfer of surplus agricultural labour through rural-urban migration.[18] The contribution of small-scale manufacturing to

---

[17] This process which took place in the public and private sectors is clearly reflected in the reports of the Industrial Development and Renovation Organization of Iran (IDRO). It is interesting to note that IDRO, which was formed in 1967 to extend technical and managerial assistance to industry, set its main priority 'to introduce into Iran the latest technology . . . in close contact with many industrial firms of international repute' (IDRO 1975, p. 14). There is no mention of the possibility to adapt the new technology to the economic conditions prevailing in Iran, and no reference to the impact of the new technology on the industrial structure as a whole.

[18] The scale and pattern of rural-urban migration during this period is discussed in appendix P.1. For an analysis of the scale of rural surplus labour see appendix M.1, section 2, and chapter 6.

Table 7.7. *Degree of mechanization and employment generation in the manufacturing sector 1963–1977*

	1963–67	1968–72	1973–7
Incremental capital/ labour ratio[a] (m Rials)	815	2791	6473
Increase in total[b] manufacturing employment (000)	297	380	785
% contribution of			
small-scale[c]	72	77	79
medium-scale[d]	10	10	11
corporate sector[e]	18	13	10
Total	100	100	100

Notes:

[a] Computed by dividing gross fixed investment in each period by the number of employees added to total employment in large-scale manufacturing (more than 10 employees).

[b] It refers to total persons engaged in small- and large-scale manufacturing in both rural and urban areas.

[c] Less than 10 persons engaged per unit.

[d] More than or equal to 10 and less than 50 persons engaged per unit.

[e] More than 50 persons per unit.

Sources: Ministry of Industry and Mines, *Trends in Industrial and Commercial Statistics* 1975(Q3), *Trends in Iranian Industrial Production* 1978, *Iranian Industrial Statistics* 1969, 1971, Central Bank, *Annual Reports* 1977, 1978.

the expansion of manufacturing employment increased from 72 per cent during the 1963–7 period to 79 per cent over 1973–7 (table 7.7).

A notable aspect of the process of structural change in the manufacturing sector was that the 5,000 or so medium-sized firms (with between ten to fifty employees) contributed no more than 10 per cent to employment generation in the sector throughout the period (table 7.7). One may expect that the combination of desirable features such as the labour intensity of production processes together with reasonable levels of labour productivity in these medium-sized firms would have made them ideal for generating some productive and gainful employment in a labour surplus economy like Iran. There were, however, various aspects of the industrial policy of the government which militated against the growth of this medium-sized manufacturing subsector. First, as we have already noted, the medium-sized firms were deprived of long-term subsidized finance, as almost the entire supply of long-term credits by the specialized banks was absorbed by the very large-scale enterprises. Secondly, the government provided no technical assis-

Table 7.8. *Key indicators in the corporate manufacturing sector 1966–1977[a]*

Indicators	1967 = 100			Average Annual Growth Rates	
	1966	1970	1977	1966–70	1970–7
Output	87	143	436	13.2	17.3
Employment	84	117	190	8.6	7.1
Productivity	103	122	231	4.6	10.2
Real wages [b]	97	114	237	4.1	11.0

Notes:

[a] Approximately corresponds to factories with more than 50 employees.

[b] Total wages and salaries bill per number of employees deflated by index of consumer prices.

Sources: Ministry of Industry and Mines 1976(Q1), *Trends in Industrial and Commercial Statistics.* Central Bank, *Annual Reports*, various issues.

tance to the medium-sized firms. The Industrial Development and Renovation Organization (IDRO), which was an extensive multi-million Rial government organization in charge of technical assistance to industry, mainly acted as a middle-man between the very large-scale domestic enterprises and the multinational companies in establishing joint ventures and licensing agreements (see IDRO, *Annual Report* 1974, 1975). Thirdly, the medium-sized firms had slender ties with the large-scale enterprises, either directly through subcontracting or indirectly through market mediated backward or forward linkages (see Radwan 1975). The large-scale enterprises in the corporate sector formed technological enclaves within the manufacturing sector depending for their raw material supplies and technology largely on imports (see the next chapter). This not only prevented the large-scale enterprises from acting as a vehicle for the diffusion of modern technology into the rest of the manufacturing sector, but also prevented the generation of demand for the rest of the sector through inter-industry linkages.[19] Finally, and related to the above point, the growth of the medium-sized sector may have been handicapped due to the competition in

[19] This situation is in sharp contrast to the case of Japan, where the medium- and small-sized firms have been making an important contribution to the industrialization process. The subcontracting relationship between the small- and large-scale industries in Japan is often quoted as an example of 'unequalled technical and managerial efficiency'. Of course government policy of acquiring foreign technology through combining selective imports with domestic research aimed at assimilating and developing the imported know-how, played an important role in the successful diffusion of modern technology in Japanese industry. See Sachs 1980, chapter 9, pp.188–240 and Kiga (1968).

Table 7.9. *Growth indicators of small-scale manufacturing 1964–1972*

Indicator	Average annual growth rates		
	1964–9	1969–72	1964–72
No. of workshops	9.7	5.5	8.1
Employment	8.8	8.2	8.6
Value added[a]	8.7	8.1	8.5
Productivity	−0.1	−0.1	−0.1

Note:
[a] Deflated by the wholesale price index.
Sources: Ministry of Industry and Mines, *Iranian Industrial Statistics* 1964, 1969, 1973.

the final product market from the highly subsidized and technologically dynamic corporate manufacturing sector.

Under these circumstances it fell upon the small-scale workshops (less than five employees) to provide the bulk of the new employment in the manufacturing sector. Ease of entry into this subsector and the possibility of work sharing through growing employment of family labour made it a repository for absorbing surplus labour[20] which could not find employment in the large-scale modern manufacturing sector.[21] The growth of this small-scale or informal manufacturing subsector therefore assumed an 'extensive' character – in the sense that it took the form of multiplication of the small workshops without major changes in their technology of production and productivity of labour. As it is shown in table 7.9, employment in the small-scale manufacturing grew *pari passu* with output and the number of workshops, with productivity of labour remaining stagnant.[22] This is in sharp contrast to the 'intensive' character of growth in the technologically dynamic corporate sector, which was characterized by rapid growth of labour productivity and real incomes. As long as there existed surplus labour in the economy one would expect the extensive character of growth

[20] Surplus labour here is defined in terms of extreme productivity differentials in the economy, with the implication that by extending the more advanced techniques known and used in the economy to the low productivity sector, labour could be removed from the sector without loss of output. This is a broader definition than the marginalist definition of the term in the sense of the existence of labour with zero marginal productivity.

[21] This point is further supported by the anti-cyclical movement of employment in the small sector during the recession of the early 1960s as shown in appendix M.1.

[22] In considering the negative productivity growth shown in the table, it should be kept in mind that the use of the wholesale price index for deflating the value added may have led to an underestimation of productivity growth. The use of the correct price index – which is not available – is unlikely to make a dramatic change in the results.

in the informal sector to continue, with its output growing with more or less the same pace as real incomes in the urban economy.[23]

Table 7.10 shows how the process of industrialization led to a growing intensification of the duality within the manufacturing sector, as is expressed in the widening gap between productivity and wages in the small-scale or informal manufacturing, and the rest of the sector – and at the same time increasing share of employment in the former. This, on the one hand, signified the fact that over the 1970s, a general shortage of labour could have hardly been a constraint to industrial growth. If anything, the problem as it presented itself in 1972 was how to generate sufficient employment in the economy in step with the growth in the supply of labour.[24] What appeared as a general shortage of labour during the 1974–6 period was a short-term phenomenon which occurred as a result of the abrupt and extremely large expansion in investment activity during the oil boom years.[25] As we have already pointed out this phenomenon which intensified the rate of introduction of labour-saving technology in the economy, if anything, intensified the problem of surplus labour from a long-term point of view. On the other hand, the growing industrial duality was an indication of the fact that the income gains from productivity growth were concentrated in the hands of a small section of the population consisting of the industrialists and workers in the corporate manufacturing sector. The growing concentration of income in turn reinforced the prevailing pattern

[23] This rate of growth depends on the income elasticity of demand for the informal sector's products. The stylized facts characterizing the 'extensive' type of growth in the informal sector of the urban economy could be formalized according to the following scenario. Assuming demand for the informal sector's output to be an increasing function of the urban sector's income as a whole, growth of the urban economy would lead to an increase in the value of output in the informal sector, and initially in the value productivity of labour and thus real incomes in that sector. This in turn induces the migration of the rural surplus labour to the urban areas, with the effect of increasing the number of workshops as well as employment in that sector. Final equilibrium is reinstated when labour productivity and real incomes in the informal sector are reduced to levels compatible with real incomes of the rural surplus labour. In the long run, with the depletion of rural surplus labour one would expect an increasing productivity of labour and real wages in small-scale manufacturing, as labour is gradually shifted into the modern sector and the products of the modern sector gradually substitute the goods and services hitherto provided by the low wage informal sector. For further elaboration of this scenario and some indication of the extent of rural surplus labour, see appendix M.1.

[24] Given the ILO (1972) estimate of 2.7 per cent natural rate of growth of the supply of labour, and assuming the trend in the productivity of labour in the economy as a whole would have remained the same as during the 1964–72 period, then a minimum rate of growth of GNP of 11 per cent was necessary to create enough employment for the new entrants to the labour market during the 1970s.

[25] In 1975, for example, total fixed investment in real terms increased by 64.6 per cent. Considering the time which is needed for both spacial and occupational movement of labour, such a massive shock was bound to produce a general shortage of labour, amongst other things.

Table 7.10. *Size composition of the manufacturing sector, urban areas 1964–1972*

	Share of value added		Share of employment[b]		Labour productivity		Wages of operatives		Ave. employee per plant[b]	
	1964	1972	1964	1972	1964	1972	1964	1972	1964	1972
Large[a]	56	65	34	32	169	184	133	138	51.2	54.7
Small	44	35	66	68	66	54	77	69	3.0	2.9
Total	100	100	100	100	100	100	100	100	4.4	4.5

Notes:
[a] Large establishments refer to those with employment of ten or more.
[b] Total persons engaged.
Sources: Ministry of Industry and Mines, *Iranian Industrial Statistics* 1964, 1972.

of structural change in the industrial sector by expanding the market for new products, in particular the new durable consumer goods, which originated in the rapid growth and diversification of consumer demand of high income groups. The question of growth and pattern of consumption, however, involves broader issues related to the availability of oil income and its contribution to the financing of investment in the economy as a whole. It is to these issues which we shall now turn before considering the specific implications of the structure of final demand for industrial growth.

7.6 Financing accumulation and the growth of consumption

The availability of ample supplies of external funds over this period, i.e., oil income and foreign capital, meant that capital formation could take place without the need to curtail the growth of consumption in the short run. In fact the use of external resources to finance the imports of capital goods for investment would have automatically increased the supply of savings in the economy as well. As is shown in table 7.11, the rapid acceleration of the rate of investment in the domestic economy, from 20 per cent in 1963 to about 47 per cent in 1977, went hand in hand with the very fast rate of growth of consumption both in the public and in the private sectors. Private consumption in real terms grew by about 8 per cent per annum over the 1960s and 14 per cent over the 1970s, while government consumption maintained a very high rate of growth close to 20 per cent throughout this period.[26] This phenomenon was only possible as a result of increasing reliance on external resources to finance domestic expenditure. As the last row of table 7.11 shows, this allowed an excess of domestic expenditure over domestic non-oil income of about 9 per cent in 1963, increasing to about 17 per cent in 1970 and 40 per cent in 1977.

The high rates of growth of consumption in this period gave rise to a rapid expansion of the domestic market. This in turn provided the demand for private industry which grew within the protected home market. However, the same phenomenon, namely the ease of access to external resources in financing capital formation, also contributed to the development of a lopsided pattern of consumption which had a profound effect on the structure of manufacturing growth and the nature of industries which developed over this period. The aim of this section is to examine the way the government through its direct income generating policies, namely its revenue raising and expenditure policies, affected the distribution of income and consumption in the economy.

[26] The question of whether such fast rates of growth of consumption were the inevitable by-products of the need to increasingly rely on external resources due to the balance of payments constraints, or whether they represented an excessive reliance on external resources to supplement domestic savings is discussed in the next chapter.

Table 7.11. *Composition of gross national expenditure 1963–1977*

	% Share of non-oil GDP[a]			Average annual growth rates	
	1963	1970	1977	1963–70	1970–7
Gross fixed capital formation					
Private sector	11.6	10.4	20.7	8.1	25.7
Public sector	8.0	15.4	26.0	20.5	22.7
Total	19.6	25.2	46.7	14.1	24.0
Consumption					
Private sector	77.3	68.6	69.1	7.9	14.0
Public sector	12.2	22.2	32.0	19.6	20.4
Total	89.5	90.9	102.0	10.0	15.8
Total domestic expenditure	109.1	116.7	140.0	10.8	16.9

Note:
[a] In real 1959 prices.
Sources: Central Bank, *Annual Report* various issues.

7.6.1 Oil revenues and income generation by the state

An important aspect of public finances over this period was the growing share of oil revenues in financing government expenditure and the low tax effort by the government. The share of oil revenues in total government revenue increased from about 50 per cent during the third plan period to more than 75 per cent over the fifth plan, while domestic taxes remained generally below 10 per cent of the GNP and showed little buoyancy (table 7.12). One implication of this was the relatively large and rapidly widening gap between government expenditure and its tax revenues, i.e., the domestic budget deficit. As is shown in table 7.12 the domestic budget deficit which represented a net generation of new incomes by the state increased from about 11 per cent to 32 per cent of the GNP between the third and fifth plan periods. The impact of the state budget on income distribution, therefore, is expected to have been mainly through the distribution of new incomes generated by the state itself, rather than a redistribution of the income generated in the private sector, as is largely the case in non-oil economies. In other words, the expenditure policy of the government is expected to have had a much more important bearing on income distribution than its taxation policy. Nevertheless, it would be illuminating to examine the

Table 7.12. *Consolidated public sector accounts 1963–1977^a*

(Per cent of GNP)

	1963–67	1968–72	1973–77
I Total income	16.7	21.5	41.0
(oil income)^b	(8.5)	(11.8)	(31.0)
(Non-oil income)^c	(8.2)	(9.7)	(10.0)
II Current expenditure^d	12.4	15.9	27.5
III Savings (I–II)	4.3	5.5	13.5
IV Capital expenditure^e	6.8	10.5	14.2
V Public sector deficit	2.5	5.0	0.7
(excluding oil income)	(10.6)	(16.8)	(32.3)
VI Financing – domestic	2.1	3.1	3.7
– foreign^f	0.4	1.9	− 3.0

Notes:
^{a} Excludes extra-budgetary accounts of the government and the budget of municipalities.
^{b} Refers to government income from the oil export sector only.
^{c} Includes all forms of taxes plus revenues from government property, exchange differentials and revenues from public enterprises and agencies.
^{d} Includes interest payments and recurrent expenditures of the Plan Organization.
^{e} Excludes recurrent expenditures.
^{f} Includes foreign investment by the government.
Sources: Central Bank, *Annual Report* various issues. World Bank, *Economic Development of Iran* 1974.

incidence of taxation – if only to form some idea of the untapped potential which existed for increasing the tax yield in the economy.

Table 7.13 presents a breakdown of central government taxes by major categories, and shows the increase in real per-capita GNP over the 1963–77 period.[27] As can be seen, despite a more than four-fold increase in real per-capita GNP, central government tax revenues remained relatively low in relation to national income and exhibited a low degree of buoyancy. A further outstanding feature of the tax structure was the very low share of direct taxes and within that the relatively low burden of taxes on property income and business profits. It is estimated that in 1965 the effective rate of

[27] The data in the table exclude the budget of the municipalities, and the central government's social security funds and extra-budgetary accounts. These are, however, very small in relation to the central government's budget. For example, in 1972 the tax revenues of the municipalities formed about 2.7 per cent of total government revenues, while the revenue of the other two budgets respectively were no more than 2.7 and 4.1 per cent of total revenues (see IMF, *Government Finance Statistics Yearbook* 1981).

Table 7.13. *Real per-capita income and central government tax revenues by major taxes 1963–1977[a]*

(Per cent of GNP)

Year	Per-capita income[b] (000 Rials)	Total taxes	Direct taxes			Indirect taxes			
			Total[c]	Private individuals income tax[d]	Corporate profit tax	Total	Import taxes[e]	Excise taxes[f]	Other taxes[g]
1963	14.8	8.0	1.1	0.5	0.1	6.9	2.6	1.2	3.1
1964	15.2	7.1	1.0	0.5	0.1	6.1	2.5	1.3	2.3
1965	16.6	8.1	1.3	0.5	0.2	6.8	2.6	1.3	2.9
1966	17.6	8.5	1.3	0.5	0.2	7.2	3.0	1.5	2.7
1967	19.2	9.1	1.4	0.5	0.2	7.7	3.3	1.5	2.9
1968	21.0	9.3	1.4	0.7	0.4	7.8	3.5	1.5	2.9
1969	22.3	9.3	1.7	0.8	0.5	7.6	3.5	1.6	2.5
1970	24.4	10.0	1.9	0.7	0.6	8.0	3.6	1.6	2.8
1971	28.5	9.9	1.9	1.0	0.5	8.0	3.6	1.6	2.9
1972	30.6	9.7	2.0	1.0	0.7	7.7	3.6	1.3	2.8
1973	41.3	7.9	1.7	0.8	0.6	6.3	3.1	1.1	2.0
1974	53.8	6.0	1.2	0.5	0.5	4.8	2.0	0.9	1.9
1975	54.0	9.5	1.5	0.7	0.6	8.0	2.6	0.9	4.5
1976	58.7	9.6	1.9	0.9	0.7	7.7	2.8	0.9	4.0
1977	58.1	10.6	2.3	1.0	1.1	8.4	3.4	1.1	4.0

Notes:

[a] Excludes special revenues of the central government, central government's social security funds and the municipalities taxes.

[b] In real 1959 prices.

[c] Includes real estate and inheritance taxes plus the other direct taxes shown in the table.

[d] Tax on wages and salaries and professions.

[e] Includes customs duties and commercial profits tax and import registration fees.

[f] Includes stamp duties.

[g] Includes receipts from government's sale of goods and services, revenues from government property, exchange differential, and revenues from public enterprises and agencies including public sector corporate profit tax.

Sources: As in table 7.12.

tax on incomes derived from property and from corporate and incorporated enterprises was about 1.5 per cent, as against 7–8 per cent on wages and salaries.[28] Though published data on the sources of income and taxation are not adequate to make similar estimates for the later years, our rough estimates based on the Central Bank's data on factor shares in national income indicate that this situation did not radically change over the period.[29]

The final incidence of taxation of course depended on the ability of different social groups to shift the burden of taxes to others through changing the price or the quantity of goods and services which they offered in the market. The mere fact that the bulk of taxes took the form of indirect taxes also did not necessarily imply a regressive tax structure: for example, the import taxes which largely fell on goods with high income elasticity of demand were likely to introduce an element of progressiveness into the tax system, while excise duties which were 90 per cent composed of fuel taxes were likely to fall more severely on low income groups. The only study which exists on the incidence of taxation in Iran is that of Mehran (1975), which measures tax incidence according to the size distribution of household incomes under eight different sets of incidence assumptions for the year 1971. Since the results only marginally differ between the different variants in Mehran's study, we have here reported one of his middle estimates of tax incidence which is shown in table 7.14. As the table shows the incidence of taxation is almost uniform amongst the income groups, being only marginally progressive for the bottom poorest and the top richest household deciles.[30] The table also provides data on average household income and consumption expenditure which help to highlight the great untapped potential which existed in the economy for increasing tax revenues by only marginal increases in the effective tax rates on high income groups. It is not difficult to calculate on the basis of the data shown in the

[28] See Kaldor 1968.
[29] Our approximate estimates for 1972 indicate an effective tax rate on wages and salaries of about 8 per cent, as against 3–4 per cent rate for property and business profit taxes in the non-agricultural private sector. These estimates are based on Central Bank's estimates of the share of gross profits, rents and interest income in private industry and services value added (see Central Bank, *Annual Report* 1974). These are rough estimates because of the deficiencies in Central Bank's factor share data, where no allowance is made for self-employed income and there is no indication whether these have been lumped with property income or with labour income. Here we have assumed that these are included in property income and thus the above 3–4 per cent estimate also includes the tax on the self-employed. It is important to note that both in these estimates and in Kaldor's estimates reported above, unearned income through capital gains has not been included in property incomes.
[30] The impact of taxation on income distribution under all the eight sets of incidence assumptions reported in Mehran's study is very marginal. The incidence of taxation reduces the GINI coefficient of expenditure inequality by 0.01 in its most progressive version, and by 0.004 in its least progressive version.

Table 7.14. *The incidence of taxation 1971*

Deciles[a]	% tax[c] incidence	Average income[b] (000 Rials)	Average expenditure (000 Rials)
Lowest 1st	9.8	19.2	19.5
2nd	7.9	34.6	31.9
3rd	7.4	46.4	41.4
4th	7.3	56.9	49.7
5th	7.3	71.3	60.4
6th	7.5	87.5	71.3
7th	7.7	113.6	92.1
8th	7.4	156.7	115.1
9th	8.1	241.4	160.1
10th	9.0	545.7	346.8
All classes	8.3	137.3	98.8

Notes:
[a] Households ranked from the lowest to highest consumption expenditure.
[b] Household broad annual income corresponding to net national income at market prices.
[c] Corresponds to middle incidence variant (D1) in the source.
Source: Mehran 1975.

table that, for example, only a 3 per cent increase in the effective tax rate on the richest 10 per cent of the households was sufficient to finance the removal of the entire taxes on the lowest 60 per cent of households and at the same time maintain the rate of savings in the economy (assuming the same average saving propensities would be maintained). Alternatively, a 3 per cent increase in the effective tax rate on the top 10 per cent of households would have been sufficient to increase national savings by an amount equivalent to more than 8 per cent of total private investment in 1971.[31] The saving propensities implicit in the data in table 7.14 and used in the above illustrative examples may be criticized on the grounds of being based on a

[31] These estimates should be treated only as illustrative examples where the margin of error may be large. There are no reliable data available on the distribution of income and savings for different household groups in Iran. Mehran's estimates reported in table 7.14 are based on household consumer expenditure data, where he assumes Pareto type functional forms for the distribution of income and consumption expenditures to derive the average propensities to save for households at each decile of the expenditure distribution. The results are finally scaled up to match the Central Bank's National Accounts estimates of income and consumption (see Mehran 1975a). Even if we allow a large margin of error, however, the results are striking enough to convey the point which is being made.

hypothetical saving function rather than being based on hard data; nevertheless the extreme concentration of consumption expenditure in the top 20 per cent of households combined with the evidence of extremely low tax yields, particularly on property and business income, incidate the potential for substantially increasing national savings through taxation without any extra burden on 80 per cent of households in lower income categories over this period.

On the basis of the above evidence one can point out the salient features of the tax system over the period under study as follows. First, the overall tax yield was low and tax revenues played an increasingly less significant part in financing government expenditure over time. Secondly, the incidence of the tax system was uniform and did not play a major part in redistributing income in the economy – with the prevailing low effective tax yields, even an extremely progressive tax system was not likely to exert a major impact on income distribution. Thirdly, there existed a great untapped potential for increasing national savings through taxation, particularly if these could be made to fall on the consumption of high income groups.

Government expenditure is expected to have exerted a more important impact than taxation on income distribution, due to its much larger size over this period. Here we shall be mainly concerned with the impact of government consumption expenditure. The impact of the development expenditure of the government in this regard works through the long-term structural changes which it creates in the economy, and its benefits are likely to be spread over many years, which make a quantitative estimation of its incidence amongst different income groups problematic.[32]

The incidence of the government consumption expenditure for the year 1971 is estimated by Mehran (1977), where he attempts to allocate the benefits from public consumption amongst the different income groups of households. As is common with such studies the benefits from categories of public expenditure are equated to the value of services provided, and measured by the net cost of their provision by the state. Though this approach has various limitations, some of which are pointed out by Mehran himself, the study nevertheless provides valuable information on different types of government expenditure and their main beneficiaries, however approximate one may assume the actual decile estimates of incidence to be.[33] Within this approach a distinction must be made between two types of

[32] For these reasons we have examined the impact of the development expenditure on income distribution in sections of the book which deal with the process of structural change in the agricultural and manufacturing sectors.

[33] For a critical review of the literature on fiscal incidence in developing countries, see De Wulf (1975).

government consumption expenditure. First is the specific or productive expenditure, such as expenditure on education and health, where the services provided could be in principle traced to particular segments of the population which benefit from them. The second type is the general or unproductive expenditure, such as general administration and defence where such an exercise in principle is not possible without resorting to certain controversial assumptions. As can be seen from table 7.15, between 60 and 70 per cent of government consumption expenditure over the 1963–77 period was absorbed by the general expenditure category, with the share of military expenditure rising from 27 per cent to almost 50 per cent of the total over the period. In estimating the incidence of the benefits of government consumption expenditure, Mehran (1977) includes the 'benefits' from these general expenditures under five alternative sets of assumptions covering a least progressive case, three middle cases, and a most progressive case of incidence.[34] However, since due to the relatively large size of these general expenditures the overall result becomes highly sensitive to the particular assumptions being made, and as these assumptions remain ultimately *ad hoc* and in any case very controversial, we shall here only concentrate on the incidence of the specific or the productive category of government expenditures. In table 7.16 we have calculated the incidence of government's specific expenditures on three consumer expenditure groups, namely the poorest 60 per cent, the top 40 per cent and the richest 20 per cent of households, on the basis of Mehran's estimates for 1971. As the table shows, a representative household in the top 20 per cent income group in absolute terms benefitted six times more than that in the lowest 60 per cent group, and with the exception of health expenditure the major share of benefits accrued to the top 40 per cent, and within that particularly to the top 20 per cent of income groups.[35] The reasons for the larger share of public consumption being absorbed by the wealthier households varies according to the type of public sector expenditure. In the case of education, for example, the wealthier households in the urban areas accounted for a much higher share of students in secondary and higher education and thus

[34] These sets of assumptions are the following: general government expenditure is divided between different household expenditure groups according to: (i) the number of households in each expenditure group, (ii) average expenditure in each group, (iii) half according to the number of households and half according to average expenditure, (iv) average income in each group and (v) square of average income in each household expenditure group.

[35] In comparing the net benefits in absolute terms, across the different household deciles allowance should be made for the average size of households. With the broad decile groups considered above, however, the average size of the household should not make a big difference to the results. In 1972, for example, the average size for the bottom 60 per cent of household groups was 5.1 as against 6.1 for the top 40 per cent.

Table 7.15. *Composition of central government consumption expenditure 1963–1977[a]*

(Percentages)

	1963	1970	1976
General expenditure	62.7	68.9	68.1
General administration[b]	36.0	30.9	19.6
Military expenditure	26.7	38.0	48.5
Specific expenditure	37.3	31.1	31.8
Education	21.1	14.6	12.2
Health	4.2	4.2	4.5
Social welfare	0.6	1.1	1.7
Agriculture[c]	1.3	2.5	6.6
Transport and communication	5.3	3.3	1.1
Miscellaneous[d]	4.6	5.3	9.1
Total	100.0	100.0	100.0
(bn Rials)	(47.2)	(135.2)	(1170.0)

Notes:

[a] Excludes extra budgetary accounts and local governments budget.

[b] Includes interest payments.

[c] Mainly consists of food subsidies.

[d] Consists of art and culture, physical education, manpower, urban and rural development, public utilities, commerce, mining and housing, environmental and regional development.

Sources: Plan and Budget Organization, *The Budget 1977–78.* World Bank, *Economic Development of Iran* 1974.

on average absorbed a larger share of benefits from free public education. Social welfare expenditure was almost totally composed of transfers to the pension fund of civil servants which belonged to the upper income groups. Expenditures under the title of agriculture in the table essentially consisted of food subsidies. As the richer households consumed more food in absolute terms they absorbed on average more of the benefits of food subsidies than the poorer ones. In the case of transport, communications and public utilities also the wealthier households were the main beneficiaries as they naturally made higher use of such facilities.[36] Despite the concentration of the benefits in absolute terms in the higher income groups, the incidence of

---

[36] For further elaboration of these points and a detailed discussion of the distribution of public consumption amongst the household expenditure deciles, see Mehran (1977).

Table 7.16. *Distribution of public consumption benefits and taxes by household decile 1971*

Household expenditure decile	Average per household (Rls/year)				Per cent share of benefit/tax				Incidence of benefit/tax[e]			
	Lowest 60%	Top 40%	Top 20%	Total	Lowest 60%	Top 40%	Top 20%	Total	Lowest 60%	Top 40%	Top 20%	Total
Type of public consumption[a]												
Education	2656	7019	10105	4401	36.2	63.8	45.9	100.0	5.0	1.8	1.6	2.4
Health	1232	974	849	1129	65.5	34.5	15.0	100.0	2.2	0.2	0.1	0.6
Social welfare	317	2051	3415	1010	18.8	81.2	67.6	100.0	0.4	0.6	0.5	0.5
Agriculture[b]	805	1372	1773	1032	46.8	53.2	34.3	100.0	1.4	0.3	0.4	0.5
Transport and com.	127	1962	3517	861	8.9	91.1	81.7	100.0	0.2	0.5	0.5	0.5
Miscellaneous[c]	610	4113	6253	2012	18.2	81.8	62.1	100.0	1.1	1.1	1.0	1.1
Total benefit[a]	5440	17390	26039	10460	33.5	66.5	49.8	100.0	10.3	4.5	4.1	5.6
Taxes	4380	31733	52594	15476	17.0	83.0	67.9	100.0	8.3	8.2	8.3	8.3
Net benefit[d]	1060	−14343	−26555	−5016	—	—	—	—	2.0	−4.3	−4.2	−2.7

Notes:
[a] Excludes general administration and defence expenditures.
[b] Largely consists of food subsidies.
[c] Includes art and culture, physical education, manpower, urban and rural development, public utilities, tourism, commerce, industry, mining and housing. Also includes interest payments.
[d] Total specific benefits minus taxes.
[e] Percentage ratio of benefit over broad income of each class as defined in table 7.14.
Source: Estimated from Mehran 1977.

public consumption was still progressive, in the sense of the share of benefits in household income being higher for the lower income households (table 7.16). This was due to the extremely skewed distribution of income amongst the households.[37] The table also shows the incidence of public consumption net of taxes, which indicates a 2 per cent net benefit for the lowest 60 per cent of households and negative net benefit for the rest of the groups. On the whole the net fiscal incidence of government specific consumption expenditure in 1971 was negative.[38] This was not surprising in view of the fact that the major share of government consumption expenditure was absorbed by general expenditure and in particular military expenditure.

In sum, the net incidence of government specific expenditure and taxes appears to have had only a small redistributive impact in 1971.[39] As to the changes of net incidence over time, there is no evidence which may suggest a dramatic change in this situation. While on the one hand the share of public expenditure on items with strong redistributive impact, such as education, declined over the period under investigation (see table 7.15), on the other hand the overall increase in government specific expenditure as a share of GNP may have counter balanced this by improving the net redistributive impact of the budget. On the basis of the existing evidence it may be plausible to assume that over the period as a whole there was a mild improvement in the redistributive effect of the net fiscal incidence as a result of the faster growth of government specific expenditures in relation to the GNP, particularly in the oil boom of the 1970s.

In the absence of deliberate policy intervention by the government aimed at redistribution of income through specific fiscal measures, there is no reason to believe that government budget, irrespective of its size, would have automatically served such a purpose.[40] This is particularly true in the case of an oil-exporting economy such as Iran: as in other economies where the growth of public expenditure has to be largely financed through taxation, there may be an in-built progressive element in the incidence of the budget as a result of the fact that high taxes cannot be afforded by the low income groups and have to be procured from high income classes. In oil-exporting economies like Iran, where a growing resort may be made to oil revenues to finance government expenditures such in-built pressures to tax

---

[37] While the lowest 60 per cent of households accounted for 33.5 per cent of public consumption, their income share was merely 17.0 per cent.

[38] This, however, is not the net fiscal incidence of public expenditure as it excludes investment expenditure and the general consumption expenditures.

[39] The impact of the net incidence of specific expenditure and taxes was to reduce the Gini coefficient of income inequality by 0.03 in 1971.

[40] Though the objective of a more equal distribution of income was mentioned in various government plan and budget documents (usually in the introduction), no specific policy measures were formulated with income redistribution as their aim.

the high income groups would be relaxed.[41] In such economies, therefore, the need for devising specific fiscal measures to alleviate income inequalities becomes paramount. The relatively large share of public sector expenditure in such economies also is not likely to bring about a drastic change in income distribution. The reason is that the higher income groups which are in a more privileged position to take advantage of public services, are likely to appropriate the *major* share of benefits from public expenditure.[42] Under such circumstances the setting up of an effective tax system appears to be an essential prerequisite for bringing about a reduction in income inequality through fiscal measures.

7.6.2 Distribution of consumption expenditure and the structure of the home market

The different aspects of the development process over the period under investigation contributed to the concentration of income in the hands of a narrow section of the population whose consumption pattern dominated the structure of the home market. As we noted in the previous chapter, the developments in the agricultural sector on the one hand led to a worsening distribution of income in the rural economy, and on the other hand gave rise to a growing number of underemployed landless labourers and very poor peasant farmers with low productivity and a meagre standard of living. The rapid flow of rural migrant labour into the urban areas, combined with high natural rates of population growth, led to a fast expansion of the urban labour force which could be only marginally absorbed in the modern industrial sector. The industrial policies of the government which encouraged the concentration of industrial investment in a relatively small number of highly capital intensive modern plants with little backward linkages to the rest of the economy, further exacerbated the problem of labour absorption in the industrial sector. The outcome of these processes as we have seen was a growing duality within the industrial sector, where a relatively small segment of the labour force was employed in the high productivity, high wage and technologically dynamic modern sector, while the major part of the labour force was absorbed by the informal sector with stagnant labour productivity and low incomes. Industrial development in this way gave rise to a concentration of income in the hands of a relatively small section of the

[41] This important feature of oil countries which was first analytically discussed by Kalecki (1966) in his paper on financing economic development, has been unfortunately totally lost in the recent literature on oil countries which has been dominated by the neo-classical issues of 'crowding out'.

[42] If, as was the case of Iran, a large share of government expenditure is absorbed by unproductive activities such as military and internal security, then the redistribution impact of government expenditure would be even less.

urban population consisting of the rentiers, capitalists and wage and salary earners in the modern sector of the urban economy. The excessive reliance of the government on oil revenues and foreign loans to finance its expenditure further exacerbated these tendencies towards growing income concentration, by removing the need to tax the high income groups.

Under these circumstances it would not be surprising to find a worsening distribution of income in the urban areas, similar to what we observed in the rural sector. The various studies which exist on income distribution in Iran, all indicate a highly unequal distribution of income by international standards, as well as rapidly growing income disparities both in the urban sector and in the country as a whole.[43] Since accurate data on either functional or personal distribution of income in Iran are not available, all these studies have used the distribution of household consumption expenditure as a proxy for income distribution. We have estimated a set of summary statistics on distribution of household expenditure in urban areas, on the basis of both the Central Bank and the Central Statistical Office (CSO) household budget surveys, which is shown in table 7.17. These results extend the period of coverage of the above studies by including the 1974–7 period, and slightly differ from the results in the above studies due to the different method of estimation used.[44] The estimates in the table confirm the conclusions of the earlier studies indicating widening disparities in the distribution of con-- sumption expenditure in the urban areas, and in particular a high and rapidly growing concentration of expenditure in the top 20 per cent of households.[45] Of course, given the higher concentration of savings expected in the top income groups, one would expect a much higher degree of inequality in the distribution of income as compared to the distribution of

[43] See Oshima (1973), World Bank (1974, vol.1), Mehran (1975a), Pesaran (1976), Pesaran and Ghahvary (1978) and Azimi (1980). Oshima's paper focussed on household income and expenditure distribution for the year 1970, and World Bank (1974) analyses income distribution for 1972. Mehran (1975a) discusses the availability of data on income distribution and gives a review of the findings of other studies. Pesaran (1976) and Pesaran and Ghahvary (1978) discuss the trends in income distribution in the country for the 1959–74 period. Azimi (1980) provides different measures of poverty and investigates income distribution trends for 1959–72.

[44] Our measures differ slightly from the above studies because of the new method of estimation of inequality indices from grouped data adopted here. The above studies use the linear interpolation method which assumes that inequality of income within each income range is zero. Here we have used the method suggested by Kakwani (1976), which involves fitting third degree polynomial curves to group expenditure intervals and Pareto curves to two open ended intervals. The application of this method to Australian income distribution data by Kakwani (1980, chapter 6) showed that it achieves a close approximation to results derived on the basis of individual data.

[45] The difference in the results derived from the Central Bank and the CSO household budget surveys is due to the different sampling procedures adopted and the different coverage of the urban population in the two surveys. The trends towards growing inequality are, however, confirmed by both surveys over the period shown in the table.

Table 7.17. *Indicators of inequality of consumption expenditure, urban area 1959–1977*

	GINI[a]	Share of top 20%	Share of middle 40%	Share of bottom 40%
Central bank surveys				
1959	0.4681	52.1	27.6	13.8
1969	0.4797	55.8	27.4	12.9
1974	0.5219	56.5	25.1	10.9
1975	0.5383	57.7	27.9	9.1
CSO surveys				
1972	0.4128	46.7	29.9	15.9
1973	0.4602	51.3	27.6	14.0
1974	0.5152	54.8	26.4	12.3
1977	0.5210	57.1	25.6	11.5

Note:

[a] The GINI coefficients and decile shares have been calculated by fitting cumulative distribution curves to the group data given in the sources below. Pareto distribution curves were fitted to the lowest and the highest open intervals and third degree polynomials to the rest of the intervals. Methods of fitting the curves as in Kakwani (1980).

Sources: Central Bank and CSO, *Household Budget Survey of Urban Areas* various issues.

expenditure. But assuming stable savings ratios for the different household expenditure groups, the trends of expenditure distribution in the table could be taken as a close proxy for income distribution trends as well. Since here we are mainly concerned with the impact of income distribution on the structure of demand, the expenditure data would in any case provide a better indicator for our purpose.

The distribution of income and its changes over time are among the important factors affecting the evolution of private consumer demand and the structure of the domestic market. This in turn is expected to have a decisive effect on the pattern of resource use in the economy as a whole. In the development economics literature, the effect of income distribution on the pattern of consumption in particular and the overall pattern of resource use in general is normally analysed in terms of the dichotomy between the 'essentials' or 'mass consumer goods', and the 'non-essentials' or 'luxury consumer goods' which form the conspicuous consumption of the higher income groups. It is argued that an unequal distribution of income would lead to a lopsided pattern of consumption dominated by the luxury consumer goods, which leads to a diversion of resources from the production of essential wage goods and producer goods and undermines the long-term growth potential of the economy (Kalecki 1979, Bharadwaj 1972, Abdel-Fadil 1980, Sachs 1980). Such arguments have been subject to criticism for being based on a closed economy framework. It may be argued that in an open economy the so-called luxury consumer goods by having a higher income elasticity of demand could achieve a better export performance than the mass consumer goods and thus prove to be more beneficial for the long-term growth performance of the economy (Borpujari 1983). A decisive factor in this argument is the extent to which the size and structure of the domestic market for different products allows the establishment of an efficient size of plant which could reap the full benefits of the economies of scale, and furthermore the extent to which the efficiency gains in production are translated into competitive prices which may induce export growth. This would require a more detailed analysis at product level, taking into account not only the level of demand at a given moment of time but also the evolution of the structure of demand over time.

The evolution of the structure of final consumer demand in Iran over this period could be viewed as the outcome of the combination of two factors: namely, the concentration of consumption expenditure in the top income groups, and the widening income disparities over time which entailed a higher than average rate of growth of consumption for these groups. The combination of these factors implied that the *growth* of total private consumption expenditure was largely dominated by the *increase* in the consumption of the high income groups. This point is highlighted by the data on growth of real consumption expenditure for the 1959–77 period which are presented in table 7.18. The table shows the growth of real household expenditure, as well as the percentage contribution to total increase in real consumption by broad household expenditure decile groups.[46] As can be seen, the combination of rapid rates of growth of average household consumption and high initial expenditure shares by the top income groups meant that the increase in consumption by these groups almost totally dominated the increase in final consumer demand. The top 40 per cent of household expenditure groups accounted for between 84 per cent

---

[46] The contribution of an expenditure decile group to the total growth of consumption is defined as the absolute increase in the decile expenditure as a percentage of increase in the absolute value of total expenditure. Since the number of households in each decile group increases at the same rate, these also correspond to the contribution of each decile group to average household consumption.

Table 7.18. *Growth of average household consumption expenditure, urban areas 1959–1977*

Household expenditure deciles[b]	Real average annual growth rates[a]		% contribution to growth of total expenditure	
	1959–71	1972–77	1959–71	1972–77
Top 20 per cent	4.2	16.0	69.8	69.0
Top 40 per cent	3.9	13.7	88.7	84.0
Middle 40 per cent	2.4	9.3	19.1	22.3
Bottom 40 per cent	1.4	5.2	5.3	6.2
Total	3.3	12.3	100.0	100.0

Notes:
[a] Real average household consumption is calculated by deflating average consumption of each household decile by its own consumer price deflator calculated on the basis of Central Bank's disaggregated price series and weights from household consumer expenditure surveys.
[b] Method of estimation of household decile expenditure as in table 7.17.
Sources: For 1959–71, Central Bank, *Household Budget Surveys of Urban Areas* 1959, 1971. For 1972–77, CSO, *Household Budget Surveys of Urban Areas* 1973, 1977.

to nearly 90 per cent of the total increase in consumption over the 1972–7 and 1959–71 periods respectively, while the contribution of the bottom 60 per cent of households was between 16 and 10 per cent over the same period. As one moves towards the top of the consumer expenditure scale this phenomenon could be observed with even higher intensity. For example, as it is shown in the table, the top 20 per cent of income groups accounted for nearly 70 per cent of the increase in total consumption, while the remaining 80 per cent of households were responsible for only 30 per cent of the increase in total consumer demand.

The growth of consumption of the high income groups is expected to have been fastest for consumer durables and high quality non-durable consumer goods with high income elasticities of demand, and in particular the new consumer products which were being introduced into the market at a rapid pace over this period. In fact, without the introduction of new products, in particular new household durable goods, such as different types of motor cars, television sets and other household electrical appliances, the fast rates of growth of average household consumption reported in table 7.18 were unlikely to be sustained over these years. Without such new products the average household consumption of the top income groups was bound to stabilize after a stage, as their needs with regard to the existing products became satiated. The available data do not allow a detailed study of the nature of the diffusion of the different consumer products among different income groups over time. The data presented in table 7.19, which give estimates of the distribution of certain groups of consumer durables, provides a snapshot of the extent of diffusion of these new consumer products for the year 1972.[47] As can be seen, more than 90 per cent of consumption of these commodities was concentrated in the top 30 per cent of households, and in particular the top 10 per cent accounted for between 50 to 80 per cent of expenditure for different products. Given the much faster rates of growth of consumption of the top income groups, they must have clearly accounted for a higher share of the *increase* of final consumer demand for these product groups than the expenditure share figures shown in the table.

It appears, therefore, that the growth of final consumer demand, specially for the new products which formed the market of the modern dynamic subsector of manufacturing production, was dominated by the consumption of a relatively small section of urban households. This meant that to sustain the growth of consumption it was necessary to continuously introduce new varieties of consumer goods to cater for the higher wants of the rich consumers, as the limited degree of diffusion of the new products amongst the majority of low income groups implied a relatively rapid satiation of the market for each new type of good. In other words the characteristics of income distribution never allowed the market for new manufacturing products to become a mass consumption market.[48] The expansion of consumer demand under these conditions is expected to assume a tendency towards increasing varieties of goods, each with a relatively limited size of market, rather than the expansion of the market through deeper diffusion of the existing products. This would imply a tendency towards fragmentation of the market instead of the strengthening of the mass consumer goods market.

The growth and structure of final consumer demand was bound to exert a

---

[47] Unfortunately for the later years the CSO household budget surveys are published at a higher level of aggregation, which does not allow a comparison of the rates of diffusion over time.

[48] The need to introduce new products in order to sustain the momentum of growth in a technologically progressive economy which is experiencing a continuous growth of per-capita incomes is emphasized in Pasinetti (1981). This implies that the growth of consumer demand in a growing economy with stationary distribution of income takes place as a result of the combinations of two factors; namely the diffusion of the existing products in successively lower income brackets, and the introduction of entirely new products. The point made above is that, due to the concentration of income gains from productivity growth in a narrow section of the population in Iran, it was the latter process which dominated the growth of consumption.

Table 7.19. *Average monthly household expenditure on selected durable consumer goods*, urban areas 1972

Expenditure decile[a]	Vehicles[b] Rials	%	Radio and TV[c] Rials	%	Refrigerators[d] Rials	%	Carpets[e] Rials	%
Lowest 1st	1.5	0.1	0.0	0.0	0.0	0.0	0.6	0.0
2nd	1.7	0.1	0.2	0.0	0.5	0.1	1.2	0.1
3rd	3.7	0.2	3.6	0.5	1.6	0.3	4.1	0.3
4th	12.4	0.7	8.7	1.3	7.8	1.5	13.1	0.8
5th	16.6	1.0	10.6	1.7	10.6	2.1	17.6	1.1
6th	22.6	1.3	25.1	4.0	21.5	4.1	37.6	2.4
7th	30.0	1.7	43.1	6.9	35.1	6.8	62.3	4.0
8th	85.9	4.9	73.4	11.7	77.5	15.0	79.5	5.0
9th	178.2	10.3	131.3	21.0	79.5	15.4	121.1	7.7
10th	1385.3	79.7	328.4	52.6	283.5	54.8	1229.8	78.5
Total	173.7	100.0	62.4	100.0	51.8	100.0	156.7	100.0

Notes:
[a] Household decile expenditure shares are derived from grouped data by linear interpolation between group averages given in household budget surveys.
[b] Includes motor cars, motor cycles, bicycles and their cost of repair and maintenance.
[c] Includes tape recorders and record players.
[d] Includes all electrical kitchen appliances including washing machines.
[e] Includes all types of floor coverings.
Sources: CSO *Household Budget Survey of Urban Areas* 1972.

significant impact on the structure of the manufacturing sector as private manufacturing relied almost totally on domestic consumer demand for its market. One discernible implication of the fragmentation of the market was the tendency towards the development of a 'branch economy', whereby numerous assembly plants were set up to cater for the increasing varieties of new consumer goods demanded by the high income classes.[49] The small size of the market made it difficult for these plants, which in the first instance were established with a limited time horizon and with a view to quick profits, to go beyond the assembly plant stage and develop into integrated

[49] For example, by the early 1970s there were ten different car assembly plants in Iran and at least four different makes of televisions were assembled in the country, where the size of the market, judged by total population and average income per head, did not probably allow for the establishment of even one integrated efficient sized factory.

production processes which could benefit from economies of scale. One effect of this was to slow down the growth of exports of the modern manufacturing sector and, as we shall see in the next chapter, to create a high degree of import dependence which threatened the viability of the growth path. A further drawback was that the availability of a protected and rapidly growing market based on the consumption of the upper income strata, did away with the need for the industrialists to transmit the productivity gains in the manufacturing sector to the consumers through lower prices, in order to expand their market through increasing demand by the lower income groups or through exports.[50] This in turn led to the retention of most of productivity gains in the modern manufacturing sector which as we have noted intensified the duality in the economy and reinforced the maldistribution of income and the lopsided market structure.[51]

7.7 Concluding remarks

As we have noted, various favourable factors both on the supply side and the demand side contributed to bring about the rapid process of industrialization over the 1963–77 period. The abundant supply of foreign exchange, being made available by the fast growth of oil exports, helped to finance the imports of capital goods and raw materials necessary for rapid industrial accumulation. The channelling of sizeable amounts of funds through industrial banks ensured the availability of large concentrations of money capital to enable the private industrialists to take advantage of the vast investment opportunities provided by the protected home market. This was complemented by direct government investment of a large part of the oil revenues in heavy industry. The availability of an abundant supply of labour combined with relatively stable food prices allowed this relatively long period of sustained accumulation to take place without major inflationary cost pressures.[52] On the demand side also, the high rates of growth of govern-

[50] For a study of the price competitiveness of Iranian manufacturing which corroborates these points, see Avramovic (1970) and World Bank (1971).

[51] We argued earlier in the discussion of agricultural terms of trade that, such a transmission appears to have happened to some extent. But, as the comparison of the relative prices and relative productivity gains in the manufacturing and agricultural sectors shows, most of the productivity gains seem to have been retained within the manufacturing sector itself. For example between 1963 and 1973 the barter terms of trade between agriculture and manufacturing (as measured by GDP price deflator) increased by only 8.8 per cent in favour of agriculture, while their labour productivity ratios increased by 24.5 per cent in favour of manufacturing.

[52] Even in the short period of the 1973–6 oil boom, when as a result of extreme overheating of the economy there was an abrupt increase in real wages, high rates of industrial investment were sustained by increasing the degree of mechanization of production techniques. As we have already noted, the possibility of intensifying the rate of introduction of more advanced technology due to higher availability of foreign exchange, in fact led to an acceleration in the rate of growth of manufacturing investment in this period.

ment expenditure, largely financed by oil revenues, led to a rapid expansion of the domestic market which helped to sustain the momentum of industrial investment throughout this period.

The industrialization process over this period, however, exhibited major weaknesses. The same factors which contributed to bring about the rapid process of industrial accumulation, namely the abundant supply of foreign exchange and external funds, also led to a neglect of the employment generation and income distribution aspects of the industrialization process. Heavy reliance on imported capital intensive technology in the modern manufacturing sector, and the lack of an adequate technology policy by the government aimed at a more widespread diffusion of benefits of advanced technology, led to a growing concentration of industrial employment in low productivity and technologically stagnant sectors. The industrial credit policy of the government, which showed a total neglect for the small- and medium-sized firms, also exacerbated this problem by stifling any initiative which may have originated in the private sector in this regard. It was believed that the fast rate of growth of the modern sector would be adequate to gradually absorb the labour force engaged in the low productivity sector. With the high rates of population growth and fast rates of rural-urban migration, however, this assumption proved wrong: as concomitant with the widening duality in the manufacturing sector, the share of employment in the low productivity sector also increased.

The taxation and expenditure policies of the government also did little to ameliorate the growing concentration of income gains from productivity growth. The availability of oil income and easy access to foreign borrowing did away with the need to tax the consumption of the high income groups in order to release resources for financing capital formation. As we have noted, the outcome of these processes was the domination of the growth of the final consumer market by the consumption pattern of a small segment of the population who exhibited relatively fast rates of growth of average consumption. This implied a tendency towards a growing fragmentation of the consumer market and weak growth of demand for items of mass consumption. Some of the likely implications of this pattern of demand for industrial efficiency and the cost/price structure of the manufacturing sector were pointed out. In the next chapter we shall examine the wider implications of the industrial structure for the long-term viability of the growth of the economy.

8

Oil income, structural bottlenecks and economic growth

8.1 Introduction

The purpose of this chapter is to examine the overall pattern of growth and structural change in the Iranian economy during the 1959–72 period, in order to identify the possible bottlenecks to the growth of the economy in the medium term, and appraise the long-term viability of the growth path beyond the lifespan of oil resources. The choice of 1972 as the terminal year is due to the fact that the impact of the oil shock during the 1973–7 period obscures certain aspects of the long-term structural changes in the economy. Although it could be shown that the inclusion of the 1973–7 period in fact reinforces the conclusions reached in this chapter about the long-term trends in the economy, this would introduce additional considerations which fall outside the purpose of the present chapter.

8.2 Structural change and the dual gap

The sectoral rates of growth and the changes in the structure of output, employment and productivity of labour for the 1959–72 period are shown in table 8.1. During this period there was a substantial change in the structure of output and employment in line with the findings of other empirical studies concerning the structural changes which normally accompany growth in the intermediate stages of economic development (see Kuznets 1971, Chenery 1960). There was a considerable increase in the share of output of the industrial sector accompanied by a comparable decline in the share of the agricultural sector in GNP. Industrial output[1] rose from 17 per cent of the GNP in 1959 – just over half of the share of the agricultural sector in that year – to about 23 per cent of the GNP, that is 5 per cent higher than

---

[1] Including, manufacturing and mining, construction, water and power. Unfortunately the Central Bank's national account statistics do not give separate estimates for the output in manufacturing and mining sectors. However, the share of mining, which should be rightly included in the primary sector together with agriculture, was very small. For example in 1968 the share of the labour force employed in the mining sector was less than 0.4 per cent of the total (see ILO 1972, pp.24–6).

the share of agriculture. There was a similar shift, though less pronounced, in the composition of employment. The industrial and service sectors increased their share of employment by 9 and 2 percentage points respectively. Despite a decline of 11 percentage points in the share of the agricultural sector, in 1972 the sector still accounted for about 43 per cent of total employment. This signified the immature structure of the Iranian economy and the existence of a large labour reserve, with a much lower level of productivity than the national average, upon which the industrial and services sector could draw during the growth process.

Comparison between the growth rates of employment and productivity of labour in the agricultural and industrial sectors during the 1959–64 and the 1964–72 periods, helps substantiate some of the arguments made in chapter 1 about the complementarity of these two sectors, and specially the dynamic role of the manufacturing sector, in the growth process. The years 1959, 1964 and 1972 were the peak years of two cycles of growth with two markedly different trend rates of growth. During these two periods one can observe an inverse relation between the rates of growth of labour productivity and employment in the agricultural sector. During the 1959–64 period when the overall rate of growth of the economy was relatively low, a high rate of growth of employment in the agricultural sector was associated with a negative rate of productivity growth in that sector. While during the high growth period of 1964–72 a high rate of growth of labour productivity in the agricultural sector was accompanied by an absolute decline in the agricultural labour force. This phenomenon partly reflected the effect of the existence of surplus labour in the agricultural sector, and partly the nature of technical progress in that sector. The shift of surplus agricultural labour to other sectors of the economy would, by definition, lead to an increase in the productivity of labour in agriculture. This could also generate secondary dynamic effects by creating a higher overall surplus in the agricultural sector which could lead to the introduction of new technology and reorganization of forms of production in that sector.

In the industrial sector on the other hand, one can observe a direct relation between growth of employment and productivity of labour. During the slow growth period of 1959–64, the rate of growth of employment and productivity of labour were both relatively low, while during the 1964–72 period high rates of growth of employment were accompanied by high rates of productivity growth.[2] A high rate of growth of the industrial sector on a

---

[2] In the manufacturing industry, the only sector for which relatively reliable annual data on employment are available, the following equations were estimated between the growth rate of real output (q), employment (e), and labour productivity (p), over the 1959–72 period.

$$p = -0.03 + 0.65q \qquad R^2 = 0.46 \qquad DW = 1.94$$
$$(-0.74) \quad (2.89)$$

sustained basis would not only lead to higher productivity growth in the sector itself but is also expected to create the conditions favourable for growth of the economy as a whole by absorbing the surplus labour and providing the goods necessary to raise productivity and incomes in the other sectors of the economy. What normally handicaps the generation of such dynamic processes in the underdeveloped economies is the limited market for the manufacturing sector and shortages of foreign exchange – both of which are related to the inefficiency of the manufacturing sector and its inability to export in the early stages of industrialization. In the Iranian economy, over this period as a whole, the sustained growth of oil exports contributed to the simultaneous alleviation of these two bottlenecks. The strength of the dynamic effects of manufacturing growth, however, depends on the type of industrialization and the kind of linkage which the manufacturing sector could establish with the rest of the economy.

By international standards the growth performance of the Iranian economy during the 1959–72 period was very impressive. Table 8.2 compares aggregate growth indicators of the Iranian economy with the upper quartile of other middle-income economies. It should be noted that the middle-income economies included in table 8.2 were amongst the fastest growing economies during the sixties and in fact the rates of growth achieved in this period had little historical precedent. The rates of growth of real GDP and real gross investment in the Iranian economy, therefore, rank amongst the highest in the world economy for this period. Taking into account the effect of cyclical fluctuations in the rate of investment during the entire period, and comparing the maximum rates of growth of investment with other middle-income mixed economies, it could be argued that during the larger part of this period (the non-recession years, i.e., the 1963–72 period)[3] the

$$e = 0.03 + 0.35q \qquad R^2 = 0.18 \qquad DW = 1.94$$
$$\quad\;\, (0.74) \;\; (1.50)$$

The low R^2, specially in the employment equation, could be partly due to the existence of surplus labour in the economy which gives a momentum of its own to the growth of employment independent of the output growth. With the exclusion of small-scale manufacturing which is mostly effected by this phenomenon, we obtain a better fit for both the equations in the following estimates:

$$p = -1.95 + 0.65q \qquad R^2 = 0.65 \qquad DW = 2.74$$
$$\quad (-0.57) \;\; (3.67)$$
$$e = 1.95 + 0.35q \qquad R^2 = 0.32 \qquad DW = 2.74$$
$$\quad\; (0.57) \;\; (1.92)$$

The value of 't' statistics are given in parentheses. (Source of data; The Ministry of Economy, *Iranian Industrial Statistics* 1972. The Ministry of Industry, *Trends in Industrial and Commercial Statistics* 1975Q4).

[3] Real annual average rate of growth of investment during the 1963–72 period was 16.8 per cent. The cyclical fluctuations in the rate of growth of investment during 1956–72 period are shown in figure 8.1(c).

Table 8.1. *Growth and structural change in the Iranian economy 1959–1972*

(Percentage)

	Average annual growth rates[a]			Structure[b]		
	1959–64	1964–72	1959–72	1959	1964	1972
Output[c]	5.1	11.7	9.1	100.0	100.0	100.0
Agriculture	1.5	4.5	3.4	32.1	29.0	18.4
Oil[d]	12.2	10.9	11.4	10.4	12.2	27.4
Manufacturing[e]	8.8	14.3	12.2	11.6	13.2	15.7
Construction	5.3	10.6	8.5	5.0	4.6	5.3
Power and water	34.3	20.4	25.6	0.4	1.3	1.6
Transport[f]	2.9	7.3	5.6	10.3	7.4	5.0
Commerce	4.6	10.3	8.1	8.6	9.0	8.3
Other services	6.6	16.4	12.5	12.8	13.8	14.6
Government	7.7	15.1	12.2	8.8	10.7	12.8
Employment	2.4	2.7	2.6	100.0	100.0	100.0
Agriculture	2.3	−0.1	0.8	53.5	53.4	42.8
Oil	5.9	2.8	4.1	0.5	0.6	0.4
Manufacturing[e]	3.2	6.7	5.3	14.5	15.1	20.5
Construction	3.0	6.2	4.9	5.9	6.1	8.0
Power and water	14.3	4.2	8.0	0.3	0.6	0.7
Transport[f]	0.8	1.8	1.4	3.3	3.1	2.8
Commerce	0.9	5.7	3.8	7.6	7.1	8.9
Other services[g]	2.0	4.2	3.3	14.3	14.1	15.8
				Relative to non-oil GDP		
Productivity[h]	2.4	8.3	6.0	100.0	100.0	100.0
Agriculture	−0.8	4.6	2.5	66.7	61.5	59.1
Oil[d]	5.9	10.9	8.9	2465.5	2474.9	8324.5
Manufacturing[e]	5.4	7.2	6.5	89.1	98.8	104.8
Construction	2.2	4.2	3.4	93.5	85.3	91.5
Power and water	17.4	15.5	16.2	133.5	243.1	320.7
Transport[f]	2.0	5.4	4.1	346.4	272.2	240.3
Commerce	3.6	4.4	4.1	125.5	144.9	127.7
Other services[g]	4.9	11.2	8.8	167.9	197.0	238.6

Notes:
[a] Refers to cumulative annual average growth rates, of real values.
[b] All variables at current prices. Domestic oil at posted prices.
[c] Real GNP including terms of trade effect.
[d] Refers to domestic oil for growth rates, national oil for the structure.
[e] Includes mining.
[f] Includes communications.
[g] Includes government.
[h] Refers to non-oil GDP.
Sources: Central Bank, *Annual Report* various issues. Plan and Budget Organization (1976).

Table 8.2. *The international growth indicators 1960–1970*

	Real annual average growth rates		No. of countries above Iran
	Iran	Upper quartile of middle-income economies[a]	
Gross domestic product[b]	8.8	6.2	1
Gross investment	12.2	9.7	4
Public consumption	16.0	8.0	0
Private consumption	10.0	6.1	1
Commodity imports	11.4	9.0	5
Commodity exports (non oil)	7.1	9.2	21

Notes:

[a] 58 countries according to the World Bank classifications, excluding the high-income oil-exporting countries.

[b] Refers to non-oil GDP for the case of Iran.

Source: World Bank, *World Development Report* 1982.

rate of investment in Iran was fairly close to the absorptive capacity of the economy.[4] This rate of investment however was heavily financed by external resources in the form of oil revenues and foreign borrowing. Oil income on average grew by the phenomenal rate of 17.9 per cent per annum in real terms[5] during the 1959–72 period. In addition about 10 per cent of gross investment during this period was on average financed by foreign borrowing.[6] As we shall shortly argue, given the structural features of the Iranian economy, this rate and pattern of growth was not viable in the long run and was subject to chronic balance of payments problems in the medium term. The important point is to identify the causal factors which created this pattern of growth and the policy prescriptions which could have been put forward for its correction. Complications however arise because of the dual contribution of the external resources.

On the one hand external resources contributed to the process of growth by covering the gap in the non-oil current account of the balance of payments. From the mid 1950s up to 1972 there was a secular increase in the share of imports financed by external resources (see table 8.3). The share of

[4] Based on the historical performance of eighty underdeveloped countries Chenery and Strout (1966) took a rate of investment growth of 12.5 per cent as a fair estimate of the normal absorptive capacity in these economies. Of course, any such strict limit on absorptive capacity is bound to be crude: but on the basis of existing evidence it is arguable that any attempt to appreciably increase the rate of investment beyond the 16.8 per cent trend during 1963–72 would have faced the human skill bottleneck (see also ILO 1972).

[5] Deflated by import price index.

[6] This figure is derived by averaging the balance of payments deficits on current account as a ratio of gross investment for the whole period.

Table 8.3. *The composition of foreign exchange earnings 1959–1972*

Year	Value of imports[a] ($ m)	Non-oil exports[b]	As percentages of imports		
			Oil sector's net earnings	Current account balance[c]	Total external resources[d]
1959	572.9	27.8	58.9	− 13.2	72.2
1960	597.3	28.3	60.1	− 11.6	71.7
1961	565.4	26.1	69.2	− 4.7	73.9
1962	527.3	25.1	80.3	5.4	74.9
1963	547.9	27.0	85.9	12.9	73.0
1964	758.9	19.2	73.2	− 7.6	80.8
1965	931.8	22.5	65.2	− 12.3	77.5
1966	1088.0	20.7	65.8	− 13.5	79.3
1967	1342.3	21.7	63.2	− 15.2	78.3
1968	1804.7	20.3	54.3	− 25.3	79.7
1969	2072.2	20.3	53.0	− 26.7	79.7
1970	2365.1	17.6	53.9	− 28.5	82.4
1971	3013.8	19.4	71.3	− 9.3	80.6
1972	3502.4	21.1	74.2	− 4.7	78.9

Notes:
[a] Imports of goods (c.i.f.) and services.
[b] Exports of goods (f.o.b.) and services.
[c] Minus sign indicates a deficit.
[d] Equals oil sector exchange earnings plus the current account deficit.
Sources: Central Bank, *Annual Reports* various issues.

imports financed by the foreign exchange proceeds from the oil sector plus foreign capital inflows,[7] rose from about 70 per cent in the late 1950s to around 80 per cent by the early 1970s.

On the other hand external resources contributed to the financing of domestic investment. During the 1960s there was a 20 per cent increase in the share of external resources in the financing of domestic investment (see table 8.4). Share of non-oil domestic savings declined from about 50 per cent to 30 per cent of gross domestic investment over this decade. This also reflected a genuine decline in the domestic savings ratio. Ratio of domestic (non-oil) savings to non-oil GNP declined from 10.5 per cent in 1959 to 7.7 per cent in 1970.[8]

[7] Measured as the deficits on the current account of the balance of payments.
[8] This is shown in a more systematic way by the elasticity of savings out of non-oil national income which was equal to 0.7. This was calculated by regressing log of non-oil domestic savings on log of non-oil GNP. The definition and derivation of non-oil domestic savings as in table 8.4.

Table 8.4. *Financing gross domestic capital formation 1959–1972*

Year	Gross investment (bn Rials)	Gross[a] domestic savings	(I) Non-oil savings	(II) Oil resources	(III) Foreign[b] savings	Total external resources[c]
			Percentage of gross investment			
1959	52.7	84.3	47.6	36.6	15.7	52.4
1960	57.8	79.9	42.9	37.0	20.1	57.1
1961	54.3	91.2	51.2	40.0	8.8	48.8
1962	47.4	111.2	61.2	50.0	−11.2	38.8
1963	51.5	112.4	58.6	53.8	−12.4	41.4
1964	63.2	95.9	38.8	57.6	4.1	61.7
1965	85.5	91.2	32.7	58.5	8.8	67.3
1966	90.0	89.1	36.8	52.3	10.9	63.2
1967	119.3	83.0	37.7	45.3	17.0	62.3
1968	136.5	77.0	31.7	45.3	23.0	68.3
1969	156.4	76.3	27.4	48.8	23.7	72.6
1970	167.3	80.1	29.0	51.1	19.9	71.0
1971	216.3	100.8	28.9	71.9	−0.8	71.1
1972	287.4	92.8	30.8	62.0	7.2	69.2

Notes:
[a] Gross domestic savings has been divided into two components; (I), gross non-oil savings, and (II), the net contribution of the oil sector. The contribution of the oil sector is assumed to be equal to the oil revenues of the central government. Non-oil savings are derived as a residual.
[b] Equals the deficit on the current account of the balance of payments.
[c] Equals (II) plus (III).
Sources: Central Bank, *Annual Reports* various issues. World Bank 1974.

The important question which has to be addressed is not whether excessive reliance on external resources was intended to alleviate a balance of payments or a savings constraint. It could be shown that, *given the production structure of the Iranian economy*, increasing reliance on external resources was due to a genuine shortage of foreign exchange which could not be removed without reducing the rate of growth of the economy much below its absorptive capacity.[9] The question is rather what factors contributed to the evolution of this particular production structure and in what ways alternative patterns of structural change could have been implemented. Had the ease of access to external resources played any part in shaping the process of structural change, or had the inevitability of this

[9] See the next section.

particular path of structural change necessitated increasing resort to external resources? It is in relation to these set of questions that it becomes important to consider both aspects of the contribution of external resources to the process of growth. As we have already noted in the previous chapter, the pattern of savings and consumption in a mixed economy could play an important part in shaping the production structure of the economy through their impact on the structure of demand. As a consequence, the purely financial aspects of the availability of external resources, e.g., the way they influence the expenditure and revenue policies of the government, could have important implications for the process of structural change as well. As was pointed out in chapter 1, neither the two-gap models nor the optimum planning models for oil economies consider such interrelations of the dual impact of external resources.

8.3 The balance of payments constraint

Despite the rapid growth of foreign exchange proceeds from the oil sector, the economy faced chronic balance of payments problems during the period under study. Two phases could be distinguished in this respect. In each phase, a period of rapid economic growth was followed by severe foreign exchange shortages which forced the government to intervene in order to slow down the rate of growth of the economy (see figure 8.1). The first phase began in the mid 1950s and ended with the severe economic and political crisis of the early 1960s.[10] The second phase began with the acceleration of economic growth after 1963 which led to a widening current account deficit and by the late 1960s forced the Central Bank to take corrective action in the form of credit and import controls[11] which created the minor recession of

[10] On the development during this period, see chapter 5.
[11] On these measures, see Central Bank, *Annual Report* 1968, 1979 and 1970. According to the Central Bank's Report (1969, p.48): 'The pressure on foreign exchange and the price level became quite clear in the first half of 1968'. Towards the end of 1968, the first set of restrictive measures were introduced to 'stem the depletion of foreign exchange reserves'. The legal reserve requirements of the commercial banks were increased by about 20 per cent, and the Central Bank's rediscount rate was raised from 5 to 7 per cent. The legal reserve requirements were increased by another 10 per cent in 1969 and a further 15 per cent in 1970. The rediscount rate was further increased to 8 per cent in 1969. Ceilings were also introduced in relation to the award of new credits to the private sector during the same year. Furthermore, in 1969 the commercial profit tax on 250 imported items was raised, and the Central Bank tightened the regulations relating to the registration of orders for imports.
    The brunt of these restrictive policies was taken by private sector investment (see figure 8.1(c)). It should be noted that despite the decline in the rate of growth of investment during these years the rate of growth of domestic absorption as a whole did not show any noticeable deviation from its long-term trends. This was due to the fact that government fiscal policy was highly expansionary throughout these years (see Central Bank, *ibid.*). This, apart from reflecting the lack of co-ordination between different aspects of government policy, is a good example of a common problem in the LDCs which arises due to their

(a)

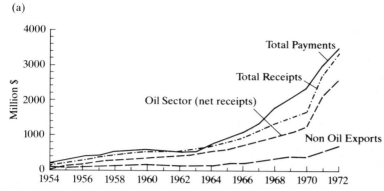

Figure 8.1a Foreign exchange receipts and payments

(b)

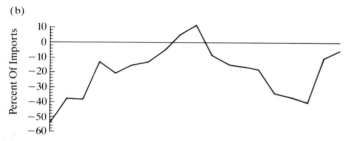

Figure 8.1b Balance of payments on current account (surplus)

(c)

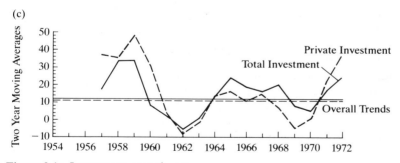

Figure 8.1c Investment growth rates

rigid fiscal structure. As a consequence, short-term demand management policies conducted with a view to the alleviation of the balance of payments problems, usually take the form of restrictive monetary and trade policies, with the result of reducing the rate of investment and the long-term development prospects of the economy. At the same time, the effectiveness of such policies in reducing total domestic absorption and relieving the balance of payment problems in the short run is dubious; the desired effects would be achieved only at the expense of a severe reduction in investment.

the 1967–9 period (see figure 8.1(c)). The minor recession of the late 1960s stopped short of turning into a full-blown economic crisis only due to the substantial rise in the oil revenues during 1970–1. The oil price hikes of 1973–4 temporarily pushed aside the preoccupations with the balance of payments problems. It however did not resolve the chronic nature of these problems and could only postpone the impending crisis which was to occur with increased intensity.

A disaggregated study of the different items of the balance of payments is necessary to delineate the underlying structural factors which created the recurring foreign exchange shortages. Table 8.5 depicts the principal components of the balance of payments during this period. It can be seen that the trade balance formed the main component of the current account deficits throughout the period. Though the balance in services also showed a perpetual deficit of increasing magnitude, it formed a relatively small item (with a decreasing share) in the overall non-oil current account deficit. It could be furthermore reasonably argued that the widening deficit on the services account was itself caused by the past deficits on the trade balance. A major part of the services deficit was composed of interest payments on long-term foreign debts which arose out of the need to finance the commodity trade deficits in the first place (see table 8.5). The primary causes of the balance of payments problems during this period, therefore, should be sought in the underlying factors of trade balance deficits.

A breakdown of the main categories of commodity exports and imports is presented in table 8.6. As the table indicates non-oil merchandise exports were mainly composed of primary commodities. During the decade, however, manufacturing exports managed to increase their share to about 40 per cent of the total. Furthermore it was the modern manufacturing rather than the traditional carpets which made the major gains. On the whole the 15.9 per cent annual rate of growth of manufacturing exports was above the average for other underdeveloped economies during the same period.[12] It should be noted however that the manufacturing exports started from a very low base, and furthermore a major part of such exports went to the Eastern European countries on the basis of barter trade.[13]

While the performance of commodity exports, in particular manufactur-

---

[12] The real rate of growth of manufactured exports from the less developed market economies during the 1959–72 period was 10.8 per cent per annum (based on the data in UN *Statistical Yearbook* 1973).

[13] According to the Central Bank (*Annual Report* 1971, p.40), 'The main buyers of Iranian manufacturing exports are the socialist countries who have clearing trade agreements with Iran'. The other important destination of Iranian modern exports was the Gulf region. It has been suggested, however, that the modern companies highly subsidized their exports to the Gulf states to comply with government requirements of export performance.

Table 8.5. *The Iranian balance of payments 1954–1972*

(US $ millions)

	1954–60	1961–64	1965–70	1971–72
Current account				
Imports (f.o.b.)	376.6	503.8	1358.3	2781.2
Exports (f.o.b.)	91.4	89.1	189.1	365.9
Non-oil trade balance	− 285.2	− 414.8	− 1169.2	− 2415.3
Services (net)	− 24.4	− 41.6	− 110.2	− 181.0
(net interest)	(− 4.7)	(− 14.8)	(− 36.6)	(− 121.7)
Oil sector (net)	230.1	460.2	920.9	2373.5
Current account balance	− 79.4	3.8	− 358.5	− 222.7
Long-term capital (net)				
Public	61.1	− 0.5	280.6	433.3
Private	0.0	1.5	17.8	55.1
Short-term capital (net)[a]	10.1	44.8	14.9	91.6
Change in reserves[b]	8.2	− 40.1	45.2	− 357.3

Notes:
The figures refer to annual averages for each period.
[a] Includes errors and omissions.
[b] Minus sign indicates an increase.
Sources: Central Bank, *Quarterly Bulletins* various issues.

ing exports, is very important in an economy like Iran from a long-term perspective, the medium-term balance of payments problems were mainly related to the rise in commodity imports. This is due to the fact that the value of imports was by far higher than non-oil exports, and no matter what rate of growth such exports could achieve, it was unlikely that they could exert an important influence on the overall trade balance in the medium run.

Table 8.6 also gives the structure and growth of imports according to their final use. During this period there was a substantial change in the composition of imports away from final consumption goods and towards the intermediate and capital goods. Despite a 10 per cent average annual rate of growth of private consumption, the rate of growth of imports of consumer goods was no more than 1.7 per cent per annum. The import substitution industrialization strategy appears to have been working effectively on these grounds. At the same time, however, there was a rapid growth in the imports of intermediate and capital goods, which as the table shows were mainly destined for the industrial sector itself. It appears that

Table 8.6. *The structure of foreign trade 1959–1972*

	Percentage shares		Real annual growth rates[a] 1959–72	
	1959–61	1970–2	(I)	(II)
Non-oil exports (f.o.b.)				
Primary products	75.8	60.5	6.1	(n.a.)
Cotton	24.3	18.6	6.9	(7.6)
Fruits	22.8	11.7	3.0	(1.7)
Hide and skins	5.9	5.5	8.2	(5.6)
Other primary	22.8	24.7	9.8	(n.a.)
Manufacturing products	24.1	39.5	15.9	(n.a.)
Carpets	21.5	20.5	9.5	(6.9)
Other manufacturing	2.6	19.0	29.9	(n.a.)
Total	100	100		
Total value (m$)	96.3	328.2	9.1	(7.5)
Imports (c.i.f.)				
Consumer goods[b]	28.0	12.5	1.4	
Intermediate goods	49.9	63.6	11.7	
Destined for:				
Industry and mining[c]	45.5	58.9	11.8	
Agriculture	0.5	1.3	17.2	
Other sectors	3.9	3.2	9.2	
Capital goods[f]	22.0	23.9	11.4	
Destined for:				
Industry and mining[c]	11.8	15.8	12.9	
Agriculture	3.3	2.1	6.4	
Other sectors	6.9	6.2	10.5	
Total	100	100		
Total value (m$)	493.7	2516.0	9.8	
Special import categories				
Food and products[d]	11.5	8.4	7.7[g]	(4.7)
Passenger cars[e]	2.4	0.4		(5.1)
Motor car bodies and parts	3.1	9.2		(16.9)

Notes:

[a] Refers to period trend rates of growth. Non-bracketed rates are derived by deflating by the general import price index. Bracketed rates are the quantum rates of growth.

[b] Include semi-processed food products.

[c] Includes water power and construction.

[d] Excludes animal and veg. oils.

[e] Excludes buses.

[f] Includes motor cars.

[g] Deflated by world trade price index for food products.

Sources: United Nations, *International Trade Statistics* 1962–72. Central Bank, *Annual Reports* 1962–73. Central Statistical Office, *Statistical Yearbook* 1968, 1975 and 1977.

the industrial trade balance was the main culprit in the balance of payments problems during the period.[14]

This point is further reinforced if we consider the behaviour of the sectoral composition of the trade balance by industrial origin during this period. Figure 8.2 presents a disaggregated picture of the trade deficit by broad sectoral origin of the traded commodities during the 1959–72 period. As the figure indicates the trade balance in primary products was fluctuating around the value of zero with very low amplitude, without showing any systematic increasing or decreasing trends during this period.

The diagram also clearly shows that oil surpluses during this period were chiefly financing the deficit in the manufacturing trade, which was widening throughout the period. As can be seen the cyclical fluctuations in the overall trade balance during the crisis of the early 1960s was a perfect mirror image of the fluctuations in the manufacturing deficit. While the minor recession of the late sixties began to bring down the manufacturing deficit, the sudden rise in oil exports prevented the repetition of the pattern of the earlier period.[15]

Figure 8.3 draws a disaggregated picture of the manufacturing trade balance. A striking fact, revealed by the figure, is that the manufacturing sector was as heavily in deficit in intermediate and consumer goods as in capital goods trade.[16] In both cases the elasticity of the trade balance deficit with respect to non-oil GDP was higher than one – though the non-capital goods sector managed to stabilize its trade balance deficit from the mid 1960s. The only two branches of manufacturing which actually managed to reduce their trade deficit as a ratio of GDP were chemicals and textiles. It is important to note that heavy chemicals was a government owned industry with a relatively homogeneous output which could be used as input in a variety of different industries, and that the textiles was an industry with a

---

[14] One may argue that a large part of what has been categorized as intermediate goods in the table is composed of agricultural products with little relation with the performance of manufacturing as such. The data on 'special import categories' at the bottom of table 8.6, however, do not support this argument. Though agricultural imports formed a relatively large part of intermediate imports (mainly composed of food grains), their rate of growth was well below the rate of growth of intermediate imports as a whole. If anything, their effect has been to pull down the average rate of growth of intermediate imports. These points are further substantiated in the following paragraph in the text.

[15] It should be, however, pointed out that a balance of payments crisis at the end of the 1960s would have had significantly different implications from the crisis of the early 1960s. During the earlier crisis the government could to some extent relieve the balance of payments pressures by curbing the imports of luxury consumer goods which formed a major share of imports. By the end of the 1960s, however, the production structure of the economy had changed with the effect that import restrictions would have inevitably led to significant reductions in the intermediate and capital goods imports resulting in a more severe slump in rate of capacity utilization and the rate of investment.

[16] The classification of manufacturing into these three broad categories is based on the UN (1971).

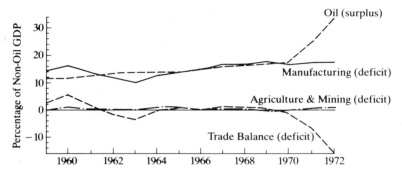

Figure 8.2 Composition of the trade balance
Sources: As for table 8.7.

mass consumption market. In both cases the existence of mass market in the domestic economy was expected to have contributed to setting up relatively well-integrated and efficient-sized plants.

8.4 Manufacturing growth and import dependence

It appears, therefore, that the main source of recurrent balance of payments problems in the Iranian economy stemmed from the imbalances in the trade performance of the manufacturing sector. Table 8.7 shows various international trade indicators for the different branches of the manufacturing sector. Together with table 8.8, which compares the structure of Iranian manufacturing with international 'norms', they throw light on some of the important aspects of manufacturing trade performance.

In twelve out of the fifteen manufacturing branches shown in table 8.7 the trade balance ratio was very close to -1 and remained more or less the same throughout the period. This signifies the paucity of the development of manufacturing exports. As the export ratio indicators show, in 1963 exports in the majority of the manufacturing branches were virtually non-existent and by 1972 still remained very rudimentary. Throughout this period more than 90 per cent of manufacturing exports were accounted for by textiles, clothing and chemical branches (see table 8.7). Given the import substitution strategy of the government and the fact that various lines of manufacturing activity were still at relatively early stages of their development, the low magnitude of export ratios may not appear surprising. It is at the later stages of import substitution industrialization, when the manufacturing sector has achieved the necessary maturity to compete in the international markets, that the export ratios are expected to rise rapidly. With the continuation of the trends observed over the period under investigation,

220

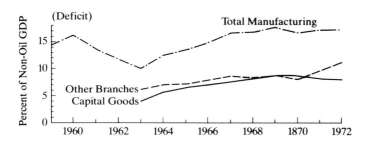

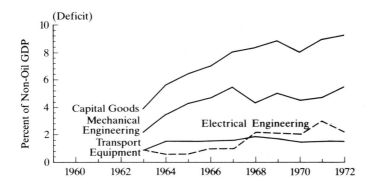

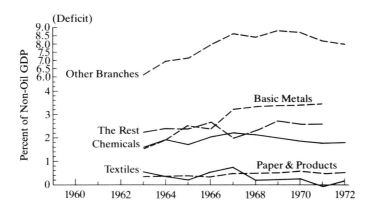

Figure 8.3 Composition of the trade balance in manufacturing
Sources: As for table 8.7.

Table 8.7. Manufacturing trade indicators 1963–1972

	(I) Trade balance ratio			(II) Import ratio			(III) Export ratio[e]			(IV) Share of imports			(V) Share of exports		
	1963	1967	1972	1963	1967	1972	1963	1967	1972	1963	1967	1972	1963	1967	1972
Total[a]	−0.849	−0.883	−0.825	31.7	33.6	32.8	3.7	3.1	4.5	100.0	100.0	100.0	100.0	100.0	100.0
Beverages and tobacco[b]	−0.019	0.308	−0.854	0.2	0.3	1.8	0.2	0.7	0.1	0.0	0.0	0.2	0.4	1.2	0.1
Textiles	−0.285	−0.228	−0.092	13.3	13.1	11.6	7.9	8.7	9.8	11.1	7.6	6.2	75.9	77.1	53.3
Clothing and footwear	0.329	0.789	0.936	1.1	0.2	0.2	2.1	1.8	4.7	0.2	0.1	0.1	4.7	10.2	16.5
Wood and paper	−1.000	−1.000	−0.990	18.2	18.7	19.9	0.0	0.0	0.1	3.9	3.1	3.5	0.0	0.0	0.2
Rubber and leather	−1.000	−1.000	−0.918	30.4	16.1	23.5	0.0	0.0	1.3	4.6	1.7	2.0	0.0	0.0	0.9
Chemicals	−0.846	−0.913	−0.658	60.4	50.5	38.8	11.3	4.4	11.6	16.5	12.9	10.3	16.8	9.5	22.2
Non-metallic minerals	−0.943	−0.899	−0.774	12.3	11.2	10.5	0.4	0.7	1.5	2.4	1.7	1.6	0.9	1.5	2.1
Basic metals	−1.000	−1.000	−0.992	83.5	76.0	59.5	0.0	0.0	0.6	14.4	18.2	17.3	0.0	0.0	0.8
Capital goods	−0.997	−0.999	−0.987	49.3	54.3	51.1	0.1	0.0	0.7	42.1	50.7	55.5	0.8	0.3	3.8
Metal products	−1.000	−1.000	−0.952	21.9	25.3	24.6	0.0	0.0	0.8	5.0	5.0	4.6	0.0	0.0	1.2
Mechanical engineering[d]	−1.000	−1.000	−0.993	97.9	92.2	85.9	0.0	0.0	2.1	20.9	27.7	27.9	0.0	0.0	1.0
Electrical engineering[d]	−1.000	−1.000	−0.992	73.3	46.3	51.1	0.0	0.0	0.4	7.8	8.8	12.2	0.0	0.0	0.5
Transport equipment	−1.000	−1.000	−0.982	26.8	37.1	32.1	0.0	0.0	0.4	8.2	9.1	10.8	0.0	0.0	1.0
Automobile[c]	−1.000	−1.000	−0.979	55.7	44.2	38.3	0.0	0.0	0.7	7.1	7.9	8.8	0.0	0.0	1.0
Misc.	−0.981	−0.990	−0.993	57.4	54.2	59.9	1.3	0.6	0.5	4.7	4.0	3.4	0.6	0.3	0.1

Notes:

Trade balance ratio = $(X_i - M_i)/(X_i + M_i)$; import ratio = $100 * M_i/D_i$; export ratio = $100 * X_i/Q_i$; share of exports = $X_i/\text{Sum}(X_i)$; where, X_i = exports of sector i's products; M_i = imports of sector i's products; share of imports = $100 * M_i/\text{Sum}(M_i)$; share of sector i's products Q_i = sector i's total domestic output; $D_i = Q_i + M_i - X_i$ = home demand.

[a] All variables are at current prices. Exports f.o.b., Imports c.i.f., and output at factor cost.

[b] Food industry is excluded.

[c] Automobile industry imports include bodies and parts.

[d] Electrical engineering includes household appliances.

[e] Output data refer to total sales.

Sources: UN, International Trade Statistics 1964–74, Ministry of Industry and Mines, Iranian Industrial Statistics 1972. The conversion of trade data from SITC to ISIC classification is based on UN 1966.

however, it is clear that the long-term viability of the growth path after the exhaustion of oil resources could not be ensured. Though in the long run the success of the import substitution strategy depends on the ability to export, the medium-term viability of the strategy depends on the possibility to bring about the necessary adjustments in the import ratios.

As the import ratio indicators in table 8.7 show, the intermediate and capital goods industries exhibited the highest potential for import substitution, and it was mainly in these lines that this process took place as signified by the reduction in import ratios between 1963 and 1972. Despite considerable reductions in import ratios in lines such as chemicals, and basic metals in this period, there was an increase in the import ratio of the manufacturing sector as a whole, and in particular in the capital goods sector. The process of import substitution, therefore, appears to have led to an increased import penetration as measured by the import ratio.[17] In this phenomenon should be sought the main explanations of the rapid expansion of manufactured imports which, as we have already noted, was the main source of recurrent balance of payments problems in the economy.

To form an idea of the possibilities of import substitution and the relative success of Iranian manufacturing in realizing such possibilities, we have compared the ratio of imports to total supplies for different manufacturing branches in Iran with the international norms for a country with similar levels of income and population, in table 8.8.[18] As the table shows, in almost all intermediate and capital goods industries (old ISIC 25–38), import coefficients were by far higher than the international norms.[19] What is more significant, however, is that the rate of decrease of import coefficients in the case of Iran is much slower than the international norms: so that by 1972 in almost all the branches the Iranian coefficient is not only much higher than the international norms but also shows a wider relative divergence from the norms than it did in 1963. In other words the growth elasticity of imports for the Iranian manufacturing sector was well above that of the international economy.[20] It is of course realized that the 'normal' ratios shown in the

[17] The term import substitution industrialization throughout this study is used in a broad sense to designate industrialization oriented towards the domestic market and supported by some type of trade restrictions, rather than in the narrow sense defined in some of the literature as absolute or relative reduction in manufactured imports. For a definition of the various meanings of the term see ECLA (1964).

[18] The international norms are derived from Chenery (1960).

[19] The reason for import ratios in 1963 being below the international standards, in the case of light industries (ISIC 23–7) and the transport industry, is mainly the concentration of a relatively large part of output in these sectors in the small artisan workshops in Iran. In Chenery's (1960) standard patterns the small sector is excluded. These small workshops, specially in the transport sector, were mainly composed of repairs shops which should be more appropriately categorized as services.

[20] The term growth elasticity is here meant to capture the effect of the rise in some composite measure of population and the GNP on imports.

Table 8.8. *Comparative structure of the Iranian manufacturing by international standards 1963–1972*

(percentages)

Old[b] ISIC code	Sector	Share of imports in total supplies				Composition of manufacturing value added				Growth of value added[d]
		Iran		'Typical' country[a]		Iran		'Typical' country[a]		1963–72
		1963	1972	1963[a]	1972[a]	1962	1972	1963[a]	1972[a]	
2–3	Total[c]	30.9	31.7	19.5	9.6	100.0	100.0	100.0	100.0	14.9
23	Textiles	12.4	10.6	21.1	7.2	34.3	20.9	26.3	17.7	11.6
24	Clothing	1.0	0.2	4.9	1.6	10.7	12.8	11.3	8.9	9.5
25–27	Wood and paper	18.2	19.9	26.0	9.8	10.2	7.9	10.7	12.4	4.9
29–30	Rubber and leather	30.4	23.3	22.9	10.3	4.6	2.6	4.0	3.9	19.7
31	Chemicals	57.5	36.0	26.5	12.6	3.9	9.8	13.4	10.6	29.9
33	Minerals	12.3	10.3	12.7	5.8	11.3	12.9	9.3	7.0	14.7
34–35	Metals	48.4	45.7	31.8	12.5	13.0	15.4	13.4	17.8	12.9
36–37	Machinery	89.7	71.0	73.4	27.8	2.3	9.4	4.6	11.3	25.5
38	Transport equip.	26.8	32.0	54.0	12.8	9.7	8.4	6.9	10.4	37.6

Notes:

[a] 'Typical country' figures are derived from regression equations run by Chenery (1960), at population levels of 23.7 and 30.5 millions and per capita income levels of $174.6 and $455.3, for the years 1963 and 1972 respectively; they refer to the actual levels of income and population attained in Iran during these two years.

[b] As defined in the UN (1956).

[c] Excludes food, beverages, tobacco, oil and coal related industries, and printing.

[d] Refers to the real annual average rates of growth of large manufacturing sector; derived from the output indices of the Ministry of Industry and Mines, using the 1967 value added weights for large manufacturing industry.

Sources: Ministry of Industry and Mines, *Trends in Industrial Statistics* 1975(Q4). Ministry of Industry and Mines, *Iranian Industrial Statistics* 1972. Table 8.7, Chenery 1960.

table are derived from cross-section data relating to the late 1950s, and may not appear entirely satisfactory in tracing the historical path of economies facing a changing set of technological and trading possibilities. However, Chenery (1960), comparing the historical experience of various countries with these cross-section results, found that there was a considerable similarity between the time series and cross-section patterns.[21] It is also important to note that the divergence between the structure of import ratios in Iranian manufacturing and in international norms is not specific to particular branches which may have arisen due to special characteristics of the natural resource base of the country, it is rather general to all industries.

One interpretation of these results may be that, due to the fast growth of oil revenues during this period, there was a perpetual disjuncture between the actual composition of output and the structure of production which domestic demand at a given level of income would have warranted. In other words, the structure of production perpetually lagged behind the rapidly changing structure of demand; the implication being that high import ratios were only a transitional phenomenon, and signified only a temporary lopsidedness in the structure of production due to the adjustment lags between a fast changing demand structure and the production structure. The existing evidence, however, does not furnish strong support for this type of argument. First, unless one assumes that the adjustment lags are increasing over time, it does not explain the widening gap in the relative performance of Iranian manufacturing compared to the 'normal' pattern. Secondly, the broad sectoral composition of manufacturing output in Iran was very close to international norms, and the divergence which existed between the two was narrowing down very rapidly through time. As the data on the composition of manufacturing value added in table 8.8 show, while during the early 1960s the structure of the Iranian manufacturing compared to the international 'norms' was heavily biased towards light industries, by 1972 it had achieved a remarkable similarity to the international norms. Despite the rapid adjustment in the structure of manufacturing production in the direction of increased alignment with the international norms between 1963 and 1972, there was an increased deviation in the import ratios, and the overall ratio in the case of Iran was

---

[21] The similarity between time series and cross-section patterns of change in the industrial structure with the rising incomes is also evidenced in Kuznets (1957), Chenery and Taylor (1968). It should be added that the proximity of the time period of the present study and Chenery's cross-section study makes it plausible to assume Iran faced similar technological and trade conditions as the thirty-eight countries represented in Chenery's sample. In the existing literature one commonly witnesses much wider time periods being considered for such comparative studies. For example, Chenery *et al.* (1962) compares the structure of the Japanese economy before the First World War with the normal patterns derived from Chenery (1960).

actually rising. This suggests that the 'adjustment lag' or 'catching up' hypothesis may not be adequate to explain the broad industry level anomalies in the import ratio. As we shall argue below many of such factors may turn out to be more permanent and 'structural' than the 'catching up' hypothesis assumes.

8.5 Oil income, structure of demand and manufacturing growth

In section 8.2 above we argued that, though the Iranian economy achieved impressive growth rates and rapid structural change, growth was financed by 'excessive' reliance on external resources – 'excessive' in the sense that in the medium term the economy was prone to severe balance of payments crises and in the long run, given the continuation of the existing pattern of structural change, the economy could not sustain itself after the exhaustion of the oil reserves. In section 8.3 we showed that the widening gap in the trade balance was the main cause of the deficits in the current account of the balance of payments, and that manufacturing balance was the main component of the trade deficit and the main source of its increase over time. We further argued that, though the low levels and relatively slow rates of growth of manufacturing exports were a main cause of concern from a long-term point of view, the main problems in the medium term were connected with the rapid rate of growth of imports. It was also shown that the main source of growth of manufactured imports was largely in semi-processed inputs and capital goods. In section 8.4 we examined the pattern of manufactured imports by branch of activity and showed that import ratios in almost all the branches of manufacturing were abnormally high, and that they increased their abnormality in relation to the international standards over the course of industrialization.

The argument thus far leads one to conclude that the process of perverse growth in the Iranian economy was the outcome of factors related to the structure of production in the economy – namely the high degree of dependence on manufactured intermediate and capital goods imports. In the terminology of the two-gap model, given this particular structure of production, external resources of the above magnitude were to a large extent necessary to cover the foreign exchange gap. Any attempts to reduce the foreign exchange requirements of the economy *under these structural conditions* would have had to reduce the rate of growth of the economy as a whole. In other words the low domestic saving propensities would follow as a matter of course, and could be regarded as only a reflection of the failure to follow a more intensive import substituting and export promoting growth path. A more intensive effort to raise the rate of domestic savings *under the existing industrial structure* would lead to under-utilization of resources rather than generating a higher rate of growth. This is a conclusion which quite often has been drawn in relation to the LDCs undergoing a similar experience of import substitution industrialization. For example according to OECD (1967, p.53), 'low saving rates are often essentially due to external trading difficulties, so that internal measures designed to increase savings may be without effect unless combined with effective measures to increase export earnings or to economize imports'.

In the short run, when the production structure of the economy may be assumed as given, the above conclusion could appear plausible. In a long-term perspective, however, this line of reasoning, which is based on a mechanical separation between the evolution of the industrial structure and the consumption and savings patterns in the economy, could lead to a one-sided view of the causes of distortion in the industrial structure. It could lead to a replication of policy prescriptions for industrial restructuring with a strong supply side bias which by themselves could prove inadequate in the case of oil-exporting economies which are experiencing a rapid growth of national income. The standard remedies emphasized by different economic schools are well known. Within the neo-classical static general equilibrium framework, anomalies in the production structure mainly arise due to distortions in the price structure. Excessive import dependence, to the extent that it could be regarded as 'abnormal' or 'undesirable',[22] arises because of the combination of high rates of protection of the domestic market and high subsidies given to the imported intermediate and capital goods (see Nelson 1970). The structural balance of payments problems which arise during the growth process are thus largely blamed on the price distortions which import substitution strategy itself creates. Devaluation of the exchange rate and a freer trade policy are advocated as the main instruments for restructuring the economy through a better use of pricing mechanism (see Kruger 1984). The structuralist school would defend import substitution industrialization on the grounds of infant industry arguments and the dynamic effects that manufacturing growth generates in the economy as a whole. They rather advocate more interventionist policies on the supply side to rationalize the industrial structure, either through direct

---

[22] It should be noted that in the neo-classical general equilibrium framework, an oil-exporting economy would *ceteris paribus* have greater manufactured import ratios than a non-oil-exporting country (Chenery 1960). The reason being that under full employment of labour, the oil-exporting country would inevitably have a higher share of its labour force in the services (non-tradables) and oil sectors, with the implication that the share of imports in the total supplies of the tradable goods would be higher. This is the gist of the theoretical arguments of the so-called Dutch Disease models (see Corden and Neary 1982). It is, however, important to note that, contrary to the predictions of such theories, the ratio of domestic production of the non-traded to traded goods in the case of Iran did not diverge from the international norms (see Kavoussi 1976). Also, as we note in chapter 7 and in appendix M.1, the full employment assumption is not realistic for the case of Iran.

investment by the government or the use of tax-subsidy methods, licensing etc., to direct private investment towards the desired lines, and to increase the competitiveness of the manufacturing sector (see Kaldor 1964, 1971, Chenery and Kretschmer 1956).[23] Industrial and trade policies which are designed without due consideration for the independent effect of the income generating activities of the oil states, however, may not be effective in creating the desired structural changes.

Taking into account the influence of the demand pattern and its dynamics on the process of structural change in the oil-exporting mixed economies, the whole chain of reasoning in the above line of argument could be reversed. It could be argued that easy access to external resources has in the first place led to the substitution of these resources for domestic savings. This could come about through various channels, which are in one way or another related to the nature of the state and the structure of power in the society. In other words, they are not the necessary preconditions for capitalist industrialization in oil economies, but rather subject to specific political determinations. Low tax effort, high wages and salaries for the state employees, substantial subsidies in the form of cheap credits, subsidized inputs, provision of free social overhead capital, and subsidized wage goods, are amongst the many mechanisms through which such a substitution, directly or indirectly (through their income generating effects in the private sector), can take place. This pattern of direct economic involvement of the state (viewed from its income generating side rather than its capacity generating aspect), would largely benefit the workers, salary earners and the property owners in the modern sector of the economy (both the state sector and private capitalist sector). In an economy which consists of a large subsistence agricultural sector this would imply the emergence of an extreme duality and a worsening distribution of income.[24] The rapid growth of the income of the few who mainly benefit from the fast rate of growth of the economy, would induce a rapid rate of growth in conspicuous consumption. The domestic market would therefore tend to be dominated by a highly differentiated and rapidly changing spectrum of luxury consumer goods. The growth of the manufacturing sector behind tariff walls would take the form of production of many commodities each having a limited market. The oligopolistic nature of the manufacturing sector would itself

[23] Chenery and Kretschmer (1956) thus define the object of development policy, independently of demand side factors, as the choice of 'techniques of production, increases in capacity import levels and export levels in such a way that the *given final demand* will be produceable in the target year with a minimum total investment and without exceeding the specified resources available' (emphasis mine).

[24] Of course the pattern of distribution of income in the economy has complex determinations, but here we are mainly concerned with those mechanisms which may assume specific significance in the trends of income distribution in the oil economies.

induce increasing product differentiation. This pattern of industrialization is bound to lead to severe balance of payments problems, for various reasons. First, from a static point of view, the production of luxury consumer goods is expected to have a higher import content than the mass consumption goods.[25] Secondly, the high degree of fragmentation of the market makes the process of the deepening of import substitution industrialization very difficult. Manufacturing production tends to take the form of last stage assemblage. Thirdly the limited market and the inability to absorb technological know-how due to the assembly plant nature of production reduces efficiency and hinders manufacturing exports. The widening gap in the balance of payments implies further reliance on external resources which in a way helps reproduce the process on an expanded scale.

Under these market conditions it is unlikely that price incentives could be very effective in bringing about the required substitutions between the domestic and imported inputs. Investment in new lines of activity in the intermediate and capital goods industries would be constrained by the size of the market. Technical substitutability between domestically produced and imported inputs thus becomes very limited.

Even if the technical possibilities of substitution are reasonably high, there is strong reason to believe that a devaluation of the exchange rate in an oil economy which is experiencing perverse growth is most likely to intensify the balance of payments problems – both in the short run and in the long run. The reason is that an immediate affect of devaluation would be to increase the oil revenues of the government in domestic currency without effecting its foreign currency value. Given the above tendencies in the behaviour of the state – i.e., the substitution of oil revenues for domestic savings and the unequal distribution of the newly generated incomes – devaluation would have an expansionary impact in the short run,[26] which would lead to a worsening in the balance of trade denominated in foreign currency, and in the long run the resulting maldistribution of income would further intensify the process of perverse growth through the mechanisms discussed above. It should be noted that the charge of the overvaluation of the exchange rate (usually made about oil-exporting countries experiencing perverse growth), in the sense of high real wages and high prices of manufactured commodities relative to raw material costs, is basically correct. But this is a problem which cannot be remedied by the devaluation of the exchange rate alone. Depending on the income generating policies of

[25] The study of Paukert *et al.* (1981) does not appear to support this hypothesis. They show that a redistribution of income towards more equality in Iran would have increased import requirements. This is, however, due to the fact that their import estimates include the second round of import growth that the expansionary effects of income redistribution would give rise to.

[26] That is if the inflationary pressures do not neutralize devaluation in the first instance.

the government, a nominal devaluation of the exchange rate could even have the paradoxical results of leading to an even higher exchange rate in real terms.

The above argument by no means implies that the rate of domestic savings (excluding oil surpluses) in oil-exporting economies should be equal to the rate of domestic investment. This would have meant that the economy should forgo the benefits provided by the availability of external resources, which is not plausible. As we noted in chapter 1 the structural rigidities in the LDCs would mean that external resources could greatly contribute to the growth of the economy. The point which is made here is that the income effects of the inflow of external resources create a perpetual distributional problem for the oil-exporting mixed economies, which unless tackled in an appropriate manner would intensify the process of perverse growth.[27] As it has turned out such distributional problems have formed one of the important aspects of capitalist industrialization in the peripheral economies during the post-war period. In oil-exporting economies like Iran, however, the problem may take a more severe and at the same time more visibly political form, as the state appears in direct charge of the distribution of a large part of the national income. This does not mean that the supply side policies, both of an indirect marked mediated type and of a more direct interventionist type, are of lesser importance in shaping the pattern of industrialization in oil-exporting economies. But it rather calls for the adoption of a policy framework which could take into account the interconnections between the income generating or demand side effects of government policy and its capacity generating impact. Within such a framework, given the evidence provided in the last two chapters, it is most likely that a more equal distribution of income through its impact on the pattern of structural change, would have allowed to maintain the overall rate of economic growth with a lower degree of reliance on oil income or foreign borrowing to finance investment – an outcome which is contrary to the conventional wisdom about the inverse relation between the degree of income inequality and the rate of growth.

[27] Kalecki (1966) discusses this problem in the context of aid-receiving countries. The dimensions of the problem for oil-exporting countries, however, is on a different scale. The need to repay the loan for the aid-receiving countries may automatically lead to a more judicious expenditure policy.

9
Conclusion

9.1 State and industrialization

Three distinct phases may be distinguished with regard to the role of state in the industrialization process in Iran. The first phase, which stretched from the early nineteenth century through to the 1920s, was a period of the disintegration of the medieval state. The significance of this phase in relation to the process of industrialization lay in what the state did not or could not accomplish rather than what it achieved. The different aspects of the transformation of the Iranian economy over this period were largely shaped by the integration of the economy into the world market under a free trade regime. The second phase, the inter-war period, witnessed the formation of the modern national state and the beginning of state intervention in the promotion of the process of industrialization. In this phase oil revenues and foreign capital made little contribution to industrial accumulation. The third phase, which began in the early 1950s and ended with the 1979 revolution, was characterized by a substantial inflow of oil revenues and foreign capital. The analysis of the changing form and functions of state institutions over these distinct phases of industrialization, helps to highlight the problems that the utilization of oil revenues posed for the state, and the way these were tackled within the institutional framework of the Iranian economy.

9.2 The phase of decline

The starting point of our analysis has been the idea that the structure of the political economy of medieval Iran and its transformation during the last century, provide some of the key elements for the understanding of the roots of backwardness as well as the nature of economic developments in later periods. This is not so much due to our belief in the persistence of the 'traditional' institutions in the 'modern' era but, on the contrary, it is because of the way the dissolution of the old structures is believed to have provided the elements for the formation of the new.[1] The contribution of this study to an understanding of the political economy of medieval Iran has been through the reinterpretation and synthesis of existing materials, by highlighting the vicissitudes of the political cycles in this period and their ramifications for the form of economic relations, especially the agrarian relations. We concentrated furthermore on political relations as constituent elements of production relations in the medieval economy. This contrasts with the usual emphasis in the literature on the role of the state in the sphere of circulation, and in particular its relation with the merchants. As we have noted, these points of emphasis play an important part in analysing the dissolution of the medieval economy under the impact of western capitalism in the nineteenth century, and the formation of new economic structures.

The integration of the Iranian economy into the world market was the prime mover in the process of socio-economic and political change which led to the dissolution of the medieval system. Economic transformation in this period, however, was very much influenced by the internal structures of the medieval system. In particular the state, forming an important mediating link in the process of integration and having a central position in medieval agrarian relations, played a dominant role in the outcome of the process of economic transformation. The failure of the attempts to restructure the state institutions, which resulted from the diffuse nature of political power in the early Qajar rule, and was reinforced by foreign political intervention, led to a cumulative process of disintegration of the traditional state, concomitant with the greater commercialization of the economy. The counterpart to the dissolution of the *ancien regime*, was the transformation of the traditional land tenure system into large-scale absentee private landlordism which characterized the agrarian scene over much of the present century.[2] The 'free trade' regime over this period also undermined the restrictive regulations of the traditional guild system; competition from cheap imported manufactures, however, did not encourage the development of higher capitalist forms of production through the internal transformation of the simple commodity producing sector which replaced the traditional guild system. A few attempts by the big merchants to establish modern industries 'from above' also ended in failure because of

[1] The idea of 'habit persistence' has been very influential in the recent studies of Iranian political economy. See Ashraf (1970) and Katouzian (1981) for two of the most notable examples, where the persistence of the traditional state structures plays a key role in the analysis of economic development over the present century.

[2] The Iranian experience in this respect may be contrasted to the case of Ottoman Turkey, where the relatively more successful attempts at reforming the central state institutions in the nineteenth century led to a totally different agrarian history in modern Turkey (see chapter 2). This brings into focus the importance of the state, and conjunctural factors such as the relative weakness or strength of the state at the time of integration into the world market, in shaping economic transformation.

the lack of necessary infrastructure and government protection. The forms of production which developed in the agricultural and manufacturing sectors over this period, therfore, not only precluded the possibility of self-sustained and mutually interacting growth in the two sectors, but also constrained their capacities to respond to external stimuli. As a consequence, the major phases of the development of the Iranian economy in the subsequent periods had their origin in changing external economic conditions and were largely initiated by the state.

9.3 The modern state and constraints to industrial accumulation

The formation of the modern state with a unified and centralized administrative and military apparatus in the 1920s heralded a new phase of state-economy interrelationships. By this time the political and economic preconditions for the formation of the modern national state were already in place. The political crisis at home and the fear of the spread of communism from the north led the traditional ruling elites, who had opposed the state reforms in the nineteenth century, to support the formation of a strong centralized state. The interimperialist rivalry between the British and Russians, which had formerly intensified the paralysis of the Qajar state, had also come to an end. Economic developments over the previous half century also played their part. The growth of foreign trade and the greater monetization of the economy had substantially expanded the possibilities for raising revenue by the government through indirect taxation. Oil revenues also provided an independent source of income for the government which contributed to the financing of the newly created military/administrative apparatus of the state.

Though the formation of the modern bureaucratic state institutions substantially enhanced the power of the state to intervene in the economy, the impact of the new state on economic development was far from the straightforward manner in which it is usually portrayed in the literature: that is, a modern state intent upon creating a new economic order with its efforts directed in a unilineal manner towards the 'modernization' of a 'traditional' economy. The rise of the authoritarian regime of Reza Shah removed from the political agenda any talk of fundamental economic reform, especially land reform which had been an important aspect of political discourse since the constitutional revolution. It enhanced the political power of the absentee landlords in the countryside and strengthened the semi-feudal relations of production in the agricultural sector, which became a major obstacle to rapid economic expansion over the next half century. The drive for industrialization initiated by the state in the 1930s also was not the result of a pre-conceived plan by the government, but was prompted rather by the pressure of circumstances arising from the world depression and the adjustment problems it created for the Iranian economy. The existence of the new state structures which was a pre-condition for the 'relative autonomy' of the state from the economically dominant classes, however, did play an important part in making the drive towards industrialization possible.

The international economic conditions in the inter-war period were characterized by the slow growth in world trade, the worsening terms of trade for primary commodity exporters like Iran, and the very limited possibilities of drawing on foreign capital to finance accumulation. The main task of the state in promoting accumulation over this period, there-fore, was the mobilization of resources for investment from a mainly agrarian and increasingly impoverished domestic economy. This was mainly achieved through indirect taxation and the creation of monopoly trading companies which led to the relatively large concentration of money capital in the hands of big merchants and in the state budget which was used for investment in infrastructure and import-substituting light industries. The state's regaining of its tariff autonomy in 1928 was another important pre-condition for the implementation of this early phase of import-substi-tuting industrialization. An important indicator of the nature of state power and the constraints to its economic intervention over this period was the way in which the burden of accumulation was shared by different social groups. Though at the national level the state was able to shift some of the burden to the landlords through indirect taxation as well as turning the terms of trade against the agricultural sector, its power of intervention at the local level was very limited because of the entrenched social position of the landlords. This severely handicapped the ability of the state to selectively distribute the burden of accumulation amongst the different social groups, for example through direct taxation. A further issue concerning political power and the financing of accumulation was the extremely low bargaining power of the government *vis-à-vis* the Anglo-Iranian Oil Company. Gov-ernment's oil revenues constituted only about 10 to 15 per cent of the value of oil exports and made little contribution to the financing of accumulation over this period. It was not until the 1950s, when oil became the central issue in the popular nationalist movement, that the government could bring about a major shift in the distribution of oil income in its own favour.

9.4 The oil era and institutional change

The post-war period witnessed important changes in the international economy and the domestic political scene which led to a significant shift in the development path of the Iranian economy. With the collapse of the authoritarian regime of Reza Shah, fundamental economic reforms such as the nationalization of the oil industry and agrarian reform became central issues on the political agenda during this period of open politics in the immediate aftermath of the war. This also coincided with the post-war restructuring of the world capitalist system under the US hegemony. The salient features of the international economic scene over this period as compared to the inter-war period were: the fast growth of world trade on a sustained basis, abundance of foreign capital both through official and private channels, and the higher degree of mobility of capital and technology through the multinational companies, particularly from the 1960s. We have seen how the combination of the new internal and external factors led to a quantum jump in oil revenues which diametrically altered the role of the state in the process of accumulation. The rapid growth of oil income together with the easy access to foreign capital during the post-1950s period eased the resource constraints to accumulation and transformed the role of the state from one of mobilization of resources for investment in the domestic non-oil economy, as in the interwar period, to one of distribution and allocation of the already centralized investible funds. In accordance, new institutions such as the Plan Organization and the Specialized Banks replaced the monopoly trading companies and the state budget as the central institutions of accumulation.

The advent of the oil era substantially increased the capacity of the state to intervene in the economy, both by increasing the magnitude of resources at the disposal of the state and by easing the structural constraints which – as we saw in the case of the inter-war period – had previously limited the field of effective economic intervention by the state. The state thus assumed a much more significant role in setting the pace and structure of growth in the oil era.

The immediate effect of the reemergence of the modern authoritarian regime after the 1953 coup was to reverse the course of the economic reforms which had begun during the period of open politics, especially in the agrarian sector. During this initial phase there was a mutual support between the regime and the traditional ruling classes, namely the landlords, the merchant bourgeoisie of the bazaar and the high clergy. While the regime benefitted from the strong social support which these classes could muster through their traditional patrimonial networks, in return it strengthened their political and economic standing by suppressing the progressive middle-class and leftist reform movements. The economic intervention of the state over this period was very much conditioned by the clientelistic relationship between the regime and the traditional ruling elite. The semi-liberal trade policies of the government together with the massive inflow of external funds led to an import boom with substantial benefit to the merchants. Though the newly created institutions such as the Plan Organization and specialized banks were instrumental in channelling a relatively large part of the external funds into productive activities, the slender capacity and backward structure of the industrial sector could not cope with the rapid increase and diversification in demand arising from the fast growth of incomes in this period. This process led to the severe balance of payments crisis of the early 1960s. Another contradiction of the process of development over this period was the sharp food price increases which resulted from the backward conditions of production in the agricultural sector, combined with the political influence of the landlords at the national level. The prevailing relations of production in the agricultural sector meant that the direction of substantial amounts of funds through the Agricultural Bank and the income gains arising from large terms of trade improvements were mainly appropriated by the absentee landlords without generating a favourable response in agricultural production.

The stabilization programme which was put into effect in the early 1960s was a short-term deflationary package which relieved the balance of payments situation at the expense of rising unemployment and further cuts in the standard of living of the lower income groups. This intensified the social tensions in the country which led to the political crisis of the early 1960s. The new policy direction which took shape over the period of the crisis reflected different aspects of state intervention which attempted to deal with some of the apparent contradictions of the previous phase of accumulation. Two major areas of such intervention were distinguished – both of which depended on a break in the alliance of the regime with the powerful traditional proprietary classes. The first major area of state intervention, i.e., the land reform, related to the internal imbalances which resulted from the backward structure of agrarian relations. The second major area of state intervention was the restructuring and renovation of the industrial sector through directing private and public investments into new lines of manufacturing production, in greater conformity with the structure of domestic demand. This involved the reversal of the semi-liberal trade policies of the earlier period, and taking measures which favoured industrial capital over the traditional merchant bourgeoisie of the bazaar, as foreign exchange receipts were increasingly channelled into financing the import requirements of the rising new industries in both the public and private sectors. This period witnessed the rise of a new industrialist class with close ties to the state and foreign capital, who increasingly relied on cheap loans from the specialized banks to invest in new industries.

The break in the alliance of the regime with the traditional propertied classes did not imply a move away from the clientelist form of representation of the state towards more democratic forms. On the contrary, after the crisis of the early 1960s, there was a tightening in the hold of the state over the society and a growing concentration of political power in the hands of a small elite, at the centre of which was the Shah and his court. The break with the traditional elite represented rather a shift towards a broadening of the state clientele, by incorporating the modern middle classes, the new peasant proprietors, and factions of the working class employed in the modern sectors of the economy. The relationship of the regime with these classes, who were totally excluded from the political process, was based on the granting of material resources and economic privileges in exchange for their passive political participation. The rapid growth of consumption of these classes laid the basis for the new model of industrial accumulation which took shape over the decades of the 1960s and 1970s.

9.5 The impact of oil revenues on growth and structural change

The impact of oil revenues on the process of growth and structural change could not be analysed in abstraction from the institutional framework of the economy, and in particular from the nature of socio-historical factors which shaped the role of the state in the economy. The provision of finance through institutions such as the specialized banks and the Plan Organization, combined with the government's protection policy which created numerous opportunities for investment, helped to generate a powerful investment drive in the economy during the oil period. The abundant supply of finance, foreign exchange and labour, combined with the fast expansion of the protected home market, led to a process of rapid industrial growth. The main source of structural imbalances in the Iranian economy over this period was not due to the 'crowding out' of the traded goods sectors by non-traded sectors, as is expounded in the recent literature on 'booming sector economies'. As we have noted, the availability of a plentiful supply of labour and the existence of a huge backlog of advanced technology which could be used to substantially increase the productivity of labour, undermined some of the basic assumptions of such theories which are based on full employment equilibrium models with given technology. The agricultural sector, likewise, benefitted from a net resource inflow of a sizeable magnitude which, combined with the institutional reforms in the sector, produced a positive, though limited, output response. On the basis of the evidence presented it is arguable that over the oil period as a whole, the unsatisfactory response in agricultural output may be due more to institutional factors and the related inefficiencies in resource utilization, rather than unfavourable terms of trade movements, or, more generally, a resource squeeze which is often claimed to have arisen from the import-substitution industrialization policy of the government.

The more serious problems relating to the pattern of structural change over the 1953–77 oil period were the lopsided nature of industrial growth which implied an excessive dependence on external resources, and the related problems of inadequate employment generation and a growing maldistribution of income.

A central issue with regard to the income distribution problem was the inability of the economic system to combine the use of advanced technology with the generation of productive and gainful employment for the major part of the labour force engaged in the backward sectors of the economy. This problem, in our opinion, was not merely a result of the 'failure' of the price mechanism to bring about the necessary factor substitutions, either due to the stickiness of wages and prices or lack of adequate technological flexibility in the production process. At a more general level, it characterized a socio-political and organizational 'failure' to make effective use of the available labour force in the economy. This problem, which is a common feature of other underdeveloped countries exhibiting a similar dual economic structure, is sometimes too conveniently brushed aside by arguing that the achievement of a reasonably fast rate of growth would be adequate for a gradual transfer of labour from the backward sectors of the economy to the advanced sectors. As the experience of Iran has shown even the achievement of rapid economic growth may not by itself be sufficient to reduce the economic duality over time. This signifies the difficult organizational task which faces the state in the developing countries with an economic structure similar to Iran, in making effective use of the abundant supply of labour available to them. The 'failure' of the Iranian state in this regard was not in its 'wrong' perception of what policies to use to tackle these problems or in the difficulties of implementation of its policies as such; the problems of growing economic duality and worsening distribution of income never received serious consideration in government policy formulation. This meant that the additional problem that the utilization of oil revenues posed for the state in this regard were also neglected. The ease of access to external resources, i.e., oil income and foreign borrowing, allowed the rapid acceleration of the rate of growth of investment and government expenditure without the need to curb the income and consumption of higher income groups. This, apart from exacerbating the problem of income inequality, created a lopsided structure of domestic demand, dominated by the consumption patterns of a small section of the population at the apex of the income distribution scale.

The domestic consumer demand, therefore, exhibited a tendency towards a growing variety of goods consumed by the higher income groups, rather than an extensive growth of mass consumption items. This, combined with the lack of adequate control over private industrial investment, and lack of selectiveness in granting protection to private manufacturing, created a tendency towards the development of a 'branch economy' in private manufacturing which was inefficient and excessively dependent on imports for its processed raw materials and capital goods supplies. As a consequence, despite the rapid growth of oil export revenues over this period, the economy developed endemic balance of payments problems which periodically interrupted the process of accumulation. This pattern of industrial growth obviously would have been difficult to sustain in the long run, when oil revenues would have started to decline, either due to the inevitable depletion of reserves or due to a prolonged slack in demand for oil in the world market as happened in the 1980s.

In the foregoing it has been possible only to concentrate on a broad characterization of the structural problems of Iranian industrialization over the oil period of 1953–77. We have tried to identify the overall features of economic development which have given rise to the process of 'perverse growth', as characterized by growing income inequalities and increasing lopsidedness of the industrial structure. Many of the complex and important issues involved in the interrelationship between economic growth and income distribution clearly need a much more detailed study which falls beyond the scope of the present work. The broad historical scope has made it possible to highlight the distinct contribution that the availability of oil income made to the process of industrialization in Iran, and in particular the significant role that the state played in this process. One of the implications of the Iranian experience may be that the functionality of the authoritarian form of the state for capital accumulation, which has been usually maintained in the development literature, may break down in the case of oil economies. It could be argued that a more democratic form of representation of the state and broader political participation may have allowed a more egalitarian distribution of income and a more stable and balanced industrialization to take place.

Appendix A.1 Measurement of the terms of trade and marketed surplus of the agricultural sector

The income terms of trade of the agricultural sector (TT) is here defined as:

$$TT = AMS \, (1/P_m - 1/P_x)$$

where AMS is the marketed surplus of the agricultural sector at current prices, and P_m and P_x are the price indices of the purchases of the agricultural sector from the rest of the economy and is marketed surplus respectively. The income terms of trade of the agricultural sector, as defined above, measures the income gains in the sector due to rising agricultural relative prices.[1]

1 Measurement of agricultural marketed surplus

We have divided the agricultural marketed surplus (AMS) into two components. The first component is the AMS of final consumption goods which includes all the food items in non-agricultural household expenditure excluding sugar and products, tobacco and beverages, tea and coffee, salt and vegetable oils. This component is measured from the expenditure side after allowing for imports of the products in question. Second is the intermediate component of AMS, measured from the production side, which includes sugar, tobacco, cotton, wool, tea, hides and skins and forest products.

1.1 Agricultural marketed surplus for final use

The CSO household budget surveys have been used to measure the final consumption component of AMS. The share of total consumption of non-

---

[1] In appendix A.2 we provide a comparative review of the different approaches to the measurement of income terms of trade. The rationale for the adoption of the above formula is that it measures the increased purchasing power of the agricultural marketed surplus in terms of outside purchases of the agricultural sector at base year prices. The adoption of this measure amongst many others which have been suggested in the literature, is here imposed by the availability of data. For further elaboration of this concept see appendix A.2.

agricultural households was calculated from the CSO surveys for the urban and rural areas separately. In the same way the share of expenditure on food (items defined above) in total expenditure of non-agricultural households was calculated for the urban and rural areas. These shares were in turn applied to the estimates of total consumption by non-agricultural households, derived from the Central Bank's National Accounts data, to arrive at total expenditure by the non-agricultural households on the final consumption component of the AMS. Since CSO data for urban areas only cover the 1969–77 period[2] – and for rural areas the 1965–77 period – the lower missing tails of the two series have had to be estimated through fitting Engel curves to the existing data. The following functional form was used.

$$Ln(FC_{na}) = a + b\ Ln(TC_{na}) + u$$

where FC_{na} and TC_{na} refer to food (items defined above) and total consumption expenditure of non-agricultural households respectively. The OLS estimates of this equation for the urban and rural areas are:

Urban: $Ln(FC) = 0.877 + 0.791\ Ln(TC)$ $R^2 = 0.99$ $DW = 2.30$
t Ratios (4.7)   (40.9)

Rural: $Ln(FC) = 0.240 + 0.880\ Ln(TC)$ $R^2 = 0.98$ $DW = 1.43$
t Ratios (0.84)   (26.7)

The estimates of urban, rural and total expenditure by non-agricultural households on the final consumption of the AMS derived in this manner are given in table A1.1. These estimates are, however, gross of value added in food industry, imports, trade and transport margins.[3] Assuming that food imports are totally consumed by non-agricultural households, the value of imports of the commodities in question is deducted from the total to arrive at its domestic component.[4] From this is subtracted value added in food manufacturing (excluding the items enumerated above) in both rural and urban areas, to arrive at the domestic *agricultural* component of food

---

[2] Though the Central Bank household budget surveys cover the whole of the 1963–77 period, the classification of the published data is such that it is not possible to separate the food consumption items defined above for the non-agricultural households.

[3] To the extent that government food subsidies lead to a reduction in consumer prices relative to producer prices, these should be also added to the above figures to arrive at the total receipts of the agricultural sector. Government food subsidies, however, mainly took the form of losses made on food imports by the government, and hence did not create any margin, over and above the trade and distribution costs, between producers' and consumer prices. Only in the case of agricultural raw materials, such as sugar, both the producers and consumers were subsidized. These latter commodities are addressed separately in the next section.

[4] The CIF value of imports (at 1963 prices) was multiplied by the consumer price index of these commodities (1963 base year), to take care of the effect of food subsidies, internal trade and transport margins, etc. See table A1.8 for the relevant raw data and further details.

consumption.[5] Finally, to arrive at the farm-gate value of *AMS* we have to subtract the value added in wholesale and retail trade and transportation from these figures. With the existing data the best available source of information on this is the annual data published by the Central Bank on value added/output ratios in retail and wholesale trade.[6] The trade and transport margin thus derived is given in table A1.8 at the end of the appendix, and the final estimate for the consumption goods components of the *AMS* is given in the fifth column of table A1.1. Since the Central Bank data on value added in retail and wholesale trade refer to the urban areas, and since trade and transport cost margins in rural areas are expected to be generally higher, there exists an element of overestimation in these figures which on the basis of the existing data cannot be remedied.

1.2 Agricultural marketed surplus for intermediate use

It is assumed that the total output of agricultural products for intermediate use is sold to the non-agricultural sector. The value of total output of such products – namely, sugar beet and cane, tobacco, cotton, wool, tea, hides and skins and forest products – measured at producer prices, is thus taken to be equal to the marketed surplus of agricultural products for intermediate use. To measure the current value of these commodities at farm-gate or producer prices, we have multiplied the volume of output by unit value estimates for each commodity – with the exception of forest products. In the case of forestry, since the sector uses little inputs from other sectors of the economy, it is plausible to assume that value added at factor cost is equal to output at farm-gate prices. Hence, national account estimates of the value added in forestry is taken as the appropriate measure of the value of output. For other commodities, with the exception of sugar beet and sugar cane, we have projected forward and backward the 1972 farm-gate prices given by CSO (*Statistical Yearbook* 1975) in proportion to the movements in the wholesale prices to arrive at estimates for farm-gate prices for the whole

---

[5] Value added in food manufacturing was calculated from the industrial surveys of the Ministry of Industry and Mines. Value added for the excluded items was estimated on the basis of the share in total output. Due to non-availability of data for 1977, the figure for 1977 was estimated, assuming that it bore the same ratio to total food consumption as in 1976.

[6] For transport costs we have used the 1965 and 1973 input-output tables to calculate the share of transport costs in the value of intermediate purchases by the agricultural sector. We have assumed the same share to apply to the sales from agricultural to non-agricultural sectors. The share for 1965 was 5.1 per cent, and that for 1973 was 6.5 per cent. We have applied the 5.1 per cent share to the whole 1963–9 period, and the 6.5 per cent transport share to the 1970–7 period. The higher share for the latter period seems plausible, since excess demand for transport and services in general over this period is expected to have increased the markups in these sectors.

Table A1.1. *Agricultural marketed surplus at current prices 1963–1977*
(billion Rials)

Year	Food consumption of non-agricultural households[a]			Food[b] imports	Agricultural marketed surplus for final use	Agricultural marketed surplus for intermed. use	Total agricult. marketed surplus
	Urban	Rural	Total				
1963	52.1	22.1	74.2	2.0	51.9	11.4	63.3
1964	57.6	25.3	82.6	2.1	56.9	12.1	69.0
1965	60.6	27.2	87.5	4.7	59.3	14.3	73.6
1966	70.6	28.5	98.6	2.7	67.2	14.4	81.6
1967	77.2	29.4	106.0	2.5	72.7	15.5	88.2
1968	89.0	31.8	120.3	4.9	81.0	19.8	100.9
1969	98.8	33.1	132.0	1.8	92.1	19.4	111.5
1970	113.2	35.3	148.5	3.4	101.8	19.9	121.6
1971	127.2	36.1	163.2	12.0	101.4	20.4	121.8
1972	155.1	36.9	192.1	12.0	119.2	25.9	145.2
1973	194.7	45.3	240.0	12.3	153.3	34.1	187.4
1974	247.2	58.8	306.0	29.4	188.6	48.2	236.8
1975	298.8	64.4	363.2	35.5	220.0	43.3	263.4
1976	366.5	80.5	447.0	42.2	276.4	52.7	329.1
1977	491.7	89.9	581.6	78.3	342.3	62.6	404.9

Notes:
[a] Refers to all food items excluding ː ɡar and products, coffee, tea and beverages, vegetable oils and salt. ·oss of imports.
[b] Imports of food products excluding the items enumerated above, valued at retail prices.
Sources: Table A1.7, A1.8, and A1.9 at the end of the appendix.

period.[7] To remove the effect of possible variations in trade and transport cost margins, we have multiplied the wholesale price indices by the trade and transport margin coefficient in each year derived from the Central Bank data in the manner explained above.[8] The 'farm-gate' unit values calculated in this way are multiplied by the volume of output for each commodity to arrive at the current values of total output shown in table A1.2. In the case of sugar beet and sugar cane, since the government provided relatively high and variable subsidies both to the producers and

[7] Since wholesale prices are composite indices of domestically produced and imported goods, we have here implicitly assumed that these two groups of goods are perfect substitutes or that there exists a high positive correlation in their price variations.
[8] All the raw data used in these calculations, together with the methods applied, are detailed in tables A1.8 and A1.9 at the end of the appendix.

consumers, the wholesale price movement of sugar is a very poor indicator of the farm-gate price variations. In the case of these commodities, therefore, output is valued at government support prices. The values of different items of the *AMS* for intermediate use are given in tables A1.2 and A1.3, at current and at 1963 prices respectively.

The value of agricultural marketed surplus for final, intermediate and total use is given in the last three columns of table A1.1. As the table indicates Iranian agriculture is still dominated by food crop cultivation, and industrial cash crops form a relatively low proportion of the marketed surplus and *a fortiori* of the total output.

2 Terms of trade of the agricultural sector

2.1 Measurement of intersectoral purchases of commodities

To measure the terms of trade between the agricultural and non-agricultural sectors we have to decompose the intersectoral purchases into their constituent commodity groupings. The years 1965 and 1973 have been chosen as the two base years for calculating the composite price indices. The sales of the agricultural sector for intermediate use has already been given in terms of its individual commodity composition in the previous section. Agricultural sales for final use have been disaggregated by the help of household budget surveys of the Central Bank (for 1965 urban areas) and the CSO (for the rest). The share of each individual group of commodities in average household expenditure on food by the non-agricultural households has been calculated from the budget surveys, for the rural and urban areas separately.[9] These shares have been applied to the aggregate estimates of *AMS* for final use to derive total expenditure on each individual group of commodities. The results are reproduced in table A1.4.

The purchases of the agricultural sector from non-agricultural sectors for intermediate use have been derived from the 1965 and 1973 input-output tables.[10] The purchases of chemicals have been further decomposed into chemical fertilizers and other chemicals by using the CSO data (*Statistical Yearbook* 1970, 1975) on the use of fertilizers in the sector.

The purchases of the agricultural sector from non-agriculture for final use have been disaggregated on the basis of the household budget surveys.

---

[9] This is of course done after deducting the value of imports of each individual commodity and applying the same trade and transport cost margin as for the aggregate case discussed above.

[10] The intermediate purchases in input-output tables are given at factor cost. The values of intermediate purchases of agriculture from trade and transport sectors have been proportionately distributed amongst other intermediate purchases to derive values at purchase prices.

Table A1.2. *Value of agricultural marketed surplus for intermediate use at current prices 1963–1977*

(million Rials)

Year	Cotton	Oil seeds	Sugar beet[a]	Tea	Tobacco	Forestry	Wool	Hide	Skin[b]	Total
1963	4675.3	180.7	1342.8	1035.5	451.5	700	2040.0	502.9	484.0	11412.6
1964	4423.1	198.9	1212.9	865.3	755.0	1300	2198.2	620.3	528.1	12101.9
1965	5637.0	204.6	1707.5	1045.0	1014.0	1000	2412.4	724.0	541.5	14285.9
1966	4209.9	189.4	2606.3	1233.1	975.0	1200	2680.4	743.1	573.4	14410.7
1967	4308.2	256.8	3219.5	1722.0	894.9	900	2790.3	787.7	626.6	15506.0
1968	6944.9	321.0	4073.6	2051.2	772.9	1800	2359.9	849.8	655.5	19828.7
1969	6106.8	594.0	4178.3	2054.9	825.2	1600	2500.3	846.9	686.6	19392.9
1970	5750.6	981.9	4608.2	2324.0	850.5	1600	2426.4	675.8	668.5	19886.0
1971	5795.5	990.6	4820.8	2260.7	1005.6	1600	2599.8	659.9	670.2	20403.2
1972	8026.2	808.0	4888.9	3127.9	1370.3	3100	2668.0	1001.0	948.0	25938.2
1973	10893.5	864.8	7508.8	3177.3	823.2	5400	2908.5	1306.8	1229.5	34112.4
1974	15055.7	1782.2	10570.0	4776.3	1118.8	7100	4404.9	2128.2	1285.5	48221.6
1975	8527.1	1640.9	14589.0	2947.2	887.6	7900	3801.3	1842.5	1193.9	43329.6
1976	12780.0	2432.6	15480.0	4020.8	1394.5	8300	5030.5	1993.9	1267.5	52699.8
1977	15181.8	2935.3	13005.0	8685.7	1804.1	11200	5898.3	2751.4	1146.4	62607.9

Notes:
[a] Includes sugar cane.
[b] Includes sheep and goat skins.
Sources: Tables A1.8, A1.9, end of the appendix.

Table A1.3. Real value of agricultural marketed surplus for intermediate use at 1963 prices 1963–1977

(million Rials)

Year	Cotton	Oil seeds	Sugar beet[a]	Tea	Tobacco	Forestry	Wool	Hide	Skin[b]	Total
1963	4675.3	180.7	1342.8	1035.5	451.5	700	2040.0	502.9	484.0	11412.6
1964	4524.1	180.7	1210.4	869.9	779.8	1120	1976.2	549.8	468.1	11679.0
1965	5675.5	180.7	1655.6	1035.5	1067.1	980	2167.5	639.3	478.2	13879.4
1966	4314.8	180.7	2510.0	1221.9	1026.0	1050	2486.2	639.3	493.4	13922.3
1967	4396.2	271.0	3085.5	1408.3	902.9	840	2103.7	639.3	508.6	14155.5
1968	6338.5	338.7	3672.9	1677.6	779.8	1400	2103.7	669.2	516.2	17496.5
1969	6047.7	587.1	3795.0	1574.0	779.8	1330	2167.5	647.9	525.3	17454.2
1970	5838.4	880.7	4177.8	1636.1	738.7	1260	2167.5	532.8	527.0	17759.0
1971	5349.9	745.2	4323.0	1346.2	738.7	1330	2231.2	520.0	528.1	17112.3
1972	7408.4	609.7	4340.8	1822.5	985.0	1960	1848.7	558.4	528.8	20062.4
1973	7268.9	643.6	4890.6	1926.1	615.6	2485	1721.2	575.4	541.4	20667.8
1974	8315.6	892.0	4983.0	1988.2	574.6	2590	1785.0	916.4	553.5	22598.2
1975	5466.2	1129.1	5349.3	1656.9	615.6	2660	1785.0	929.2	602.1	20193.2
1976	5931.4	1467.8	5676.0	1822.5	779.8	2660	1785.0	967.5	615.1	21705.1
1977	6222.2	1185.5	4768.5	2402.4	615.6	3220	1785.0	1393.8	580.7	22173.7

Notes:
[a] Includes sugar cane.
[b] Includes sheep and goat skins.
Sources: Tables A1.8, A1.9, end of the appendix.

Table A1.4. *Intersectoral exchange of commodities 1965 and 1973*

(million Rials)

Purchased by agriculture from non-agriculture			Sold by agriculture to non-agriculture		
	1965	1973		1965	1973
for intermediate use			*for intermediate use*		
Fertilizers	874.3	4254.2	Cotton	5637.0	10893.5
Other chemicals[a]	318.8	5576.8	Oil seeds	204.6	864.8
Fuel	296.6	2594.0	Tea	1045.0	3177.3
Metal products	279.0	5732.5	Tobacco	1014	823.2
			Hides	724.0	1306.8
			Skins	541.5	1229.5
			Wool	2412.4	2908.5
			Sugar beet[b]	1707.5	7508.8
			Forestry	1000.0	5400.0
for final use			*for final use*		
Sugar	5689.5	6377.9	Cereals	18470.1	51601.2
Edible oil	1748.6	2933.0	Meat	16411.2	44781.3
Cigarettes	1359.7	2212.0	Pulses	2911.4	6800.9
Spices (salt)	365.0	368.2	Eggs and dairy products	8550.3	22141.1
Clothing	9377.5	15934.8	Fruit and vegetables	17362.3	36650.4
Fuel and light	5990.0	7143.1			
Medical care	3523.4	7470.4			

Notes:
[a] Includes pesticides, insecticides and drugs for work animals.
[b] Includes sugar cane.
Sources: CSO, *Household Budget Survey of Rural Areas* 1965, 1973. Central Bank, *Surveys of Urban Areas* 1965. UN, *Yearbook of International Trade Statistics* 1965, 1974. Table A1.9, end of the appendix.

The share of each individual item in average household consumption of agricultural households has been applied to aggregate consumption of agricultural households, to derive the total value of each item. The name of the commodity groups and their estimated values are given in table A1.4.

2.2 Price indices

To measure the terms of trade of the agricultural sector we need appropriate price indices for the sales and purchases of the agricultural sector in commodity groupings enumerated above. Any alternative price indices which can be plausibly assumed to have a high degree of correlation with the prices of these commodity groupings, could equally serve as a good proxy.

In the case of agricultural sales for intermediate use we have already discussed the derivation of appropriate prices for measuring the value of marketed surplus in the previous section.[11] In the case of agricultural purchases for intermediate use we have used the wholesale price indices published by the Central Bank – with the exception of fertilizers which were highly subsidized and directly sold to the farmers by the government. The price index for fertilizers was calculated from official price and consumption data on seven categories of chemical fertilizers (see table A1.9 at the end of the appendix).

It could be plausibly assumed that prices received by the agricultural sector are highly correlated with wholesale prices, barring two qualifications. First, due to possibly faster growth of productivity in trade and transport services and improvement of marketing services in the rural areas (e.g., the introduction of rural co-operatives), there may be a long-term tendency for the trade and transport cost margins for agricultural sales to decline over time. Secondly, the trade and transport bottlenecks which were created after the 1973 surge in domestic demand, is expected to have increased the trade and transport cost margins in the wholesale prices. To remove the likely effects of these two factors in distorting the correlation between the wholesale prices and agricultural sales prices, we have again deflated the wholesale prices by the trade and transport cost factors, derived from the Central Bank data as discussed above.

In the case of the agricultural households' purchases for final use, consumer price indices are more suitable than wholesale price indices, in particular since the government's consumer subsidies on commodities such as sugar, cigarettes and tea created a large and variable gap between the wholesale prices and consumer prices over the different years. Though the consumer price indices published by the Central Bank only cover the urban areas, it would be plausible to assume that rural retail prices, while being different from the prices in the urban areas, fluctuate in harmony with the latter, in particular in the case of easily tradable and non-perishable commodities being considered here.

In the case of agricultural sales for final use, we have also used the wholesale price indices, subject to the above discussed trade and transport margins. Though the government provided large consumers subsidies on different categories of food items, as mentioned above, these subsidies largely took the form of losses made on import of foodstuffs and therefore could not create a substantial margin between the wholesale prices and

---

[11] In the case of forestry the implicit GDP deflator at factor cost is taken as the appropriate price index.

Table A1.5. *Composite inter-sectoral price indices 1963–1977*

(1963 = 100)

Year	Sales of agricultural sector to non-agriculture			Purchases of agricultural sector from non-agriculture		
	Intermediate use	Final use	All uses	Intermediate use	Final use	All uses
1963	100.0	100.0	100.0	100.0	100.0	100.0
1964	103.2	112.0	110.4	101.1	102.0	102.0
1965	103.2	112.3	110.6	103.7	100.3	100.5
1966	103.0	111.0	109.5	101.3	99.9	100.0
1967	109.3	109.0	109.1	105.0	100.7	100.9
1968	113.0	110.1	110.6	105.5	102.4	102.6
1969	111.0	115.4	114.6	100.6	104.5	104.3
1970	111.2	118.0	116.7	99.8	106.2	105.8
1971	119.9	133.7	131.3	110.6	110.5	110.5
1972	132.8	138.9	137.9	115.0	114.1	114.4
1973	169.4	156.8	159.0	128.4	125.6	126.4
1974	218.4	210.0	211.4	146.2	136.9	139.7
1975	213.6	204.3	205.9	142.2	146.7	145.3
1976	246.7	235.9	237.7	169.7	157.6	161.2
1977	283.0	283.9	283.7	189.6	176.5	180.4

agricultural producer prices, over and above the trade and transport margins.

The data on the disaggregated price indices used, and more details on sources and methods are given in table A1.9 at the end of the appendix.

Using the 1965 and 1973 intersectoral purchases (table A1.4) and the disaggregated price series, we have measured the composite price indices for the sales and purchases of the agricultural sector, and the terms of trade of the sector, which are shown in tables A1.5 and A1.6. As the tables show the agricultural terms of trade, both in the case of intermediate inputs and final products, follow a clear upward trend which particularly intensifies from 1971 onwards. This may reflect the effect of the substantial increase in government subsidies, both to producers and consumers, as a result of the oil revenue increases of the early 1970s. Agricultural producers benefitted from such subsidies both as producers (e.g., support prices on sugar beet, etc.) and as consumers. The magnitude of income terms of trade effect, i.e., real income gains (1963 prices) is given in the last column of table A1.6.

Table A1.6. *Indices of the terms of trade of the agricultural sector 1963–1977*

(billion Rials)

Year	Net barter terms of trade			Income terms of trade
	Intermediate use	Final use	All products	
1963	100.0	100.0	100.0	0.0
1964	102.1	109.8	108.2	5.2
1965	99.5	112.0	110.1	6.7
1966	101.7	111.1	109.6	7.1
1967	104.0	108.3	108.1	6.5
1968	107.1	107.5	107.8	7.1
1969	110.3	110.4	109.9	9.6
1970	111.5	111.0	110.3	10.7
1971	108.3	121.0	118.8	17.4
1972	115.5	121.7	120.5	21.6
1973	131.9	124.9	125.7	30.3
1974	149.4	153.4	151.3	57.5
1975	150.2	139.3	141.7	53.3
1976	145.4	149.7	147.5	65.7
1977	149.3	160.8	157.2	81.7

Table A1.7. *Number of households, consumption and agricultural value added data 1963–1977*

Year	TH	TUH	TRH	TAH	ARH	AUH	TCC	CCU	CCR	TRC	RCU	RCR	AVCAGR	AVCRU	ACAGU	AGR	RAGR
1963	4646.7	1682.7	2964.0	1946.5	1818.2	128.3	262.1	143.9	118.2	262.1	143.9	118.2	3546.0	3278.0	n.a.	98.4	98.4
1964	4769.1	1770.7	2998.4	1953.6	1821.5	132.1	294.7	161.2	133.5	284.3	154.4	129.9	3791.0	3478.0	n.a.	110.6	100.5
1965	4896.6	1863.3	3033.3	1960.7	1824.8	135.9	312.5	169.7	142.8	295.8	162.0	133.8	4078.0	3770.0	n.a.	120.0	108.4
1966	5029.3	1960.7	3068.6	1968.0	1828.1	139.9	348.6	202.2	146.4	332.7	191.6	141.1	4365.0	3988.0	n.a.	121.7	112.2
1967	5167.5	2063.2	3104.3	1975.3	1831.4	144.0	371.6	222.6	149.0	359.1	209.1	150.0	4965.0	4386.0	n.a.	128.4	121.1
1968	5311.6	2171.1	3140.4	1982.9	1834.7	148.1	423.1	262.3	160.8	402.8	242.8	160.0	4383.0	4005.0	n.a.	139.6	130.4
1969	5461.6	2284.7	3177.0	1990.5	1838.0	152.5	463.7	294.9	168.8	432.8	263.7	169.1	4043.0	3957.0	n.a.	147.8	134.5
1970	5618.0	2404.1	3213.9	1998.3	1841.4	156.9	522.6	344.4	178.2	477.3	304.0	173.3	4210.0	4179.0	n.a.	160.6	140.7
1971	5781.2	2529.8	3251.3	2006.2	1844.7	161.5	572.0	392.4	179.6	493.0	327.4	165.7	4603.0	4985.0	n.a.	172.3	135.6
1972	5951.3	2662.1	3289.1	2014.2	1848.0	166.2	676.9	495.5	181.4	550.2	385.8	164.4	5108.0	4940.0	6627.0	201.8	143.1
1973	6128.7	2801.3	3327.4	2022.4	1851.4	171.0	875.9	650.8	225.1	639.4	455.9	183.5	6109.0	5985.0	7989.0	234.4	151.0
1974	6313.9	2947.8	3366.1	2030.7	1854.7	176.0	1166.4	867.8	298.6	738.1	527.0	211.1	11487.0	11044.0	15999.0	303.3	159.9
1975	6507.2	3102.0	3405.3	2039.2	1858.1	181.2	1411.4	1085.4	326.0	816.2	604.8	211.4	13549.0	12861.0	21468.0	333.9	170.3
1976	6709.1	3264.2	3444.9	2047.9	1861.4	186.5	1799.9	1385.9	414.0	920.0	682.6	237.3	12598.0	12678.0	24654.0	426.3	179.7
1977	6919.8	3434.9	3484.9	2056.7	1864.8	191.9	2437.5	1975.1	462.4	1055.3	823.8	231.5	17344.0	17267.0	27770.0	485.0	177.3

Notes:

TH = total number of households (in 000s). TUH = total number of urban households (in 000s). TRH = total number of rural households (in 000s).

TAH = total number of agricultural households (in 000s). ARH = total number of rural agricultural households (in 000s). AUH = total number of urban agricultural households (in 000s). CCU = total private consumption at current prices in urban areas (in bn Rials). CCR = total private consumption at current prices in rural areas (in bn Rials). TCC = total private consumption at current prices in rural areas (in bn Rials). RCU = total private consumption at 1963 prices (in urban areas (in bn Rials). RCR = total private consumption in the rural areas at 1963 prices (in bn Rials). TRC = total private consumption in the rural areas in 1963 prices (in bn Rials). AVCAGR = average monthly consumption of agricultural households in rural areas (in Rials). AVCRU = average consumption per month of all the households in rural areas (in Rials). ACAGU = average monthly consumption of urban agricultural households (in Rials). The data for 1963 average rural consumption were calculated on the basis of the National Account estimates of the Central Bank. Average agricultural rural consumption for the year 1963 was calculated as a fixed ratio of average rural consumption on the basis of the average ratio for the subsequent three years. AGR = value added in the agricultural sector at current prices. RAGR = value added in the agricultural sector at 1963 prices (in bn Rials).

Sources: CSO, *National Census for Population and Housing* 1956, 1966, 1976. The data for intervening years have been estimated on an exponential growth line. CSO, *Iranian Statistical Yearbook* 1969, 1977, 1979, CSO, *Household Budget Surveys of Rural Areas* and *Household Budget Surveys of Urban Areas* various issues, Central Bank, *Annual Reports* various issues.

Table A1.8. *Average food consumption, food imports, trade and transport margins, and volume of agricultural raw materials*

Year	AVFCNR	AVFCNU	AVCNAR	AVCNAU	FIMP	TRS	TRDE	TTAG	TJMP	COT	OSEED	TEA	TBCO	SUGBT	SUGCAN	WOOL	HIDE	SKIN	GSK
1963	1582.5	2755.0	3277.7	7338.6	2.0	5.1	18.6	77.5	129.1	402	16	50	11	1191.0	248.0	32	11.8	21.4	8.2
1964	1743.7	2888.5	3659.4	7790.8	2.0	5.1	18.4	77.6	128.8	389	16	42	19	1028.0	292.0	31	12.9	20.1	8.4
1965	1831.4	2882.5	3869.3	7770.3	4.5	5.1	18.1	77.9	128.3	488	16	50	26	1411.0	392.0	34	15.0	20.0	9.0
1966	1853.0	3188.3	3921.3	8826.0	2.5	5.1	17.9	78.1	128.0	371	16	59	25	2280.0	383.0	39	15.0	21.0	9.0
1967	1862.9	3305.1	3945.0	9236.8	2.3	5.1	17.2	78.8	126.9	378	24	68	22	2830.0	430.0	33	15.0	22.0	9.0
1968	1972.0	3616.3	4208.5	10348.8	4.2	5.1	17.2	78.8	126.9	545	30	81	19	3410.0	450.0	33	15.7	22.5	9.0
1969	2037.3	3810.4	4367.1	11055.6	1.5	5.1	16.9	79.1	126.5	520	52	76	19	3480.0	530.0	34	15.2	23.1	9.0
1970	2115.2	4140.2	4557.2	12278.2	2.8	6.5	16.1	78.8	126.9	502	78	79	18	3860.0	540.0	34	12.5	25.0	7.6
1971	2108.2	4412.7	4540.2	13308.3	10.2	6.5	17.5	77.5	129.1	460	66	65	18	3980.0	580.0	35	12.2	25.2	7.5
1972	2105.3	5109.1	4533.0	16015.1	11.1	6.5	18.9	76.2	131.3	637	54	88	24	3918.0	700.0	29	13.1	25.5	7.3
1973	2520.1	6085.2	5560.3	19974.1	14.0	6.5	18.9	76.2	131.3	625	57	93	15	4240.0	1050.0	27	13.5	26.2	7.4
1974	3199.1	7329.8	7291.1	25269.7	50.5	6.5	19.0	76.1	131.5	715	79	96	14	4300.0	1100.0	28	21.5	27.0	7.4
1975	3421.2	8408.2	7868.6	30055.1	62.0	6.5	19.2	75.9	131.8	470	100	80	15	4670.0	1100.0	28	21.8	27.9	9.2
1976	4179.5	9787.0	9877.7	36412.4	56.2	6.5	19.1	76.0	131.6	510	130	88	19	5200.0	800.0	28	22.7	28.5	9.4
1977	4560.1	12461.7	10905.6	49412.4	82.4	6.5	19.0	76.1	131.5	535	105	116	15	4150.0	1000.0	28	32.7	29.3	7.0

Notes:

AVFCNR, AVFCNU = average monthly food consumption of non-agricultural households in rural and urban areas respectively, excluding sugar and products, vegetable oil, tea and coffee, tobacco, and beverages (in Rials). AVCNAR, AVCNAU = average monthly consumption of non-agricultural households in rural urban areas respectively (all items in Rials per month). FIMP = CIF value of food imports (excluding the above defined items, in bn Rials). TRS = percentage ratio of transport costs to the factor cost value of intermediate inputs used in agriculture. TRDE = percentage ratio of value added to total turnover in wholesale and retail trade. TTAG = percentage of retail value of agricultural sales accruing to the agricultural sector. Calculated from the following formula: TTAG = (100 + TRS)/(100 − TRDE). TIMP = factor for converting the CIF value of imports into retail values (in percentages). Calculated from the following formula: TIMP = (100 − TRDE)/(100 + TRS). The rest of the variables are production volumes in thousand metric tonnes of: cotton (COT), tea, tobacco (TBCO), sugar beet (SUGBT), sugarcane (SUGCAN), wool, hide, sheep skin (SKIN), and goat skin (GSK).

Sources: UN, *International Trade Statistics 1963–79*, Central Bank, *Annual Report* various issues, CSO, *Iranian Statistical Yearbook 1966–79*.

Table A1.9. Disaggregated price indices of various commodity groupings

Year	FERT	OCHM	FUEL	METL	COTN	OSED	TEA	SUGB	WOOL	TBCO	SKIN	FRST	CERL	PULS	EGS&	MEAT	FVEG	EOIL	MEDC	LIGH	SUGR	CLOTH	CIGR
1963	100.0	100.0	100.0	100.0	100.0	100.0	100.0	100.0	100.0	100.0	100.0	100.0	100.0	100.0	100.0	100.0	100.0	100.0	100.0	100.0	100.0	100.0	100.0
1964	99.0	97.3	106.0	105.9	97.8	109.8	99.5	100.2	111.2	96.8	112.8	116.1	113.4	144.4	107.8	112.4	106.7	105.8	103.7	103.5	97.3	102.7	101.4
1965	102.4	96.5	108.9	109.6	99.3	112.6	100.9	103.1	111.3	95.0	113.2	102.0	123.3	121.1	107.0	117.9	96.3	106.2	104.6	98.8	92.6	102.7	103.7
1966	97.1	97.3	109.9	108.8	97.6	104.0	100.9	103.8	107.8	95.0	116.2	114.3	113.4	103.5	106.1	117.4	106.1	101.2	105.7	97.7	91.7	103.2	103.7
1967	101.3	97.4	115.3	113.3	98.0	93.2	122.3	104.3	132.6	99.1	123.2	107.1	101.6	94.6	107.9	124.7	105.1	104.0	108.8	99.4	91.6	102.9	103.7
1968	100.6	96.3	124.1	110.8	109.6	93.2	122.3	110.9	112.2	99.1	127.0	128.6	97.8	97.4	109.8	131.5	105.1	107.2	112.4	104.1	91.0	103.2	104.9
1969	75.8	95.8	127.1	148.1	101.0	99.1	130.5	110.1	115.4	105.8	130.7	120.3	103.2	75.7	113.3	135.7	117.1	107.6	115.7	108.3	90.8	105.5	105.3
1970	74.7	92.8	123.7	152.4	98.5	109.6	142.0	110.3	111.9	115.1	126.9	127.0	119.8	86.2	114.4	134.0	107.9	121.2	117.4	107.2	91.0	108.0	105.3
1971	74.0	90.9	123.7	151.1	108.3	132.9	167.9	111.5	116.5	136.1	126.9	120.3	136.6	122.4	128.0	139.6	127.9	136.9	118.9	107.5	91.1	111.6	105.3
1972	79.2	90.8	124.0	161.0	108.3	134.8	171.6	112.6	144.3	139.1	179.3	158.2	121.8	182.8	137.0	158.3	132.2	134.6	123.8	110.1	91.9	117.7	105.3
1973	86.4	89.7	124.8	198.9	149.9	136.7	165.0	153.5	169.0	133.7	227.1	217.3	145.9	169.4	136.8	193.6	136.9	159.0	132.3	113.9	94.8	136.7	105.3
1974	86.3	91.7	126.6	252.5	181.1	203.5	240.2	212.1	246.8	194.7	232.2	274.1	235.8	160.5	159.5	243.5	172.4	172.7	146.4	119.9	97.3	153.7	105.3
1975	86.2	94.3	126.5	237.3	156.0	148.4	177.9	272.7	213.0	144.2	198.3	297.0	181.3	134.8	169.3	262.8	199.2	168.9	166.3	124.8	100.6	167.4	105.3
1976	86.3	179.2	126.7	241.8	215.5	169.0	220.6	272.7	281.8	178.8	206.1	312.0	210.9	240.6	184.4	295.7	228.2	179.3	179.1	127.6	102.2	186.1	106.2
1977	86.3	200.6	137.9	278.9	244.0	252.1	361.5	272.7	330.4	293.1	197.4	347.8	236.4	381.7	209.5	359.4	285.1	195.1	215.1	138.9	106.2	209.2	109.7

Notes:

FERT = fertilizer price index. Composite index of seven types of chemical fertilizers at government subsidized prices. OCHM = price index of other chemicals used in agriculture. FUEL = wholesale price index of fuels other than crude petroleum. METL = wholesale price index of metal products. COTN = wholesale price index of cotton, 1974–7 based on export prices. OSED = price index of oil seed. 1963–8 based on wholesale prices of raw materials of vegetable origin, 1969–77 based on the wholesale price index of oilseeds. TEA = tea price index. 1963–7 refers to producer prices calculated by dividing the value of output by its volume, 1963–7 refers to wholesale prices of raw materials of vegetable origin. SUGB = farmgate price of sugar beet at government subsidized prices. WOOL = export price index of wool. TBCO = price index of tobacco, as for tea. SKIN = wholesale price index of skin and hides. FRST = implicit GDP deflator of forestry at factor cost. CERL = wholesale price index of cereals. PULS = wholesale price index of pulses. EGS& = consumer price index of dairy products and eggs. MEAT = consumer price index of meat and products. FVEG = consumer price index of fresh fruits and vegetables. EOIL = consumer price index of edible oil. MEDC = consumer price index of medical care. LIGH = consumer price index of fuel and light. SUGR = consumer price index of sugar and products. CLOTH = consumer price index of clothing. CIGR = consumer price index of cigarettes and tobacco.

Sources: CSO, *Iranian Statistical Yearbook* 1966–79, Central Bank of Iran, *Quarterly Bulletins* various issues, 1962–79.

Appendix A.2 Measurement of net agricultural surplus

1. Net agricultural surplus at current prices

Following Millar (1970), net agricultural surplus here is defined as gross value added in the agricultural sector minus the consumption of the households who are directly involved in agricultural production. It refers to resources made available by the agricultural sector for gross investment within the sector itself and utilization in the other sectors, including exports. Using the following notations; Q_a, C_a, I_a, X_a, and M_a, referring respectively to gross output, consumption, gross investment, marketed surplus, and non-agricultural purchases of the agricultural sector, we can define net agricultural surplus (S_a) and agricultural surplus ratio (R_a) as:

$$S_a = (Q_a - C_a) = (I_a + X_a - M_a), \qquad\qquad 1$$

$$R_a = (S_a \,/\, Q_a). \qquad\qquad 2$$

Net agricultural surplus, in other words, refers to gross investment within the agricultural sector plus the surplus in the balance of trade of the agricultural sector with the rest of the economy. The agricultural sector here includes farming, animal husbandry, fishing and forestry.

The number of agricultural households, within both the rural and urban areas, is calculated from population censuses (a log-linear trend has been used to obtain population estimates for the missing years). Average monthly consumption, for total households as well as those within the agricultural sector, is derived from the household budget surveys of the Central Statistical Office (CSO) for both rural and urban areas. These data have been used to derive the ratio of agricultural households' consumption to total consumption both within the urban and rural areas. These ratios have in turn been applied to the Central Bank's National Account data on private consumption in rural and urban areas to derive the current annual consumption of agricultural households within these two areas.[1] The sum

---

[1] CSO data for the urban sector are only available for the years 1969–77. For the years prior to that we have taken the average consumption of rural agricultural households to

of these two annual consumptions has been subtracted from value added in the agricultural sector to give the net agricultural surplus at current prices as defined above. The results are shown in the first four columns of table A2.1 and the primary data used are reproduced in table A1.7 at the end of the appendix A.1.

A likely source of error in these estimates arises from the inaccuracies of the Central Bank's data for private consumption, particularly for the rural sector. The Central Bank's National Accounts estimates of private consumption are derived as a residual and divided into rural and urban components on the basis of estimates of the level of economic activity in the two regions. The aggregate consumption data therefore incorporates all the measurement errors in the other components of national accounts. If such measurement errors remain proportionately fixed over time, the error involved in the trend growth rates may not be very serious. A more serious source of error in the Central Bank's data on private consumption, in our opinion, arises from the procedure adopted for the division of private consumption into its rural and urban components. There is strong evidence to suggest that the Central Bank's estimates of rural consumption over the 1970–7 period exhibit a significant underestimation of the trend growth rates.[2] This may be due to growth of consumption in rural areas being financed by migrant labour remittances over the 1970s, which would not be taken into account in the Central Bank's procedure of division of total consumption between the rural and urban areas. Though it is possible to attempt alternative estimates of rural consumption based on CSO household budget surveys, we have preferred to retain the original Central Bank's estimates since all of our arguments in the main text which rely on the behaviour of the net agricultural surplus would be *a fortiori* correct at lower levels of net agricultural surplus for the 1970s.

Apart from the possible inaccuracies in the Central Bank's consumption data, two other sources of error which arise due to the difficulties in classifying consumption expenditures by the sector of activity should be borne in mind. First, the rural households classified under non-agricultural activities may participate in part-time agricultural work – or some members of the household may be full-time agricultural workers (households are

represent those of urban agricultural households as well. Since urban agricultural households form a very small section of total agricultural households, the underestimation of agricultural household consumption involved in this procedure is expected to be marginal, of the order of 1 to 2 per cent.

[2] The CSOs rural household budget surveys exhibit trend growth rates which are substantially at variance with the Central Bank's rural consumption during the 1970s. Furthermore, Central Bank's data produce highly paradoxical results – e.g., estimates of food consumption in rural areas based on Central Bank's data show a deceleration in trend rates of growth over the 1970–7 period as compared to 1963–70 period, which is not plausible.

classified according to the major activity of the head of the household). This leads to an overestimation of agricultural surplus as measured above, since part of the consumption of this group of households, according to our definition of net surplus, should be subtracted from the above measure. Secondly, the agricultural households may have alternative sources of income, implying that some of the members of the household may not be directly involved in agricultural production and hence their consumption according to our definition should be included in the net agricultural surplus. The data provided by the household budget surveys of the CSO on the different sources of rural income allow a quantification of these magnitudes for the 1975–6 period.[3] According to this source, the share of agricultural incomes accruing to non-agricultural households varied between 6.8 and 6.1 per cent between the years 1975 and 1976, while the share of non-agricultural income of agricultural households remained stable at around 12.6 per cent for these two years.

It is, however, quite possible to believe that these estimates had been significantly affected by the oil boom years of 1972–7. The share of non-agricultural income in the agricultural households income must have risen during this period, as these were the years of booming carpet weaving and construction related industries, such as brick making in the rural areas.[4] For similar reasons the share of non-agricultural workers in agricultural income must have declined during the same period. These points are clearly supported by the fact that, after the revolution, with the end of the economic boom in 1979/80 the share of non-agricultural income in agricultural households income declined to 9 per cent from its peak pre-revolution level of 12.5 per cent and the share of income of non-agricultural households from agricultural income rose from 6.8 per cent to 8.9 per cent.

The incorporation of these two sources of income and consumption in the above notion of net agricultural surplus encounters various conceptual and measurement problems due to the impossibility of strict categorization of households by sector of economic activity. Under a specific set of assumptions, the measure of agricultural surplus reported in the table can be shown to incorporate these. If it is assumed that agricultural income accruing to non-agricultural households is totally composed of rentiers income, then it could be treated as part of the surplus as defined above. If in addition it is assumed that the consumption of agricultural households corresponds to a certain desired or necessary norm which is invariant to the level of their non-agricultural income (in other words employment of some members of the

[3] In the case of urban agriculture, due to the relatively small magnitude involved, such considerations will not be worth pursuing.

[4] See Madjd (1980, pp.26–8). According to this source, in the Nishapur region for example, between 30 and 40 per cent of small farmers were also involved in carpet weaving.

household in non-agricultural activities does not affect the consumption level of the household), then this latter source of income also becomes immaterial to the measurement of agricultural surplus as defined above. This assumption would be plausible for example when it is the case that non-agricultural income accrues to the very poor peasantry and is necessary for the reproduction of the peasant household as an effective unit of agricultural production. Under these assumptions the introduction of the above sources of income does not affect the measure of surplus reported in table A2.1.

It is possible to estimate alternative measures of net agricultural surplus on the basis of different sets of assumptions regarding these two sources of income and consumption. We estimated two such alternative measures under assumptions which were radically different from those made above. Since these two measures turned out to be very close to the estimates reported in table A2.1, we have not reported them here.[5]

The following observations could be made on the basis of the results presented in table A2.1. First, the net agricultural surplus ratio remained relatively stagnant during the 1963–7 period which was a period of slow growth of agricultural productivity, and then grew rapidly during the fourth plan period up to 1972, which was a period of relatively faster growth of labour productivity. The rising trend of the agricultural surplus ratio may be indicative of the fact that much of the productivity growth in agriculture was accounted for by large commercial farms and the well-to-do peasantry. In addition during the whole of the post-land reform period there was a trend towards higher concentration of land ownership and greater use of wage labour which would be expected to lead to higher surplus ratios. Furthermore, during this period, there was a noticeable improvement in the agricultural terms of trade, which as we have already observed led to sizeable increases in real agricultural incomes rendering the sector capable of affording higher surpluses. Since food and agricultural raw materials form a high percentage of consumption of poorer households, such income gains from terms of trade improvements are expected to have a highly skewed distribution in favour of the richer households, which again contributes to rising surplus ratios.

During the oil boom of post 1972, however, there was a sharp reversal in these trends. Two factors which may go a long way in explaining this phenomenon were the rapid growth of non-agricultural incomes of rural households, and the sharp wage increases for agricultural labour over this period. The former would tend to reduce the surplus ratio in the case of

[5] The estimated deviation of these measures from that reported in table A2.1 in most of the years was below 1 per cent of agricultural value added with the maximum deviation being 3.3 per cent for the year 1975.

Table A2.1. *Net agricultural surplus at current prices 1963–1977*

Year	Annual agricultural household consumption			Agr. value added	Net agr. surplus	Agr. surplus ratio
	Rural	Urban	Total			
1963	78.4	5.5	84.0	98.4	14.4	14.7
1964	88.4	6.1	94.5	110.6	16.1	14.6
1965	92.9	6.7	99.7	120.0	20.3	16.9
1966	95.5	7.4	102.9	121.7	18.8	15.5
1967	99.5	7.0	106.5	128.4	21.9	17.0
1968	102.8	7.9	110.7	139.6	28.9	20.7
1969	99.8	7.5	107.3	147.8	40.5	27.4
1970	102.9	8.0	110.9	160.6	49.7	31.0
1971	94.1	9.0	103.1	172.3	69.2	40.1
1972	105.4	13.4	118.8	201.8	83.0	41.1
1973	127.8	16.6	144.5	234.4	89.9	38.4
1974	171.1	34.3	205.4	303.3	97.9	32.3
1975	187.4	47.3	234.7	333.9	99.2	29.7
1976	222.3	55.9	278.2	426.3	148.1	34.7
1977	248.5	64.8	313.4	485.0	171.6	35.4

Notes:
Values are in bn. Rials and ratios in percentages.
Sources: Table A1.7 at the end of appendix A1.

independent peasant farmers through the demonstration effect of the new consumption habits which it inevitably generates in the countryside, and the latter through reducing the surpluses of commercial farms with predominant use of wage labour.

2 Real net agricultural surplus

Denoting real values by lower case letters, equation 1 could be expressed as:

$$P_s s_a = P_i i_a + P_x x_a - P_m m_a, \qquad\qquad 3$$

where P_i, P_x and P_m are the related price indices of the variables defined as in equation 1, and P_s is the price index for real agricultural surplus. Assuming $P_s = (I_a + X_a - M_a)/(i_a + x_a - m_a)$, this gives us the real agricultural surplus from the point of view of the economy as a whole, i.e.:

$$s_a = i_a + x_a - m_a. \tag{4}$$

From the point of view of the agricultural sector itself, however, real net agricultural surplus (s'_a) should also incorporate the terms of trade effect (TT), that is:

$$s'_a = s_a + TT. \tag{5}$$

Assuming $P_s = P_i = P$, where P is the particular price index for net surplus which incorporates the terms of trade gains, then equation 3 could be written as:

$$
\begin{aligned}
s'_a &= i_a + x_a(P_x/P) - m_a(P_m/P), \\
&= (i_a + x_a - m_a) + x_a(P_x/P - 1) + m_a(1 - P_m/P), \\
&= s_a + TT.
\end{aligned}
$$

This is the general form of expression of the terms of trade effect. The choice of an appropriate price index (P) has been subject to an old and as yet unresolved controversy in the literature.[6] As we noted in appendix A.1, the choice for us has been decided by the availability of data. If we assume that $P = P_m$ we arrive at the terms of trade equation which was measured in appendix A.1, that is:

$$TT = x_a(P_x/P_m - 1).$$

Table A2.2 shows the real consumption, real income, and real net surplus of the agricultural sector. Subtracting the real consumption of agricultural households from the gross value added in the sector at factor cost, gives the real net agricultural surplus from the point of view of the economy as a whole (s_a), which is presented in column 6 of the table. Column 7 of the table shows the substantial income gains in the sector due to terms of trade improvements, which particularly accelerated during the 1970s decade. In fact, as a comparison between columns 5 and 7 of the table show, income gains in the sector due to the terms of trade improvements during the 1963–77 period exceed those procured through the normal growth of agricultural output. Such income gains to some extent reflect the benefits accrued to the agricultural sector from productivity growth in other sectors of the economy, but largely they were made possible by the rapid growth of the oil export revenues of the country and reflect a major channel through which such revenues were transmitted to the agricultural sector. Finally, to derive the net surplus from the point of view of the agricultural sector itself (s'_a) we have added the income terms of trade to the real net surplus of the sector which is shown in column 8 of table A2.2.

[6] See Stuvel (1956), UN (1968), Kurabayashi (1971) and Gutmann (1981).

Appendix A.2

Table A2.2. *Net agricultural surplus in real terms at 1963 prices 1963–1977*

(billion Rials)

Year 1	Real consumption of agricultural households			Real value added in agri-culture	Net agr. surplus in real terms	Income terms of trade of agri-culture	Real net surplus accrued to agri-culture
	Rural 2	Urban 3	Total 4	5	$6 = 5 - 4$	7	$8 = 7 + 6$
1963	78.4	5.5	84.0	98.4	14.4	0.0	14.4
1964	86.0	5.8	91.9	100.5	8.6	5.2	13.8
1965	87.1	6.4	93.5	108.4	14.9	6.7	21.6
1966	92.0	7.0	99.0	112.2	13.2	7.1	20.3
1967	100.0	6.6	106.8	121.1	14.3	6.5	20.8
1968	102.0	7.3	109.6	130.4	20.8	7.1	27.9
1969	100.0	6.7	106.7	134.5	27.8	9.6	37.4
1970	100.0	7.1	107.1	140.7	33.5	10.7	44.3
1971	86.8	7.5	94.3	135.6	41.2	17.4	58.7
1972	95.5	10.4	106.0	143.1	37.1	21.6	58.8
1973	104.0	11.6	115.8	151.0	35.1	30.3	65.5
1974	121.0	20.8	141.8	159.9	18.1	57.5	75.6
1975	122.0	26.4	147.9	170.3	22.4	53.3	75.7
1976	132.0	27.5	159.5	179.7	20.2	65.7	85.9
1977	124.0	27.0	151.5	177.3	25.8	81.7	107.5

Sources: Tables A1.7, A1.8, A1.9, at the end of appendix A1.1.

Appendix I.1 Determinants of private investment

1 Introduction

In this appendix we shall attempt to specify and estimate a private investment function based on the theoretical arguments put forward in chapters 4 to 7. There, we argued that government investment was likely to exert a strong positive influence on private investment, through its complementarities and backward and forward linkages as well as inducements on the demand side through its multiplier effects. It was also argued that government investment did not exert a 'crowding out' impact on private investment from the financial side. On the contrary, government expenditure being mainly financed by oil revenues, and budget deficits being covered by foreign borrowing or domestic monetary expansion, periods of rapid growth of government investments were normally accompanied by the fast expansion of the monetary base and an increase in the availability of credit to the private sector through the banking system. It was furthermore argued that the availability of credit had a significant bearing on private investment, specially in the case of Iran where the rapid growth of investment in new enterprises implied a high degree of reliance on external funds.

In what follows we shall attempt to incorporate these ideas into a private investment function on the basis of a stock adjustment model of the investment process. The procedures adopted for specifying the investment function have been tailored to take into account the specificities of Iranian financial institutions as well as the inadequacies in the available data. Consider a flexible stock adjustment investment process of the following form:

$$IP_t = \alpha(K_t^* - K_{t-1}) + \beta K_{t-1}, \tag{I.1}$$

where IP, K^* and K respectively refer to gross investment, desired capital stock and actual capital stock in the private sector. The α coefficient

Appendix I.1

specifies the speed of adjustment of private capital stock and β is the coefficient of depreciation.[1]

We shall assume that desired capital stock is a function of the output of the private sector, which in turn depends on total investment through the multiplier process.[2] Assuming a linear relationship we have:

$$K_t^* = k + gIG_t + pIP_t \tag{I.2}$$

where IG refers to public sector investment.

Cost of capital is not here considered as a determinant of desired capital stock, due to the backwardness of the capital market in Iran and controlled bank interest rates which were well below the market rates of interest. The supply of credit, at fixed interest rates, is taken here rather as a constraint to private investment which directly affects the speed of adjustment of private capital stock. This assumes that due to credit rationing there is always a backlog of private investment projects which could be quickly implemented with finance becoming available. Assuming a linear relation between the speed of adjustment of the capital stock, and the availability of bank credit (CR) relative to a desired net investment, we can express a as:

$$a = b + c(CR_t/(K_t^* - K_{t-1})). \tag{I.3}$$

Substituting I.2 and I.3 into I.1 we get the following linear regression model for private investment:

$$IP_t = a_1 + a_2 IG_t + a_3 CR_t + a_4 K_{t-1} + u_t, \tag{I.4}$$

where:

$$a_1 = kb/1 - bp \quad a_2 = bg/1 - bp \quad a_3 = c/1 - bp \quad a_4 = \beta - b/1 - bp.$$

The coefficients a_1, a_2 and a_3 are expected to be positive. The sign of a_4 can be positive or negative depending on whether $\beta > b$ or $\beta < b$.

One may also allow for the influence of the supply of foreign capital to the private sector (FOR) by incorporating FOR in an analogous manner to the availability of domestic bank credit (CR) in equation I.2, to get:

---

[1] There is a large body of literature on theoretical underpinning of this type of investment function and its economic estimation, see Jorgenson (1971), Lund (1971), Rowley and Trivedi (1975). For an application of a modified version of the accelerator theory of investment to the case of a selected number of developing countries, see Wai and Wong (1982).

[2] Exports formed a negligible part of private output in Iran over this period. Considering that public sector output was non-competing with private output, it can be treated in the same way as non-competing imports as long as the private sector is concerned on the demand side. Assuming private and public consumption taxes and imports are linear functions of total output, one can easily derive a linear multiplier relation between private output and total investment.

Determinants of private investment

$$PI_t = b_1 + b_2 GI_t + b_3 CR_t + b_4 FOR_t + b_5 K_{t-1} + u_t, \tag{I.5}$$

where all the coefficients are the same as in I.4 except for $b_4 = f/1 - bp$. The coefficient of foreign capital is expected to be positive and it may be particularly significant in countries facing foreign exchange shortages.

Estimation

The data for real investment are based on the Central Bank's National Account estimates of real gross fixed investment in public and private sectors. The data for domestic credits to the private sector (CR) are based on the IMF, *International Financial Statistics (IFS)* Yearbook 1983, and refer to the change in the claims of the banking system on the private sector. The data on foreign capital inflow in the private sector (FOR) are derived from Central Bank, *Quarterly Bulletin*, 1962–77. Both CR and FOR series are deflated by the private investment price deflator. Real private sector capital stock has been measured by cumulatively adding real gross private fixed investment to the estimate of real private fixed capital stock in 1959, after allowing for capital depreciation in each year. The base year value of real capital stock has been calculated by assuming the capital output ratio in that year being equal to the incremental capital-output ratio over the 1959–71 period. There are no data available on capital depreciation and the procedure adopted for measuring the base year capital stock may also involve large measurement errors. Due to these problems we have used different depreciation rates (varying between 5 and 10 per cent) as well as initial capital values (-30 per cent and $+30$ per cent of the estimated values), to assess the sensitivity of regression coefficients to variations in these magnitudes. The results of these sensitivity tests are reported in table 1.2 at the end of the appendix. Since the variation of these magnitudes does not seem to substantially affect the estimated regression coefficients, in what follows we only discuss the results obtained by setting the depreciation coefficient at 7 per cent and retaining our original estimate of initial capital stock. The data are shown in table I.1.

Ordinary Least Square method was applied to equations I.4 and I.5, and the following results were obtained for the 1959–77 period:

$$IP_t = 23.7 + 0.99 IG_t + 0.36 CR_t - 0.08 K_{t-1} \quad R^2 = 0.98 \tag{I.4}$$
$$\quad (3.10)\ (3.83) \quad\ (2.13) \quad (-1.80) \qquad DW = 1.92$$

and

$$IP_t = 26.8 + 0.81 IG_t + 0.45 CR_t + 1.09 FOR_t - 0.08 K_{t-1} \quad R^2 = 0.98 \tag{I.5}$$
$$\quad (3.32)\ (2.68) \quad\ (2.41) \quad\ (1.12) \quad (-1.67) \qquad DW = 1.75.$$

Table I.1. *Real investment, real private sector capital stock, foreign capital and domestic credit inflows to the private sector*

Year	Real investment[a] Public sector	Real investment[a] Private sector	Real private capital stock[a]	Change in net claims of banks on private sector	Long-term foreign capital to private sector
1959	20.8	31.9	82.2	9.6	—
1960	18.4	37.1	114.1	8.5	—
1961	20.8	34.2	151.2	6.7	—
1962	18.4	31.0	185.4	− 1.6	0.2
1963	22.6	32.7	216.4	12.0	0.3
1964	23.1	40.1	249.1	14.6	0.1
1965	40.5	44.1	289.2	12.4	0.4
1966	38.8	49.2	333.3	18.0	1.5
1967	55.1	58.0	382.5	16.1	1.3
1968	70.4	55.9	440.5	25.4	1.5
1969	79.3	52.5	496.4	19.0	2.1
1970	83.4	56.3	548.9	33.1	3.2
1971	101.6	77.7	605.2	30.8	3.5
1972	110.2	108.7	682.9	57.3	4.9
1973	135.9	109.8	791.6	81.1	9.9
1974	181.1	123.2	901.4	88.7	16.5
1975	248.5	252.5	1025.6	172.8	21.6
1976	323.0	282.5	1277.1	183.0	18.5
1977	350.0	278.7	1560.6	114.3	39.9

Notes:
[a] Real values are in 1959 prices, in bn Rials.
Sources: As specified in the text.

In both equations bank credits and particularly government investments exert a positive and highly significant influence on private investment. The coefficient of foreign investment in the second equation is not significant, and its inclusion does not affect the overall goodness of fit of the equation. This result may be due to multicollinearity between CR_t and FOR_t, as a substantial part of long-term foreign capital flow to the private sector was channelled through the specialized banks. To alleviate this effect we have reestimated equation I.5 by subtracting specialized banks' credits from CR. The new estaimate (I.5″) which uses non-specialized banks' credits ($NSCR$) instead of CR is given below. The coefficient for FOR in the new equation still remains insignificant. The insignificance of the coefficient of foreign capital may be due to the fact that the direct foreign exchange requirements for private investment over this period was supplied by the oil sector, and

Table I.2. *Results of sensitivity analysis for equation I.5*

	b_1	b_2	b_3	b_4	b_5	R^2	DW
$K_0 = 82.2$							
$\beta = 0.05$	27.6	0.96	0.46	1.16	-0.10	0.98	1.71
(*t* ratio)	(3.32)	(3.48)	(2.13)	(1.10)	(-2.15)		
$\beta = 0.06$	27.6	0.96	0.46	1.16	-0.10	0.98	1.71
(*t* ratio)	(3.32)	(3.48)	(2.12)	(1.10)	(-2.15)		
$\beta = 0.07$	27.6	0.96	0.46	1.16	-0.10	0.98	1.70
(*t* ratio)	(3.32)	(3.47)	(2.11)	(1.10)	(-2.15)		
$\beta = 0.08$	27.6	0.96	0.46	1.16	-0.10	0.98	1.70
(*t* ratio)	(3.31)	(3.47)	(2.11)	(1.10)	(-2.15)		
$\beta = 0.09$	27.7	0.96	0.46	1.16	-0.10	0.98	1.70
(*t* ratio)	(3.31)	(3.47)	(2.11)	(1.10)	(-2.15)		
$\beta = 0.10$	27.7	0.97	0.46	1.16	-0.10	0.98	1.70
(*t* ratio)	(3.31)	(3.46)	(2.10)	(1.10)	(-2.15)		
$\beta = 0.07$							
$K_0 = 106.9$	28.7	0.81	0.45	1.10	-0.08	0.98	1.75
(*t* ratio)	(3.22)	(2.68)	(2.41)	(1.12)	(-1.68)		
$K_0 = 57.5$	25.3	0.96	0.46	1.16	-0.10	0.98	1.70
(*t* ratio)	(3.35)	(3.47)	(2.12)	(1.10)	(-2.14)		

the private sector had unlimited access to foreign exchange for its foreign purchases of investment goods.[3]

$$IP_t = 27.6 + 0.96 IG_t + 0.46 NSCR_t + 1.16 FOR_t - 0.1 K_{t-1} \quad R^2 = 0.98 \text{ (I.5'')}$$
$$(3.31)\ (3.42) \quad (2.12) \qquad (1.10) \quad (-2.15) \qquad DW = 1.70$$

[3] In periods when balance of payments problems were pressing (as in the 1967–9 period) the Central Bank would resort to overall credit restrictions and direct import controls rather than foreign exchange rationing (see chapters 5 and 8).

Appendix M.1 Surplus labour and the dual structure of the manufacturing sector

1 Identification of duality

In this appendix we shall attempt to further substantiate the arguments put forward in chapter 7 about the duality of the manufacturing sector and the existence of surplus or slack labour supply within the sector itself. Table M1.1 shows the size composition of private manufacturing in the urban areas in 1964. Two categories of large and small establishments are distinguished according to the total employment criterion – large establishments are defined to be those employing more than ten persons and small establishments less than ten persons each. As the table shows more than 80 per cent of total employment in private manufacturing in 1964 was in the small establishments employing less than 2.8 persons on average. The hourly wages of unskilled labour in the large establishments were on average 170 per cent higher than the wages of the same category of workers in the small workshops. The quoted source defines unskilled labour as the 'labour which needs no skills or prior experience, and requires neither general training nor on-the-job training'. Such distinct wage differences as exist, therefore, could not be due to variations in skills, efficiency or other personal attributes of the workers. There remains to be examined, however, whether these average wage differentials arise due to the concentration of the small workshops in specific low pay and low productivity industries or in particular backward regions, or whether they could be explained by the high concentration of female labour in the small workshops. As we shall see below none of these factors could explain the wage differentials between the large and small subsectors of manufacturing in a significant way.

Table M1.1 shows also the average wage differentials across different industries. With the exception of three industries (namely food (31), paper (34), and non-metallic minerals (36)) the wage differentials across different industries have a very low dispersion around the overall average. The table also shows that the main source of divergence of wage differentials across the different industries arises from the variation of wages in the small subsector. The across industry wage structure for the large sector is remarkably uniform. A closer inspection of the data shown in the table indicates that the main source of variation in the small sector wage structure is due to the variation of the size of the establishments across the different industries. The correlation coefficient between the size of the workshops and the hourly wages in the small subsector is 0.82. It could be easily seen from the table that the three industries in which the small sector wage rate is much higher than the overall average, also exhibit much higher than average size of the establishments. The relatively high average wages in the small establishments in these industries could be due to the *ad hoc* definition of small establishments. The ten employee threshold which turns out to be appropriate for revealing the dual wage structure in most industries, does not seem to be appropriate for this purpose in the case of these three industries. A redefinition of the size criteria could reveal a similar pattern of duality in these three lines of activity as in other industries. The available data, however, do not allow such an undertaking. It is nevertheless sufficiently clear that the duality in the wage structure is common to almost all manufacturing sectors.

The data shown in table M1.1 also indicate that the observed wage differentials between the small and large subsectors cannot be due to an over-concentration of female labour in the small sector. Though the average share of female labour in the small sector (12.1 per cent) is higher than the large sector (9.8 per cent), the difference is not large enough to explain the wide disparities in the wage rates. Furthermore, with the exception of textiles, the share of female employment in the large sector is well above their counterpart in the small sector in every industry. Therefore with the exception of the textile industry where the high share of female labour in the small workshops could have played some part in producing the observed wage differentials, it appears that the effect of female employment, if anything, has worked towards the reduction of wage differences in the rest of the industrial branches.

It finally remains to see whether the wage differences between the large and small establishments have been due to the concentration of the small workshops in specifically backward regions with low general wage levels. The 1964 survey of the Ministry of Labour does not furnish the necessary data for testing this hypothesis. We have to rely on the 1969 survey of the Ministry of Industry and Mines where data concerning both the size and regional distribution of manufacturing are given. Table M1.2 shows the annual wage rates in the manufacturing sector as a whole by the size of the establishments and the province of their location. This table depicts a similar picture of the duality in the manufacturing sector as the previous table. About 66 per cent of total manufacturing employees in 1969 were working in small workshops with less than 2.9 employees on average and

Table M1.1. *Size composition of urban private manufacturing by sector 1964*

					ISIC CODE					
Indicator	3 Total	31 Food	32 Textile	33 Wood	34 Paper	35 Chemicals	36 Minerals	38 Mechanical	384 Transport	39 Misc.
Number of establishments										
Small scale	118453	13046	57092	12429	832	1431	2034	17021	9085	5381
Large scale	2384	430	1223	86	63	77	233	144	113	15
Total employees										
Small scale	340133	57310	157569	23995	3367	3549	12337	51284	24156	11223
Large scale	83836	8336	51740	1100	2186	6362	6625	4126	2778	583
Percentage of female employees										
Small scale	12.1	2.0	26.1	0.0	0.8	0.7	0.0	0.2	0.0	0.0
Large scale	9.8	8.7	12.4	0.0	2.7	7.8	2.3	4.9	0.0	27.7
Average employee per workshop										
Small scale	2.8	4.4	2.7	1.9	4.0	2.5	6.1	3.0	2.7	2.1
Large scale	35.1	19.4	42.3	12.8	34.7	82.6	28.4	28.6	24.6	38.9
Unskilled labour										
Small scale	35972	6587	12433	2023	433	384	3060	6920	4097	1273
Large scale	12577	2321	3927	166	192	2077	2716	952	226	20
Hourly wages (unskilled labour)										
Small scale	2.4	4.0	1.8	1.9	5.3	2.5	4.7	2.0	1.8	2.0
Large scale	6.5	6.0	6.5	8.1	7.8	7.7	6.6	6.5	6.5	7.2

Notes:
Small scale refers to workshops employing less than ten employees.
Hourly wages refer to those of unskilled labour, values in Rials.
Mechanical (38) excludes transport equipment (384).
Source: Ministry of Labour and Social Affairs, *Yearbook of employment statistics*, No.7 1964.

Table M1.2. *Size composition of urban manufacturing by province 1969*

Indicator	Whole Country	(1)	(2)	(3)	(4)	(5)	(6)	(7)	(8)	(9)	(10)	(11)	(12)	(13)
No. of workshops														
Small scale	172588	60663	6530	9035	15023	4790	9397	1478	10474	7105	5300	13652	28255	886
Large scale	5066	2324	217	204	836	92	142	19	202	153	82	362	407	26
Total employees														
Small scale	499923	181720	19213	22241	42943	10969	27684	4032	30869	27067	16406	44257	69559	2963
Large scale	256755	126776	10584	17601	22930	2638	5318	572	9366	7501	6337	14090	32648	394
Average employee per workshop														
Small scale	2.9	3.0	2.9	2.5	2.9	2.3	2.9	2.7	2.9	3.8	3.1	3.2	2.5	3.3
Large scale	50.7	54.6	48.8	86.3	27.4	28.7	37.5	30.1	46.4	49.0	77.3	38.9	80.2	15.2
Value added per employee														
Small scale	62.5	78.1	46.9	44.0	44.9	21.0	43.6	54.3	95.6	59.6	35.4	32.2	69.8	59.7
Large scale	218.4	309.5	120.9	131.2	64.7	110.3	145.7	636.4	244.1	188.8	181.8	101.6	123.8	33.0
Annual wage rate														
Small scale	30.9	42.7	23.8	26.8	24.9	26.9	21.1	26.5	41.2	28.9	18.3	22.5	17.6	16.8
Large scale	62.0	73.2	103.0	61.2	29.8	44.0	44.5	60.2	84.7	81.4	20.4	37.9	40.9	19.1

Notes:

* Province codes are in the following order; 1 = Central, 2 = Gilan, 3 = Mazandaran, 4 = East Azarbaijan, 5 = West Azarbaijan, 6 = Kermanshahan, 7 = Kurdestan, 8 = Khuzestan, 9 = Fars, 10 = Kerman, 11 = Khorasan, 12 = Esfahan, 13 = Sistan & Baluchestan.

** All values in thousand Rials. Wages refer to total remuneration of labour, both wages and salaries.

Source: Ministry of Industry and Mines, *Iranian Industrial Statistics* 1969.

wage rates below 50 per cent of the workers in the large establishments.[1] Similar wage differentials between the large and small sectors could be observed across the different provinces. As one would have expected, the variations, both in the absolute level of wages and in the wage differentials between the two sectors across the different provinces, are much wider than the inter-industry variations in the same variables. It is not, however, the case that small-scale employment is concentrated in the low wage provinces. On the contrary, there is a strong positive correlation between the wage rates and the share of the small-scale employment across the different provinces (the correlation coefficient is $+0.55$). Tehran with a dominating share of total employment in the small establishments has the lowest wage differentials and the highest wage rates in the small sector. Even across the different provinces, the variation in the wage differentials between the large and small sectors is highly correlated with the relative size of the establishments. The rank correlation coefficient between the wage differentials (measured by the ratio of wage rate in large establishments to those of the small workshops in each province) and the relative size of the establishment (measured by the ratio of workers per establishment in the large sector to those in the small sector in each province) is 0.47.

2 The internal structure of the small manufacturing sector

To understand the functional role of the small-scale manufacturing sector in the process of industrialization it is necessary to further examine the internal structure of the sector, with a view to the prevalent social and technical conditions of production within that sector. Table M1.3 reproduces a few summary statistics concerning the small manufacturing sector during the 1964–73 period. As the table shows, the use of wage labour in the small establishments was very limited. On average, wage labour per establishment was no more than 1.7. As it would be reasonable to assume the major part of wage labour to be employed in the relatively larger establishments within the sector, one may conclude that the majority of the small workshops barely employed any wage labour.[2]

It appears therefore that small-scale manufacturing was predominantly composed of a large number of artisan workshops where the owner-

[1] The lower ratio of workers employed in the small sector in 1969 compared to the figure of 80 per cent in 1964 shown in table M1.1, is mainly due to the fact that the 1964 data exclude the workers in large public enterprises.

[2] The alternative assumption of wage labour being thinly spread over the workshops, would imply a structure where in each workshop besides the owner producer and one family worker or apprentice, there are one or two wage labourers employed as well. This assumption is less plausible than the one made above. It does not, however, basically alter the nature of the arguments we make on the conditions of production in the small workshops.

Table M1.3. *Small-scale manufacturing indicators 1964–1973*

	1964	1969	1973
Average employee per workshop	2.8	2.9	3.0
Average wage earner per workshop	1.6	1.7	1.7
		In percentages	
Share of total manufacturing wage labour	53.4	54.9	49.5
Share of total manufacturing value added	43.9	35.8	29.3

Sources: Ministry of Industry and Mines, *Iranian Industrial Statistics* 1964, 1969, 1973.

producers with the help of family labour and barely one or two wage labourers were engaged in commodity production. The social and material conditions of production which characterize these 'simple commodity producing' units, introduce a qualitative distinction between them and the capitalist form which characterizes the modern manufacturing sector.[3] In the modern manufacturing sector the direct producers predominantly appear in the form of wage labourers. The implication being that the means of production also appear in the form of 'free' capital – free in the sense that the employer is liberated from manual labour and the means of production under his control are no longer tied to his own personal skills and crafts-manship. An additional characteristic, which is in a way a pre-condition for the above to hold, is that the ownership of the means of production should entitle the owner/employer to a revenue above his own subsistence. It is only under these conditions that capital can be alternatively used as a source of revenue in either purely financial transactions or by being redeployed in different lines of production irrespective of the personal skills and abilities of the owner. This has the important implication of introducing commercial calculation and capitalist rationality into the field of production and exposes it to the dynamic effects of what has come to be known as the profit maximizing behaviour of the capitalist.

This form of economic rationality cannot be generalized to incorporate all production units irrespective of their size and social form of production. In the small artisan workshops or in production units where family labour and casual wage labour work side by side with the owner producers, the concept of profit or net revenue has neither a material existence for the owner of the means of production nor is it theoretically amenable to unambiguous definition. Under such conditions the relations of production

[3] The definition of, and distinction between, 'simple commodity production' and 'capitalist' form of production is based on Marx (1976, chapters 11–15). Since here we are mainly concerned with the conditions of production in the small sector, capitalist production is defined in its simplest form, namely 'simple co-operation', cf. *ibid.*, chapter 13.

are highly intertwined with family relations. Accumulation, improvement in production methods and work discipline – whether or not the technological conditions and external market relations are favourable – being highly influenced by the needs of the family, or the subjective whims of the owner-producer need not be subject to the same economic rationality as in the modern capitalist sector. Modern book-keeping and accounting methods are non-existent in the simple commodity producing sector, and the accounts of the workshop as a unit of production are usually indistinguishable from the expenses of the household. The means of production owned by the owner-producer in the small workshop are tied to the personal skills of the owner, and their market value, barring such skills, is negligible. Similarly, in the absence of employment opportunities in the modern organized sector, the labour of the producer (or the family as a unit of production as a whole) can barely command a market wage above the subsistence needs of the family. The means of production under such circumstances should be viewed as the means of procurement of the subsistence of the family, rather than as 'capital' which flows freely into different fields of activity motivated by the criteria of profitability and forces of competition.

The productivity of labour in small-scale manufacturing is very low. As can be observed from table M1.2, overall labour productivity in small-scale manufacturing was barely above the level of wages in the large-scale sector. If we allow for the depreciation and other overhead expenses, as well as rents and interest payments, the per-capita net value added appropriated by the direct producers in the small sector would be well below the wage rates in the large sector. The possibility of financing accumulation from within the sector, therefore, appears to be very limited.

The very low levels of labour productivity in the small artisan workshops is to some extent explained by their limited market power. The subordinate position of the small producers in setting the terms of exchange, both in the sale of their output and the purchase of their inputs, and their lack of access to organized money markets, create systematic channels of surplus transfer from that sector.[4] This, however, could only to a limited extent explain the vast productivity differentials between large- and small-scale manufacturing. The main reason for the extremely low levels of labour productivity in small-scale manufacturing should be sought in their backward technology and the inefficient methods of production and work practices which mainly arise due to the extremely small size of the workshops. Significant changes in the productivity of labour necessitates the adoption of advanced tech-

---

[4] Of course only the unequal exchange in the input and output markets are reflected in the low observed productivity levels in the small sector. Interest payments only affect the level of retained incomes in the sector. For a discussion of systematic mechanisms of surplus transfer from the informal sector, see Gerry (1974), Beinfeld and Godfrey (1978).

Table M1.4. *Growth indicators of small-scale manufacturing 1964–1972*

Indicator	Average annual growth rates		
	1964–9	1969–72	1964–72
No. of workshops	9.7	5.5	8.1
Employment	8.8	8.2	8.6
Value added[a]	8.7	8.1	8.5
Productivity	−0.1	−0.1	−0.1

Note:
[a] Deflated by the wholesale price index.
Sources: As in table M1.3

nology which requires a different form of organization of labour and a much larger size of workplace than the existing simple commodity producing workshops could provide. The growth of output in the small sector is, therefore, most likely to take place in the form of duplication of workshops with similar technical and social conditions of production and the same level of labour productivity. This is clearly reflected in the patterns of growth of output, employment and productivity in the small-scale manufacturing sector in the Iranian economy (see table M1.4). During the 1964–72 period real output in small-scale manufacturing grew by an average annual rate of 8.5 per cent, while the number of workshops and employment grew by 8.1 and 8.6 percentage points respectively. The growth of labour productivity during this period was hardly above zero.[5]

Small-scale manufacturing, therefore, appears to have little dynamism of its own and its growth is of an extensive rather than intensive nature. As long as there exists surplus labour in the economy the small or informal sector will reproduce itself, growing more or less with the same pace as the modern sector of the urban economy.[6]

[5] In considering the negative growth of productivity shown in the table, one should keep in mind that the use of the wholesale price index for deflating the value added may have led to an underestimation of productivity growth. The use of the correct price index – which is not available – however, should not make a dramatic change in the result.
[6] This type of growth in the small-scale manufacturing – or the informal sector of the urban economy as a whole – could be easily formalized by assuming the demand for the informal sector's output to be an increasing function of the urban income as a whole. Growth of the urban economy as a whole would thus lead to an increase in the output of the informal sector and initially in the productivity of labour in that sector. This in turn induces the migration of rural surplus labour to the urban areas, with the effect of increasing the number of establishments as well as employment in the informal sector. Final equilibrium is reinstated when labour productivity, and by implication real incomes, in the informal sector are reduced to levels compatible with real incomes of the rural surplus labour.

This is not to deny that to a certain degree the process of accumulation and technical change could originate within the small sector itself, through the internal differentiation of the small producers. The process of differentiation and structural transformation of the simple commodity producers is said to have played a major role in the genesis of industrial capital in the west.[7] This process of structural change through internal differentiation of the artisan sector, however, does not play as important a role in the industrialization of the present day LDCs as it did historically in the west. The already existing advanced technology in the industrial countries, which could be imitated by the LDCs, reduces the significance of that kind of gradual transformation of the productive structure. The use of modern technology necessitates a prior concentration of financial capital, and its adoption takes place at a point in time and virtually from above and outside the artisan sector – transforming the productive structure in an abrupt manner.[8]

It may be concluded that the main function of the small commodity producing or informal sector in the Iranian economy has been to act as a source of sustenance for the surplus or slack labour in the urban areas (that is, the labour which cannot find employment in the modern sector).[9] This argument is further reinforced if one examines the behaviour of manufacturing employment during the crisis of the early 1960s. As table M1.5 shows, during the years of the crisis, employment in the large-scale manufacturing sector declined by more than 20 per cent, while employment in the small-scale or informal sector kept on growing. Between the years 1959 and 1962, employment in small-scale manufacturing had grown by more than 23 per cent. This is suggestive of the fact that the informal sector during the crisis years had been accommodating the urban unemployed labour force. This would have implied a large degree of work sharing and a noticeable decline in the productivity of labour and the level of real incomes in that sector.[10]

The above conclusion is not to imply that the informal sector plays an entirely passive role in the process of growth. One may suggest two main areas in which the small manufacturing sector could make important

[7] See Marx (1972, vol.3, chapter XX, 1976, chapters 14, 15, 31), Dobb (1972, chapter 4), Takahashi (1952). For a detailed discussion of this process in the light of the Russian experience, see Lenin (1977, chapters V, VI, VII). For more recent studies, see Kreidte *et al.* (1981), Berg (1980).

[8] See Takahashi (1952), where he counterposes this way of the genesis of the industrial capital in the late-comers like Japan to the classical case of Britain epitomized by Marx (1972).

[9] This obviously excludes specific traditional handicrafts such as carpets, which are valuable precisely because they are handmade. The major part of urban small-scale manufacturing, however, does not fall into this category.

[10] Unfortunately the quoted source in the table does not give any data on the value added in the small-scale manufacturing during this period.

Table M1.5. *Indices of manufacturing employment 1958–1962*

	1958	1959	1960	1961	1962
Large scale[a]	100.0	122.6	121.9	106.9	100.1
Small scale[b]	100.0	140.3	154.1	165.3	172.9

Notes:
[a] Between 10 and 500 employees.
[b] Less than 10 employees.
Source: CSO, *Statistical Yearbook of Iran* 1968.

contributions to the growth of modern manufacturing. First, it could contribute to the lowering of labour costs in the modern sector by producing cheap wage goods. Secondly, during the early stages of industrialization in a surplus labour agrarian economy, the small artisan workshops could play an important role in the transition of unskilled and non-disciplined rural labour into the disciplined and urbanized labour force of the modern sector. Further research may well suggest other areas in which the informal sector contributes to the process of industrialization (e.g., through direct linkages).[11] This is not, however, the main issue of concern here. The main purpose of this appendix has been twofold. First to study the different dimensions of duality in the manufacturing sector; and secondly, to examine the conditions of production in the so-called informal or small-scale sector. A conclusion which stands out clearly is that the extremely low levels of labour productivity in the small sector cannot be improved without transforming the productive structure of the sector itself. This in turn, or rather tautologically, implies the eradication of surplus labour in the economy – that is, the expansion of the modern sector to the extent that it can productively absorb the disguised unemployed in the urban and rural informal sectors.

3 The scale of rural surplus labour

A major presupposition which has been lurking behind most of the above arguments is the existence of a large army of surplus labour in the rural sector – in the sense of having a productivity within the same range as in the urban informal sector. In chapter 8 we referred to the wide productivity gap between the agricultural sector and other sectors of the economy as an

[11] It is equally conceivable that in certain cases the small-scale manufacturing could play a negative role in the process of industrialization by out-competing the more technologically dynamic production units. This could take place, for example, through the over-exploitation of labour in the sweat shops.

indication of this phenomenon. However, this may not be totally adequate; since as we have already noted for the case of the manufacturing sector, there is expected to exist wide productivity differentials within the different sectors of the economy as well. Furthermore, a large part of the rural surplus labour belong to the category of non-agricultural labourers.

There exists a number of studies on the structure of rural employment which indicate similar patterns of duality in the rural sector to those we observed in the urban sector (see Ashraf 1982, Pesaran and Karshenas 1983). These studies, however, provide only partial answers to the question we are addressing here. First they are in the main concerned with the agricultural sector rather than the rural economy as a whole. Secondly, they are not concerned with the comparison of productivity and pay in the rural and urban sectors. Such a comparison is necessary for substantiating the arguments based on the interconnections between the labour markets in the two sectors. This, however, involves numerous complications which cannot be convincingly tackled given the available data. Indicators at the level of production, such as wage rates, hours of labour, productivity and patterns of ownership of land etc., are not in themselves entirely adequate for this purpose, since in the rural areas, as in the urban informal sector, it is the income or productivity of the family as a unit of production and subsistence which is relevant. The problem could be exacerbated in the rural areas, as each working member of the family may have more than one source of income (e.g., casual labour, subsistence farming, etc.). More difficulties arise due to the fact that the unit of migration may be the entire household or alternatively the individual members of the household. In both cases the decision to migrate may be based on the needs and aspirations of the household or the individual member of the household as the effective decision-making unit. Further complications arise due to the fact that the measurement of income and the productivity effect of the withdrawal of a family member is not unambiguous. These problems arise in any attempt to identify the origins of rural migrant labour and to study the mechanisms of rural/urban migration. It is, nevertheless, possible to give an overall picture of the scale and intensity of the economic push which underlies the process of migration by comparing household incomes across the different income classes in the rural and urban areas. Having already formed an idea of the dimensions of economic duality in the urban areas, this could help bring into perspective the scale of surplus labour in the rural areas and give some indication of the productivity of labour in the rural informal sector.[12]

[12] Of course the relations of production in the rural sector are much more complicated than the formal/informal dichotomy could capture. The terminology is, however, useful for the type of overall comparison between the rural and urban labour markets we are interested in here.

We have used the 1972 household expenditure survey to estimate the distribution of households, individuals and the employed labour force across the different consumption expenditure classes in the rural and urban areas (see figure M1.1). The use of consumption rather than income classes for classification is due to the fact that the income data are notoriously unreliable, and that monthly consumption is a better indicator of the income 'norms' than the actual monthly income data – specially in the lower income groups which interest us here.

As the graph clearly indicates in all the three distributions, there is an overwhelming concentration in the lower end of the distribution in the rural areas. The huge gap between the overall average consumption expenditure (per household or per head) between the rural and urban areas is in fact due to the concentration of the rural population in the lower income brackets rather than being the result of the differentials in average consumption between each income class in the two regions (see table M1.6). This brings into clear relief the scale of the rural surplus labour and the significantly larger size of the rural 'informal' sector than its urban counterpart. To get an idea of the orders of magnitude involved, one may compare the concentration of the employed labour force in the three lowest income classes in rural and urban areas. Without trying to estimate the exact income class location of the employed labour force in the urban informal sector, it would be fair to assume that the three lowest expenditure classes – incorporating about 18 per cent of the urban employed labour force – contain the poorest sections of the workers in the urban informal sector. This hypothesis is clearly supported by the fact that more than 60 per cent of urban manufacturing employment was in the informal sector. A much larger share of the rural employment, however, fell within the three lowest income classes. More than 46 per cent of total employment in the rural areas fell within these three income categories. Some of the implications of this situation could best be grasped in a hypothetical comparative static construct. In a hypothetical situation, where enough new jobs are created in the high productivity sector of the urban areas to absorb the bottom 18 per cent of the urban labour force, there would remain the huge army of low productivity and low income rural labour force to refill the old positions in the urban informal sector.[13]

This is not to imply that in actual fact migrant labour wholly originates in the lowest income brackets, or that the process of migration takes place by a gradual promotion of low productivity labour to high productivity jobs in a hierarchic manner. Contrary to the common assumption in some of the

[13] For the sake of comparability of the above figures which are given in terms of percentage of the rural and urban labour force, it should be pointed out that in 1972 the rural labour force was more than 60 per cent of the total in the country.

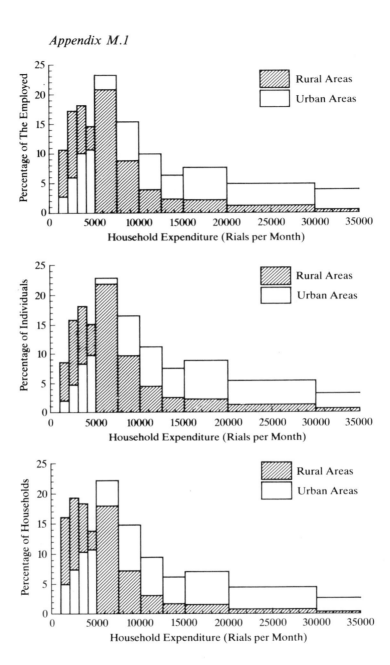

Figure M1.1 Distribution by household expenditure
Sources: As for table M1.6.

Table M1.6. *Distribution of households, individuals, and the employed by household expenditure class, rural and urban areas 1972*

Household expenditure classes (Rials/month)	Percentage of households		Percentage of individuals		Percentage of the employed		Average household expenditure		Average individual expenditure	
	Urban	Rural	Urban	Rural	Urban	Rural	Urban	Rural	Urban	Rural
Total	100.0	100.0	100.0	100.0	100.0	100.0	9313	4872	1830	947
Below 2000	4.9	16.1	1.9	8.6	2.7	10.6	1585	1506	793	550
2000–2999	7.4	19.3	4.8	15.8	5.9	17.2	2640	2552	803	606
3000–3999	10.3	18.3	8.3	18.1	10.0	18.1	3595	3495	881	687
4000–4999	10.7	13.8	9.7	15.1	10.6	14.6	4582	4470	989	795
5000–7499	22.2	17.9	22.8	21.8	23.1	20.8	6289	6052	1204	967
7500–9999	14.7	7.2	16.5	9.6	15.3	8.8	8737	8659	1536	1259
10000–12499	9.4	3.1	11.1	4.5	9.9	3.9	11291	11114	1875	1504
12500–14999	6.2	1.7	7.4	2.5	6.2	2.3	13781	13626	2242	1760
15000–19999	7.0	1.5	8.8	2.2	7.6	2.1	17328	17284	2740	2320
20000–29999	4.5	0.8	5.4	1.2	4.8	1.2	24101	23802	3894	2840
30000 and more	2.7	0.3	3.3	0.6	3.9	0.5	48447	45715	7748	5091

Sources: CSO, *Household Budget Survey of Rural Areas* and *Household Budget Survey of Urban Areas 1972.*

most well-known models of migration,[14] one would expect a considerable proportion of the rural/urban migration to originate in the middle or even high income brackets of the rural sector. Here we shall not labour this issue any further. The origins of rural migrant labour and the mechanisms of rural/urban migration are immaterial for the purpose of our present argument. No matter what the origins of rural migrant labour, it is clear that the removal of a large reserve of labour with extremely low productivity levels will not, under normal circumstances, significantly reduce the level of output and is most likely to lead to an improvement in the overall productivity of labour. It should be noted that the evidence presented in this section is only indicative of the existence of surplus labour in the rural areas, and should be treated as complementary to the specific studies of the rural labour market.

[14] See Harris and Todaro (1970), Todaro (1969). One reason why such an assumption could have appeared plausible may be the static treatment of the supply of labour in these models. Once the significance of the new entries in the labour market is taken into account, however, the plausibility of this assumption would clearly fade away.

Appendix P.1 Measurement of rural-urban migration

1 General indicators

In this appendix we shall attempt to highlight the scale of rural/urban migration and the contribution of migrant labour to the total supply of the urban labour force. Table P.1 gives the rate of growth of the rural and urban populations during the intervals between the three national population censuses of 1956, 1966 and 1976. The much lower than national average rates of growth of rural population is suggestive of a high degree of rural/urban migration, specially during the latter period.[1]

Below we shall try to use the statistics on registered deaths and births in the rural and urban areas to estimate the flow of rural/urban migration over the 1956–76 period. Though the reliability of the available data is poor, it still may not be entirely pointless to make such an effort. This may not produce highly accurate estimates, but it can highlight the problems involved and the shortcomings of the data, and could give more or less reasonable estimates of changing migration trends over time.

2 Rural-urban migration trends

The three population censuses of 1956, 1966 and 1976 have been used to estimate the rural, urban and total populations during the 1956–76 period. Constant cumulative growth rates have been assumed for calculation of the annual population figures during the two intervals between the three census years. The data are given table P.2.

To give an idea of the comparability of the data on registered deaths and

---

[1] Two points should be made about the comparability of the three national census statistics. First, while the 1956 and 1966 census statistics only include the settled populations, the 1976 census covers the nomadic tribes as well. While this may introduce a slight overestimation in the rural and total population growth rates during the 1966–76 period, it will not affect the urban population statistics nor our estimates of rural/urban migration in the following section. Secondly, the status of some rural settlements – defined as those with less than 5,000 inhabitants – may have changed during the three censuses. This is likely to over-exaggerate the scale of rural/urban migration.

Table P.1. *Population growth rates 1956–1976*

	Structure			Annual average growth rates	
	1956	1966	1976	1956–66	1966–76
Rural	68.6	61.9	53.0	2.0	1.1
Urban	31.4	38.1	47.0	5.1	4.9

Sources: CSO, *National Census of Population and Housing* 1956, 1966, 1976.

births with the population census data, we have calculated a second series for total population based on the former data. To do this we have taken the census data on total population in a year as a benchmark, and calculated total population for the succeeding year from the registered deaths and births data. The new series is given in column 8 of the table, with discrepancies from the census series in column 9. As the table shows the annual discrepancies fluctuate around the value of less than one percentage point of total population, with a persistent positive bias throughout the period. Though the annual discrepancies may appear to be relatively small, their cumulative effect over the whole period is quite noticeable (from 1956 to 1976 it adds up to about 8 per cent overestimation of total population). This is not an unexpected finding. Though a reasonable degree of accuracy may be assumed with regard to the data on registered births, it is commonly known that many deaths, specially in the rural areas, remain non-registered. Keeping this source of bias in mind, and specially its cumulative effect over time, we can proceed to estimate the annual flow of rural/urban migration on the basis of the vital statistics provided by the Central Statistical Office. For ease of exposition we shall use the following notations.

P_t = Total urban population at time t

M_t = Total stock of rural migrant population in urban areas at time t

$NM_t = (P_t - M_t)$ = Total stock of non-migrant urban population at time t

m_t = Flow of rural/urban migration during the $\{ (t-1), t \}$ interval

B_t = Total number of births in urban areas during the $\{ (t-1), t \}$ interval

D_t = Total number of deaths in urban areas during the $\{ (t-1), t \}$ interval

Year beginning March	Registered births		Registered deaths		Population[a]		Total population		Discrepancy (T2−T1)/T1	Rural/urban migration flow
	Urban	Rural	Urban	Rural	Urban	Rural	T1	T2		
1956	155.4	222.8	54.1	92.8	5953.6	13001.1	18954.7	—	—	—
1957	159.7	262.9	56.7	111.7	6259.2	13270.5	19529.6	19208.9	−0.016	202.6
1958	174.1	305.9	59.9	118.1	6580.4	13545.4	20125.8	19831.6	−0.015	207.0
1959	249.4	625.0	57.4	117.5	6918.2	13826.0	20744.2	20825.3	0.004	145.7
1960	273.7	625.7	58.1	110.5	7273.2	14112.4	21385.7	21475.0	0.004	139.5
1961	393.6	621.3	61.7	90.0	7646.6	14404.8	22051.4	22148.9	0.004	141.4
1962	400.7	712.4	60.0	89.8	8039.0	14703.2	22742.3	23014.7	0.012	51.8
1963	329.8	591.0	64.5	71.7	8451.6	15007.9	23459.5	23526.9	0.003	147.3
1964	322.1	792.9	66.6	77.2	8885.4	15318.8	24204.2	24430.7	0.009	178.3
1965	408.0	731.6	71.8	101.4	9341.4	15636.1	24977.6	25170.6	0.008	119.8
1966	360.3	741.3	67.7	112.7	9820.9	15960.1	25781.0	25898.8	0.005	186.9
1967	359.0	661.0	69.0	111.0	10302.7	16140.0	26442.8	26221.0	0.007	191.8
1968	386.0	656.0	70.0	105.0	10808.2	16322.0	27130.2	27309.8	0.007	189.5
1969	377.0	714.0	72.0	96.0	11338.4	16506.1	27844.5	28053.2	0.007	225.2
1970	419.0	770.0	71.0	92.0	11894.7	16692.2	28586.9	28870.5	0.010	208.3
1971	450.0	782.0	65.0	85.0	12478.2	16880.4	29358.7	29668.9	0.011	198.6
1972	422.0	714.0	67.0	87.0	13090.4	17070.8	30161.2	30340.7	0.006	257.2
1973	449.0	763.0	73.0	86.0	13732.7	17263.3	30955.9	31214.2	0.007	266.2
1974	464.0	785.0	71.0	79.0	14406.4	17457.9	31864.3	32094.9	0.007	280.7
1975	522.0	821.0	73.0	76.0	15113.2	17654.8	32767.9	33058.3	0.009	257.8
1976	557.0	845.0	77.0	78.0	15854.6	17853.8	33708.5	34014.9	0.009	261.5

Notes:

[a] Based on the population census.

T1, based on the population census. T2, based on vital statistics.

Sources: CSO, *Statistical Yearbook of Iran* 1968, 1977. CSO, *National Census of Population and Housing* 1956, 1966, 1976.

Appendix P.1

$DNM_t =$ Total incidence of deaths amongst non-migrant urban
population during the $\{ (t-1), t \}$ interval
$DM_t =$ Total incidence of deaths amongst migrant urban
population during the $\{ (t-1), t \}$ interval

The following identities clearly hold:

$$NM_t = NM_{t-1} + B_t - DNM_t$$
$$M_t = P_t - NM_t$$
$$m_t = M_t + DM_t - M_{t-1}$$

Knowing the value of M_{t-1} at a base year (The Ministry of Labour's survey puts the stock of rural migrant population in the urban areas at 985.4 thousands), one can proceed to estimate the value of both the stock and flow of migrant population in the urban areas from the above identities. There are, however, two major problems involved in estimating the value of the *stocks* in this manner. The first one is the cumulative effect of the non-registered urban deaths, which after the first few years will totally dominate the value of such stock estimates, and makes them highly unreliable. The second problem is that for the estimation of the *stocks* one needs to know the incidence of death amongst the urban migrant and non-migrant populations separately (i.e., DNM_t and DM_t). It is possible to estimate these variables by using the available data on the age structure of the two categories of urban population, and applying age specific death ratios to divide the total death incidence between the two categories. The inaccuracies in the total number of registered deaths, however, makes entering into such complications unrewarding. We therefore confine our calculations to the *flow* of migrant labour over time, which is relatively less susceptible to these problems. The following identity could be easily derived by simple manipulation of the above identities:

$$m_t = (P_t - P_{t-1}) + (D_t - B_t)$$

We have used the urban population estimates from the national census data, together with the vital statistics published by the Central Statistical Office, to calculate m_t from the above identity. The results are shown in the last column of table P.2. As can be seen from the above equation the measurement errors in D_t and B_t are not cumulative over time. Furthermore, part of the underestimation in D_t would be cancelled out by its counterpart in B_t. Despite these considerations, the calculated values of m_t may still be far from (and generally an underestimation of) its true value by a large margin.[2] Though the absolute values of the estimated migration

---

[2] The most important source of error in these estimates arises perhaps due to lack of accurate annual data on urban population. The size of total urban population relative to the

flows shown in the table may not be entirely reliable, they could nevertheless be reasonably accurate in reflecting the changes in migration trends over time.[3]

Two interesting points are observed in the behaviour of the migration trends shown in the table. The first one is that the medium-term cyclical movements in rural/urban migration are closely associated with the fluctuations in the level of economic activity.[4] The second point is that the commonly held view of associating the high degree of rural/urban migration during the latter half of the 1960s and the early 1970s with the effects of the land reform programme, may be mistaken. This view could have arisen due to a mistaken comparison between the relatively low migration activity during the 1959–62 period – which was mainly due to low level of economic activity in that period – with the post-land reform trends. Our evidence, however, suggests that even in the pre-land reform period – during the investment boom of the late 1950s – there was a comparatively high degree of rural/urban migration.

3 The scale and composition of migrant labour force

The 1964 and 1972 manpower surveys of the Ministry of Labour provide data on the size and composition of the stock of migrant labour in the urban areas. In 1972 the number of employed migrant labour in the urban areas was about 1,506.9 thousand, which formed more than 50 per cent of total employed urban labour force (see table P.3). Evidently, not all of the urban migrant labour came from the rural areas. During the period concerned, there was a general flow of migration from the rural to urban areas, as well as intra-provincial urban migration which took place from the less to the more prosperous urban centres.[5] The breakdown of migrant labour by the sector of activity before migration, however, shows that both in 1964 and 1972, the majority came from the primary sector (see table P.3). If we omit the category of 'activities not adequately described', which is mainly

migration flows is so large that a small measurement error in the former would totally overshadow the value of the latter calculated from the above identity.

[3] Providing the proportion of non-registered deaths and births bear a relatively stable relation to their respective totals.

[4] It should be pointed out that these cyclical fluctuations may to some extent have been exaggerated due to the assumption of a constant cumulative growth rate which was used to estimate the urban population series from the census statistics. The effect has been the transmission of much of the fluctuations in the birth rates directly to our calculated migration flows. This has been particularly important for certain years such as 1957–8 and 1962, when the registered birth statistics have shown sharp deviations from their overall trends.

[5] This is reflected in the highly differentiated rates of growth of population across different provinces and urban centres.

Table P3. *Distribution of employed urban migrant workers by type of activity before and after migration*

(per cent)

Activity	1964		1972		
	Before migration	After migration	Before migration	After migration	Per cent of urban employment
Total	100.0	100.0	100.0	100.0	50.9
Primary	27.8	3.5	25.0	3.9	28.5
Manufacturing	10.0	20.5	7.1	24.3	44.3
Public utilities	0.3	0.8	0.3	1.4	45.6
Construction	3.8	10.8	3.4	12.4	59.5
Trade and banking	7.0	18.9	5.0	17.9	48.0
Transport and communications	3.2	8.9	2.4	8.7	53.6
Other services	15.4	35.4	11.5	30.6	61.8
Activities not adequately described[a]	36.3	1.1	45.3	7.2	0.6

Note:

[a] Includes the unemployed and those outside the labour force before migration.

Sources: Ministry of Labour, *Manpower Survey 1972*, Tehran. CSO, *Statistical Yearbook of Iran 1968*, Tehran.

composed of those who were unemployed or outside the labour force before migration, then it turns out that more than 40 per cent were involved in agricultural activities before migration. The post-migration sector of activity seems to be more evenly distributed in both years, though construction and services employ about 80 per cent of migrant labour in both years. Construction and services are also the sectors in which the share of migrant labour in total employment is higher than the average. This may be an indication of the fact that the majority of migrant workers are of the rural origin, since these sectors are the most likely sectors in which the unskilled rural labour can find employment.

Bibliography

Abdel-Fadil, M. (1980), *The Political Economy of Nasserism: A Study in Employment and Income Distribution Policies in Urban Egyt, 1952–72*, Department of Applied Economics, Occasional Papers, 52, Cambridge University Press.

(1980a), *Development, income distribution and social change in rural Egypt*, Department of Applied Economic Papers, Occasional Paper, 45, Cambridge University Press.

Abrahamian, E. (1974), 'Oriental despotism: the case of Qajar Iran', *International Journal of Middle Eastern Studies*, 5: 3–31.

(1982), *Iran Between Two Revolutions*, Princeton: Princeton University Press.

Abrahamian, E, and Kazemi, F. (1978), 'The non-revolutionary Peasantry of modern Iran', *Iranian Studies*, 11: 259–304.

Adamiyyat, F. (1945), *Amir Kabir va Iran* (Persian), Tehran: Payman.

(1976), *The Ideology of the Constitutional Revolution*, Tehran: Payam.

Adamiyyat, F. and Nategh, H. (1977), *Social, Political and Economic Thought in the Unpublished Manuscripts of the Qajar Period*, Tehran: Agah.

Adler, J. (1965), *Absorptive capacity and its Determinations*, Washington DC: The Brookings Institution.

Afshar, H. (1981), 'An assessment of agricultural development policies in Iran', *World Development*, 9, 11/12: 1097–1108.

Agah, M. (1958), *Some Aspects of Economic Development of Modern Iran*, Ph.D. thesis, Oxford University.

Ahari, H. and Johnson, V.W. (1963), *The Agricultural Bank of Iran in an Expanding Economy*, Tehran: The Agricultural Bank of Iran.

Ajami, I. (1973), 'Land reform and modernization of the farming structure in Iran', *Oxford Economic papers*, 11, 2.

Amuzegar, J. (1977), *Iran: An Economic Profile*, Washington DC: The Middle East Institute.

Amuzegar, J. and Fekrat, M.A. (1971), *Iran: Economic Development Under Dualistic Conditions*, Chicago: University of Chicago Press.

Anderson, P. (1979), *Lineages of the Absolutist State*, London: New Left Books.

Arasteh, A.R. (1962), *Education and Social Awakening in Iran: 1850–1968*, Leiden: E.J. Brill.

Ardahali, A. (1966), *San'at-e Ajor Sazi Dar Iran*, The Committee for Non-metallic Mineral Industries, Abdm, 1345, Tehran.

288

Bibliography

Ashraf, A. (1970), 'Historical obstacles to the development of bourgeoisie in Iran', in M.A. Cook (ed.), *Studies in the Economic History of the Middle East from the Rise of Islam to the Present Day*, Oxford University Press.

(1980), *Mavane-e Tarikhi-e Roshdeh Sarmayeh Dary Dar Iran: Dowreh-e Qajarieh* (Historical Obstacles in the Development of Capitalism in Iran: Qajar Period), Tehran: Zamineh, 1359.

(1982), 'Dehghanan, Zamin va Enghelab', *Ketab-e Agah*, Tehran: Amir Kabir.

Ashraf, A. and Banuazizi, A. (1980), 'Policies and strategies of land reform in Iran', in B. Inayatulah (ed), *Asian Experiences*, Kualalampur: APDAC.

Ashraf, A. and Safai, H. (1977), *The Role of Rural Organizations in Rural Development: The Case of Iran*, Tehran: Plan and Budget Organization.

Avramovic, D. (1970), 'Industrialization of Iran: the records, the problems and the prospects' in *Tahqiquat-e Eqtesadi*, 18, Tehran, 14–47.

Azimi, H. (1980), *Aspects of Poverty and Income Distribution in Iran: 1960–72*, Ph.D. thesis, Oxford.

Baer, W. and Kerstenetsky, H. (eds.) (1964), *Inflation and Growth in Latin America*, Homewood, Illinois: Irwin.

Bairoch, P. (1981), 'The main trends in national economic disparities since the Industrial Revolution', in P. Bairoch and P. Levy-Leboyer (eds.), 3–17.

Bairoch, P. and Levy-Leboyer, M. (eds.) (1981), *Desparities in Economic Development Since the Industrial Revolution*, London: Macmillan.

Bakhash, S. (1978), *Iran: Monarchy, Bureaucracy and Reform Under the Qajars: 1858–1896*, London: Ithaca Press.

Baldwin, G.B. (1967), *Planning and Development in Iran*, Baltimore: Johns Hopkins Press.

Banani, A. (1961), *The Modernization of Iran: 1921–1941*, Stanford: Stanford University Press.

(1978), 'Reflections on the social and economic structure of Safavid Persia at its zenith', *Iranian Studies*, 11: 83–116.

Bank Melli Iran (1957), *Balance Sheet: Accounts and General Report of The National Bank*, Tehran: Bank Melli Press.

Bashiriyeh, H. (1984), *The State and Revolution in Iran: 1962–82*, London: Croom Helm.

Beinfeld, M. and Godfrey, M. (1978), 'Surplus labour and underdevelopment', *Working Papers*, 138, Institute of Development Studies, Sussex.

Benab, Y.P. (1979), 'Political organizations in Iran; a historical review', *Review of Iranian Political Economy and History (RIPEH)*, 3, 1.

Benedick, R.E. (1964), *Industrial Finance in Iran*, Boston: Harvard University Press.

Berard, V. (1910), *Revolution de la Perse: les provinces, les peuples et le gouvernement du roi des rois*, Paris: Colin.

Berg, M. (1980), 'Proto-industry, political economy and the division of labour, 1700–1800', *Warwick Economic Research Papers*, 170, August.

Bharadwaj, K. (1972), 'Notes on political economy of development: the Indian case', *Economic and Political Weekly*, August: 317–28.

(1979), 'Towards a macroeconomic framework for a developing economy: the Indian case', *Manchester School*, September: 270–302.

289

Bharier, J. (1971), *Economic Development in Iran, 1900–1970*, Oxford University Press.

Borpujari, J.G. (1983), 'Consumption and productivity patterns and the implications for the production structure', IMF research paper.

Brenner, R. (1976), 'Agrarian class structure and economic development in pre-industrial Europe', *Past and Present*, 30–75.

(1977), 'The origins of capitalist development: a critique of neo-Smithian Marxism', *New Left Review*, July–August: 25–92.

Central Bank of Iran (1959–77), *Household Budget Surveys of Urban Areas*, 1959, 1965, 1971, Tehran.

(1962–77), *Annual Report & Balance Sheet*, Tehran.

(1963–83), *Quarterly Bulletin*, 7, May–June 1963 to 107/108, Spring/Summer 1983, Tehran.

(1969), *National Income of Iran, 1962–67*, Economic Research Department, Bank Markazi, September.

(1974), *National Accounts of Iran, 1959–72*, Tehran.

Central Statistical Office (CSO) (1956–76), *National Census of Population and Housing*, 1956, 1966, 1976, Tehran.

(1963–77), *Household Budget Survey of Rural Areas*, Tehran.

(1966–79), *Statistical Yearbook of Iran*, Tehran.

(1968–77), *Household Budget Survey of Urban Areas*, Tehran.

(1976), *Results of the Agricultural Census, Second Stage, 1974*, No. 722, Tehran.

(1976), *Bayan-e Amary-e Tahavollat-e Eghtesady Va Edjtemai-e Iran* (Statistical Representation of the Economic and Social Changes in Iran), No. 627, 2535 (1975), Mordad.

(1977), *Preliminary Results of Agricultural Census*, Tehran.

Chakravarty, S. (1987), *Development Planning: The Iranian Experience*, Oxford University Press.

Chambers, J.D. and Mingay, G.E. (1966), *The Agricultural Revolution 1750–1880*, London: Batsford.

Chenery, H.B. (1960), 'Patterns of industrial growth', *American Economic Review*, 50: 624–54.

Chenery, H.B. and Kretschmer, K.G. (1956), 'Resource allocation for economic development', *Econometrica*, 24, October: 365–99.

Chenery, H.B., Shishido, S. and Wantabe, T. (1962), 'The patterns of Japanese growth, 1914–1954', *Econometrica*, 30: 98–139.

Chenery, H.B. and Strout, A. (1966), 'Foreign assistance and economic development', *American Economic Review*, 56, 4: 679–733.

Chenery H.B. and Taylor, L. (1968), 'Development patterns: among countries and over time', *Review of Economics and Statistics*, 50, November: 391–416.

Cohen, G. (1978), *Karl Marx's Theory of History: a Defence*, Oxford: Clarendon Press.

Corden, W.M. (1984), 'Booming economic sector and Dutch disease economics: survey and consolidation', *Oxford Economic Papers*, 36: 359–80.

Corden, W.M. and Neary, J.P. (1982), 'Booming sector and de-industrialization in a small open economy', *Economic Journal*, 92, December: 825–48.

Bibliography

Cottam, R.W. (1979), *Nationalism in Iran*, Pittsburgh: University of Pittsburgh Press.

Cripps, T.F. and Tarling, R.J. (1973), *Growth in Advanced Capitalist Countries 1950–1970*, Cambridge University Press.

Currie, L. (1971), 'The exchange constraint on development – a partial solution to the problem', *Economic Journal*, 81: 886–903.

Dasgupta, P., Eastwood, R. and Heal, G. (1978), 'Resource management in a trading economy', *Quarterly Journal of Economics*, 92: 297–306.

De Wulf, L. (1975), 'Fiscal incidence studies in developing countries: survey and critique', IMF, *Staff Papers*, 22: 61–131

Demin, A.I. (1971), 'Selskoe Khzyaistvo Sovremennogo Irana', in C. Issawi (1971).

Diamond, M. (1978), 'Towards a change in the economic paradigm through the experience of developing countries', *Journal of Development Economics*, 5: 19–53.

Dobb, M. (1969), *Essays on Economic Growth and Planning*, 2nd edn., New York: Monthly Review Press.

(1972), *Studies in the Development of Capitalism*, London: Routledge and Kegan Paul.

Draper, H. (1978), *Karl Marx's Theory of Revolution*, New York: Monthly Review Press.

Eckaus, R.S. (1955), 'The factor proportion problems in underdeveloped areas', *American Economic Review*, 45, 4: 539–65.

(1972), 'Absorptive capacity', in J., Bhagwati and R.S. Eckaus (eds.), *Development and Planning: Essays in Honour of Paul Rosenstein Rodan*, London: Allen and Unwin, 79–108.

Economic Commission for Latin America (1964) (ECLA), 'Growth and decline of import substitution in Brazil', *Economic Bulletin for Latin America*, 9, 1, March: 1–60.

Ensafpour, G.R. (1977), *The Structure of State in Iran: From Islamic Times to The Mongol Invasion*, Tehran: Sepah Publishers.

Entner, M.L. (1965), *Russo-Persian Commercial Relations, 1828–1914*, University of Florida Monographs No. 28.

Eshag, E. (1971), 'The relative efficiency of monetary policy in selected industrial and less developed countries', *Economic Journal*, June: 294–305.

Evans, P.B. and Rueschemeyer, D. (1985), 'The state and economic transformation: toward an analysis of the conditions underlying effective intervention', in P.B. Evans, P. Rueschemeyer and T. Skopol (eds.), 44–78.

Evans, P.B., Rueschemeyer, P. and Skopol, T. (1986), *Bringing the State Back In*, Cambridge University Press.

Farmanfarmayan, H. (1968), 'The forces of modernization in nineteenth-century Iran: a historical survey', in W.R. Polk and R.L. Chambers (eds.), *The Beginnings of Modernization in the Middle East: the 19th-Century*, Chicago: University of Chicago Press.

Feldman, M. (1928), 'On the process of economic growth', *Planavoe Khoxiaistvo*, November. See, E.D. Domar (ed.), *Essays in the Theory of Economic Growth*, 1957, New York: Oxford University Press, 223–61.

Bibliography

Fesharaki, F. (1976), *Development of the Iranian Oil Industry; International and Domestic Aspects*, New York: Praeger.

Findley, R. (1971), 'The foreign exchange gap and growth in developing economies', in J.N. Bhagwati, R.W. Jones, R.A. Mundell and J. Vanek (eds.) (1971), *Trade Balance of Payments and Growth*, London: North Holland.

Fisher, W.B. (1961), *The Middle East*, London: Butler and Tanner.

Fisher, W.B. (ed.) (1968), *The Cambridge History of Iran, Vol. 1, The Land of Iran*, Cambridge University Press.

Fitzgerald, E.V.K. (1974), *The Public Sector in Latin America*, Cambridge: Working Papers No. 18, Center for Latin American Studies.

(1977), 'The state and capital accumulation in Mexico', *Journal of Latin American Studies*, 10, 2: 263–82.

(1978), 'The fiscal crisis of the Latin American state', in J.F.J. Toye (ed.), *Taxation and Economic Development*, London: Frank Cass.

(1983), 'The state and the management of accumulation in the periphery', in D. Tussie (ed.), *Latin America in the World Economy & New Perspectives*, Aldershot: Gower.

Food and Agricultural Organization 1972, 1979 (FAO), *Trade Yearbook*, Rome.

Friedman, B.M. (1978), 'Crowding out or crowding in? Economic consequences of financing government deficits', in *Brooking Papers on Economic Activity*, 3: 593–655.

Furtado, C. (1970), *The Economic Development of Latin America*, Cambridge University Press.

Gablot, H. (1962) 'Le probleme de l'eau en Iran', in C. Issawi (1971).

Garthwaite, G.R. (1978), 'Pastoral nomadism and tribal power', in *Iranian Studies*, 9: 173–99.

Gerry, C. (1974), 'Petty producers and the urban economy: A case study of Dakar', *International Labour Office*, Geneva.

Gerschenkron, A. (1962), *Economic Backwardness in Historical Perspective*, Cambridge, Mass.: Harvard University Press.

Gharatcheh-Daghi, S. (1967), *Distribution of Land in Varamin: An Opening Phase of the Agrarian Reform in Iran*, Germany: Leske Verlag Opladen.

Gilbar, G. (1977), 'The big merchants and the Persian constitutional revolution of 1906', *Asian and African Studies*, 2: 275–303.

(1976), 'Demographic developments in late Qajar Persia, 1870–1906', *Asian and African Studies*, 125–56.

(1978), 'Persian agriculture in the late Qajar period, 1860–1906: some economic and social aspects', *Asian and African Studies*, 12: 312–65.

Gomulka, S. (1971), *Inventive Activity, Diffusion, and the Stages of Economic Growth*, AARHUS.

Groseclose, E. (1947), *Introduction to Iran*, New York: Oxford University Press.

Grove, T.J. (1970), *The Iranian Tax System*, Tehran: IMDBI.

Gutmann, P. (1981), 'The measurement of terms of trade effects', *Review of Income and Wealth*, Series 27: 433–53.

Hadary, G. (1951), 'The agrarian reform problem in Iran', *Middle East Journal*, 5, 2.

Hakimian, H. (1985), 'Wage labour and migration: Persian workers in southern

Russia, 1800–1914', *International Journal of Middle Eastern Studies*, 17, 4, November.

Halliday, F. (1979), *Iran: Dictatorship and Development*, New York: Penguin.

Hambly, G. (1964), 'An introduction to economic organization of early Qajar Iran', *Iran; Journal of the British Institute of Persian Studies*, 2.

Harris, J.R. and Todaro, M.P. (1970), 'Migration, unemployment and development: a two-sector analysis', *American Economic Review*, 60, 1: 126–42.

Hershlag, Z.Y. (1964), *Introduction to the Modern Economic History of the Middle East*, Leiden: E.J. Brill.

Hilton, R. (1978), *The Transition From Feudalism to Capitalism*, London: Verso.

Hindess, B. and Hirst, P.Q. (1975), *Modes of Production and Social Formation*, London: Macmillan.

Hirschman, A.O. (1958), *The Strategy of Economic Development*, New Haven: Yale University Press.

Hirschman, A.O. and Lindblom, C.E. (1962), 'Economic development, research and development policy making: some converging views', *Behavioural Science*, 7: 211–22.

Hurewitz, J.C. (1956), *Diplomacy in the Middle and Near East: A Documentary Record, 1914–56*, Princeton: Van Nostrand.

Ibn Khaldun (1967), *The Mugadimah: An Introduction to History*, translated by F. Rosental, edited by N.J. Dawood, London: Routledge and Kegan Paul.

Industrial and Development Renovation Organization (IDRO) (1974, 1975), *Annual Report*, Tehran.

Industrial and Mining Development Bank of Iran (IMDBI) (1960–77), *Annual Report*, Tehran.

Industrial Credit Bank, Iran (ICB) (1960–77), *Annual Report*, Tehran.

International Bank of Reconstruction and Development (IBRD) (1974), *Appraisal of the Industrial and Mining Development Bank of Iran*, January, 259a-IRN.

International Labour Organization (ILO) (1972), *Employment and Income Policies for Iran*, Geneva.

(1973), *Employment and Income Policies in Iran*, Geneva.

International Monetary Fund (IMF) (1981, 1983), *Government Finance Statistics Yearbook*, Washington DC.

(1963–79), *International Financial Statistics: Yearbook*, Washington DC.

Ishikawa, S. (1978), *Labour Absorption in Asian Agriculture*, Asian Regional Programme for Employment Promotion, Bangkok: ILO.

Issawi, C. (1966), *The Economic History of the Middle East: 1800–1914*, Chicago: University of Chicago Press.

(1970), 'The decline of Middle Eastern Trade', in D.S. Richards (ed.), *Islam and the Trade of Asia: A Colloquium*, Philadelphia: University of Pennsylvania Press.

(1971), *The Economic History of Iran: 1800–1914*, Chicago: University of Chicago Press.

(1980), *The Economic History of Turkey: 1800–1914*, Chicago: University of Chicago Press.

(1981), 'Egypt, Iran and Turkey, 1800–1970: patterns of growth and development', in P. Bairoch and M. Levy-Leboyer (eds.), 65–77.

Issawi, C. and Yeganeh, M. (1962), *Economics of Middle Eastern Oil*, London: Praeger.

Ivanov, M.S. (1977), *Tarikh-e Novin-e Iran* (The Modern History of Iran), Stockholm: Tudeh Publishing Center (in Persian).

Jamalzadeh, M.A. (1917), *Ganj-i Shayegan*, Berlin.

Jazayeri, A. (1987), *The Economic Impact of Oil Revenues and Development Policies in Two Oil-Exporting Countries: The case of Iran and Nigeria; 1970–82*, Ph.D. Thesis, Institute of Development Studies, Sussex.

Jessop, B. (1982), *The Capitalist State*, Oxford: Martin Robertson.

Jorgenson, D.W. (1971), 'Econometric studies of investment behaviour: a survey', *Journal of Economic Literature*, 9, 4: 1111–48.

Joshi, V. (1970), 'Saving and foreign exchange constraints', in P. Streeten (ed.), 111–34.

Kakwani, N. (1976), 'On the estimations of income inequality measures from grouped observations', *Review of Economic Studies*, 43: 483–92.

  (1980), *Income Inequality and Poverty: Methods of Estimation and Policy Applications*, Oxford University Press.

Kaldor, N. (1957), 'A model of economic growth', *Economic Journal*, 67, December: 591–624.

  (1962), 'The Role of Taxation in Economic Development', in N. Kaldor (1964), *Essays in Economic Policy*, vol. 1, London: Duckworth.

  (1964), 'Dual Exchange Rates and Economic Development', in N. Kaldor (1980), vol. II, chapter 19: 178–203.

  (1967), *Strategic Factors in Economic Development*, New York: Cornell University.

  (1968), 'Economic and taxation problems in Iran', in N. Kaldor, *Reports on Taxation*, vol. 2, 1980, London: Duckworth.

  (1971), 'The role of industrialization in Latin American inflation', in N. Kaldor (1978), chapter 8: 119–38.

  (1972), 'Capitalism and industrial development: some lessons from Britain's experience', in N. Kaldor (1978), chapter 10: 154–75.

  (1972a), 'Advanced technology in a strategy of development', in N. Kaldor (1978), chapter 9: 138–54.

  (1977), 'The effect of devaluation on trade in manufactures', in N. Kaldor (1978), chapter 7: 99–119.

  (1978), *Further Essays in Applied Economic*, London: Duckworth.

  (1980), *Essays in Economic Policy*, vols. 1 and 2, London: Duckworth.

Kalecki, M. (1953), 'The Problems of Financing Economic Development', in M. Kalecki (1979), chapter 5: 41–64.

  (1966), 'Forms of foreign aid: an economic analysis', in M. Kalecki (1979), chapter 6: 64–98.

  (1972), *Essays on the Growth of the Socialist and Mixed Economy*, Cambridge University Press.

  (1979), *Essays on Development Economics*, Brighton: Harvester Press.

Karpat, K.H. (1968), 'The land regime, social structure, and modernization in the

Ottoman empire', in W.R. Polk and R.L. Chambers (eds.), *Beginnings of Modernization in The Middle East, The Nineteenth Century*, Chicago: University of Chicago Press.

Katouzian, H. (1978), 'Oil versus agriculture: a case of dual resource depletion in Iran', *The Journal of Peasant Studies*, 347–69.

(1981), *The Political Economy of Modern Iran, Despotism and Pseudo-Modernism, 1926–1979*, London: Macmillan.

Kavoussi, R.M. (1976), *Structural Change in the Iranian Manufacturing Industry, 1959–72*, Ph.D. thesis, Harvard University.

Kazemi, F. (1980), 'The Military and Politics in Iran: The Uneasy Symbiosis', in E. Kadourie and S.G. Haim (ed), *Towards a Modern Iran*, London: Frank Cass, 217–41.

Kazemzadeh, F. (1968), *Russia and Britain in Persia 1864–1914, A Study in Imperialism*, New Haven: Yale University Press.

Keddie, N. (1968), 'The Iranian village before and after land reform', *Journal of Contemporary History*, 3, 3.

(1972), 'Stratification, social control, and capitalism in Iranian villages: before and after land reform', in Keddie (ed.) (1980).

(1980), *Iran: Religion, Politics and Society*, London: Frank Cass.

(1981), *Roots of the Revolution*, London: Yale University Press.

Keyder, C. (1979), 'The political economy of Turkish democracy', *New Left Review*, May–June: 3–39.

Khamsi, F.S. (1968), *The Development of Capitalism in Rural Iran*, M.A. Dissertation, Faculty of Political Science, Colombia University.

Khosravi, K. (1979), *The Peasant Community in Iran*, Tehran: Payam.

Kiga, K. (1968), *Characteristics of Japan's Economic Growth*, Centre for Afro-Asian Research of the Hungarian Academy of Sciences, Budapest.

Kreidt, P., Medick, H., and Schlumbohm, J. (1981), *Industrialization Before Industrialization: Rural Industry in the Genesis of Capitalism*, Cambridge University Press.

Kruger, A.O. (1984), 'Trade policies in developing countries', in R.W. Jones and P.B. Kenen (eds.), *Handbook of International Economics*, Amsterdam: North Holland.

Kurabayashi, Y. (1971), 'The impact of change in terms of trade on a system of national accounts', *The Review of Income and Wealth*, 3: 285–99.

Kuznets, S. (1957), 'Quantitative aspects of the economic growth of nations: industrial distribution of national product and labour force', *Economic Development and Cultural Change*, 5, July, Supplement.

(1966), *Modern Economic Growth: Rate, Structure and Speed*, New Haven: Yale University Press.

(1971), *Economic Growth of Nations: Total Output and Production Structure*, Cambridge, Mass.: Harvard University Press.

Lambton, A.K.S. (1943), 'Some Aspects of the Situation in Persia', *Asiatic Review*, 39–49.

(1953), *Landlord and Peasant in Persia: a study of land tenure and land revenue administration*, London: Oxford University Press.

(1954), *Islamic Society in Persia*, London: Oxford University Press.

(1962), 'Justice in the medieval Persian theory of kinship', *Studies Islamica*, 17.

(1969), *Persian Land Reform, 1962–66*, London: Oxford University Press.

(1969a), 'Land reform and cooperative societies in Persia', *Royal Central Asian Journal*, 56.

(1970), 'Persian trade under the early qajar', in D.S. Richards (ed.), *Islam and the Trade of Asia: A Colloquiuim*, Philadelphia: University of Pennsylvania Press.

Lefeber, L. (1972), 'Income distribution and agricultural development', in J. Bhagwati and R.S. Eckaus (eds.), *Development and Planning*, London: Allen and Unwin: 133–51.

Lenin, V.I. (1977), *The Development of Capitalism in Russia*, Moscow: Progress Publishers.

Lewis, B. (1937), 'The Islamic Guilds', *Economic History Review*, 8: 20–37.

Lewis, W.A. (1978), *Growth and Fluctuation: 1870–1913*, London: Allen and Unwin.

Lockhart, L. (1959), 'The constitutional laws of Persia: an outline of their original and development', *Middle East Journal*, 13: 372–88.

Lorenze, J.H. (1971), 'Iran's great reformers of the nineteenth century: an analysis of Amir Kabir's reforms', *Iranian Studies*, Spring-Summer, Boston.

Lowe, A. (1976), *The Path of Economic Growth*, Cambridge University Press.

Lund, P.J. (1971), *Investment: The Study of an Economic Aggregate*, San Francisco: Holden-Day.

Maddison, A. (1984), *Phases of Capitalist Development*, Oxford University Press.

Madjd, M.H. (1983), 'Land reform and agricultural policy in Iran, 1962–78', *International Agricultural Economics Study*, Dept. of Agricultural Economics, Cornell University, New York.

Mahalanobis, P.C., (1953), 'Some observations on the growth of national income', *Sankhia*, September.

Mahdavy, H. (1965), 'The coming crisis in Iran', *Foreign Affairs*, 44, October: 134–46.

(1970), 'The patterns and problems of economic development in rentier states: the case of Iran', in M.A. Cook (ed.), *Studies in the Economic History of The Middle Eastern*, London: Oxford University Press.

(1982), 'The thirty year evolution of a village in Gorgan Plains', *Ketabe Agah*, Tehran: Amir Kabir.

Marris, R. (1970), 'Can we measure the need for development assistance?', *Economic Journal*, 80, September: 650–68.

Marx, K. (1859), 'The Eighteenth Brumaire of Louis Bonaparte', in K. Marx and F. Engels, *Collected Works*, vol. 2, London: Laurance and Wishart, 99–197.

(1936), *The Poverty of Philosophy*, Moscow: Foreign Languages Publishing House.

(1972), *Capital: a Critical Analysis of Capitalist Production*, vol. 3, London: Lawrence and Wishart.

(1976), *Capital: A Critique of Political Economy*, vol. 1, Harmondsworth: Penguin.

(1977), *Grundrisse: Introduction to the Critique of Political Economy*, edited by M.

Nicolaus, Harmondsworth: Penguin.

Marx, K. and Engels, F. (1965), *The German Ideology*, London: Lawrence and Wishart.

Maynard, G. (1963), *Economic Development and the Price Level*, London: Macmillan.

McKinnon, R.L. (1964), 'Foreign exchange constraints in economic development and efficient aid allocation', *Economic Journal*, 74: 388–409.

Mead, J.E. and Russel, E.A. (1957), 'Wage rates, the cost of living, and the balance of payments', in *Economic Record*, April: 23–8.

Mehran, F. (1975), *Taxes and Income: Distribution of Tax Burdens in Iran*, ILO, Working Paper, WEP 2-23/WP 33.

(1975a), *Income Distribution in Iran: The Statistics of Inequality*, ILO, Working Paper, WEP 2-23/WP 30.

(1977), *Distribution of Benefits From Public Consumption Expenditures Among Households in Iran*, ILO, Working Paper, WEP 2-23/WP 57.

Meredith, C. (1971), 'Early Qajar administration: an analysis of its development and functions', *Iranian Studies*, Spring-Summer, Boston.

Merrington, J. (1975), 'Town and country in transition to capitalism', *New Left Review*, 93, September-October.

Michalopulous, C. (1975), 'Production and substitution in two-gap model', *Journal of Development Studies*, July, 11, 4: 343–57.

Millar, J.R. (1970), 'Soviet rapid development and the agricultural surplus hypothesis', *Soviet Studies*, 22: 77–91.

Ministry of Interior Affairs (1960), *National Agricultural Census*, Department of Agricultural Statistics, Tehran.

Ministry of Industry and Mines (1955), *Statistics on Industrial and Mining Activities*, Bureau of Statistics, Information and Standards, 1334, Tehran.

(1964–73), *Iranian Industrial Statistics*, 1964, 1969, 1972, 1973, Tehran.

(1967), *Industrial Development of Iran*, Research Centre for Industry and Trade Development, Tehran.

(1972–76), *Trends in Industrial and Commercial Statistics*, 1972(Q1), 1975(Q1,Q4), 1976(Q1,Q4), Tehran.

(1978) *Trends of Iranian Industrial Production*, Tehran.

Ministry of Labour (1947), *Statistical Survey of Iranian Industries*, Tehran.

Ministry of Labour and Social Affairs (1964), *Yearbook of Employment Statistics*, 7, Tehran.

(1972), *Manpower Survey*, Tehran.

Minorsky, V. (1980), *Tadhkirat Al-Muluk: A Manual of Safavid Administration*, Cambridge: E.J.W. Gibb Memorial Trust.

Miroshnikov, L. (1964), *Iran in World War I*, Moscow: Nauka.

Moameni, B. (1980), *The Agrarian Question and Class War in Iran*, Tehran: Payvand.

Moghaddam, G.R. (1956), *Iran's Foreign Trade Policy and Economic Development in the Inter-War Period*, Ph.D. thesis, Stanford University.

Motamen, H. (1979), *Expenditure of Oil Revenue; An Optimal Control Approach to the Iranian Economy*, London: Francis Pinter.

Mouzelis, N. (1980), 'Capitalism and the development of the Greek state', in R. Scase (ed.), *The State in Western Europe*, New York: St. Martin's Press.

Nazim al-Islam Kermani (1960), *The History of the Awakening of the Iranians*, Tehran.

Nelson, R. (1970) 'The effective exchange rate employment and growth in a foreign exchange constrained economy,' *Journal of Political Economy*, 78, 3: 546–65.

Nirumand, B. (1969), *Iran: The New Imperialism in Action*, New York: Monthly Review Press.

Noamani, F. (1972), 'The origin and development of feudalism in Iran', *Tahgigat-e Egetesadi*, 9, 27 and 28.

—— (1981), *The Evolution of Feudalism in Iran*, Tehran: Amir Kabir.

Nowshirwani, V.F. (1976), *Technology and Employment Programme; Agricultural Mechanization in Iran*, ILO, Working Paper, WEP 2-22/WP 28.

Nowshirwani, V.F. and Bildner, R. (1973), 'Direct foreign investment in the non-oil sectors of the Iranian economy', in *Iranian Studies*, Spring-Summer: 66–109.

Nowshirwani, V.F. and Knight, A. (1975), 'The beginning of commercial agriculture in Iran', *Discussion Paper No. 255*, Economic Growth Center, Yale University.

Nuti, D.M. (1979) 'Contradictions of socialist economies', *Socialist Register*, London: Merlin Press, 228–73.

Okazaki Shoko (1968), *The Development of Large-Scale Farming in Iran: The Case of Province of Gorgan*, Tokyo.

Olson, R.T. (1980), 'The mazandaran development project and Haji Mohammad Hasan: a study in Persian entrepreneurship, 1884–1898', in E. Kedourie and S.G. Haim (ed.), *Towards a Modern Iran*, London: Frank Cass, 38–56.

—— (1981), 'Persian gulf trade and the agricultural economy of southern Iran in the nineteenth century', in M.E. Bonine and N.R. Keddie (eds.), *Continuity and Change in Modern Iran*, New York: State University of New York Press.

Ono, M. (1967), 'On socio-economic structure of Iranian villages', *Developing Economies*, 5: 446–62.

Oshima, H. (1973), 'Income distribution', *Mission Working Paper No. 11, Employment and Income Policies in Iran, World Employment Programme Research*, Geneva: ILO.

OECD (1967), *Quantitative Models as an Aid to Development Assistance Policy*, Organization for Economic Co-operation and Development, Paris.

Pasinetti, L.L. (1981), *Structural Change and Economic Growth: A Theoretical Essay on the Dynamics of the Wealth of Nations*, Cambridge University Press.

Paukert, F., Skolka, J., and Maton, J. (1981), *Income Distribution, Structure of Economy and Employment*, London: Croom Helm.

Pavlovich, M.P. (1910), 'The agrarian question in Iran', in M. Hooshiar (ed.), *The Constitutional Revolution*, Tehran: Roodaki.

Pegulevskaya, N.V., Yakubovsky, A.Y., Petrushevsky, I.P., Belenitsky, A.M., and Stroeva, L.V. (1975), *Iranian History: From Antiquity to the 18th Century*, Persian Text (translated by K. Keshavarz from Russian), Tehran: Payam.

Pesaran, M.H. (1976), 'Income distribution and its major determinants in Iran', in J.W. Jacqz (ed.), *Iran, Past, Present and Future*, Colombia: Aspen, 267–86.

Pesaran, M.H. and Ghahvary, F. (1976), 'Growth and income distribution in Iran', in R. Stone and W. Peterson (eds.), *Econometric Contribution to Public Policy*, London: Macmillan, 231–48.

Pesaran, M.H. and Karshenas, M. (1983), 'Islamic government and the Iranian economy', Paper presented at the 17th Annual Conference of The Middle East Studies Association, Chicago, November.

Petrushevsky, I.P. (1968), 'The socio-economic conditions of Iran under the Ilkhans', in J.A. Boyle (ed.), *The Cambridge History of Iran, vol. 5*, Cambridge University Press, 483–538.

(1978), *Agrarian relations in the Mongol Period in Iran*, Persian Text (Translated by K. Keshavarz), vols. 1–2, Tehran: NIL Press.

Plan and Budget Organization of Iran (PO) (1964), *Report on the Implementation of the Second Seven-Year Plan*, Tehran.

(1965), *Outline of the Third Plan: 962–67*, Isfand, 1344.

(1968), *Development Plan Laws; a Collection*, Isfand, 1347.

(1969), *Budget of Public Enterprises*, Supplement No. 3 to the 1349 (1970) Budget, Bahman, 1348, Tehran.

(1975), *The Budget 1977–78*, 2535, Tehran.

(1976), *Economic Statistics and Trends*, 3rd Edition, Statistical Research Unit, Tehran.

(1977), *Budget of Public Enterprises*, Supplement No. 3 to the 2536 (1976) Budget, Tehran.

Poulantzas, N. (1973), *Political Power on Social Classes*, London: New Left Books.

Price, O.T.W. (1975), *Towards a Comprehensive Iranian Agricultural Policy*, IBRD, Agricultural and Rural Development Advisory Mission, Iran, September.

Przeworski, A. (1985), *Capitalism and Social Democracy*, Cambridge University Press.

Radwan, S. (1975), *Employment Implications of Capital Intensive Industries in Iran*. A Report on the ILO Mission to Iran; 20 December 1974–27 January 1975, Geneva.

Raj, K.N. and Sen, A.K. (1961), 'Alternative patterns of growth under conditions of stagnant export earnings', *Oxford Economic Papers*, 13: 43–62.

Rawandi, M. (1977), *The Social History of Iran From the Early Ages to the Present*, Tehran: Amir Kabir.

Razavi, H. (1982), 'Optimal rate of oil production for OPEC-member countries', *Resources and Energy*, 4, London: North Holland, 291–305.

(1983), 'An analysis of Iran's oil production policy: a welfare maximization approach', *Applied Economics*, 15: 243–54.

Rosenberg, N. (1976), *Perspectives on Technology*, Cambridge University Press.

Rowley, J.C. and Trivedi, P.K. (1975), *Econometrics of Investment*, New York: John Wiley and Sons.

Rustow, D.A. and Mugno, J.F. (1976), *OPEC; Success and Prospects*, London: Martin Robertson and Co. Ltd.

Sadigh, P. (1975), *Impact of Government Policies on the Structure and Growth of Iranian Industry*, Ph.D. thesis, London School of Oriental and African Studies.

Sachs, I. (1980), *Studies in Political Economy of Development*, New York: Pergamon Press.

Safi Nezhad, J. (1977), *Boneh*, 3rd edn., Tehran: Toose.

Saikal, A. (1980), *The Rise and Fall of The Shah*, Princeton: Princeton University Press.

Satwatmanesh, S. (1980), *Determination of Iran's Agricultural Trade, 1960–75*, Ph.D. thesis, London.

Sawer, M. (1977), *Marxism and the Question of the Asiatic Mode of Production*, The Hague: Martinus Nijhoff.

Seers, D. (1962), 'A theory of inflation and growth', *Oxford Economic Papers*, June: 174–97.

Sen, A.K. (1968), *Choice of Techniques*, 3rd edn., Oxford: Blackwell.

Seyf, A. (1984), 'Technical changes in Iranian agriculture, 1800–1906', *Middle Eastern Studies* 20, 4, October.

Shafa-eddin, S.M. (1980), *A Critique of Development Policies Based on Oil Revenues in Recent Years in Iran*, Ph.D. thesis, Oxford.

Shams, H. (1973), *Allocation of Resources Under Agrarian Reform in Iran*, Ph.D. thesis, Cambridge.

Sharafi, S. (1977), *Bahsi Dar Nezam-e Budgeh Rizi-e Iran*, Plan and Budget Organization, 1–5, Mordad 2436.

Sheikholeslami, A.R. (1971), 'Sale of offices in Qazar Iran', *Iranian Studies*, Spring–Summer.

    (1978), 'The patrimonial structure of Iranian bureaucracy in the late 19th century', *Iranian Studies*, 10: 199–258.

Singer, W.H. (1965), 'External aid: for plans or projects?', *The Economic Journal*, September: 539–45.

Skopol, T. (1985), 'Bringing the state back in: strategies of analysis in current research', in P.B. Evans and D. Rueschemeyer (eds.), 3–44.

Smith Jr., J.M. (1978), 'Turanian nomadism and Iranian politics', *Iranian Studies*, 11: 57–81.

Stewart, F. (1976), 'Capital goods in developing countries', in A. Cairncross and M. Puri (eds.), *Employment, Income Distribution and Development Strategy: Problems of the Developing Countries*, London: Macmillan, 120–39.

Stork, J. (1975), *Middle East Oil and the Energy Crisis*, New York: Monthly Review Press.

Strassmann, W.P. (1956), 'Economic growth and income distribution', *Quarterly Journal of Economics*, 70: 425–40.

Streeten, P. (ed.), (1970), *Unfashionable Economics: Essays in Honour of Lord Balogh*, London: Weidenfeld and Nicolson.

Stuvel, G. (1956), 'A new approach to the measurement of terms of trade effects', *The Review of Economics and Statistics*, August: 294–307.

Takahashi, K. (1952), 'A contribution to the discussion', in R. Hilton (ed.) (1978), 68–98.

Taylor, L. (1983), *Structuralist Macroeconomics: Applicable Models for the Third World*, New York: Basic Books.

Tockman, V.E. (1971), 'An exploration in the nature of informal-formal sector interrelationships', in *Programa Regional Del Empleo Para America Latin Y El Caribe*, Geneva: ILO.

Todaro, M.P. (1969), 'A model of labour migration and urban unemployment in less developed countries', *American Economic Review*, 59, 1: 138–48.

United Kingdom, Department of Overseas Trade (UK, DOT) (1923–48), *Report on Economic and Commercial Conditions in Iran*, 1923, 1925, 1948, London.

United Nations (1940–79), *Yearbook of International Trade Statistics* (UN, YITS), Washington DC.

(1951), *Public Finance Information Papers: Iran*, Tehran.

(1955), 'Economic development in the Middle East, 1954–1955', Supplement to *World Economic Survey*, Supplement, Washington DC.

(1956), 'Economic development in the Middle East, 1955–1956', *World Economic Survey*, Supplement, Washington DC.

(1957–73), *Statistical Yearbook*, Washington DC.

(1958), 'Economic development in the Middle East, 1957–1958', *World Economic Survey*, Supplement, Washington DC.

(1961), 'Economic development in the Middle East, 1956–1961', *World Economic Survey*, Supplement, Washington DC.

(1961a), *Monthly Bulletin of Statistics*, June, New York.

(1965), *World Economic Survey: 1964*, New York.

(1966), *World Economic Survey: 1965*, New York.

(1966a), *Classification of Commodities by Industrial Origin, Relationship of the SITC and International SIC*, Statistical papers, Series M, No. 43, Washington DC.

(1968), 'A system of national accounts', *Studies in Methods*, Series F, No. 2, Rev. 3.

(1971), *Classification by Broad Economic Categories*, Statistical papers, Series M, No. 53, Washington DC.

(1979), *World Industry Since 1969: Progress and Prospects*, UNIDO, Vienna, E.79.ll.B.3.

Veblen, T. (1932), 'On the nature of capital', in T. Veblen (ed.), *The Place of Science in Modern Civilization, and Other Essays*, New York, 324–86.

Von Furstenberg, G.M. and Malkiel, B.G. (1977), 'The government and capital formation: a survey of recent issues', *Journal of Economic Literature*, September.

Vreeland, H. (ed.) (1957), *Country Survey Series: Iran*, New Haven: Human Relations Area Files.

Wai, T. and Wong, C.H. (1982), 'Determinants of private investment in developing countries', *Journal of Development Studies* 19, 1: 19–37.

Walton, T. (1980), 'Economic development and revolutionary upheavals in Iran', *Cambridge Journal of Economics*, 4: 271–92.

Weber, M. (1978), *Economy and Society: An Outline of Interpretative Sociology*, Berkeley: University of California Press.

Wells, J.P. and Malan, P.S. (1981), 'Structural models of inflation and balance of payments disequilibria in semi-industrialized economies: some implications for stabilization and growth policies', paper presented to International Economic

Association Conference on, *Problems of Changes in Relative Prices*, September.

Westwood, A. (1960), 'Elections and Politics in Iran', *Middle East Journal*, 15: 379–415.

Wilber, O.N. (1963), *Contemporary Iran*, New York: Praeger.

(1976), *Iran: Past and Present*, 8th edn., Princeton: Princeton University Press.

Wittfogel, K.A. (1967), *Oriental Despotism: A Comparative Study of Total Power*, London: Yale University Press.

World Bank (1971), *Industrial Policies and Priorities in Iran*, Washington DC.

(1974), *Economic Development of Iran*, 1–4, Washington DC.

(1982), *The World Development Report*, Washington DC.

Yaganegi, E.B. (1934), *Recent Financial and Monetary History of Persia*, New York: Columbia University Press.

Young, A. (1928), 'Increasing return and economic progress', *Economic Journal*, 38, December: 527–42.

Zonis, M. (1971), *The Political Elite of Iran*, Princeton: Princeton University Press.

Index

Index

capital accumulation (*cont.*)
  constraints to 233–4
  role of Plan Organization 94–7
capital formation, and structural change 176–87
capital mobility 125
capital/labour ratio 181
capitalist production 25, 50–1, 143; see also manufacturing, corporate
Cereal Organization 129
Chakravarty, S. 24n
Chardin 34n, 46
Chenery, H.B. 13, 18, 207, 211n, 223n, 225, 228
class theories of state 26
constitutional monarchy 60
Constitutional Revolution (1906–9) 45, 58, 60–2
consumer demand 201–5, 238
consumption,
  data 255–6
  distribution of expenditure on 198–205
  growth of food 157–8, 162
  private and public sector 187, 194–7
Corden, W.M. 116
Cottam, R. W. 89n
coups,
  (1921) 64
  (1953) 84, 85, 88, 235
credit; see also financial institutions
  controls 112, 214
  expansion 114–15, 173–5
  government intervention 120
Cripps, T.F. 12
crowding out effect 173, 198n, 237
customs duties and tariffs 47n, 117–18, 167, 178n, 234

D'Arcy concession 81
Dasgupta, P. 7
demand, structure of 225, 226–30
descriptive analysis 24
development plans 105–7, 171; see also Plan Organization
Diamond, M. 9
distributional problems 230
Dobb, M. 8
domestic budget deficit 136, 188
dual-gap models 9–10, 18–21, 226–7
duality 207–14, 266–70

Eckaus, R.S. 13
economic growth, see growth
economic waste 127–9, 136, 152
Egypt 47n, 127, 167, 168
employment,

agriculture 161, 165n
  composition of 208
  manufacturing 181–2, 184
  and productivity 208–9
Entner, M.L. 48, 59
Evans, P.B. 27, 28
exchange rate system 98n, 117
exports,
  commodity 216
  manufacturing 216, 220
  oil share 69n
  stagnation 70–1, 131, 133

famines 56, 58
Farm Corporations 147
Fath-Ali Shah 42
Feldman, M. 8
Fesharaki, F. 86
feudal dismemeberment 35
finance (see also) credit
  government provision 125–7
financial crisis 45–6
financial institutions 92, 97–105, 125, 176, 235, 237
Findley, R. 20
Fitzgerald, E.V.K. 9, 22, 23, 25n
food,
  consumption 157–8, 162
  imports 157, 162
  inelastic supplies 130–1
  prices 4, 128–9, 140, 156–7, 236
  subsidies 241n
  urban supply 155–9
foreign debt,
  investment financed by 211–12
  private and public sector 137
  and state role in investment 92, 94, 171, 235
foreign exchange; see also exchange rate systems
  oil revenue 11, 18
  reserves 134, 137
  revaluation 17, 98, 115
  in structuralist models 8
foreign skills 16, 119–20
foreign trade; see also exports; imports
  free trade 46–51, 69–83, 232
  pattern 49, 69–70, 72–3, 218, 219
  state control of 71, 74
Furtado, C. 8, 9

Gerschenkron, A. 25n, 92
Ghahvary, F. 199n
Gharatcheh-Daghi, S. 53, 61
Gilbar, G. 45, 48, 55, 56, 59
government, see state

304

Index

Index

Index